International Trade in Services and Intangibles in the Era of Globalization

Studies in Income and Wealth
Volume 69

National Bureau of Economic Research
Conference on Research in Income and Wealth

International Trade in Services and Intangibles in the Era of Globalization

Edited by **Marshall Reinsdorf and Matthew Slaughter**

The University of Chicago Press

Chicago and London

MARSHALL REINSDORF is senior research economist at the U.S. Department of Commerce, Bureau of Economic Analysis. MATTHEW SLAUGHTER is professor of international economics at the Tuck School of Business at Dartmouth College, and a research associate of the National Bureau of Economic Research.

The University of Chicago Press, Chicago 60637
The University of Chicago Press, Ltd., London
© 2009 by the National Bureau of Economic Research
All rights reserved. Published 2009
Printed in the United States of America

18 17 16 15 14 13 12 11 10 09   1 2 3 4 5
ISBN-13: 978-0-226-70959-8 (cloth)
ISBN-10: 0-226-70959-0 (cloth)

Library of Congress Cataloging-in-Publication Data

International flows of invisibles : trade in services and intangibles in the
    era of globalization / edited by Marshall Reinsdorf and Matthew
    Slaughter.
        p. cm. — (Income and wealth ; vol. 69)
    Papers from the conference entitled International Service Flows
convened under the auspices of the Conference on Research in
Income and Wealth and the National Bureau of Economic Research,
held in Bethesda, Maryland on April 28–29, 2006.
    Includes bibliographical references and index.
    ISBN-13: 978-0-226-70959-8 (cloth : alk. paper)
    ISBN-10: 0-226-70959-0 (cloth : alk. paper) 1. Service
industries—Congresses. 2. International trade—21st century—
Congresses. 3. Contracting out—Congresses. I. Reinsdorf,
Marshall B. II. Slaughter, Matthew J. (Matthew Jon) III. Series.
    HD9980.5.I58 2009
    382'.45—dc22

                                                    2008039264

Relation of the Directors to the
Work and Publications of the
National Bureau of Economic Research

1. The object of the NBER is to ascertain and present to the economics profession, and to the public more generally, important economic facts and their interpretation in a scientific manner without policy recommendations. The Board of Directors is charged with the responsibility of ensuring that the work of the NBER is carried on in strict conformity with this object.

2. The President shall establish an internal review process to ensure that book manuscripts proposed for publication DO NOT contain policy recommendations. This shall apply both to the proceedings of conferences and to manuscripts by a single author or by one or more co-authors but shall not apply to authors of comments at NBER conferences who are not NBER affiliates.

3. No book manuscript reporting research shall be published by the NBER until the President has sent to each member of the Board a notice that a manuscript is recommended for publication and that in the President's opinion it is suitable for publication in accordance with the above principles of the NBER. Such notification will include a table of contents and an abstract or summary of the manuscript's content, a list of contributors if applicable, and a response form for use by Directors who desire a copy of the manuscript for review. Each manuscript shall contain a summary drawing attention to the nature and treatment of the problem studied and the main conclusions reached.

4. No volume shall be published until forty-five days have elapsed from the above notification of intention to publish it. During this period a copy shall be sent to any Director requesting it, and if any Director objects to publication on the grounds that the manuscript contains policy recommendations, the objection will be presented to the author(s) or editor(s). In case of dispute, all members of the Board shall be notified, and the President shall appoint an ad hoc committee of the Board to decide the matter; thirty days additional shall be granted for this purpose.

5. The President shall present annually to the Board a report describing the internal manuscript review process, any objections made by Directors before publication or by anyone after publication, any disputes about such matters, and how they were handled.

6. Publications of the NBER issued for informational purposes concerning the work of the Bureau, or issued to inform the public of the activities at the Bureau, including but not limited to the NBER Digest and Reporter, shall be consistent with the object stated in paragraph 1. They shall contain a specific disclaimer noting that they have not passed through the review procedures required in this resolution. The Executive Committee of the Board is charged with the review of all such publications from time to time.

7. NBER working papers and manuscripts distributed on the Bureau's web site are not deemed to be publications for the purpose of this resolution, but they shall be consistent with the object stated in paragraph 1. Working papers shall contain a specific disclaimer noting that they have not passed through the review procedures required in this resolution. The NBER's web site shall contain a similar disclaimer. The President shall establish an internal review process to ensure that the working papers and the web site do not contain policy recommendations, and shall report annually to the Board on this process and any concerns raised in connection with it.

8. Unless otherwise determined by the Board or exempted by the terms of paragraphs 6 and 7, a copy of this resolution shall be printed in each NBER publication as described in paragraph 2 above.

Contents

Prefatory Note

This volume contains revised versions of most of the papers and discussions presented at the Conference on Research in Income and Wealth entitled "International Service Flows," held in Bethesda, Maryland on April 28–29, 2006.

Funds for the Conference on Research in Income and Wealth are supplied by the Bureau of Economic Analysis, the Bureau of Labor Statistics, the Census Bureau, the Federal Reserve Board, the Internal Revenue Service, and Statistics Canada. We are indebted to these organizations for their support.

We thank Marshall Reinsdorf and Matthew Slaughter, who served as conference organizers and editors of the volume.

Introduction

Marshall Reinsdorf and Matthew Slaughter

International trade in services is an increasingly important feature of the U.S. economy. Anecdotal evidence abounds on the rapid growth of new types of services imports made possible by information and communications technology (ICT)—for example, call centers, software programming, legal services, and even medical services such as radiology diagnostics. Moreover, predictions by some economists about the eventual effects of this new type of trade in services indicate that it may shape the future of the U.S. economy in ways that once would have been unimaginable. Now that the ability to deliver services over a wire has circumvented the traditional constraint on the growth of trade in services imposed by the need for physical proximity, what is to prevent trade in services from expanding to a scale that would have large effects on labor markets and on the U.S. balance of payments?

Although news stories, controversies, and even novels about life as a call center worker have given new types of trade in services high visibility, other types of international service transactions also have important roles in the evolving structure of global production. Besides advances in ICT, growth in trade in services has been promoted by liberalized or favorable treatment of services-related foreign direct investment (FDI) by some host countries, by the growing importance of services in general in advanced economies, and by the growing fragmentation of the production process into chains of specialized activities, each of which is located where it can be

Marshall Reinsdorf is chief of the national economic research group at the U.S. Bureau of Economic Analysis. Matthew Slaughter is associate dean of the MBA program and professor of international economics at the Tuck School of Business at Dartmouth College, and a research associate of the National Bureau of Economic Research.

done most efficiently (Feenstra 1998). As a result of these trends, world trade as a whole has grown faster than world production of goods and services, and the services component of trade has tended to grow faster than the goods component.

The importance of services in overall economic activity in the United States means that if services activities are becoming more tradable, the effects on the U.S. economy could be profound. As of April 2007, fully 115.2 million U.S. payroll jobs—83.7 percent of the 137.7 million total— were in service-producing industries. Indeed, many industries within the service sectors individually accounted for more American jobs than the 14.1 million jobs found in all of manufacturing; as an example, professional and business services, which contains many occupations that van Welsum and Reif (chapter 9, this volume) find to be vulnerable to offshoring, had 17.9 million jobs. Clearly, the structure of services employment matters greatly for the overall performance of the American economy.

Changes in sort of services that are tradable could also have important effects on the current account balance of the United States. The United States has maintained a revealed comparative advantage in services trade for some time. In 2007, for example, the overall U.S. trade deficit of $708.5 billion masked a deficit in goods of $815.4 billion that was partly offset by a services surplus of $106.9 billion. It has long been argued that this surplus in services reflects U.S. comparative advantage in activities intensive in human capital. Given its advantages in the production of tradable services, the expanding span of these services could bring the United States new or improved export opportunities. Yet at the same time, expansions in the span of tradable services are also likely to alter trade flows in ways that impart new pressures on some segments of the U.S. labor market and that reduce incentives to invest within the United States in human capital and other assets needed to produce tradable services.

Finally, at the macroeconomic level, the sustainability of large U.S. current-account deficits—which peaked at $811.5 billion in 2006—is a long-standing concern. Greater tradability of services might foster an additional margin of adjustment for the U.S. economy, in terms of expanding the set of "tradable" activities to which resources must shift for production of exports.

To explore the economic and measurement implications of new types of trade in services and of growing international flows of invisibles of all types, we organized a conference under the auspices of the Conference on Research in Income and Wealth (CRIW) and the National Bureau of Economic Research. The conference, entitled "International Service Flows," was held in Bethesda, Maryland on April 28–29, 2006.

Happily, the authors who wrote papers for the conference chose to interpret the topic of services in the conference title broadly. This book's title of *International Trade in Services and Intangibles in the Era of Globalization* conveys the breadth of topics covered more clearly than the title used at the conference itself. For example, a theme of several of the papers was the importance of international transactions involving the creation, use, or ownership of intangible assets such as intellectual property in the emerging globalized economy. This result builds on the papers at a previous CRIW conference on *Measuring Capital in the New Economy* (Corrado, Haltiwanger, and Sichel, eds., 2005), which revealed the role of intangible assets as key constituents of the capital stock of a modern service-oriented economy. Besides services and intangibles, another category of invisibles considered by some of the papers is the income recorded in the current account. (Invisibles comprise all elements of the current account in the balance of payments other than merchandise trade.)

Progress on Measurement Challenges

The globalized economy presents some new kinds of measurement challenges for our statistical system, which the papers presented at the conference help us to meet. Equally important, the papers allow us to assess our progress and to identify the gaps and limitations of the data that hinder our ability to understand the emerging globalized economy and to analyze key policy questions. For nominal flows of invisibles, notwithstanding such problems as tax-related distortions of economic flows or transactions in intangibles whose country of residence can be ambiguous, the overall picture is reasonably optimistic. In the face of formidable measurement difficulties, however, development of the price indexes needed to deflate nominal flows is proceeding more slowly. Poorly measured real flows of international services may therefore become an increasingly serious obstacle to knowing how globalization is affecting the U.S. economy.

Nominal Flows

Research that Ascher and Whichard (1991) presented at the 1989 CRIW conference "International Economic Transactions" documented the development at the U.S. Bureau of Economic Analysis (BEA) of comprehensive measures of trade in services.(Data on trade in some services, such as shipping and passenger travel, had long been available for the United States and other countries, as documented by Hoeksta and Stern [1991].) Research attention next turned to products delivered through foreign affiliates of multinationals—which are especially key in the case of services— and the development of the ownership-based framework of the current account. The usefulness of ownership-based accounting in a world where trade is increasingly conducted through affiliates and where intangibles with no definite geographic location are increasingly important was highlighted in 1995 at the CRIW conference "Geography and Ownership as Bases for Economic Accounting" (Baldwin, Lipsey, and Richardson 1998.)

With these accomplishments behind us, research on trade in services can now be focused on particular commodities that are emerging in importance, changing in character, or where improved measurement techniques have become available. Among such topics covered at the "International Service Flows" conference were trade in banking and insurance services (Borga, chapter 2, this volume), business' use of offshored services (Yuskavage, Strassner, and Madeiros, chapter 8, this volume), and intangible assets such as R&D (Moris, chapter 5 this volume) and intellectual property in general (Robbins, chapter 4, this volume). Measures of R&D and intellectual property transactions are important both because of these products' key role in the modern economy and because of the role of R&D assets in the forthcoming revision of the international guidelines for the preparation of national accounts of the 1993 System of National Accounts (SNA93).[1]

Reassuringly, no evidence was presented at our conference to corroborate suspicions that imports of ITC-enabled of services may have been missed in the U.S. accounts. Nevertheless, the conference uncovered some important gaps in the data and provided striking evidence of ways in which those data that are available could be misleading. In a case study of an important U.S. export, motion pictures, Hanson and Xiang (chapter six, this volume) find that UN Comtrade data misses most of the value of this trade, and that even though BEA data are better, private data sources must be used to obtain the geographic detail needed to study the drivers of this trade. Furthermore, Lipsey (chapter 1, this volume) and Mutti and Grubert (chapter 3, this volume) suggest that some reported patterns of trade in international transactions in intangible assets and their services are heavily influenced by the tax treatment of transactions with affiliates located in tax havens, which could lead to a distorted picture of the true economic flows. Lipsey also notes how the lack of geographical nexus of international transactions in services and other invisibles makes measurement more challenging.

Prices

In the case of the prices needed to deflate international service flows, the recent measurement story is, unfortunately, one of growing ignorance. This is especially disappointing in light of the good foundation laid by ear-

1. Information on the forthcoming revision of the SNA, including draft chapters, is available on the United Nations Statistics website at http://unstats.un.org/unsd/sna1993/snarev1.asp.

lier progress on price measurement for traded goods and for nontraded services. For goods, the CRIW conference "International Economic Transactions" included a paper on the development by the Bureau of Labor Statistics (BLS) of comprehensive sets of export and import price indexes (Alterman 1991) and a paper on measuring international trade price competitiveness (Lipsey, Molinari, and Kravis 1991). For domestic services, the suspicion that poor price measures for the growing service sector could help to account for a puzzling slowdown in measured productivity growth (Griliches 1992, 3) sparked much research, including CRIW conferences "Output Measurement in the Service Sectors" (Griliches, ed. 1992), "Medical Care Output and Productivity" (Cutler and Berndt 2001), and "Hard-to-Measure Goods and Services" (Berndt and Hulten 2007). Enough progress was made so that the important contribution of the service sector in the post-1995 productivity speedup (see Bosworth and Triplett [2007] and Triplett and Bosworth [2004], chapter 2) could be discovered.

For internationally traded services, as of 2007, BLS's international price program had developed and released indexes covering only passenger air transportation, air freight, ocean liner freight (inbound only), crude oil tanker freight (inbound), travel and tourism exports, and education services exports. The development of these last two indexes, and of additional new indexes for trade in services, were topics of a paper (not included in this volume) that Kelley Khatchadourian and Alice Wiesner (2006) presented at the "International Service Flows" conference. Subsequently, budget cuts compelled BLS to cease research on indexes for trade in services and to cease producing the just-developed indexes for travel and tourism and education services exports, along with older indexes for inbound ocean liner freight and inbound tanker freight. Missing price information for traded services is thus likely to pose an increasingly serious obstacle to measuring U.S. real output and productivity, to gauging inflationary pressures on the economy, to estimating the substitutability of internationally sourced services for U.S. production, and to assessing trends in U.S. competitiveness. Besides the information lost in the recent reversals at BLS, we lack price indexes for trade in business, professional, and technical (BPT) services. Yuskavage, Strassner, and Medeiros (chapter 8, this volume) note that these indexes are needed to measure these services in real terms, a task that is becoming important for accurate measurement of the growth of the U.S. economy. Prices of BPT service imports may be rising rapidly because dollar-denominated costs are climbing and capacity constraints are tightening in key supplying countries like India, or they may be flat because cost pass-through is low, or they may be falling because new sources of supply are providing increased competition. We simply do not know.

Defining Trade in Services

Besides providing hard evidence on new and emerging trends in trade that have the potential to dramatically reshape the economies of developed and developing nations alike, this book provides background on the key conceptual issues in measuring trade in invisibles. One such issue is the definition of trade in services. Though this question might seem to be rather technical, its importance was made clear by a recent controversy over a large discrepancy between India's reported exports of BPT services to the United States and the imports of BPT services from India reported by the BEA. A Government Accountability Office (2005) report refers to an estimate of $8.7 billion for India's exports to the United States in 2003, when BEA's estimate of corresponding imports was just $423 million. (Dossani [2006, 249] reports Indian exports in the $2.5 to $3.6 billion range in 2002 to 2004, based on Indian data.) The main explanation turned out to be the definition of trade in services that had been used in calculating India's exports, as Borga (chapter 2, this volume) notes.

To define trade in services requires an answer to the question of what kinds of transactions constitute services and the question of which service transactions constitute trade. Note that trade in services is a broader concept than offshoring of services or international outsourcing of services. Offshoring and outsourcing include only types of services formerly or usually produced in the domestic economy. Moreover, many authors regard the meaning of the term "international outsourcing" as an even narrower concept than "offshoring." They include in the former only purchases from *unaffiliated* establishments of inputs that were formerly produced in house, and use the term "insourcing" for the services produced in a foreign affiliate of a multinational corporation (MNC).

Which Transactions are Services?

Hill (1977, 317–18) observes that services change the condition of a good or person, illustrating this concept with examples of shipment of goods, repairs, cleaning, hairdressing, and dental care. The forthcoming revision of the SNA follows a similar approach. It defines a service as a production activity that changes the condition of a good or a person or that facilitates the exchange of products or financial assets (United Nations 2007, paragraphs 6.17–6.18).

The "production activity" requirement of the definition in the revised SNA is not a topic of controversy, but it can present difficulties. Distributions of property income such as dividends and interest paid to providers of finance are examples of transactions that are excluded from services by this requirement, as passive owners of property used by a business are not themselves engaged in a production activity.[2] Yet we must be careful about using the label given to a transaction to decide whether its economic substance is a production activity. Lease payments, for example, normally represent service transactions, but leases that are merely financing arrangements, known as financial leases, are functional equivalents of collateralized loans and must be treated as such. The opposite kind of reclassification can be needed as well. In a chapter in this volume, Maria Borga discusses research on recognizing how interest, including interest that is foregone, can substitute for the explicit payments of premiums or fees in the financial services industries of insurance and banking. Implicitly purchased services are therefore included in the production activities of these industries.

A point of controversy in the definition of services is the line between services and goods. A succinct definition of a service that well describes the practice in official statistics is that a service is any produced item that is not a good, where goods are material in nature (e.g., IMF 2008, paragraph 10.6). Such a definition by exclusion of all that is material leaves room for considerable diversity in the types of transactions included in services. Indeed, even the subset of internationally traded services that can be transmitted over a wire includes, besides the transmission itself, items as dissimilar as motion pictures, financial or legal contracts, information of various sorts, software, data processing, and telephone assistance. Even sales of patents are included in exports of R&D services in the latest edition of the Balance of Payments and International Investment Position Manual (IMF 2008, paragraph 10.134).[3]

Identifying such a broad set of items as services based on their immateriality is, in Hill's (1999) view, a mistake. Instead, he contends that the definition of a service ought to hinge on whether consumption occurs after production or simultaneously. Goods have to be produced before they are consumed and hence exist at least momentarily as inventories. Services, on the other hand, cannot be put into inventories because their production and consumption are simultaneous (Hill 1999, 437). Hill therefore divides the conventional two categories of goods and services into three categories consisting of ordinary goods, intangible goods, and services. Intangible goods would include immaterial products that are available for use after they have been produced, such as the text of a book, an artistic original, a

---

2. Originally BEA's international transactions accounts classified as services all current account items other than goods and unilateral transfers. Ascher and Whichard (1991, 207) discuss how this treatment was changed.

3. At present, BEA's practice is generally to record them as services exports of royalties and license fees, though in some cases they are included in the capital account rather than the current account (Yorgenson 2007, 27, fn. 38).

scientific formula, the design for a new machine, or a new computer program.

The concept of stockpiles of services seems paradoxical, but the potential for timing differences between the production and sale of intangible products that Hill highlights means that stocks of these products, either as inventories or as fixed assets, must be recognized if we are to record current production correctly. Moreover, Griliches (1992, 5) identifies as distinctive features of service transactions a lack of change of ownership and the participation of the purchaser in the production process, either directly or as a supplier of an input. These criteria are adopted by the IMF *Balance of Payments and International Investment Position Manual* (IMF 2008, paragraph 10.60) when it excludes goods sent abroad for processing from trade in goods and instead classifies the processing fee as trade in services.

A change in ownership is the very thing that distinguishes transactions in intangible assets themselves from transactions for the use, or services, of such assets. Nonetheless, when the forthcoming revision of the SNA introduces a new category of intangible products called "knowledge-capturing products," it classifies sales of these products as services (UN 2007, paragraph 6.22). As a practical matter, transactions in the use of intangible assets (such as a royalty to a patent holder) may be difficult to separate out from sales of the intangible asset itself in the available source data. Furthermore, their immateriality is not the only conceptual reason for classifying knowledge-capturing products as services. These products have the service-like properties of changing the condition of the user and of requiring the participation of the user in the production process. For example, a research report written under contract makes the buyer better-informed, but the buyer must provide inputs of the time and effort to read it. Thus, although transactions in intangible assets do not fit neatly into either of the categories of goods and services, their inclusion in trade in services is appropriate.

Which Service Transactions Constitute Trade?

The next question is how to distinguish services transactions that constitute international trade from those that are purely domestic. For goods, physical movement across a border can usually be used to identify trade, but a service can be consumed in the country where it is produced yet still be considered as traded. This occurs when either its consumer or its producer is a nonresident. As a result, the General Agreement on Trade in Services (GATS) recognizes four modes of trade in services: (a) cross-border supply; (b) consumption abroad, such as by tourists or students; (c) commercial presence of foreign affiliates of multinational companies; and (d) presence of natural persons.

The establishment of foreign affiliates by MNCs (Mode 3) and movement of natural persons across borders (Mode 4) are, of course, important elements of globalization. They are also important parts of the picture of international trade in services because many types of services can only be delivered via physical presence. Indeed, for the United States, sales and purchases of services delivered by foreign affiliates have substantially exceeded cross-border trade in services since the late 1990s (Koncz and Flatness 2007). Nevertheless, the movements of productive factors across borders referenced in GATS Modes 3 and 4 tend to blur the significance of national boundaries in ways that raise questions in the construction and interpretation of measures of international transactions. In the Mode 4 case, for example, migration of natural persons across a border changes their residency, but temporary visits (defined in official statistics as remaining in the host country for a less than a year) do not. Whether to treat both parties to a service transaction as residents of the host country or whether to count the transaction as trade can be unclear, either because the length of stay is uncertain (Lipsey, chapter 1, this volume) or because the purpose for which the data are being compiled calls for an alternative approach.

In the case of GATS Mode 3, foreign affiliate trade in services (FATS), the affiliate is unambiguously a resident of its host country. Services that foreign affiliates provide to host country residents are therefore not included in the definition of exports from the standard geography-based accounting framework of national accounts. Yet products delivered through affiliates can be substitutes for cross-border trade and are part of the overall trade picture. An ownership-based accounting framework for international transactions allows insight into the activities of foreign affiliates, as Landefeld, Whichard, and Lowe (1993) and Baldwin and Kimura (1998) explain. This accounting framework shows the combined receipts from exports and the investment income that sales of foreign affiliates generate for their U.S. parent. In interpreting these receipts caution may sometimes be warranted, however, because Mutti and Grubert (chapter 3, this volume) show that some transactions between foreign affiliates have been accounted for in a way that allows the U.S. parent to report smaller receipts of income from them.

Another problem in defining trade in services arises in the treatment of rentals of fixed capital assets. Rentals of such assets are accounted for as service flows from the owner of the asset to the user of the asset. As a result, operating leases for movable capital assets with nonresident lessors are included in imports of services, and those with nonresident lessees are included in exports of services. Ireland, for example, had exports of aircraft leasing services amounting to €3.3 billion—representing more than 2 percent of its GDP—in 2005 (Central Statistics Office 2006.)

On the other hand, the adjective "domestic," represented by the middle letter in GDP, implies that that concept includes any production that occurs within the borders of a country and excludes any production that occurs outside those borders. A capital asset located within a country's borders seems pretty clearly to be producing its services within those borders, even if its owner resides elsewhere. To resolve the tension between the need to account for rentals as purchases of services from asset owners and the need for a geographically defined measure of total production, the services of immovable fixed capital assets such as land or structures are always deemed to be provided by a resident of the country where they are located.[4] For example, when a rented structure is owned directly by a nonresident, a notional resident affiliate is effectively credited with receiving the rent, and the payment to the nonresident is classified as a distribution of income. This prevents services of structures leased from foreign owners from being counted as imports of the country where the structure is located.

Royalties and license fees paid to owners of intellectual property (IP) are analogous to payments for the use of fixed capital assets, except that in this case the asset is an intangible one.[5] A treatment parallel to that given to movable fixed capital assets is generally appropriate for international transactions in royalties and license fees. The services furnished to the user of an IP asset resemble the services that tangible capital assets furnish to their users. Furthermore, transactions for the use of IP often include assistance from the owner of the IP, such as the furnishing of copies of originals, oversight, or advice.

Nevertheless, chapters in this book by Lipsey and by Mutti and Grubert raise questions of whether certain payments for the use of IP have any rationale beyond the shifting of taxable income to a jurisdiction with a low tax rate.[6] These payments are substantial enough in value to suggest the need for future research on a possible alternative treatment, modeled on the treatment presently given to immovable fixed assets, for certain international transactions for the use of IP. Intangible IP assets share with services the characteristic of the lack of a physical presence in a particular location. This can make it hard to be sure whether an IP asset that is reported to have been acquired by an overseas affiliate via a purchase or cost-sharing arrangement has really been exported. For example, when a U.S. pharmaceutical manufacturer transfers ownership of patents resulting from R&D performed in the United States to a tax haven affiliate, the production attributable to that IP (as measured by royalty payments to the foreign affiliate) counts as an import of services by the United States. Yet the tax haven will often have no material role in either the production of the drug itself or

4. International Monetary Fund (1993), paragraphs 64 and 316.
5. The forthcoming revision of the SNA recommends that the IP created by R&D activities be recognized as an intangible capital asset. This gives a natural interpretation to royalties and license fees paid for the use of these assets as payments for services that these assets produce.
6. In some cases the IRS has determined that the answer to this question is "no." See Drucker (2006). Another example of payments to an overseas affiliate for the use of IP—which have not been challenged by the IRS—is discussed in Simpson (2005b).

in the underlying R&D. Under these circumstances, a portrayal of the transaction as an export of a service by the tax haven probably captures its economic significance less well than a portrayal that adopts the view that the IP in question is still within the United States, so that the payments to the offshore affiliate really represent income transactions.

The Chapters in this Volume: Four Main Themes

The chapters of this volume have been grouped into four noteworthy themes. First, the measurement of trade in services presents some unique challenges. Keeping classification schemes for collecting and organizing measures of services trade up-to-date is difficult when new types or patterns of trade in services emerge.[7] A paper by Pierre Sicsic (2006) presented at our conference (but not included in this volume) found, for example, that in French data, call centers were sometimes reported in business services (where they are supposed to be) and sometimes reported in communications services. As another example, Borga (chapter 2, this volume) reports that an additional probing question and a sample size expansion were needed in the United States to address an undercount of new kinds of trade in services. Some other measurement challenges arise from the unique features of services trade. The definitions of the price, volume, and even expenditures on many traded services may involve difficult conceptual and analytical questions. Moreover, in the case of services, no physical object exists whose movement across a border can be tracked, and the true country of residence of the financial, intangible, or mobile capital assets that render or facilitate the service, or even of the transactors, may be ambiguous or of dubious meaning. This partly reflects the ease with which items with no tangible presence can be lodged for legal and tax purposes far from the location where they originated.

For example, when a multinational corporation transfers ownership of intellectual property created in the United States to a tax haven affiliate that then collects royalty payments from the United States, do those royalty payments really represent production in the tax haven of intermediate inputs used by U.S. producers? The answer to this question has implications for the interpretation of measures of GDP for both of the trading partners, because even production that consists entirely of capital services is included in the GDP of the host country, not in the GDP of the country of residence of the ultimate beneficial owners of the capital assets used in that production.

A second theme is that, in contrast to trade in goods, where the United States runs large deficits, the production of services for export by affiliates

---

7. Adoption of the North American Industrial Classification System (AICS) has, however, helped with keeping up with evolving universes of services.

of MNCs and others continues to be an area of strength for the American economy. Production of some traded services cannot move to other countries because they can only be produced in the country where they are consumed (tourism or servicing of visiting aircraft, for example). Other services require concentrations of specialized expertise and resources that would be difficult to recreate in most countries outside the United States. The U.S. trade advantage in services also reflects the way production is now organized for many goods, with research, development, and testing services, as well as some managerial and financial services performed in the United States, while the physical product assembly occurs offshore. These arrangements often involve affiliates of MNCs, including ones based outside the United States.

A third theme is that patterns of trade in services have some unique drivers. The role of improvements in communications and information technology in facilitating offshore sourcing is clear, but questions of job characteristics—whether an activity is entirely codifiable rather than dependent on discretion, judgement, and tacitly communicated knowledge—and the presence of educational, language, or cultural barriers can also be key. Growth in some other kinds of traded services is linked with growth of foreign direct investment and the establishment of foreign affiliates of MNCs because these services are delivered via physical presence in a foreign host country. In other instances, tax and regulatory considerations may be key drivers—or perhaps distorters—of services trading patterns. Finally, some important traded services (such as wholesaling, merchanting, financing, insuring, and shipping) are complementary to trade in goods, with the growth causality running in both directions. In the nineteenth century Alfred Marshall noted that the railroad had made fresh fish available inland in England for the first time, but now shipping and transport technologies allow fresh-cut flowers to be picked on one continent and sold on another.

The fourth and final theme of this volume is that new ways of trading some kinds of services can intensify international competition for jobs, capital investment, economic growth, and tax revenue. Offshore outsourcing of employment in such functions as call centers, technical support, back office functions, and tax preparation is the example of this that looms large in the mind of the general public. However, differences between jurisdictions in the tax, legal, or regulatory environment can also influence foreign direct investment flows sufficiently to cause large shifts in the location of production of capital-intensive services.

As examples, exports of services such as licensing of intellectual property and leasing of aircraft have flourished in the nonburdensome tax and regulatory environment offered by Ireland. They are part of the growth process that took Ireland from among the poorest countries in Europe in the 1980s as measured by GDP per capita to the richest in 2004, excluding countries with populations below five million. Exports of another asset-intensive service, insurance, have long thrived in the favorable tax and legal environment of Switzerland, but in recent years Caribbean tax havens have also become large exporters of such services.

Part I: Challenges in Measuring Trade in Services

An overview of the topic of international transactions in services, including a conceptual and historical background on trade in services, is provided by Robert Lipsey's chapter, "Measuring International Trade in Services." Measured by exports, world services trade rose from just over 20 percent of goods trade at the end of 1970s to just under 30 percent in 2003, though the official statistics on services trade may overstate their growth because data collection has improved. For the United States, services exports now amount to over 40 percent of goods exports. Imports of services have grown more modestly relative to imports of goods on a balance of payments basis: in the United States they have been flat at about 20 percent of imports of goods since 1987, although they have risen relative to GDP.

Lipsey next examines problems in the measurement of U.S. trade in services. Unlike goods trade, which is often defined in practice by physical movement across a border, trade in services must be defined by reference to the residency of the transactors or owner of the capital asset used to deliver the service.[8] Yet even this criterion does not resolve all the ambiguities. An example comes from U.S. exports of education services. The nonresident status of the consumers of these services can be questionable, as many of them intend to remain in the United States at the conclusion of their studies.

Some recent developments in international transactions in services, including shifting patterns of location of intellectual property assets and of exports of rights to the use of these assets, also raise questions of interpretation. Lipsey documents some oddities in trade patterns for tax haven countries, and in asset and profit ratios for affiliates that suggest the presence of tax-related distortions in some reported values of trade and foreign direct investment. The values of the financial assets and intellectual property assets attributed to foreign affiliates based in tax havens seem implausible. As a result, residency-based measures of trade in such services as insurance and royalties and license fees may be less meaningful than the alternative ownership-based international transactions accounts.

The data on trade in services published by the BEA and research on improving and expanding that information are the topics of a chapter by Maria Borga entitled "Improved Measures of U.S. International Services:

---

8. Even for ordinary goods, change in ownership is the conceptually correct basis for defining trade, even when movement across a border is the more practical alternative. See SNA93, paragraph 14.55.

The Cases of Insurance, Wholesale and Retail Trade, and Financial Services." The published data cover the two channels of international delivery
of services: cross-border trade in services, and sales of services through locally established direct investment enterprises or affiliates. In 2006, the
United States exported private services of $404 billion and it imported ser-
vices of $308 billion. The fastest growing categories were royalties and li-
cense fees and other private services (a category that includes finance, insurance, education, telecommunications, and business, professional, and
technical services), with import growth slightly outpacing export growth
both for these specific categories and for services in the aggregate. The
rapid rates of growth of trade in services are exceeded by the growth rate of
sales of services by affiliates, however, implying that international services
are increasingly delivered through a commercial presence in the customers' country.[9] In contrast to cross-border trade in services, where the
U.S. advantage is narrowing, the majority-owned foreign affiliates of U.S.
MNCs are growing faster than the majority-owned U.S. affiliates of foreign
MNCs.

Borga next reports on research on new measures of trade in services,
starting with insurance. Until 2003, the measurement concept for cross-
border insurance services was premiums less claims. Now the concept is
premiums less expected losses plus investment earnings on technical reserves ("premium supplements") plus auxiliary services, which are separate international transactions for items like actuarial services or claims
and adjustment services. The new approach has reduced the volatility of
the measures of insurance exports and imports, and on average it has
raised their level. Borga also develops a new method that could be used to
estimate the value of insurance services provided by U.S. affiliates of foreign MNCs. The older measure of output of insurance affiliates did not
deduct claims, so the effect of the new method is to cut the estimated value
of these services by roughly half.

Borga's research measures of trade in services include two further types
of services. First, in official statistics on exports and imports of goods,
wholesale and retail trade margins that cover the cost of distributive services are combined with amounts paid to producers of goods, primarily
manufacturers. Supplementary measures of the distributive services included in statistics on goods trade are therefore needed to discern the role
of the distributive industries in international trade. Second, for banks,
measures of implicitly priced services are included in national and industry accounts, but not yet in the ITAs. Banking services are purchased im-

---

9. An appendix to Borga's chapter discusses an alternative ownership-based presentation
of the current account that highlights the income receipts that services sales of affiliates generate for their parents. As explained previously, affiliates' sales in their host country are not
included in the definition of exports and imports.

plicitly by depositors who accept a lower rate of interest than would be obtainable from an investment that conferred no services, and by borrowers who pay interest rates that include a spread over the banks' cost of funds.

Part II: R&D and Intellectual Property

Readers who want to delve more deeply into the question of effects of tax incentives on measures of trade in services and of location of intellectual property assets should turn to John Mutti and Harry Grubert's chapter, "The Effect of Taxes on Royalties and the Migration of Intangible Assets Abroad." Tax-induced distortions in international sourcing of income are not a new phenomenon—see Grubert and Mutti (1998)—but over the past ten years, a number of developments have enabled U.S. MNCs to attribute more of their global income to affiliates located in tax havens. One of these is a regulation issued by the Internal Revenue Service (IRS) in 1997 that has been nicknamed "check-the-box." The name refers to a box that can be checked if the MNC filing the tax return wants to consolidate multiple controlled foreign corporations (CFCs) into a single hybrid entity. Transactions between the CFC affiliates wrapped up in a hybrid are invisible to the IRS, including transactions that would otherwise be covered by the antiabuse provisions in the Internal Revenue Code covering royalty payments between siblings of an MNC. Check-the-box does *not* prevent the affiliates of the MNC from filing separate *foreign* tax returns, so the affiliate in the high-tax country can continue to claim its royalty payments as a deductible expense.

The authors discover some patterns in the data that indicate that MNCs have responded to the check-the-box regulation by paying royalties and license fees to tax haven affiliates for the use of the affiliate's intellectual property, such as software or patents. These patterns include rapid growth of: (a) nondividend income of CFCs in low-tax countries; (b) payments of royalties by foreign affiliates reported in BEA's surveys; (c) receipts of royalties by tax haven affiliates as measured by BEA surveys; and (d) direct investment service payments. The direct investment service payments are an indicator of cost-sharing for the development of intellectual property that entitles the tax haven affiliate to royalties from the users of the intellectual property. The authors also find that the share of the benefits of parent R&D retained by foreign affiliates after making royalty payments to the parent grew after check-the-box, and that parent R&D became strongly associated with cost-sharing payments instead of with royalty payments.

Although these findings imply a reduction in tax revenues, check-the-box may also have some beneficial effects. It may help prevent the migration of R&D activity offshore by allowing MNCs to conduct their R&D in a nontax haven country yet still receive the associated royalty income in a tax-advantaged location. Indeed, Mutti and Grubert find that MNCs have not shifted the location of actual R&D activities to low tax countries, and that relatively little R&D activity has migrated away from the United States.

A general picture of royalty payments and license fees for the use of IP assets from an industry perspective is the topic of the chapter by Carol Robbins, "Measuring Payments for the Supply and Use of Intellectual Property." Totals of explicit purchases of the services of IP assets do not come close to being a comprehensive estimate of the overall importance of such assets in the U.S. economy: intangible assets are often used internally, leaving no record of a transaction that directly measures their services. Still, if intangible IP assets represent an important share of society's true capital stock, as argued by Corrado, Hulten, and Sichel (2005, 2006), transactions for their use can be expected to occur frequently. Robbins confirms the growing importance of IP property transactions, finding, for example, that IRS totals for royalty receipts have a ten-year average growth rate of 11 percent per year, compared with a growth rate of 6 percent per year for services as a whole.

Robbins' analysis of BEA surveys of international transactions in royalties and license fees in 2002 shows that industrial processes (which include patents and trade secrets) and general use software account for the bulk of U.S. receipts from unaffiliated parties. In payments to unaffiliated parties, industrial processes licensed by the pharmaceutical industry stand out as important, but in IRS data both this industry and the computer and electronics industry are important recipients of licensing receipts.

Robbins also finds that trade in royalties and license fees is predominantly conducted through affiliates and that the United States has a large trade surplus in both these categories. For royalties and license fees this surplus is $25 billion in 2002, compared with a trade surplus in services as a whole of $61 billion. This is consistent with the picture of a reorganized structure of production in which manufacturers separate the location of the research, development, and testing functions from that of the more rote function of product assembly, retaining only the former within the United States.

Next, Robbins investigates the supply and use of royalties and license fees by U.S. industries, including domestic transactions. One mystery is why royalty receipts in the industry data from the Economic Census for 2002 are so low. The Census Bureau royalty receipts total $24 billion, compared with $115.9 billion in receipts tabulated from business tax returns by the Statistics of Income (SOI) program of the IRS. Also, respondents to BEA surveys covering just receipts from foreign sources report $44.5 billion in royalties. The SOI estimates could be affected by double-counting of pass-through transactions, and they include some royalties received by foreign affiliates of MNCs that file consolidated tax returns, so the undercount in the Economic Census is not as great as might be surmised from comparing it with the SOI figure. Moreover, the BEA royalties include general licenses for the use of software, which, unlike the licenses to reproduce software, do not belong in the intermediate input category of royalties that Robbins and the Census Bureau are trying to measure. Nevertheless, the Census data omit some types of establishments, and in cases of reciprocal arrangements such as cross-licensing agreements they appear to reflect only net payments, not the gross payments and receipts collected by BEA. On the whole, Robbins finds that the SOI data are more complete than the Census data as a basis for estimation of the industries' supply and use of rights to benefit from intellectual property.

The production of much of the intellectual property associated with royalty payments requires R&D. International transactions in research, development, and testing (RDT) services are the topic of a chapter by Francisco Moris, "R&D Exports and Imports: New Data and Methodological Issues." An extensive literature exists on spillovers and disembodied flows of knowledge across borders. Yet in contrast to these implicit transactions, explicit transactions in knowledge between the United States and other countries have not been analyzed in any detail. Moris' study fills this gap in the literature. He finds that MNCs have a large role in the performance of RDT in the United States: out of $208 billion of RDT expenditures in 2004, $152 billion was done by U.S. MNCs at home and $30 billion was done by U.S. affiliates of foreign MNCs. Particularly noteworthy is the role of U.S. affiliates of foreign MNCs as performers of R&D for their parents. These affiliates export a substantial fraction of the RDT that they perform, and their exports of RDT services far exceed their imports. Indeed, they account for most of the overall U.S. trade surplus in RDT services, with the remainder accounted for by U.S. MNC parents. As MNCs segment their production process into activities that can be parceled out among countries in a cost-effective manner, the United States evidently continues to have a comparative advantage in the performance of RDT.

Moris also develops a classification scheme for business R&D and for trade in RDT services. An influential previous proposal, found in the Organization for Economic Cooperation and Development's (OECD's) 1993 and 2003 Frascati Manual, considers only funding and performance of R&D, while measures of trade in business R&D services consider just the use and performance of these services. Moris finds that all three dimensions are important for understanding international transactions in R&D, however. In a comprehensive set of measures that includes the performance, the funding, and the use of R&D, U.S. transfers to fund foreign R&D are seen to be $31 billion. Unfortunately, data on transfers from abroad to US performers of R&D are unavailable, which prevents an estimate of net transfers to performers of R&D or one of the overall net effect of R&D services transactions on the U.S. balance on current account. However, the United States uses less R&D services than it performs, leaving it with a trade surplus of almost $4 billion in this item in 2004.

A distinctive feature of trade in intellectual property services and other information products is the degree to which export success may hinge on the ability to overcome barriers posed by cultural and linguistic differences. In "International Trade in Motion Picture Services" Gordon H. Hanson and Chong Xiang estimate a modified version of the gravity model of trade to investigate the effect of such trade barriers on one of the most successful export products of the United States. To carry out their study, Hanson and Xiang use data from a commercial source to construct measures of trade in motion picture services based on box office receipts by country of origin. Hanson and Xiang also develop indexes of language closeness to English that serve as measures of linguistic and cultural distance from the United States.

Box office revenues for U.S. films in Europe are quite large compared to revenues from domestic sources, with much variation across countries. Econometric models of the sources of variation in the revenues grossed by American movies relative to domestic films confirm that trade costs arising from linguistic and cultural differences have large, statistically significant effects. Hanson and Xiang also find that countries that are better situated to produce domestic films themselves have smaller relative consumption of U.S. films. As is predicted by theories of scale effects for the production of differentiated products, a large domestic market as measured by a country's GDP relative to the United States confers important advantages in motion picture production. Finally, explicit trade barriers to film imports for European countries are found to have a significant effect in one of the specifications.

Part III: Offshoring of Services

Employees who manufacture goods in wealthier countries have long had to worry about losing their job to a low-wage overseas competitor. Recently, however, advances in information and communications technology (ICT) have led to the phenomenon of offshore sourcing of many service functions previously located in a domestic establishment. As a result, displacement by foreign labor has also become conceivable for many employees in the service sector of wealthier countries. In a global economy where millions of educated employees are willing to work at considerably lower wages than predominate for service workers in the U.S. and where information transmittal has become close to costless, predictions reminiscent of Presidential candidate Ross Perot's "giant sucking sound" of jobs and capital being drained from the American economy have reentered the debate.

Yet two of the chapters in this volume carefully analyze the effects of services offshoring that has already occurred and obtain results that are in stark contrast with the dramatic future that has been imagined. The first chapter on this subject, "Does Service Offshoring Lead to Job Losses? Evidence from the United States," by Mary Amiti and Shang-Jin Wei, notes that news stories on job losses due to offshore outsourcing numbered in the thousands in 2004, suggesting that this phenomenon is quite important. To see if this is so, Amiti and Wei assemble detailed data covering input-output (I-O) tables, trade, and domestic labor markets to estimate effects of offshore outsourcing on domestic employment from 1992 to 2000. In regressions covering 96 manufacturing industries, with instrumental variables techniques to control for endogeneity in changes in imported materials and services inputs, they find no evidence of negative employment effects from growth in imported inputs. Effects at aggregate levels are, however, expected to be smaller than at disaggregated levels because in the flexible labor markets of the United States, labor is mobile across industries. Indeed, after disaggregating the data into 450 industries, services offshoring is found to have a statistically significant negative effect on employment. Nevertheless, the implied effect on manufacturing employment is a modest −0.4 percent over the period covered by the investigation.

A chapter by Robert E. Yuskavage, Erich H. Strassner, and Gabriel W. Medeiros, "Outsourcing and Imported Services in BEA's Industry Accounts" also uses I-O accounts data to study employment effects of offshore outsourcing. This chapter also provides a guide to where specific types of information on trade in services may be found in the three different sets of accounts at BEA: the ITAs; the National Income and Product Accounts (NIPAs); and the Annual Industry Accounts (AIAs), which include the annual input-output (I-O) accounts and the integrated GDP-by-industry accounts. The differences in treatment of trade in services between these accounts are not always obvious. For example, duties on imported goods are excluded from imports in ITAs and the NIPAs, where goods trade is on a free-on-board (f.o.b.) basis. Yet in the I-O accounts–where we can find commodity detail on imports in the use of commodities tables–duties are included in the value of the goods. To prevent a discrepancy in total imports between the I-O accounts and the NIPAs and ITAs, the duties added to the value of goods imports are subtracted from imports of wholesale trade services, leaving the I-O accounts with a smaller measure of overall imports of services than the NIPAs or the ITAs.

The I-O accounts include the bulk of imported services in a line labeled "noncomparable imports." The term "noncomparable" means that the imported item has no domestic counterpart, so it is tempting to conclude that imported services are largely not in direct competition with services produced in the United States and hence have little potential to displace domestic employment. This would be a mistake, however, because business, professional, and technical (BPT) services that are outsourced by MNCs to a foreign affiliate are often classified as noncomparable imports. The authors therefore develop corrected estimates of total imports of BPT services that include those treated as noncomparable imports in the I-O accounts.

The authors next use the AIAs to estimate the use by industries of outsourced services and of outsourced services from foreign sources. They find that offshore outsourcing of services is indeed growing rapidly, so that the imported component of the outsourcing-related services doubled between 1997 and 2004. Nevertheless, it has not yet become large enough to account for much of the slowdown in the competing domestic industry that occurred after 2000 or to have substantial effects on domestic employment. For manufacturing, imports supply only 5 percent of all outsourced BPT services in the years after 2001, and for private industries in the aggregate imports supply around 3 percent of these services.

Even though the studies of offshore outsourcing find that its effects thus far on U.S. labor markets and industrial structure have been modest, Blinder (2006) argues that in the not-so-distant future imports of newly tradable types of services may expose tens of millions of employees here to foreign competition, with potentially drastic effects on U.S. labor markets. The potential effect of offshore outsourcing on labor markets in the United States and other OECD countries is the topic of Desirée van Welsum and Xavier Reif's chapter, entitled "We can Work it Out: The Globalization of IT-enabled Services." As background for their inquiry, the authors provide evidence from trade and FDI patterns from many countries pointing to trends toward increasingly globalized production of both services in general and outsourcing-related services (defined as business services plus computer and information services) in particular. To discern the outer limit of where these trends could take us in terms of labor market impacts on OECD countries, we can consider what percentage of jobs is potentially offshorable. The authors estimate these percentages based on counts of employees engaged in detailed occupations that have four offshorability attributes: (a) intensive use of information and communication technologies (ICTs); (b) an output that can be transmitted by ICTs; (c) highly codifiable knowledge content; and (d) no requirement of face-to-face contact.

For the OECD countries that have sufficiently detailed data to be included in the analysis, the results show that 18 to 20 percent of total employment is potentially offshorable. (This estimate is slightly above the share of employment in tradable services found for the United States by Jensen and Kletzer [2006], but the difference is in the range that might be expected given the upper bound interpretation of van Welsum and Reif's results.) For less-skilled offshorable occupations, declines in employment shares in Canada, Australia, and especially the United States suggest that effects of offshoring are already being felt, though other factors, such as technology adoption, could also be responsible for these declines.

The authors next fit fixed effect regressions explaining offshorable employment as functions of indicators of openness, use and production of ICT goods, flexibility of product markets, and the importance of services in the economy. The results show that exports of business and other information services are associated with increased employment in offshorable occupations, while imports of these services are associated with decreased offshorable employment. Thus, trade in such services does seem to matter in the expected direction. In addition, outward FDI and ICT intensity are associated with increased employment in skilled offshorable occupations and decreased employment in unskilled ones, perhaps because of needs for headquarters staff and complementarities between skill and ICT use and production. Finally, inflexibilities introduced by regulation are negatively associated with employment in both skilled and unskilled offshorable occupations, perhaps because they slow an economy's evolution away from declining goods-producing industries that have little offshorable employment. This finding, together with the finding of a positive association between the importance of services and skilled offshorable occupations, suggest that the future evolution of the economy will tend to increase the share of employment that is potentially offshorable.

Part IV: Topics in the Measurement of Price and Productivity

Several studies have used data from the Annual Industry Accounts published by BEA to investigate industries' contributions to aggregate productivity growth. Another strand of the productivity literature has focused on MNCs, reporting evidence that their productivity level exceeds that of purely domestic firms and that foreign affiliates' adoption of productivity-enhancing technologies creates spillovers for the host economy as domestic firms learn about these technologies and adopt them as well. In "The Contribution of Multinational Corporations to U.S. Productivity Growth, 1977–2000" Carol Corrado, Paul Lengermann, and Larry Slifman unite these two strands of the literature, melding detailed industry data from the AIAs with BEA's data on MNC parents and affiliates to examine the role of MNCs in the productivity performance of the United States.

A striking speedup in productivity growth after 1995 has been credited primarily to the production and use of IT and to an improved performance of wholesale and retail trade brought about by innovations in distribution technologies and organization. Using the merged data set to decompose the private business sector in a different way, the authors discover, however, that MNC parents or affiliates located in the United States played a major role in the productivity speedup. (These estimates are not necessarily inconsistent with the earlier findings: some of the outperformance of the MNCs can be attributed to their overrepresentation in IT manufacturing, for example.) Furthermore, although the MNC sector represented about 25 percent of the gross product of all nonfarm private businesses and about 40 percent of nonfinancial corporate gross product, it accounted for more than half of the increase for all nonfarm private businesses and all of the increase in the labor productivity of nonfinancial corporations in the late 1990s. This finding raises intriguing questions about the productivity growth advantages that come from having overseas affiliates or an overseas parent. These may include increased ability to benefit from international flows of knowledge or intellectual property, the ability to replicate best practices on a global scale, and the ability to offshore activities with low labor productivity levels. It also raises questions about whether their high productivity levels and growth rates mean that MNCs are destined to play an increasingly dominant role in U.S. economic activity.

References

Alterman, W. 1991. Price trends in U.S. trade: New data, new insights. In *International economic transactions: Issues in measurement and empirical research,* Studies in income and wealth, vol. 55, ed. P. Hooper and J. D. Richardson, 109–43. Chicago: University of Chicago Press.

Ascher, B., and O. G. Whichard. 1991. Developing a data system for international sales of services: Progress, problems and prospects. In *International economic transactions: Issues in measurement and empirical research,* Studies in income and wealth, vol. 55, ed. P. Hooper and J. D. Richardson, 203–36. Chicago: University of Chicago Press.

Baldwin, R. E., and F. Kimura. 1998. Measuring U.S. international goods and services transactions. In *Geography and ownership as bases for international accounting,* Studies in income and wealth, vol. 59, ed. R. Baldwin, R. Lipsey, and J. D. Richardson, 9–35. Chicago: University of Chicago Press.

Baldwin, R. E., R. E. Lipsey, and J. D. Richardson, eds. 1998. *Geography and ownership as bases for economic accounting,* Studies in income and wealth, vol. 59. Chicago: University of Chicago Press.

Berndt, E. R., and C. R. Hulten. 2007. *Hard-to-measure goods and services: Essays in honor of Zvi Griliches,* Studies in income and wealth, vol. 67. Chicago: University of Chicago Press.

Blinder, A. S. 2006. Offshoring: The next industrial revolution? *Foreign Affairs* 85 (Mar/April): 113–28.

Bosworth, B. P., and J. E. Triplett. 2007. Services productivity in the United States. In *Hard-to-measure goods and services: Essays in honor of Zvi Griliches,* Studies in income and wealth, vol. 67, ed. E. R. Berndt and C. R. Hulten, 413–447. Chicago: University of Chicago Press.

Central Statistics Office of Ireland. 2006. Aircraft leasing in Ireland—treatment in the macroeconomic accounts. Personal communication, September.

Corrado, C., J. Haltiwanger, and D. Sichel, eds. 2005. *Measuring capital in the new economy,* Studies in income and wealth, vol. 65. Chicago: University of Chicago Press.

Corrado, C. A., C. R. Hulten, and D. E. Sichel. 2005. Measuring capital and technology: An expanded Framework. In *Measuring capital in the new economy,* Studies in income and wealth, vol. 65, ed. C. Corrado, J. Haltiwanger, and D. Sichel, 11–46. Chicago: University of Chicago Press.

Corrado, C. A., C. R. Hulten, and D. E. Sichel. 2006. Intangible capital and economic growth. Working Paper no. 11948. Cambridge, MA: National Bureau of Economic Research, NBER January.

Cutler, D. M., and E. R. Berndt, eds. 2001. *Medical care output and productivity,* Studies in income and wealth, vol. 62. Chicago: University of Chicago Press.

Dossani, R. 2006. Globalization and the offshoring of services: The case of India. In *Brookings trade forum: 2005 offshoring white-collar work—The issues and implications,* ed. L. Brainard and S. M. Collins, 241–67. Washington, D.C.: Brookings Institution Press.

Drucker, J. How Merck saved $1.5 billion paying itself for drug patents. *Wall Street Journal,* September 28.

Feenstra, R. 1998. The integration of trade and disintegration of production in the global economy. *Journal of Economic Perspectives* 12 (Fall): 31–50.

Government Accountability Office. 2005. International Trade: U.S. and India data on offshoring show significant differences. Report number GAO-06-116 (October). Available at: www.gao.gov/cgi-bin/getrpt?GAO-06-116

Griliches, Z. 1992. Introduction. In *Output Measurement in the Service Sectors.* Studies in income and wealth, vol. 56. Chicago: University of Chicago Press.

———, ed. 1992. *Output measurement in the service sectors,* Studies in income and wealth, vol. 56. Chicago: University of Chicago Press.

Hill, P. 1999. Tangibles, intangibles and services: A new taxonomy for the classification of output. *The Canadian Journal of Economics / Revue canadienne d'Economique* 32 (2): 426–46.

Hill, T. P. 1977. On goods and services. *The Review of Income and Wealth* 23 (4): 315–38.

Hoekman, B. M., and R. M. Stern. 1991. Evolving patterns of trade and investment in services. In *International economic transactions: Issues in measurement and empirical research,* Studies in income and wealth, vol. 55, ed. P. Hooper and J. D. Richardson, 237–90. Chicago: University of Chicago Press.

International Monetary Fund. 1993. *Balance of payments manual,* fifth edition. Washington, D. C.: International Monetary Fund.

International Monetary Fund. 2008. *Balance of payments and international investment position manual,* sixth edition. Washington, D. C.: International Monetary Fund.

Jensen, J. B., and L. G. Kletzer. 2006. Tradable services: Understanding the size and scope of services outsourcing and its impact on American workers. In *Brookings trade forum: 2005 offshoring white-collar work—The issues and the implications,* ed. S. M. Collins and L. Brainard, 75–116. Washington, D. C.: Brookings Institution.

Khatchadourian, K., and A. Wiesner. 2006. International price program's services price indexes. Paper presented at the CRIW conference on International Service Flows. 28–29 April, Bethesda, MD.

Koncz, J., and A. Flatness. 2007. U.S. international services: Cross-border trade in 2006 and sales through affiliates in 2005. *Survey of Current Business* October: 94–146.

Landefeld, J. S., O. G. Whichard, and J. H. Lowe. 1993. Alternative frameworks for U.S. international transactions. *Survey of Current Business* 73 (December): 50–61.

Lipsey, R. E., L. Molinari, and I. B. Kravis. 1991. Measures of prices and price competitiveness in international trade in manufactured goods. In *International economic transactions: Issues in measurement and empirical research,* Studies in income and wealth, vol. 55, ed. P. Hooper and J. D. Richardson, 144–202. Chicago: University of Chicago Press.

Mutti, J., and H. Gruber. 1998. The significance of international tax rules for sourcing income. In *Geography and ownership as bases for international accounting.* Studies in income and wealth, vol. 59, ed. R. Baldwin, R. Lipsey, and J. D. Richardson, 259–80. Chicago: University of Chicago Press.

Sicsic, P. 2006. Are there more and more missing imports of services in the French balance of payments? Paper presented at the CRIW conference on International Service Flows. 28–29 April, Bethesda, MD.

Simpson, G. R. 2005a. Microsoft unit is no. 1 earner in Ireland. *Wall Street Journal,* December 20.

Simpson, G. R. 2005b. Wearing of the green: Irish subsidiary lets Microsoft slash taxes in U.S. and Europe. *Wall Street Journal,* November 7.

Triplett, J. E., and B. P. Bosworth. 2004. Productivity in the U.S. services sector. Washington, D. C.: Brookings Institution.

United Nations. 2007. *1993 SNA, Revision 1.* Draft available online at: http://unstats.un.org/unsd/sna1993/draftingPhase/ChapterIssueMatrix.asp

Yorgenson, D. R. 2007. Treatment of international research and development as investment: Issues and estimates. Bureau of Economic Analysis, Working Paper. U.S. Department of Commerce: Washington, D.C. (October).

I

Challenges in Measuring Trade in Services

Measuring International Trade in Services

Robert E. Lipsey

1.1 Introduction

Most of the literature on international trade that has accumulated over the last 300 years has dealt with trade in goods, and almost every country has had in place for many years a system of collecting information on such trade. In the mercantilist era, a surplus of exports over imports of goods was sought as a way of acquiring gold, and imports of goods were carefully watched and counted as a source of tax revenue. As a result, there has been an apparatus in place for measuring the inflow and outflow of goods in every country for centuries, based on counting and appraising the value of goods as they crossed the country's borders. Trade in goods among regions of a country is often studied by trying to approximate the movement of goods across regional, provincial, or state borders. Only recently, with the establishment of the single market in the European Union, have some major trading countries moved away from the traditional reliance on customs declarations at borders and been forced to invent other ways of measuring trade in goods (OECD 2001, 3).

The collection of data on trade in goods is governed by recommendations set forth in United Nations (2004), which interprets, for compilers of trade data, the methodological guidelines adopted by the United Nations

Robert E. Lipsey is a professor of economics, emeritus, at Queens College and the Graduate Center, City University of New York, and a research associate and director of the New York office of the National Bureau of Economic Research.

I am indebted to Jing Sun for assistance in all phases of the research, to J. David Richardson and Marshall Reinsdorf for comments and suggestions at the conference and afterwards, some of which are incorporated here, and to Maria Borga of the Bureau of Economic Analysis for help in understanding the BEA service trade data. Also to Deoin Wilson of the Bermuda Government Department of Statistics for clarification of the Bermuda data.

Statistical Commission. One of the principal recommendations is that countries use ". . . crossing the border rather than change of ownership as the basic principle for compilation of trade statistics . . ." (p. 5). The geographical basis of the data is emphasized by the recommendation that the data should "record all goods which add to or subtract from the stock of natural resources of a country by entering (imports) or leaving (exports) its economic territory" (p. 74), and by the definition of the partner in terms of the "statistical territory of each country" (p. 75) or, when free zones are involved, the economic territory if the reporting country uses "the strict version of the special system of trade." The definitions are all based on geography rather than ownership.

The measurement of trade in goods for the balance of payments has a different objective. That is the measurement of changes in the ownership of goods between residents and nonresidents of a country. Because the great majority of such changes in ownership take place in connection with the physical movement of the goods, the measures are quantitatively close, and the balance of payments measures are mainly dependent on the data for the physical movement of goods and also very close to them. However, since imports are reported on a cost, insurance, and freight (c.i.f.) basis in the goods trade data, and the balance of payments concept separates freight and insurance costs from the value of the physical commodities, one adjustment that is required is to peel off those costs and, if they are purchased from foreigners, transfer them to the trade in services account.

Most of the differences between trade statistics and balance-of-payments measures for trade in goods involve the dependence of the balance of payments accounts on change of ownership rather than physical movement. Thus, the trade statistics include, and the balance of payments data exclude, goods purchased by travelers and brought home; while there is a change in location, there is no change of ownership. Trade data include, but balance of payments figures exclude, exports transferred under U.S. military agency sales contracts. Other adjustments involve, for example, timing in terms of change of ownership rather than terms of the change in the location of goods.

In contrast to exports and imports of goods, exports and imports of services do not have alternative measurements based on either physical movements or ownership. Exports and imports of services exist only in the balance of payments universe. As is observed in United Nations (2002a) and similarly in the Organization for Economic Cooperation and Development (OECD 2001), "measurement of trade in services is inherently more difficult than measurement of trade in goods.[. . .] Unlike trade in goods, for trade in services there is no package crossing the customs frontier with an internationally recognized commodity code, a description of the contents, information on quantity, origin, and destination, an invoice and an administrative system based on customs duty collection, that is practiced at assembling these data" (p. 5). The difference is more than a question of documentation. Exports or imports of services often involve no crossing of an international boundary by the service, but only a crossing of a border by the consumer of the service. Some exports or imports of services are geographically domestic transactions made international solely by a difference in country of residence between the buyer and the seller of the service. It is a balance of payments concept more than a physical trade concept, and the definition of residence plays a crucial part in defining what trade in services is.

United Nations (2002a), following the precedent of the General Agreement on Trade in Services (GATS), broadens its concept of international trade in services beyond the balance of payments definition. The broadening adds to the balance of payments definition, the supply of services through GATS mode 3 and part of GATS mode 4. The GATS mode 3 is the supply of services ". . . by a service supplier of one [WTO] Member through commercial presence in the territory of any other Member . . ." (p. 11). The GATS mode 4, some of which is included in the balance of payments, is the supply of a service ". . . by a service supplier of one [WTO] Member through presence of natural persons of a Member in the territory of any other Member . . ." (p. 11).

Because data on foreign affiliate provision of services are very limited in most countries and there is no suggestion of a similar expansion of the concept of trade in goods in United Nations (2004), the comparisons to trade in goods here are confined to the conventional balance of payments definition, including in service trade only exports and imports of services.

The chapter begins with a discussion of the size of exports and imports of services, and their composition, by type of service. It continues with an attempt to judge how fast the growth in service exports and imports has been, relative to trade in goods and to the production of services. The next topic is the problems that arise from the lack of any accounting for flows of human capital. The final topic is the problems in the measurement of service exports and imports caused by the ambiguities in defining the location of service production, particularly service production based on intangible and financial assets. If the location of production is ambiguous, the distinction between home production and imports of services is correspondingly ambiguous, as is the distinction between home consumption and exports. These ambiguities then infect measures of the current balance and of domestic production. The measurement difficulties are exacerbated by the deliberate manipulation of the apparent location of production; for the avoidance or reduction of corporate taxes by appearing to move production to low-tax locations. The chapter ends with suggestions for measurements of service trade that would reduce some of these ambiguities.

1.2   The Size and Growth of World Exports and Imports of Services

Exports and imports of services have been something of an orphan in international measurement of trade. The report on *The Network of World Trade*, mostly by Folke Hilgerdt (League of Nations 1942) hardly mentioned exports and imports of services, except to suggest that exports and imports probably offset each other for most countries. Interest in service trade has grown recently, especially since services became part of international trade negotiations, but it is hard to say just how large these exports and imports of services are because the completeness of reporting varies greatly across countries. Some countries publish data that cover only limited types of services.

Some important participants in trade in financial services, such as Bermuda and the Cayman Islands, did not report to the International Monetary Fund (IMF) at all for many years. Bermuda announced (Bermuda 2006) that it was bringing its reporting into substantial compliance with IMF standards, and data on that basis are now available on the Bermuda Department of Statistics website, beginning with 2006. Bermuda omits from its balance of payments transactions on the income account of what it calls "exempted companies." These are firms whose business is outside Bermuda, and are not permitted to do business in Bermuda except by special license. Their contribution to Bermuda's gross national product is based only on expenditure in Bermuda. Because they are considered non-resident companies, their income is omitted from Bermuda's national accounts, including the balance of payments. However, the sales of services by these companies outside Bermuda are counted as imports from Bermuda by the countries purchasing them, although Bermuda does not consider them exports. Other offshore financial centers, such as the Cayman Islands, remain nonreporters to the IMF.

Many countries that report to the IMF do not report service exports and imports. Those that do reported exports of $US 2,487 billion and imports of $US 2,371 billion in 2005 (table 1A.1). Of these countries, the 150 that reported both goods and services exports and imports reported exports of services that were 25.4 percent of exports of goods, and imports of services that were 24.1 percent of imports of goods (table 1A.1), close to one quarter.

It is hard to judge how fast exports and imports of services have been growing because the number of countries measuring them has increased, and the number of categories covered by surveys and reporting has been growing over time, but to inconsistent degrees in different countries. For twenty-two countries that have reported service exports and imports to the IMF since 1972, and accounted for close to half of "world" exports of services in 2005, the reported ratio of service exports to goods exports grew from 21 to 28 percent between 1972–76 and 2002–6. The corresponding

Table 1.1   **Service exports and imports as percent of goods exports and imports**

	22 Countries[a]		30 Countries[b]	
Year	Credit	Debit	Credit	Debit
1972–1976	21.02	23.94	n.a.	n.a.
1977–1981	20.93	24.26	21.93	24.69
1982–1986	23.92	25.19	23.33	25.52
1987–1991	25.36	25.23	24.66	26.87
1992–1996	27.20	26.05	26.01	28.00
1997–2001	27.56	25.00	26.22	26.29
2002–2006	28.40	24.77	27.65	25.78

Source: Appendix table 1A.1.

Note: n.a. = not available.

[a] The 22 countries include Australia, Austria, Barbados, Canada, Colombia, Dominican Rep., Germany, Haiti, Israel, Italy, Jordan, Malta, Netherlands, New Zealand, Romania, Saudi Arabia, Singapore, South Africa, Sweden, United Kingdom, United States, and Venezuela.

[b] The 30 countries include the 22 countries, plus Argentina, Belgium-Luxembourg, Brazil, Denmark, Finland, France, India, and Japan.

ratio for imports barely changed, staying at 24 to 25 percent over that same period (table 1.1). For a larger group of thirty countries that have reported service exports and imports since 1977, and accounted for two thirds of "world" service exports in 2005, the ratio of service exports to goods exports grew from about 22 to 28 percent between 1977–81 and 2002–6. The ratio for imports grew from 24 to 25 percent to a peak of 28 percent in 1992 through 1996, and has since settled back to around 26 percent. Thus, there is some indication of an upward trend in the reported ratio of service to goods exports and imports since the 1970s.

Many countries are dropped from the recent IMF Balance of Payments CDs for years before 1972, presumably because the definitions and measures of service exports and imports did not match the current definitions. However, it is possible to put together series extending back to 1961 for twenty-four of the larger countries from earlier IMF data (IMF 1991). These show a decline from 27 to 25 percent on the export side and 32 to 28 percent on the import side. The extension suggests, if anything, a somewhat smaller increase in the ratio on the export side and a larger decline on the import side, but no very large changes over more than forty years.

A further indication of the trend in the world importance of service exports and imports can be gleaned from estimates for 1950 to 1954, purportedly covering the whole world (Woolley 1966, table 3). The ratios quoted here exclude investment income, treated as service trade in the source). On the export side, they show service exports 21.6 percent of goods exports, below the 1961 ratio, but almost the same as the average ratio for the first five years, starting in 1972, in table 1.1. On the import side, the estimated ratio in 1950 to 1954 is over 24 percent, again below the 1961 ratio, but almost exactly the average of 1972 to 1976 in table 1.1. Thus, there is little indication of a strong trend in the ratio in the last fifty years if we assume that the adjustments made to the data for the earlier period by Woolley had been adopted in the official data by 1972, or at least by 2002. However, if the same omissions in the official services data remain, and they are equally important in the later period, some long-term rise in the service/goods export and import trade ratios is implied.

For the more distant past, before 1950, the picture is even dimmer. Viner (1924) claimed that Argentina was the only country for which ". . . comprehensive statistics of export and import services are officially collected and published . . ." but that the British Board of Trade "had recently begun the collection of similar statistics . . ." (p. 63, fn 1). He did report, for freight costs alone, ratios from several sources of freight charges to world imports of goods, derived by what he referred to as "Hobson's method," based on the world excess of reported imports over reported exports. This ratio fluctuated mainly between 6 and 9 percent from 1901 through 1912, but with no obvious trend.

One reason for being suspicious about the apparent rising trend in service trade relative to goods trade is that not only has the number of countries reporting service trade to the IMF risen over the last fifty years, and even the last thirty years, but among those reporting, the number reporting particular types of service trade has increased even more. While the number of countries reporting total service exports to the IMF has not changed greatly from 1985 to 2005, the number reporting exports of, for example, construction services, rose from seven to 88; financial services, ten to 105; computer and information services, one to 100; and personal, cultural, and recreational services, four to 91 (table 1.2). In some cases, the services may not have existed in the particular countries, or may not have been exported at all. In other cases, they might have been reported under "other business services." Neither of these reasons would imply any bias in the overall ratios. However, it seems more likely that at least some of these services were traded, but no device was in place for collection of data on them, in which case the increasing numbers of reporters would imply upward bias in the measured ratios of service exports and imports to goods trade.

The same information for imports of services is provided in table 1.3. In most cases, collection and reporting of data on particular imports and exports moved together, but there were exceptions. Reports of freight imports increased faster than those on freight exports, and the same was true for reports on insurance imports and construction imports. In general, however, types of services poorly reported in import records were the same as those poorly reported in export records, and the biases are probably similar on the two sides of the account.

Table 1.2   **Number of countries reporting trade in various services from the export side**

	1975	1985	1995	2005
Total services	61	146	157	150
Transportation	60	137	153	146
Passenger	39	99	111	117
Freight	49	111	111	119
Other transportation	55	113	116	118
Travel	60	138	151	147
Government services, n.i.e.	56	119	139	138
Other services				
Communications	8	19	94	127
Construction	3	7	54	88
Insurance	44	100	117	130
Financial	2	10	61	105
Computer and information	0	1	43	100
Royalties and license fees	19	35	66	91
Other business services	60	139	145	136
Personal, cultural, and recreational	3	4	43	91

Source: IMF (2007)

Table 1.3   **Number of countries reporting trade in various services from the import side**

	1975	1985	1995	2005
Total services	62	146	157	150
Transportation	62	145	155	148
Passenger	44	102	115	123
Freight	61	145	136	133
Other transportation	51	106	113	109
Travel	60	140	154	147
Government services, n.i.e.	57	125	143	143
Other services				
Communications	9	21	92	126
Construction	4	6	64	102
Insurance	57	139	142	141
Financial	3	10	69	113
Computer and information	0	2	47	111
Royalties and license fees	26	55	85	120
Other business services	60	141	154	143
Personal, cultural, and recreational	6	10	53	99

Source: IMF (2007)

Reported imports of services were about 10 percent larger than reported exports in 1950 to 1954 (Woolley 1966, table 3). The same was true among twenty-two countries until the 1990s, sometimes by 10 percent or more, but the totals have been much closer in size since then. That same trend is shown in the data for thirty countries since 1977, with the latest figures showing exports and imports almost equal in size (table 1A.1). Either comparative advantages in service production have shifted toward these groups of twenty-two and thirty countries or there have been more improvements in measuring service exports than in measuring service imports.

If there has not been any strong trend in world service exports and imports relative to world goods trade over the last half century, as is suggested by these estimates, the growth of service exports and imports has outpaced the growth of world GDP, since the ratio of goods trade to GDP has risen substantially. The world ratio of goods exports to GDP was under 10 percent in 1960 and 1970 but had risen to more than 20 percent by 2000 to 2006 (table 1.4). World production appears to have moved from goods-producing industries (half the total in 1960, but less than a third in 2000 to 2006) to service-producing industries (table 1.5); one might have expected a corresponding shift in the composition of exports and imports from goods to services. The absence of any obvious shift in that direction implies that the growth of exports and imports relative to output has been slower in services than in goods.

The rough stability in the ratio of service exports and imports to goods exports and imports may reflect the fact that we are comparing nominal rather than deflated or real values of the two types of trade. If prices of traded services have fallen relative to prices of traded goods, the stability of the nominal ratio may conceal a more rapid growth in real service exports and imports. If relative prices of traded services have risen, on the other hand, the stability of the services/goods trade ratio would imply a decline in the importance of service trade in real terms. That question is dis-

Table 1.4   **World exports of goods as percent of world GDP**

Year	World GDP ($US billions)	Exports of goods ($US billions)	Percent (%)
1960[a]	1,504	130	8.6
1970[a]	3,275	317	9.7
1970	3,402	312	9.2
1970–1979	6,250	847	13.6
1980–1989	14,584	2,230	15.3
1990–1999	27,282	4,620	16.9
2000–2006	38,213	8,353	21.9

Sources: GDP: UN (1993b); IMF World Economic Outlook Database (2007). Exports: 1960–1984: GATT (1985); 1985–1990: GATT (1994); 1991–2006: WTO (2007).
[a]Estimates from UN(1993b).

Table 1.5   **World goods and service output as percent of world GDP**

Year	Goods[a]	Services
1960[b]	49.6	50.4
1970[b]	50.9	49.1
1970	48.4	51.6
1970–1979	47.5	52.5
1980–1989	42.6	57.4
1990–1999	35.3	64.7
2000–2006	32.0	68.0

Sources: UN (1993b); UN National Accounts Main Aggregates Database, downloaded on Dec. 19, 2007.
[a]Construction is classified as goods.
[b]Data are from UN (1993b).

cussed more fully following, in connection with U.S. trade, for which we have slightly more data. However, for the world as a whole, it should not be assumed that the rise in service prices relative to goods prices typically found in domestic price comparisons applies to prices of internationally traded services. Domestic prices of services are heavily weighted with labor-intensive services, but the composition of internationally traded services may be very different. For example, the commodity market integration that took place in the nineteenth century and continued in the twentieth has been associated with, among other determinants, ". . . changes in the technologies of communication, transaction, and transport," according to a recent study (Jacks 2006, 405). These are not the predominant components of domestic service price indexes. The same study also suggested that trade costs were ". . . more responsive to changes in monetary regimes and commercial policy than changes in the underlying technology of transport" (p. 405), even further removed from the elements of domestic service price indexes.

A rough idea of the composition of world service trade and changes in composition over the last twenty years, as reported by the IMF, is given by table 1.6. The three major elements are "transportation," "travel," and "other business services." The major change in composition that is visible in both exports and imports is the decline in importance of "Freight" and "Other transportation," reduced by about one third. Some of this reduction may be an effect of containerization and other productivity improvements, but some may be an artifact of the improvement in the reporting of "Other services" that can be seen in tables 1.2 and 1.3. The share of passenger transportation held up better than that of goods transportation. There was also a large decline in the importance of "Government services, n.i.e.," which include ". . . services (such as expenditures of embassies and consulates) associated with government sectors or international and regional organizations and not classified other items" (IMF 2004, xxvi).

Table 1.6   The composition of world service trade, 1985 and 2005 (%)

	Exports		Imports	
	1985	2005	1985	2005
Total services	100	100	100	100
Transportation[a]	27	21	31	26
Passenger	5	4	4	5
Freight	13	9	19	14
Other transportation	8	5	8	5
Travel	28	27	23	26
Government services, n.i.e.	7	3	9	3
Other services[b]	39	50	37	45
Communications	1	2	1	2
Construction	2	2	1	2
Insurance	2	2	3	4
Financial	2	6	1	3
Computer and information	0	4	0	2
Royalties and license fees	3	5	2	6
Other business service	25	24	21	22
Personal, Cultural, and Recreational	0	1	0	1

Sources: IMF (2007); Republic of China (Taiwan) (1987).

[a]The imports and exports of component services under "Transportation" do not add up to the imports and exports of "Transportation", presumably because not all countries report the components.

[b]The imports and exports of "Other services" are calculated by subtracting the imports and exports of transportation, travel, and government services from total services. The "Other services" total includes Taiwan, but the breakdown does not.

The composition of reported imports is considerably different from that of reported exports. The direction and size of the discrepancies between reported export and reported import totals vary across service categories, probably because reporting by developed countries is more complete than that by developing countries. Thus, reported imports of freight transportation are larger than reported exports, probably because imports of freight transportation services are mainly by developed countries, and the exports, at least nominally, from developing countries.

On the other hand, for "Financial" and "Computer and Information" services, reported exports are larger than reported imports, presumably because these are mainly export items for developed countries. "Insurance" services are an exception among business services in that reported exports are smaller than reported imports. One reason may be that exports are, relative to country size, disproportionately concentrated in Bermuda, which did not report to the IMF at all. That situation may not change much because Bermuda treats some international operations as outside its economy and excludes such transactions from its reported national income and product accounts and trade data, while the importing countries will report importing these services from Bermuda (Bermuda 2006).

Over twenty years, the main trend in the direction of service export and import flows is that the share of industrial countries in exports has declined, while their share of service imports has risen. The share in imports of the Euro area rose, and that accounted for most of the increase in industrial country imports.

1.3   The Size and Growth of U.S. Trade in Services

The United States has been a leader in measuring service trade, perhaps because it offers a more cheerful picture of the U.S. international position than the goods trade account. In 2006, the United States reported a surplus of exports over imports in service trade of $US 88 billion, in contrast to a deficit in goods trade of $US 850 billion (U.S. Department of Commerce, Bureau of Economic Analysis [henceforth, BEA] 2007).

Services have recently been much larger relative to goods in U.S. exports (over 40 percent) than in U.S. imports (a little under 20 percent), presumably reflecting U.S. comparative advantage in service industries (fig. 1.1). Service exports were about 60 percent as large as service imports during the 1930s, became larger than imports during World War II, fell back to half in the early 1950s, and then began to grow faster. By the early 1970s service exports began to surpass imports and have done so ever since.

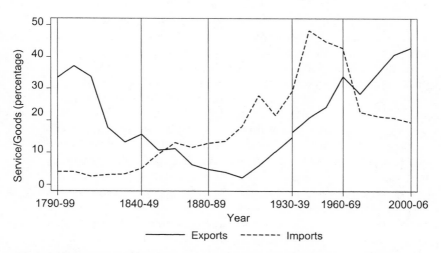

Fig. 1.1   U.S. exports and imports of services as percent of U.S. exports and imports of goods, current dollars, by decades: 1790–1999 and average of 2000–2006
Source: Table 1A.2

However, in the last five years, service import growth has outpaced service export growth (table 1A.2).

The large current importance of services relative to goods in U.S. exports is not unprecedented. In the first thirty years of balance of payments records, 1790 to 1819, U.S. service exports averaged about a third of goods exports. Two of the early periods shown in figure 1.1, 1800 to 1809 and 1810 to 1819, were affected by the Napoleonic Wars and the accompanying blockades and embargos, as Marshall Reinsdorf reminded me in a personal communication. It is not obvious how these would have affected the values of service exports and imports associated with trade, as compared with the value of trade itself, given the impacts on prices as well as quantities of trade and services, as discussed in several recent articles (e.g., O'Rourke 2006).

After the 1820s, the importance of service exports relative to goods exports trended downward, reaching a level of only 2 percent of exports of goods in the early 1900s. Then service exports began a long rise in importance, leading to the current high levels (fig. 1.1).

Services were more important in U.S. exports than in U.S. imports in the early days of the United States, usually more than twice as important through the 1840s. After the Civil War, the relation was reversed, and services were generally much more important in imports than in exports in the latter half of the nineteenth century and through the 1960s, reaching well over 40 percent of goods imports during the years when goods imports were affected by World War II and the postwar recovery. As goods imports grew rapidly starting in the 1970s, the ratio of service to goods imports receded to around 20 percent, where it has remained since the 1970s (fig. 1.1).

Services have often been treated as nontradables, and they are, in fact, less traded than goods, relative to their output. That is, exports and imports of services have been much smaller relative to the U.S. domestic output of services, than exports and imports of goods, relative to the U.S. domestic production of goods, at least since 1869. Aside from World War II, service exports were almost always less than 2 percent of domestic service output until the 1960s, according to contemporary estimates (later revised to almost 3 percent for the 1960s). Since then, they have grown to usually about 5 percent of service output. Goods exports have generally been much larger relative to goods output during the same period, often 10 to 14 percent before World War I, falling back to 7 or 8 percent from 1929 through the 1960s and then rising, to above 20 percent in most of the last decade (fig. 1.2). Service imports in current dollars were over 3 percent of U.S. domestic service output during the 1960s, and reached over 4 percent of U.S. service output in recent years. Goods imports were 10 percent of domestic goods output in most of the late nineteenth century, ranged from 5 to 8 percent of goods output most years from then through the 1960s, and

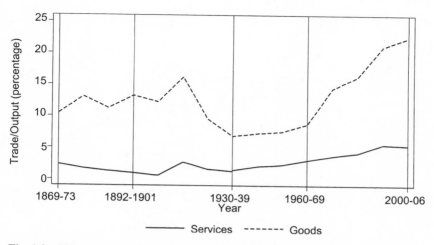

Fig. 1.2   U.S. exports of goods and services as percent of U.S. domestic output of goods and services, current dollars, by decades: 1869–1999 and average of 2000–2006

Source: Tables 1A.3 and 1A.4.

then soared, to reach 35 to 40 percent of domestic goods production since 2000 (fig. 1.3).

The relation of service to goods exports and imports and the different movements of trade/output ratios in the two sectors may reflect differences in price movements. As David Richardson pointed out in his comments at the conference, the official data on implicit prices underlying GDP and those for exports both show prices of services rising relative to those for goods. For example, between 1929 and 2006, domestic prices for services rose by over three times as much as domestic prices of goods, and export prices of services rose almost two-and-a-half times as fast as export prices of goods (table 1A.8). If we accept these price estimates, they present a very different picture of the relation of service to goods exports and imports from that in the nominal data, in some respects. In particular, they show the ratio of services to goods in U.S. exports fairly stable from the 1960s through the early 1990s, and then declining, instead of rising sharply through the 1970s and the 1980s. And they show the ratio in U.S. imports to have fallen throughout the 1990s, instead of being stable (fig. 1.4).

The translation from nominal to real, or constant dollar, terms makes much less difference to the comparisons of exports and imports to output in goods and services than to the comparison of services to goods exports and imports (figs. 1.5 and 1.6). The reason is that the reported disparity in price movements between goods and services in trade is very similar to that in domestic production.

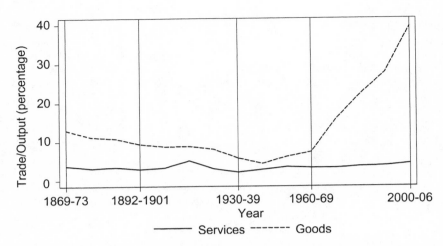

Fig. 1.3 U.S. imports of goods and services as percent of U.S. domestic output of goods and services, current dollars, by decades: 1869–1999 and average of 2000–2006

Source: Tables 1A.3 and 1A.4.

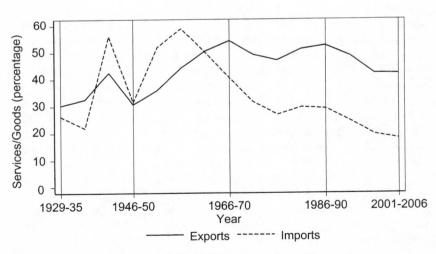

Fig. 1.4 U.S. exports and imports of services as percent of U.S. exports and imports of goods in 2000 prices

Source: Table 1A.5.

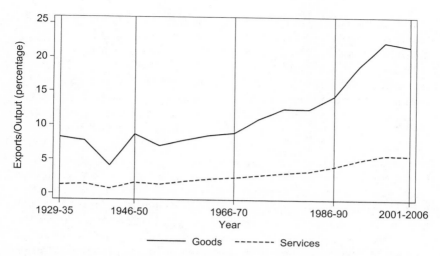

Fig. 1.5   U.S. exports as percent of U.S. domestic output of goods and services in 2000 prices

Source: Tables 1A.6 and 1A.7.

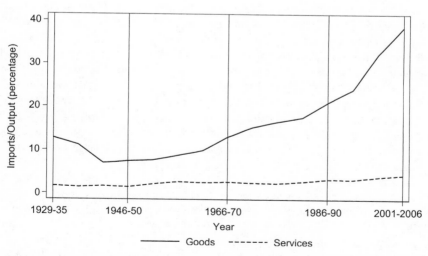

Fig. 1.6   U.S. imports as percent of U.S. domestic output of goods and services in 2000 prices

Source: Tables 1A.6 and 1A.7.

One problem with all of these comparisons in constant dollars, or in real terms, is that price measurement in the service sector, and corresponding quantity measurement, are the weakest parts of the national accounts. Two volumes of the Conference on Research in Income and Wealth (CRIW) series, Griliches (1992) and Cutler and Berndt (2001), devoted a great deal of attention to the problems of measurement of prices and output in this sector. It is hard to have much confidence in the existing measures. The problems for trade in services are worse than for domestic production, because the collection of prices for service trade is at a very early stage, as indicated in the paper by Khatchadourian and Wiesner (2006). They mention that the BLS International Price Program has collected service price indexes that cover ". . . approximately 8 percent of export service trade and 23 percent of import services trade" (p. 2). In the absence of extensive price collection, the BEA has used various crude proxies, described for earlier years in United States, BEA (1987). For freight transportation, values were extrapolated by tonnage, implying that value per ton measured price movements, and for fees and royalties and other private services, the implicit price deflator for GDP was used.

The long-term history of costs of freight transportation, one of the largest segments of international services trade (about one third of all service trade in 1950 to 1954, according to Woolley [1966]) suggests that they were falling relative to prices of goods in general. The evidence includes convergence of prices between origin and destination countries and calculations of freight rates themselves, documented in papers by many authors, some of which are discussed and summarized in Mohammed and Williamson (2004). For other major parts of international service trade, such as communication and business services, it is difficult to find price records. However, they do not seem likely candidates for large increases in price relative to goods; communication costs were almost certainly falling.

The ratios of trade to output, particularly for goods, exaggerate the importance of trade somewhat, because while the production figures are output net of purchases from other industries, export and import figures are gross of such purchases. Because such purchases are more important in goods industries than in service industries, the exaggeration of the importance of trade is greater for goods than for services.

Estimates of U.S. service trade are still a work in progress. A report by the Office of Technology Assessment (OTA) estimated that exports of services, excluding banking services, were about 60 percent higher than "Official U.S. Government figures" in 1983 and 1984, and that imports of services were 40 to 50 percent higher in those years (U.S. Congress, Office of Technology Assessment 1986, table 1). The latest official BEA calculations of service exports and imports are quite close to the OTA estimates for those years, but somewhat larger for 1984 (Sauers and Pierce 2005, table 1).

The path to the revised, and much higher, estimates of trade in services was described in the appendix to Whichard and Borga (2002). That path began with new legislation in 1984 that permitted BEA to conduct surveys of trade in services. The first benchmark survey was carried out for 1986, and annual follow-up surveys began in 1987. Also in that year, medical service exports were estimated for the first time and primary insurance services were added to previous estimates of reinsurance transactions. Estimates of expenditures by foreign students in the United States and U.S. students abroad started in 1989. In 1990, services were redefined to exclude investment income. In 1992, trade in services between U.S. and foreign parents and their affiliates was placed on a gross, instead of a net, basis (increasing both exports and imports of services), coverage of transportation services was increased, and some new services were added to the 1991 benchmark. Truck transportation services between the United States and Canada were added to the service trade account in 1995. In 1996, BEA began what is known as the "Benchmark Survey of Financial Services Transactions Between U.S. Financial Services Providers and Unaffiliated Foreign Persons." Since then, there have been other improvements (described in Borga and Mann [2003, 2004] and in articles in later October issues of the *Survey of Current Business*) in measures of transportation services and reclassifications of software royalties and license fees, leasing of transportation equipment, compensation of employees, new sources for exports of medical services, imports of travel, and various other items.

One consequence of all these improvements in data collection and expansions in the list of services covered is that historical comparisons over long periods are questionable. The earliest estimates of U.S. service exports included only shipping earnings, and later also port charges on foreign ships, and foreign tourist expenditures in the United States. The closest approximation to these items in the current accounts, travel and transportation services, accounted for only 38 percent of service exports in 2006 (Koncz and Flatness 2007, 114). The same items cover more of the current imports of services, a little over half (pp. 104, 115).

Many services in the early United States were performed by foreign companies' agents or by affiliates of foreign firms, which possessed skills not common in the United States at that time. Wilkins (1989) quotes a letter to Alexander Hamilton, referring to Virginia to the effect that "'the trade of this state is carried on chiefly with foreign (British) capital. Those engaged in it [the trade] hardly deserve the name of merchants, being factors, agents, and Shop-keepers of the Merchants and Manufacturers of Great Britain . . .'." Wilkins goes on to say that the passage does not reveal whether these were ". . . salaried, or partners in the British firms," in which case they might have represented imports of services into the United States, or ". . . financially independent units that acted for British houses on a purely commission basis" (p. 40), in which case they might have represented U.S. exports of services. Wilkins also reports that America's national banking legislation of 1864 to 1865 ". . . had not provided a satisfactory basis for the largest American banks to participate in foreign trade financing . . ." and that as a result, ". . . to finance much of that trade, American enterprises depended on foreign (mainly British) banking services" (p. 463). Outside of banking, Wilkins notes that ". . . in 1914, the United States had to rely on foreign-owned shipping, foreign-owned cables, and foreign-owned radio communication" (p. 524). Shipping services were recorded in the balance of payments, but not the others.

Of course, many of the services traded currently, such as telecommunications and film and television tape rentals, did not exist very long ago, but there apparently were many services that did exist and were not recorded. It is therefore difficult to be sure how much of the apparent trend in the share of service trade in total U.S. trade is genuine.

1.4   The Definition of Residence and Trade in Educational Services

The measurement of trade in more and more services places a great deal of weight on the definition of residence, because the identification of residence can change what is, on the face of it, a domestic transaction into an international transaction. One case in which the attribution of residence changes a domestic demand on a country's resources into an international demand is that of foreign students, who are treated in the U.S. accounts as residents of the country from which they come, with the result that their costs of education and living expenses become a service export of the United States. The service that is simply domestic production and consumption or investment in human capital if a student is a resident of the United States is an export of educational services if the student is classified as a foreign resident. In other countries, the criteria for defining foreign students are diverse, including citizenship, ". . . nationality, place of birth, former domicile . . .", and in some cases can include students born in the host country (Larsen, Martin, and Morris 2002, 852).

Since many students choose to stay in the host country after their education is completed, the services exported to those students' home countries never leave the host countries. The service exports are reimported when the students become host country residents, an item missed in the balance of payments. Alternatively, the exported educational services could be thought of as turning into an import of human capital by the host country, a type of import that is not recognized in the balance of payments.

The U.S. exports of educational services more than doubled in value between 1992 and 2006, reaching $14.6 billion (Koncz and Flatness 2007), but there are no comprehensive data on what proportion of these service exports in fact never leave the United States. A hint that the share staying in the United States might be important is provided by data on intentions to stay expressed by foreign recipients of science and engineering doctorates in the United States. There are data on "intentions to stay," and on "definite plans to stay." Among students from countries accounting for about three quarters of such doctorates between 1985 and 1996, an intention to stay in the United States was expressed by half in 1985, rising to 70 percent in 1995 and 1996. Among degree recipients from all countries, "plans to stay" were expressed by 68 percent in 1992 to 1995, 72 percent in 1996 to 1999, and 74 percent in 2000 to 2003. A "firm plan to stay," meaning that the student had accepted a definite offer of a postdoctoral appointment or employment in the United States, was reported from 36 to 46 percent of the doctoral recipients over 1985 through 1996, and "definite plans to stay" was reported from 35 percent in 1992 to 1995, to 46 percent in 1996 to 1999, and 51 percent in 2000 to 2003 (National Science Foundation 1998b, 2006, appendix table 2-33).

The data on plans to stay do not reveal outcomes. Some indication of the fulfillment of these plans is that of about 8,000 temporary residents receiving science and engineering doctorates in 1998, over 60 percent were still in the United States in 2003 (National Science Foundation 2006, table 3-24).

Recipients of doctorates were only a small part of the 13 percent foreign-born share in R&D scientists and engineers in the United States in 1993, although the foreign-born were more important among PhDs than among those with less education. At all degree levels, about two-thirds of the foreign-born scientists and engineers employed in the United States had received their training in the United States (National Science Foundation 1998a, table 1), for the most part, probably, from U.S. exports of educational services.

If some substantial part of education exports remains in the United States, there is no clear way to recognize that fact in the current balance of payments framework. Presumably, the students' financial assets and liabilities should enter the accounts when they become residents. The estimated total was fairly small, under $1 billion in 2002, when it was noted that the average immigrant is relatively young—younger and less wealthy than the average emigrant (Bach 2003, 43–44). Students deciding to stay permanently in the United States are in the category classified by the BEA as "legal, adjusted-status immigrants" (Bach 2006, 43). The BEA apparently estimates the assets transferred by assigning to each immigrant his or her nationality, multiplied by the average income in that country, multiplied by the average ratio of wealth to income in that country (Bach 2006, 42–43).

The former students among these adjusted-status immigrants may differ substantially from the other members of that group. For one thing, they may have more debt, although that is not necessarily the case. Of over 36,000 science and engineering doctorate recipients reporting, almost three-quarters reported no undergraduate debt at the time of graduation and almost two-thirds reported no graduate debt. The average graduate had about $6,000 in undergraduate school debt and about $11,000 in graduate school debt (National Science Foundation 2006, appendix table 2-23). These should enter the balance of payments at the time of deciding on U.S. residence.

What would be required to complete the account for this transaction, but does not exist, is some accounting for flows of human capital. The decisions of alien importers of U.S. education to settle in the United States would then be treated as an import of human capital, analogous to the standard flows of financial capital.

The impact of exports of education services may go beyond the tendency of students to stay in the countries where they receive higher education. Even if students do not stay after graduation, they may return as immigrants, carrying back the previously exported education services. One study of immigration found that student flows explained migration to the United States more consistently than ". . . traditionally highlighted economic variables. . . ." Similar relationships could be observed for migration to a cross-section of OECD countries (Dreher and Poutvaara 2005, 17).

The idea that there is a human capital flow missing from the balance of payments data was suggested a long time ago by Alfred Marshall: "England exports to India a good many able young men: they do not enter in India's list of imports; but it is claimed that they render to her services whose value exceeds that of her total payments to them. They return to England (if they come back at all) after their best strength has been spent: they are unreckoned exports from England. But that part of their incomes, which they have saved, is likely to come back sooner or later in the form of material goods which enter into her imports. On the other hand, India counts those material goods among her exports to England: but of course she makes no entry among her imports for the expensive young men who have been sent to her" (Marshall 1923, 134–35).

1.5   Tax Havens and the Measurement of Trade in Services

There is a considerable literature, some of which is summarized in Hines (2005) and in Desai, Foley, and Hines (2006), which describes the effect of low rates of host country taxation in attracting investment and economic activity by multinationals from the United States and probably even more from other countries. Some of the activity attracted is production, but much of it involves the shifting of income to avoid or reduce taxes. Hines refers to "an impressive concentration of financial activity in tax havens" (p. 78). The thirty tax havens he lists accounted in 1999 for 0.7 percent of the world's population and 2.1 percent of world GDP, but for 4.8 percent of net property, plant, and equipment of U.S. affiliates, 3.4 percent of employee compensation, and 3.7 percent of employment. These shares probably represent production taking place in the tax havens and are not of concern in connection with the measurement of their production or export of services. However, these same tax haven affiliates accounted for 15.7 percent of gross foreign assets of U.S. affiliates, 13.4 percent of sales, and ". . . a staggering 30 percent of total foreign income . . ." (p. 78). "Much of reported tax haven income consists of financial flows from other foreign affiliates that parents own indirectly through their tax haven affiliates. Clearly, American firms locate considerable financial assets in foreign tax havens, and their reported profitability in tax havens greatly exceeds any measure of their physical presence there" (p. 78). Hines goes on to suggest that firms in other countries, such as Germany and the Netherlands, which largely exempt their firms' foreign income from taxation, have even stronger incentives to locate investment and income production in tax havens (p. 79). Desai, Foley, and Hines (2003, 68) refer to this flexibility as ". . . the ability of multinational firms to adjust the reported location of their taxable profits." While this literature refers to American firms, there has now been a series of papers describing the similar tax-minimizing activities of European firms (e.g., Ramb 2007; Egger, Eggert, and Winner 2007; Overesch 2006; and Weichenrieder 2007).

Why is this of interest in understanding trade in services? This ability of firms to shift the location of assets and profits by paper transactions internal to the firm, whether or not the transactions are reported at market values, makes the location of the firms' production ambiguous. That is true in industries, such as banking and other financial services, in which production is intangible, and assets are mostly financial and intangible assets. It is also the case in other industries in which output is intangible, or based on intellectual property. And it is the case in tangible goods industries in which much of the value of the tangible goods stems from intangible assets. The ambiguity in the location of production produces a corresponding ambiguity in measures of exports and imports, particularly in services, where there is no physical movement to observe. But even in industries where physical movements of output can be observed, it is difficult to identify the location or locations of the value added, if intangible inputs are important.

Reported service exports by U.S. affiliates, worldwide and from main regions, and a few selected countries, are shown in table 1.7, with comparisons to the service exports reported by the same countries, mainly to the IMF. The affiliate exports are not reported as exports in the BEA surveys, but as sales by affiliates other than local sales, divided between sales to the United States and sales to other areas outside the host countries. The comparisons are very imprecise for a number of reasons. The U.S. affiliate nonlocal sales of services are incomplete in several respects. One is that they do not include banking—an important part of service exports worldwide—because the BEA surveys of banks do not include the extensive list of questions asked of nonbanking parents and their affiliates. Secondly, the BEA

Table 1.7 Exports of services reported by U.S. firms' affiliates and by host countries ($US, millions)

	1999		2005	
	Sales by nonbank majority-owned affiliates to U.S. and other foreign countries	Exports of services reported by host countries	Sales by nonbank majority-owned affiliates to U.S. and other foreign countries	Exports of services reported by host countries
All countries[a]	52,167	1,159,948	134,336	2,158,986
Canada	2,482	36,117	7,919	55,313
Europe	27,639	731,685[b]	70,832	1,341,060[b]
Ireland	1,577	15,688	5,755	59,920
Netherlands	2,715	52,023	7,893	80,087
Switzerland	648	29,277	5,957	47,225
United Kingdom	12,440	119,068	33,536	209,435
Latin America and other Western Hemisphere	11,652	54,801[c,d]	23,885	82,379[c]
Central and South America	1,883	41,139[d]	4,158	65,341
Other Western Hemisphere[e]	9,769	13,662[c]	19,727	17,038[c]
Barbados	(D)	1,029	253	1,457
Bermuda	6,311	1,486	13,908	1,163
United Kingdom Islands, Caribbean[f]	881	n.a.	2,388	n.a.
Western Hemisphere, n.e.c.[g]	(D)	8,296[c]	(D)	10,504[c]
Barbados and Western Hemisphere, n.e.c.[g]	2,577	9,326[c]	(D)	11,962[c]

Middle East	586	24,656[h]	1,147	47,725[h]
Asia Pacific	8,899	270,846[i]	27,391	547,381[i]
China	118	26,248	1,103	74,404
Hong Kong	1,536	35,625	3,913	63,762
Singapore	1,562	24,933	2,946	52,742

Sources: Nonbank majority-owned affiliates sales are from U.S. Department of Commerce, Bureau of Economic Analysis, www.bea.doc.gov (downloaded in Nov. 2007). Exports of services reported by host countries are from IMF (2007). Exports of services reported by host countries for Bermuda in 1999 are from United Nations (2002b). Exports of services reported by host countries for Bermuda in 2005 are from website of Statistics Department of Bermuda, www.statistics.gov.bm (downloaded in Sept. 2007).

Notes: (D) refers to the suppression of data. n.a. = not available.

[a]U.S. is excluded.

[b]Data exclude Andorra, Gibraltar, Greenland, Liechtenstein, Serbia, Turkmenistan, and Uzbekistan in both years and in 2005, Montenegro and Slovakia are excluded also.

[c]Data include all the countries in "Western Hemisphere, n.e.c." except Cuba, French Islands (Caribbean), and United Kingdom Islands (Atlantic).

[d]French Guiana is excluded.

[e]"Other Western Hemisphere" refers to Barbados, Bermuda, Dominican Republic, United Kingdom Islands (Caribbean), and Western Hemisphere, n.e.c.

[f]"United Kingdom Islands, Caribbean" refers to British Antilles, British Virgin Islands, Cayman Islands, and Montserrat.

[g]"Western Hemisphere, n.e.c." refers to Anguilla, Antigua and Barbuda, Aruba, Bahamas, Cuba, Dominica, French Islands, (Caribbean), Grenada, Haiti, Jamaica, Netherlands Antilles, St. Kitts and Nevis, St. Lucia, St. Vincent and the Grenadines, Trinidad and Tobago, and United Kingdom Islands (Atlantic).

[h]United Arab Emirates are not available.

[i]In 1999, data exclude Bhutan, Brunei, Macau, Fiji, French Islands (Indian Ocean), French Islands (Pacific), Laos, Marshall Islands, Micronesia, Nauru, Papua New Guinea, Samoa, and Tonga; in 2005, the same set of countries are excluded except Macau, Papua New Guinea, Samoa, and Tonga.

data are confined to majority-owned affiliates, because minority-owned affiliates are not asked the questions about destination of sales. Third, the BEA data are heavily suppressed in publication, with very little country detail available for Caribbean countries that account for much of trade in financial services.

The data reported by the countries to the IMF have other deficiencies. They lack detail, and more important, several important countries in international trade in services, such as the Cayman Islands and Bermuda, did not report to the IMF at all in these years. However, Bermuda did report exports and imports of services in its national accounts. For the world as a whole, sales of services outside their host countries reported by U.S. affiliates account for 6 percent or less of exports of services reported by host countries. For western hemisphere countries outside of Central and South America, reported sales outside the host countries by U.S. affiliates were larger than the aggregate service exports reported by the host countries in 2005. That was particularly the case for Bermuda in both 1999 and 2005. Either Bermuda did not consider these sales to be exports or it did not consider these affiliates part of the Bermuda economy.

Table 1.8 gives some hints about the peculiarities of U.S. affiliates in various host countries in 1999. Affiliates in the area called "Other Western Hemisphere," essentially islands in the Caribbean, owned enormous assets relative to their labor input, measured by employment or employee compensation. For example, while the average ratio of assets to employment around the world was about $700,000 per employee, the ratios in the three European countries shown were all over $1.7 million per employee, and those for affiliates in "Other Western Hemisphere" were $9 million per employee. Within that group, affiliates in Bermuda had assets of over $16 million per employee[1] and those in the UK Islands in the Caribbean, $28 million per employee. While worldwide, U.S. affiliates owned assets twenty-one times their payrolls, those in "Other Western Hemisphere" had assets over 300 times their payrolls. Their activities appear to be very capital-intensive types of production.

Capital/labor ratios could differ across countries because the industry composition of production differs, even if they were identical within industries. In fact, the country differences are evident within industries. Table 1.8 shows the ratios for depository institutions and for finance (except depository institutions), and insurance. In the case of depository institutions, in which the worldwide average assets per employee in U.S. affiliates was $10 million, U.S. affiliates in "Other Western Hemisphere" owned $117 million of assets per employee. Their assets were more than 2,000

---

1. That exceptional level for Bermuda, in terms of the direct investment position rather than total assets, was pointed out in Mataloni (1995, 46), and attributed to the use of Bermuda as an intermediate step for investment eventually located elsewhere.

Table 1.8   **Ratios of total assets to other input measures: U.S. affiliates in all industries, 1999**

	All industries		Depository institutions		Finance (except depository institutions) and insurance	
	Employment[a]	Compensation of employees	Employment[a]	Compensation of employees	Employment[a]	Compensation of employees
All countries	696	21	10,245	168	6,637	97
Canada	360	11	2,744	106	(D)	(D)
Europe	941	22	11,766	147	11,131	121
Ireland	1,010–2,020	(D)	3,570–8,922	(D)	15,089	268
Netherlands	1,710	37	(D)	(D)	(D)	(D)
Switzerland	2,131	31	6,970	55	22,222	175
United Kingdom	1,784	38	20,080	195	13,608	121
Latin America and other Western Hemisphere	556	34	12,013	264	5,015	137
Central and South America	253	16	2,394	53	1,488	50
Other Western Hemisphere	9,375	335	117,367	2,347	(D)	378
Bermuda	16,287–32,574	(D)	0	0	27,725	398
UK Islands, Caribbean[b]	28,157	462	153,283	1,703	63,540	304
Other, Western Hemisphere[c]	4,116–8,233	(D)	(D)	(D)	(D)	(D)
Middle East	1,078	25	16,593	215	(D)	(D)
Other Middle East[d]	3,967	100	(D)	(D)	(D)	(D)
Asia Pacific	563	20	7,434	155	3,334	51
China	112	17	8,653	288	489–978	(D)
Hong Kong	1,357	35	6,402	130	4,342	30
Singapore	1,204	37	15,921	195	(D)	(D)

Source: U.S. Department of Commerce, Bureau of Economic Analysis, www.bea.doc.gov (downloaded on Sept. 23, 2005).

Note: (D) refers to the suppression of data.

[a]Thousands of dollars per employee.

[b]"United Kingdom Islands, Caribbean" comprises British Antilles, British Virgin Islands, Cayman Islands, and Montserrat.

[c]"Other, Western Hemisphere" refers to Anguilla, Antigua and Barbuda, Aruba, Bahamas, Cuba, Dominica, French Islands (Caribbean), Grenada, Haiti, Jamaica, Netherlands Antilles, St. Kitts and Nevis, St. Lucia, St. Vincent and the Grenadines, Trinidad and Tobago, and United Kingdom Islands (Atlantic).

[d]"Other Middle East" refers to Bahrain, Iran, Jordan, Kuwait, Lebanon, Oman, Qatar, Syria, and Yemen.

times their employee compensation, as compared with about 168 times employee compensation worldwide.

In "other finance and insurance," U.S. affiliates worldwide owned $6.6 million in assets per employee while those in Switzerland owned assets of over $22 million per employee, those in Bermuda, almost $28 million per employee, and those in "Other UK Islands," over $60 million per employee. Worldwide, U.S. affiliates in this industry owned assets almost 100 times their payrolls, but those in Switzerland had assets 175 times their payrolls and those in "Other Western Hemisphere," had assets 300 to 400 times their payrolls (table 1.8).

The data for the two finance sectors make it clear that the loading of assets on to U.S. affiliates in Switzerland and the Caribbean is not simply a result of the industry composition of investment in those countries, but represents a choice by parent companies in financial service industries to attribute assets to these locations.

The assets of U.S. affiliates, in countries where the ratio of assets to labor inputs is particularly high, are not primarily physical assets, as can be seen from table 1.9. The worldwide ratio of total assets to net property, plant, and equipment in U.S. nonbank affiliates was 5.6 in 1999, but the ratio in the Netherlands was almost 14; in Switzerland, 23; in Bermuda, 27; and in UK Islands in the Caribbean, 34. Most of the assets of these asset-rich affiliates were financial assets or other assets, such as intangible or intellectual property. It would be hard to define the location of these assets, and if they are the basis for most of the output of these affiliates, one could say that only statistical convention places that output in these affiliates' host countries.

Table 1.10 displays the "profit-type return" relative to labor compensation, for those affiliates that are not only nonbank, but also majority-owned for both 1999 and 2005. Profit-type return ". . . measures profits before income taxes, and it excludes nonoperating items (such as special charges and capital gains and losses) and income from equity investments" (U.S. Bureau of Economic Analysis 2004, M-19). These ratios are clearly related to the asset/labor ratios of table 1.8, even though they exclude income on equity investments. While the worldwide ratios of profit-type return to payrolls were 56 and 84 percent in the two years, those for Ireland were 396 and 664 percent, and those for "Other Western Hemisphere" were over 600 percent in 1999 and almost twice that in 2005. They were around 1,300 and then 3,600 percent for affiliates in Bermuda, 3,000 percent and more for those in Barbados, and well over 1,000 percent in UK Islands and other countries in the Caribbean area. The extremely high ratios of capital income to labor income were achieved by placing large amounts of financial and intangible capital in the affiliates in these countries, although the capital may be far away from where an innocent observer might think production took place.

Table 1.9   **Ratio of total assets to net property, plant, and equipment by nonbank affiliates of nonbank U.S. parents, 1999**

	Ratio of total assets to net property, plant, and equipment
All countries	5.65
Canada	4.22
Europe	7.44
Ireland	10.78
Netherlands	13.95
Switzerland	23.20
United Kingdom	8.59
Latin America and other Western Hemisphere	4.66
Central and South America	3.11
Other Western Hemisphere	15.40
Barbados	(D)
Bermuda	27.57
United Kingdom Islands, Caribbean[a]	34.33
Other, Western Hemisphere[b]	4.04
Bermuda and other, Western Hemisphere[b]	13.10
Middle East	2.19
Other Middle East[c]	1.49
Asia Pacific	4.56
China	2.90
Hong Kong	7.86
Singapore	7.02

Source: U.S. Bureau of Economic Analysis (2004)

Note: (D) refers to the suppression of data.

[a]"United Kingdom Islands, Caribbean" comprises British Antilles, British Virgin Islands, Cayman Islands, and Montserrat.

[b]"Other, Western Hemisphere" refers to Anguilla, Antigua and Barbuda, Aruba, Bahamas, Cuba, Dominica, French Islands (Caribbean), Grenada, Haiti, Jamaica, Netherlands Antilles, St. Kitts and Nevis, St. Lucia, St. Vincent and the Grenadines, Trinidad and Tobago, and United Kingdom Islands (Atlantic).

[c]"Other Middle East" refers to Bahrain, Iran, Jordan, Kuwait, Lebanon, Oman, Qatar, Syria, and Yemen.

In the case of one service imported into the United States, insurance services, data are available for imports in recent years from all sources, not only from U.S. affiliates (table 1.11). A few islands in the Caribbean, with small populations and labor forces, were responsible for over half of U.S. imports of insurance services in 2001 and 2004, and almost half in other years. Extreme specialization is not impossible, but it is hard to think of what resources in these islands produced all these insurance services. One might suspect that the labor input took place in the home countries of the firms nominally operating in Bermuda and that the capital input was from financial assets that had no real geographical location and were under the

Table 1.10   **Ratio of profit-type return to compensation of employees by majority-owned nonbank affiliates of U.S. nonbank parents**

	1999	2005
	Ratio of profit-type return to compensation of employees	Ratio of profit-type return to compensation of employees
All countries	0.557	0.840
Canada	0.586	0.848
Europe	0.439	0.579
Ireland	3.964	6.639
Netherlands	0.793	0.878
Switzerland	0.867	1.614
United Kingdom	0.333	0.291
Latin America and other Western Hemisphere	0.771	1.555
Central and South America	0.466	0.978
Other Western Hemisphere	6.161	11.709
Barbados	30.884	34.967
Bermuda	13.007	36.062
United Kingdom Islands, Caribbean[a]	4.249	8.833
Other, Western Hemisphere[b]	1.655	6.347
Bermuda and other, Western Hemisphere[b]	6.714	15.794
Barbados and other, Western Hemisphere[b]	4.798	8.008
Middle East	1.084	1.837
Other Middle East[c]	5.887	9.403
Asia Pacific	0.755	1.178
China	0.670	1.498
Hong Kong	0.898	0.953
Singapore	1.420	2.978

Sources: U.S. Bureau of Economic Analysis (2004) U.S. Department of Commerce, Bureau of Economic Analysis, www.bea.doc.gov (downloaded Sept. 2007).

[a]"United Kingdom Islands, Caribbean" comprises British Antilles, British Virgin Islands, Cayman Islands, and Montserrat.

[b]"Other, Western Hemisphere" refers to Anguilla, Antigua and Barbuda, Aruba, Bahamas, Cuba, Dominica, French Islands (Caribbean), Grenada, Haiti, Jamaica, Netherlands Antilles, St. Kitts and Nevis, St. Lucia, St. Vincent and the Grenadines, Trinidad and Tobago, and United Kingdom Islands (Atlantic).

[c]"Other Middle East" refers to Bahrain, Iran, Jordan, Kuwait, Lebanon, Oman, Qatar, Syria, and Yemen.

control of the parent companies, but could be placed under the ownership of any affiliate, anywhere.

The allocation of financial assets to low tax countries is probably the most common distortion of the location of production, and along with production, exports and imports. However, other intangible assets are subject to similar manipulation and the creation of phantom flows of trade. Ireland and Bermuda have been favorite locations for transfers of such as-

Table 1.11   **U.S. payments for insurance services, 2001–2006 ($US, millions)**

	2001	2002	2003	2004	2005	2006
All countries	16,706	22,150	25,234	29,090	28,540	33,582
Canada	343	554	498	664	652	645
Europe	7,121	11,915	12,404	11,836	14,618	17,177
Netherlands	110	142	166	41	11	15
Switzerland	1,232	2,316	2,574	3,029	4,928	5,594
United Kingdom	2,978	3,848	4,134	3,344	3,186	3,134
Latin America and other						
Western Hemisphere	9,082	9,462	12,110	16,334	12,988	15,437
Other Western Hemisphere	9,032	9,383	12,059	16,257	12,935	15,334
Bermuda	7,167	7,499	10,034	11,805	10,227	12,685
Other, Western Hemisphere[a]	1,867	1,884	2,025	4,450	2,708	2,648
Africa	2	4	1	24	30	18
Middle East	4	3	5	12	8	11
Asia and Pacific	132	205	201	206	240	286

Sources: Borga and Mann (2004); Nephew et al. (2005); Koncz, Mann, and Nephew (2006); Koncz and Flatness (2007).

[a]"Other, Western Hemisphere" refers to Anguilla, Antigua and Barbuda, Aruba, Bahamas, Cuba, Dominica, French Islands (Caribbean), Grenada, Haiti, Jamaica, Netherlands Antilles, St. Kitts and Nevis, St. Lucia, St. Vincent and the Grenadines, Trinidad and Tobago, and United Kingdom Islands (Atlantic).

sets as software and drug patents (see, e.g., Simpson [2005], which lists many companies' Irish affiliates).

Publicly available data do not report individual company transactions, but these moves by various firms seem to have made their mark in a number of places in aggregate data. It is difficult to compare 1994 and 1999 BEA numbers by industry because of the shift from the Standard Industrial Classification (SIC) to North American Industry Classification System (NAICS) industry classifications, but this and similar transactions may have figured in the more than tenfold growth over that period in the sales of U.S. affiliates in Ireland classified as "Electronic and Other Electric Equipment" or "Services" in 1994, or as "Computers and Electronic Products" or "Professional, Scientific and Technical Services" in 1999, from $2.5 billion to $26 billion (U.S. Bureau of Economic Analysis 1998, 2004). There was a considerable growth in employment also, but only from 14,000 to 36,000 (BEA 1998, 2004). Software is not the only corporate asset subject to international shifting for tax purposes. One news article on such shifts referred to ". . . patents on drugs, ownership of corporate logos, techniques for manufacturing processes and other intellectual assets . . ." and quoted a tax lawyer as calling such moves routine, "'international tax planning 101.'" He added that "'most of the assets that are going to be relocated as part of a global repositioning are intellectual property . . . that is where most of the profit is. When you buy a pair of sneakers for $250, it's the swoosh symbol, not the rubber, you pay for" (Johnston 2002).

1.6 The Definition of Residence: What does the Current Account Balance Measure?

The U.S. Review Committee for Balance of Payments Statistics (1965) suggested that "balance of payments data are peculiarly elusive" because "[t]he basic criterion for a balance of payments transaction is that it is between a domestic and a foreign 'resident.' [. . .] The application of this set of concepts to concrete situations may involve subtle distinctions, and it is often difficult to determine residence even when all the facts are known.[. . .] Distinctions based on the balance of payments concept of residence have not ordinarily been important in the affairs of business firms, governments, or households; the concept, therefore, is not normally reflected in their records. The balance of payments statistician seeking data on international transactions from these records finds himself asking questions that are likely to be new and alien to the company's or the agency's normal way of thinking" (pp. 16–17).

As the importance of intangible assets has grown, particularly for the United States, it may no longer be true that questions of residence are new or alien to the thinking of companies, but the way they have become familiar to companies is different from the way that economists think of them. For companies, issues of residence, or the location of intangible assets, are important as tools for minimizing taxes, and companies can manipulate the residence of assets in ways that do not fit with economists' concepts of trade and production.

What are the economist's concepts of trade and the current balance? Meade (1951) defined exports as an element of ". . . demands for goods and services which directly or indirectly cause a demand for factors of production (i.e. for the productive services of land, capital, enterprise and work) . . ." whose incomes are recorded in the national income. Imports, correspondingly, lead to a demand for ". . . the productive resources of other countries" (p. 34)

If the object in the balance of payments is not to measure the physical movement of goods or services, and trade in services does not involve a change in ownership, what is the goal of the measurement? Writings about the balance of trade, and particularly about the balance of payments, have often had a whiff of mercantilism about them. That used to be especially clear in the references to "favorable" or "unfavorable" balances. These terms have virtually disappeared, but they reflected the traditional purpose of the calculations, which was to know whether a country was gaining or losing gold. In an international regime aiming at stability of exchange rates, the substitute was the question of demand for and supply of a country's currency. One reflection of that aim was the effort to define "autonomous" and "accommodating" transactions, as in Meade (1951, 11–16). In the United States, there was a search for the appropriate measure of balance-of-payments deficits or surpluses, the need for which stemmed from the fact that "leading countries have established fixed parities for their currencies and have undertaken to maintain exchange rates within prescribed margins of those parities" (U.S. Review Committee for Balance of Payments Statistics 1965, 2). That purpose too has become obsolete. The Bureau of Economic Analysis, describing concepts underlying the balance of payments in 1990, does not provide a purpose for the calculation, but defines it simply as ". . . a statistical summary of international transactions . . . defined as the transfer of ownership of something that has an economic value measurable in monetary terms from residents of one country to residents of another" (U.S. Department of Commerce 1990, xiii). The article explaining alternative frameworks for the international accounts (Landefeld, Whichard, and Lowe 1993) refers to the "standard balance of payments" as providing ". . . indicators of returns to domestic versus foreign factors of production . . ." (p. 51), echoing Meade's description.

A more recent textbook defines a country's current account balance as ". . . the change in the value of its net claims on the rest of the world—the change in its net foreign assets" (Obstfeld and Rogoff 1996, 4). The issue of residence remains. An intangible or financial asset has no real geographical location; its only definite location is its ownership. A multinational corporate owner can choose to move the ownership of an intangible asset to an affiliate anywhere in the world. By moving a piece of paper from one pocket to another, the firm changes the apparent geographical location of an asset, of production from that asset, and the direction of trade flows from its output. Production that had been taking place in the home country now takes place in the country of assignment of the asset. The home country, or other former nominal location of the asset, which had been credited with its output, is now reported to be importing that output. Has anything really happened? Can we accept that there has been a change in the reality we are trying to measure, or are we being fooled into thinking that some economic event has taken place when it has not?

In the cases of international service trade based on intangible assets, if the assets producing these services are exported to some countries by placing them on the books of the affiliates incorporated there, what local resources are used in producing these services? What is the flow of services from these exporters that is equivalent to the flow of goods measured in the goods trade accounts? What would be the significance to the U.S. economy of a rise in the deficit from these imaginary international flows?

If there are what appear to be large distortions in the service trade data, or extreme flexibility in assigning production of services to locations, they raise questions about the meaning and purpose of the balance of payments accounts. The producers of the accounts often justify procedures by conformity with IMF (1993) and the SNA (United Nations 1993a), without much discussion of the underlying purposes of the measurement. They rarely discuss the implications, if any, of moving from a world in which production and trade consist mostly of goods produced by physical capital and labor to a world in which most output is in the form of services, much of it produced by intangible assets, and much of goods output, also, is from intangible inputs. And they rarely discuss the implications of moving from a world in which production within a firm is located in a firm's home country to a world in which production within a firm combines inputs located in many countries or worse, inputs with no definite geographical location.

The issue here is not what tax havens and the shifting of assets do to home and host country tax revenues. The focus is on the tiny tax havens, because some of them have so little production outside of tax avoidance activities that it is relatively clear what is going on there. However, much the same problem in measuring flows of services must exist, more hidden, in larger countries. The question is whether we are, by our ways of measuring, creating phantom international flows of some services that may not be crossing international borders at all. Services that are produced and consumed entirely within the United States without crossing borders may appear to be produced in some Caribbean Island or other tax-favored location and exported to the United States. What do we learn about the economy of the United States or of the exporting country from observing these phantom flows? Some host countries have answered that question by excluding from their national accounts the activities of these offshore enterprises.

The possibility that some imports or exports of services do not actually cross international borders was illustrated by a recent court proceeding in a bankruptcy case (*Wall Street Journal* 2006b). "Funds flowed freely between the Bermuda entity and New York units and throughout Refco . . . it employed no one at all at its headquarters address in Bermuda. New York-based employees ran the unit." An arrangement recently challenged by the IRS involved a transfer of major drug patents to a subsidiary in Bermuda that caused the U.S. parent company to pay royalties to a Bermuda subsidiary although the patents had been developed by the parent company in the United States (Drucker 2006).

Various ways have been suggested for incorporating production by foreign affiliates into international accounts by producing accounts on what is referred to as an ownership rather than a residency basis. One such suggestion was proposed in National Research Council (1992) by a national Academy of Sciences panel chaired by Robert E. Baldwin, and amplified in Baldwin and Kimura (1998) and Kimura and Baldwin (1998). While such accounts are not intended as replacements for the standard balance of payments accounts, and are intended for different purposes, they do, in the process, escape from counting transactions that do not really take place by combining the operations of parent firms with those of their foreign affiliates. The Bureau of Economic Analysis now regularly publishes an ownership-based current account for the United States, explained in Landefeld, Whichard, and Lowe (1993). The latest of these is U.S. Bureau of Economic Analysis (2006).

These alternative measures are based on the ownership of the productive resources or of the firms in which production takes place, rather than the location of the resources. In this way, they net out the effects of some of what are described here as phantom transactions, although they do not remove them from the standard accounts. However, the cost is that these accounts provide no information on the location of production.

Given the ease with which the nominal location of production, imports, and exports from financial and intangible assets can be manipulated, is there a better method for tracing the path of these variables? The problem is similar to that faced by the European Commission in suggesting the need for an agreed way of allocating profits among a firm's locations, overriding the allocations on the firms' books (see, e.g., *Wall Street Journal* 2006a).

For an individual firm, the actual location of production might be better represented by ignoring the nominal geographical location of financial and intangible assets on the firm's books, attributing to parent companies the ownership of these assets, the production from them, and the trade from that production. That could be done by the statistical authorities of any of the few countries that survey the outward direct investment activities of their countries' firms, as the BEA does for the United States.

The simplest case is that of affiliate holdings in other foreign affiliates, which clearly do not contribute to production and exports in the affiliate's host country. They probably do not distort the reported host country export data, but they inflate affiliate income in those countries by including income earned elsewhere. For U.S. affiliates worldwide, these holdings were 23 percent of total assets in 2005, but they were almost half in the Netherlands and in affiliates in "Other Western Hemisphere, n.e.c.", and over a third in Switzerland and Bermuda (U.S. Department of Commerce, BEA 2007).

Under the extreme assumption that all assets other than inventories and property, plant, and equipment should be attributed to the parent firm, on the grounds that they have no specific geographical location and could be placed anywhere by the parent firm, the effect on affiliate assets would be much larger. For U.S. affiliates worldwide, assets would be reduced to 12 percent of the reported total. In Ireland and Switzerland, they would be only 6 percent. In Barbados, less than 2 percent of reported assets would remain and in Bermuda and U.K. Islands in the Caribbean, only 1 percent. From the published data, one cannot match the asset holdings with the exporters of services, as opposed to goods. It would be possible, with access to the original questionnaires, to match the portfolio holdings with the exports of goods and of services and identify firms whose service exports were produced essentially without local labor and with only assets that had no clear geographical location.

While this way of estimating exports of services could be carried out for trade with U.S.-owned affiliates, it does not solve the problem of trade with other countries' affiliates. Some host countries exclude affiliates that operate only outside the country from their national accounts. In that case, their sales of services abroad do not appear in host country export data. However, they can still be counted in the imports of services by other countries from that host country. Unless the home countries of the affiliates' parents survey their own foreign investors, there is no obvious way to attribute these imports to the country where they are actually produced.

1.7   Summary and Conclusions

Exports and imports of services are more difficult to define and measure than trade in goods, and as a consequence, their size and growth are much less certain. The reported world total value in 2005 was about 2.5 trillion of exports and a similar amount of imports, approximately one-quarter of world trade in goods.

The trend in the importance of service exports and imports is even harder to measure, because the number of services covered and the number of countries measuring service exports and imports has increased, especially since 1975. Despite those increases, there is only slight evidence of a rise in the importance of service exports and imports relative to goods trade.

Since the United States has been a leader in measuring service exports and imports, the U.S. data are more complete than those for the world. Service exports have recently been over 40 percent of goods exports, while service imports have been only about 20 percent of goods imports. However, service imports have recently been growing faster than service exports.

Attempts to translate these trends in nominal ratios of service to goods trade into ratios in real terms face the almost complete absence of data on prices of traded services. Use of domestic price measures as proxies faces the problem that even domestic service prices are poorly measured and subject to many criticisms, and the fact that the composition of domestic service production and consumption is very different from that of internationally traded services.

Relative to goods and services output, U.S. service exports and imports are much smaller than goods exports and imports, especially the imports. Service exports and imports are about 4 to 5 percent of services output, while goods imports are almost 40 percent and goods exports are over 20 percent of goods output. Both goods and services exports are at historically high levels relative to output, compared to the period since 1869, and the same is true for goods imports, which have risen steadily since 1950 after a long secular decline from 1869 to World War II. Changes in services imports relative to services output have been much smaller: the ratio for 1990 to 1999 was almost identical to that for 1869 to 1873, but the ratio for 2000 to 2006 was 15 percent higher.

The measures of service trade, because they are not anchored in any observation of physical movement, are, much more than those of goods trade, determined by the definition of residence, since residence, rather than an observed movement of a final product, determines what is an export or import. The problem is illustrated by the case of trade in educational services, because the determination that an ostensibly domestic transaction is an import or export rests on a difference in residence between the provider and the acquirer of the service. A paradoxical aspect of this definition is that, especially in the United States, much of the exported educational service never leaves the United States because the recipients decide to become U.S. residents. What would be necessary to close this gap between the service trade measure and reality would be an account for flows of human capital that would show the service imported into the United States in the form of human capital. An alternative would be to treat the educational expenditure as an internal trade within the United States until the recipient crossed the border to return home, if he or she did so, and then enter it into exports of services. A drawback of this scheme is that it would not account for the reimport of previously exported services when the recipient of a U.S. education returned to the United States at a later date.

A serious problem for the measurement of service trade, and also for the measurement of the location of output of both goods and services, is the growing importance of intangible inputs, including intellectual assets, in production, because these assets do not have a clear geographical location. The same is true for financial assets. One consequence of this growth is the expanding use by parent firms of the placement of intangible and financial assets in low tax jurisdictions. Since the assets are intangible, including financial assets, patents, trademarks, rights to designs, and corporate logos, they have no particular geographical location, and their ownership can be moved by the parent company of a multinational to any of its affiliates. The result is that the output and exports stemming from these assets can also be attributed to geographical locations almost at will, subject to some limited regulation by tax authorities, without any relation to the actual location of any physical aspect of the production. A large part of service production, exports, and imports, and some part of goods production can begin to consist of phantom production and trade that makes no use of factors of production actually resident in the countries to which they are attributed. If that takes place to an important degree, the measures of the current balance and national output begin to lose their meaning.

For trade with U.S. affiliates, it is possible to consolidate the operations of multinational parents and their affiliates in the data, counting as trade only transactions outside the multinational firm, between segments of the firm and unaffiliated entities. The closest approximation to this is the ownership-based accounts of the BEA. However, these are not incorporated into the international transactions accounts or national accounts in general and, as they are constructed, provide no data on the geographical location of production.

It may be that the calculation of trade flows, particularly for services—but to some extent for goods as well—and the related calculations of the location of production, have reached the stage that calculations of capital consumption reached many years ago. That stage was the decision by statistical agencies to abandon the reliance on corporate accounting for capital consumption, because corporate accounts were too distorted by differences in assumptions and by tax considerations, and to substitute statistical and econometric estimation of capital consumption based on other types of data.

Appendix

Table 1A.1   Goods and service exports and imports by fixed sets of countries, five-year averages, 1972–2006, and year, 2005 ($US, billions)

	22 Countries[a]				30 Countries[b]			
	Goods		Services		Goods		Services	
Year	Credit	Debit	Credit	Debit	Credit	Debit	Credit	Debit
1972–1976	375.8	355.4	79.0	85.1	n.a.	n.a.	n.a.	n.a.
1977–1981	806.1	776.0	168.7	188.3	1,101.9	1,071.3	241.7	264.5
1982–1986	924.1	964.9	221.1	243.1	1,312.9	1,305.3	306.3	333.0
1987–1991	1,512.9	1,563.1	383.7	394.3	2,167.4	2,122.4	534.4	570.3
1992–1996	2,140.8	2,164.3	582.2	563.7	3,058.0	2,925.1	795.3	819.1
1997–2001	2,739.6	2,914.7	755.0	728.6	3,810.5	3,851.7	999.2	1,012.6
2002–2006	3,785.1	4,200.7	1,072.6	1,031.2	5,272.5	5,539.5	1,456.6	1,414.8
2005	4,353.0	4,798.4	1,216.9	1,169.1	6,047.1	6,382.9	1,681.6	1,617.0

	World: 150 Countries			
	Goods		Services	
	Credit	Debit	Credit	Debit
2005	9,779.1	9,856.4	2,486.7	2,370.8

Source: IMF (2007).

Note: n.a. = not available.

[a]The twenty-two countries include Australia, Austria, Barbados, Canada, Colombia, Dominican Rep., Germany, Haiti, Israel, Italy, Jordan, Malta, Netherlands, New Zealand, Romania, Saudi Arabia, Singapore, South Africa, Sweden, United Kingdom, United States, and Venezuela.

[b]The 30 countries include the twenty-two countries, plus Argentina, Belgium-Luxembourg, Brazil, Denmark, Finland, France, India, and Japan.

Table 1A.2 U.S. trade in goods and services, decade averages, 1790–1999 and average of 2000–2006 ($US, millions)

Year	Services		Goods	
	Exports	Imports	Exports	Imports
1790–1799[a]	14.5	2.2	43.5	53.9
1800–1809	28.2	3.9	75.9	96.4
1810–1819	20.2	2.1	59.8	82.0
1820–1829[b]	12.4	2.3	69.7	74.1
1830–1839	13.0	3.9	98.7	118.0
1840–1849	18.4	5.8	118.0	113.8
1850–1859	24.8	26.3	231.6	277.1
1860–1869[c, d]	29.4	43.5	263.6	333.7
1870–1879	35.2	60.8	566.7	525.9
1880–1889	36.8	91.9	780.8	714.3
1890–1899	37.6	104.2	980.3	770.0
1900–1909[e]	36.8	209.6	1,705.1	1,157.7
1910–1919	251	642	4,255	2,304
1920–1929	530	869	5,151	4,034
1930–1939	398	659	2,710	2,261
1930–1939	440	660	2,700	2,260
1940–1949	1,610	2,200	7,730	4,550
1950–1959	3,570	5,310	14,760	11,840
1960–1969	9,390	9,890	27,740	23,130
1970–1979	28,270	24,490	99,730	108,710
1980–1989	86,870	73,320	251,370	344,090
1990–1999	223,890	150,350	550,550	724,790
2000–2006	348,843	275,843	813,329	1,423,786

Sources: 1790–1860: North (1960, tables A-4, B-2, and B-3); 1861–1900: Simon (1960, table 27); 1901–1939: U.S. Bureau of the Census (1975, table U 1–25, 864–66; 1930–2006: BEA website, http://www.bea.gov/bea/di1.htm (downloaded on Dec. 24, 2007).

[a]From 1790 to 1819, exports of services include only freight earnings; imports of services include only payments for insurance; exports of goods include exports of merchandise and sales of ships.

[b]From 1820 to 1860, exports of services include freight earnings, port charges, and tourist expenditures; imports of services include freight payments to foreign ships and tourist expenditures; exports of goods include exports of merchandise and sales of ships.

[c]Exports and imports of goods in 1860 include specie.

[d]From 1861 to 1900, exports of services are equal to total shipping income plus foreign tourist expenditures plus port outlays of foreign passenger steamships; imports of services are equal to total shipping payments plus U.S. tourist expenditures. Exports of goods are the sum of exports of merchandise and the sales of ships.

[e]From 1901 to 1970, exports of services are sums of transportation, travel, and other transactions; imports of services are sums of transportation, travel, direct military expenditures, and other transactions.

Table 1A.3 **U.S. trade in and output of services, current prices, 1869–2006**

Year	Exports ($US, millions)	Imports ($US, millions)	Output of services ($US, billions)	Output (%) Exports	Output (%) Imports
1869–1873	37	59	1.6	2.34	3.74
1872–1881	35	64	2.1	1.68	3.12
1882–1891	38	100	3.0	1.27	3.38
1892–1901	36	112	3.9	0.93	2.86
1902–1911	43	249	7.7	0.55	3.23
1912–1921	405	766	15.1	2.68	5.07
1922–1931	450	854	28.7	1.57	2.98
1930–1939	398	659	31.6	1.26	2.09
1930–1939	440	660	31.6	1.39	2.09
1940–1949	1,610	2,200	79.6	2.02	2.76
1950–1959	3,570	5,310	156.2	2.29	3.40
1960–1969	9,390	9,890	310.9	3.02	3.18
1970–1979	28,270	24,490	771.7	3.66	3.17
1980–1989	86,870	73,320	2,074.8	4.19	3.53
1990–1999	223,890	150,350	4,040.2	5.54	3.72
2000–2006	348,843	275,843	6,458.1	5.40	4.27

Sources: Exports and Imports 1869–1900: Ten-year averages calculated from Simon (1960). Exports and Imports 1901–1939: Ten-year averages calculated from U.S. Bureau of the Census (1975, table U 1–25, 864–66). Exports and Imports 1930–2006: Ten-year averages calculated from BEA website, http://www.bea.gov/bea/di1.htm (downloaded on Dec. 24, 2007). Output of Services 1869–1931: U.S. Bureau of the Census (1975, table F 71–97, 231). Output of Services 1930–2006: Ten-year averages calculated from BEA website, http://www.bea.gov/bea/dn1.htm (downloaded on Dec. 24, 2007).

Table 1A.4   **U.S. trade in and output of goods, current prices, 1869–2006**

Year	Exports ($US, millions)	Imports ($US, millions)	Output of goods ($US, billions)	Output (%) Exports	Output (%) Imports
1869–1873	438	545	4.2	10.45	13.01
1872–1881	656	561	5.0	13.09	11.20
1882–1891	783	751	7.0	11.26	10.80
1892–1901	1,099	777	8.3	13.23	9.35
1902–1911	1,829	1,299	14.9	12.26	8.71
1912–1921	5,140	2,781	31.7	16.22	8.77
1922–1931	4,487	3,761	46.9	9.56	8.01
1930–1939	2,710	2,261	39.5	6.86	5.72
1930–1939	2,700	2,260	39.5	6.83	5.72
1940–1949	7,730	4,550	106.1	7.29	4.29
1950–1959	14,760	11,840	195.5	7.55	6.06
1960–1969	27,740	23,130	317.5	8.74	7.29
1970–1979	99,730	108,710	691.0	14.43	15.73
1980–1989	251,370	344,090	1,544.2	16.28	22.28
1990–1999	550,550	724,790	2,611.8	21.08	27.75
2000–2006	813,329	1,423,786	3,615.6	22.49	39.38

Sources: Exports and Imports 1869–1900: Ten-year averages calculated from Simon (1960). Exports and Imports 1901–1939: Ten-year averages calculated from U.S. Bureau of the Census (1975, table U 1–25, 864–66). Exports and Imports 1930–2006: Ten-year averages calculated from BEA website, http://www.bea.gov/bea/di1.htm (downloaded on Dec. 24, 2007). Output of Services 1869–1931: U.S. Bureau of the Census (1975, table F 71–97, 231). Output of Services 1930–2006: Ten-year averages calculated from BEA website, http://www.bea.gov/bea/dn1.htm (downloaded on Dec. 24, 2007).

Table 1A.5   **U.S. exports and imports of services and goods in 2000 prices, five-year averages, 1929–2000 and average of 2001–2006 ($US billions)**

	Goods Exports	Goods Imports	Services Exports	Services Imports	Services/goods (%) Exports	Services/goods (%) Imports
1929–1935	17.8	27.6	5.4	7.3	30.39	26.28
1936–1940	21.5	31.2	7.0	6.8	32.59	21.88
1941–1945	18.0	30.6	7.7	17.2	42.59	56.01
1946–1950	44.5	38.2	13.7	12.0	30.72	31.50
1951–1955	42.4	46.5	15.3	24.2	36.00	51.94
1956–1960	53.7	60.1	23.8	35.3	44.37	58.81
1961–1965	69.2	80.1	35.0	40.1	50.57	50.08
1966–1970	91.4	134.5	49.6	54.5	54.30	40.57
1971–1975	134.1	186.6	66.0	59.0	49.26	31.63
1976–1980	183.7	243.7	86.6	65.7	47.12	26.97
1981–1985	208.8	295.2	107.2	87.7	51.34	29.71
1986–1990	298.4	437.1	157.0	127.7	52.61	29.22
1991–1995	452.3	577.0	221.0	142.7	48.86	24.73
1996–2000	682.8	989.7	289.0	194.6	42.32	19.67
2001–2006	786.4	1,403.2	331.8	253.7	42.19	18.08

Source: BEA website, http://www.bea.gov/bea/di1.htm (downloaded on Sept. 25, 2007).

Table 1A.6	U.S. exports and imports of goods and output of goods in 2000 prices, five-year averages, 1929–2000 and average of 2001–2006

	Output of goods ($US, billions)	Exports and imports of goods as percent of output	
		Exports	Imports
1929–1935	215.3	8.24	12.84
1936–1940	278.5	7.72	11.21
1941–1945	439.3	4.09	6.97
1946–1950	513.5	8.66	7.43
1951–1955	606.2	6.99	7.67
1956–1960	687.3	7.82	8.74
1961–1965	811.5	8.53	9.87
1966–1970	1,031.9	8.85	13.03
1971–1975	1,221.8	10.97	15.27
1976–1980	1,476.1	12.45	16.51
1981–1985	1,685.3	12.39	17.52
1986–1990	2,083.2	14.32	20.98
1991–1995	2,403.1	18.82	24.01
1996–2000	3,070.9	22.24	32.23
2001–2006	3,641.4	21.59	38.53

Source: BEA website, http://www.bea.gov/bea/di1.htm (downloaded on Sept. 25, 2007).

Table 1A.7	U.S. exports and imports of services and output of services in 2000 prices, five-year averages, 1929–2000 and average of 2001–2006

	Output of services ($US, billions)	Exports and imports of services as percent of output	
		Exports	Imports
1929–1935	441.6	1.22	1.64
1936–1940	505.5	1.39	1.35
1941–1945	1,073.3	0.71	1.60
1946–1950	870.6	1.57	1.38
1951–1955	1,149.3	1.33	2.10
1956–1960	1,336.6	1.78	2.64
1961–1965	1,646.0	2.13	2.44
1966–1970	2,111.9	2.35	2.58
1971–1975	2,460.7	2.68	2.40
1976–1980	2,854.0	3.03	2.30
1981–1985	3,259.1	3.29	2.69
1986–1990	3,923.7	4.00	3.26
1991–1995	4,459.1	4.96	3.20
1996–2000	5,079.0	5.69	3.83
2001–2006	5,899.6	5.62	4.30

Source: BEA website, http://www.bea.gov/bea/di1.htm (downloaded on Sept. 25, 2007).

Table 1A.8   **Implicit price indexes for goods and services in U.S. output, exports, and imports, five-year averages, 1929–2000, and average of 2001–2006 (2000 = 100)**

	Goods			Services		
	Output[a]	Exports	Imports	Output[b]	Exports	Imports
1929–1935	17.41	15.31	8.37	7.03	7.23	9.34
1936–1940	16.92	15.57	8.31	6.81	8.42	10.40
1941–1945	20.91	22.63	11.37	7.54	15.01	14.22
1946–1950	27.09	28.59	17.97	10.33	17.18	18.72
1951–1955	30.35	31.83	23.62	12.33	19.57	19.67
1956–1960	32.77	33.64	23.20	14.48	21.09	19.52
1961–1965	34.47	34.78	22.77	16.19	22.47	20.99
1966–1970	38.23	39.46	24.54	19.22	25.26	23.44
1971–1975	46.94	55.47	40.58	25.86	33.79	33.67
1976–1980	63.82	85.39	74.69	37.42	48.08	53.37
1981–1985	82.83	106.26	100.28	55.23	67.20	68.87
1986–1990	90.43	104.92	101.71	68.65	77.15	79.40
1991–1995	99.38	107.13	106.44	83.11	90.00	92.30
1996–2000	100.47	101.80	99.62	94.98	96.71	97.98
2001–2006	100.30	103.60	102.83	112.11	106.48	110.95

Source: BEA website: http://www.bea.gov/bea/dn1.htm (downloaded on September 25, 2007).
[a]Output of goods is measured as final sales.
[b]Includes government consumption expenditures, which are for services (such as education and national defense) produced by government. In current dollars, these services are valued at their cost of production.

References

Bach, C. L. 2003. Annual revision of the U.S. international accounts, 1992–2002. *Survey of Current Business* 83 (7): 32–45.
———. 2006. Annual revision of the U.S. international accounts, 1995–2005. *Survey of Current Business* 86 (7): 36–48.
Baldwin, R. E., and F. Kimura. 1998. Measuring U.S. International Goods and Services Transactions. In *Geography and Ownership as Bases for Economic Accounting,* Studies in income and wealth, vol. 59, ed. R. E. Baldwin, R. E. Lipsey, and J. D. Richardson, 9–36. Chicago: University of Chicago Press.
Bermuda Department of Statistics. 2006. *Bermuda balance of payments, quarter ending December 2005.* Bermuda Department of Statistics.
Borga, M., and M. Mann. 2003. U.S. international services: Cross-border trade in 2002 and sales through affiliates in 2001. *Survey of Current Business* 83 (10): 58–77.
———. 2004. U.S. international services: Cross-border trade in 2003 and sales through affiliates in 2002. *Survey of Current Business* 84 (10): 25–76.
Cutler, D. M., and E. Berndt, eds. 2001. *Medical care output and productivity,* Studies in income and wealth, vol. 62. Chicago and London: University of Chicago Press.
Desai, M. A., C. F. Foley, and J. R. Hines Jr. 2003. Chains of ownership, regional tax competition, and foreign direct investment. In *Foreign direct investment in the*

real and financial sector of industrial countries, ed. H. Hermann and R. E. Lipsey, 61–98. Berlin-Heidelberg: Springer-Verlag.

———. 2006. Taxation and multinational activity: New evidence, new interpretations. *Survey of Current Business* 86 (2): 16–22.

Dreher, A., and P. Poutvaara. 2005. Student flows and migration: An empirical analysis. Center for Economic Studies & Ifo Institute for Economic Research CESifo Working Paper No. 1490, and Institute for the Study of Labor IZA, IZA Discussion Paper no. 1612.

Drucker, J. 2006. How Merck saved $1.5 billion paying itself for drug patents. *Wall Street Journal,* September 28.

Egger, P., W. Eggert, and H. Winner. 2007. Saving taxes through foreign plant ownership. CESifo Working Paper no. 1887, January.

General Agreement on Tariffs and Trade (GATT). 1985. *International trade, 1984/85.* Geneva.

———. 1994. *International trade, trends and statistics.* Geneva.

Griliches, Z. 1992. *Output measurement in the service sectors,* Studies in income and wealth, vol. 56. Chicago and London: University of Chicago Press.

Hines, J. R. Jr. 2005. Do tax havens flourish? In *Tax policy and the economy 19,* ed. J. M. Poterba, 65–99. Cambridge, MA: MIT Press.

International Monetary Fund. 1991. *International financial statistics yearbook.* Washington, D.C.: International Monetary Fund.

———. 1993. *Balance of payments manual, 5th edition.* Washington, D.C.: International Monetary Fund.

———. 2004. *Balance of payments statistics yearbook, 2004, part 1, country tables.* Washington, D.C.: International Monetary Fund.

———. 2007. *Balance of payments yearbook CD-ROM.* Washington, D.C.: International Monetary Fund.

Jacks, D. S. 2006. What drove 19th century commodity market integration? *Explorations in Economic History* 43 (3): 383–412.

Johnston, D.C. 2002. Key company assets moving offshore. *New York Times,* November 22.

Khatchadourian, K., and A. Wiesner. 2006. International price program's (IPP's) services price indexes. Paper presented at CRIW Conference on International Service Flows. 28–29 April, Bethesda, MD.

Kimura, F., and R. E. Baldwin. 1998. Application of a Nationality-Adjusted Net Sales and Value-Added Framework: The Case of Japan. In *Geography and ownership as bases for economic accounting,* R. E. Baldwin, R. E. Lipsey, and J. D. Richardson, 49–80. Chicago: University of Chicago Press.

Koncz, J., and A. Flatness. 2007. U.S. international services: Cross-border trade in 2006 and sales through affiliates in 2005. *Survey of Current Business* 87 (10): 94–113.

Koncz, J., M. Mann, and E. Nephew. 2006. U.S. international services: Cross-border trade in 2005 and sales through affiliates in 2004. *Survey of Current Business* 86 (10): 18–74.

Landefeld, J. S., O. G. Whichard, and J. H. Lowe. 1993. Alternative frameworks for U.S. international transactions. *Survey of Current Business* 73 (12): 50–61.

Larsen, K., J. P. Martin, and R. Morris. 2002. Trade in educational services: Trends and emerging issues. *World Economy* 25 (6): 849–68.

League of Nations. 1942. *The network of world trade.* Geneva: League of Nations.

Lindner, A., B. Cave, L. Deloumeaux, and J. Magdeleine. 2001. Trade in goods and services: Statistical trends and measurement challenges. Statistics Brief no. 1, October. Paris: Organization for Economic Cooperation and Development.

Marshall, A. 1923. *Money, credit, and commerce.* Repr., New York: Augustus M. Kelley, 1965.

Mataloni, R. J. Jr. 1995. A guide to BEA statistics on U.S. multinational companies. *Survey of Current Business* 75 (3): 38–55.

Meade, J. E. 1951. *The theory of international economic policy: Vol. 1, the balance of payments.* London: Oxford University Press.

Mohammed, S. S., and J. G. Williamson. 2004. Freight rates and productivity gains in British tramp shipping 1869–1950. *Explorations in Economic History* 41 (2): 172–203.

National Research Council, Panel on Foreign Trade Statistics. 1992. *Behind the numbers: U.S. trade in the world economy,* ed. A. Y. Kester. Washington, D.C.: National Academy Press.

National Science Foundation. 1998a. *International mobility of scientists and engineers to the United States—Brain drain or brain circulation?* Division of Science Resources Studies Issue Brief, Washington, D.C., Directorate for Social, Behavioral, and Economic Sciences, June.

———. 1998b. *Statistical profiles of foreign doctoral recipients in science and engineering: Plans to stay in the United States.* Division of Science Resources Studies, Washington, D.C., Directorate for Social, Behavioral, and Economic Sciences, November.

———. 2006. *Science and engineering indicators, 2006.* Division of Science Resources Studies, Washington, D.C., Directorate for Social, Behavioral, and Economic Sciences.

Nephew, E., J. Koncz, M. Borga, and M. Mann. 2005. U.S. international services: Cross-border trade in 2004 and sales through affiliates in 2003. *Survey of Current Business* 85 (10): 25–77.

North, D.C. 1960. The United States balance of payments, 1790–1860. In *Trends in the American economy in the nineteenth century,* Studies in income and wealth, vol. 24, ed. W. N. Parker, 573–627. Princeton: Princeton University Press.

Obstfeld, M., and K. Rogoff. 1996. *Foundations of international macroeconomics.* Cambridge, MA: MIT Press.

O'Rourke, K. H. 2006. War and welfare: Britain, France, and the United States, 1807–14. IIIS Discussion Paper 119. Institute for International Integration Studies, The Sutherland Centre, Trinity College, Dublin.

Overesch, M. 2006. Transfer pricing of intrafirm sales as a profit shifting channel-evidence from German firm data. Discussion Paper no. 06-084. Centre for European Economic Research (ZEW).

Ramb, F. 2007. Corporate marginal tax rate, tax loss carryforwards, and investment functions—empirical analysis using a large German panel data set. Frankfurt am Main, Deutsche Bundesbank Discussion Paper Series 1: Economic Studies no. 21/2007.

Republic of China (Taiwan). 1987. Statistical yearbook of the Republic of China, 1987. Directorate-General of Budget, Accounting, and Statistics, Executive Yuan, Republic of China, Taipei, Taiwan.

Sauers, R. M., and K. K. Pierce. 2005. U.S. international transactions: First quarter of 2005. *Survey of Current Business* 85 (7): 72–121.

Simon, M. 1960. The United States Balance of Payments, 1861–1900. In *Trends in the American economy in the nineteenth century,* Studies in income and wealth, vol. 24, ed. W. N. Parker, 629–711. Princeton: Princeton University Press.

Simpson, G. R. 2005. Irish subsidiary lets Microsoft slash taxes in U.S. and Europe. *Wall Street Journal,* November 7.

United Nations. 1993a. *A system of national accounts.* Studies in Methods, series F, no. 2, rev. 3. New York: United Nations.

———. 1993b. *MSPA handbook of world development statistics.* Long-Term Socio-Economic Perspectives Branch, Macroeconomics and Social Policy Analysis Division, Department of Economic and Social Policy Analysis. New York: United Nations.

———. 2002a. *Manual on statistics of international trade in services.* Statistical Papers, series M, no. 86. Geneva, Luxembourg, New York, Paris, Washington, D.C.: UNCTAD, European Commission, United Nations, OECD, IMF, and WTO.

———. 2002b. *National accounts statistics: Main aggregates and detailed tables, 2000.* New York: United Nations.

———. 2004. *International merchandise trade statistics compilers manual.* Department of Economic and Social Affairs, Statistics Division. New York: United Nations.

U.S. Bureau of the Census. 1975. *Historical statistics of the United States, colonial times to 1970.* Washington, D.C.: U.S. Government Printing Office.

U.S. Congress, Office of Technology Assessment. 1986. *Trade in services: Exports and foreign revenues-special report,* OTA-ITE-318. Washington, D.C.: U.S. Government Printing Office, September.

U.S. Department of Commerce, Bureau of Economic Analysis. 1987. *Foreign transactions methodology paper series MP-3.* Washington, D.C.: GPO.

———. 1990. *The balance of payments of the United States: Concepts, data sources, and estimating procedures.* Washington, D.C.: GPO.

———. 1998. *U.S. direct investment abroad: final results from the 1994 benchmark survey.* Washington, D.C.: GPO.

———. 2004. *U.S. direct investment abroad: final results from the 1999 benchmark survey.* Washington, D.C.: GPO.

———. 2006. An ownership-based framework of the U.S. current account, 1993–2004. *Survey of Current Business* 86 (1): 43–45.

———. 2007. BEA website. Available at www.bea.gov.

U.S. Review Committee for Balance of Payments Statistics. 1965. *The balance of payments statistics of the United States: A review and appraisal.* Report of the Review Committee for Balance of Payments Statistics to the Bureau of the Budget, Washington, D.C., April.

Viner, J. 1924. *Canada's balance of international indebtedness, 1900–1913.* Cambridge, MA: Harvard University Press.

Wall Street Journal. 2006a. EU bid to unify tax code may overcome objections. April 6.

Wall Street Journal. 2006b. Offshore disturbance: Behind big Wall Street failure: An unregulated Bermuda unit. July 3.

Weichenrieder, A. J. 2007. Profit shifting in the EU: Evidence from Germany. CESifo Working Paper no. 2043, July.

Whichard, O. G., and M. Borga. 2002. Selected issues in the measurement of U.S. international services. *Survey of Current Business* 82 (6): 36–56.

Wilkins, M. 1989. *The history of foreign investment in the United States to 1914.* Cambridge, MA: Harvard University Press.

Woolley, H. B. 1966. *Measuring transactions between world areas.* New York: National Bureau of Economic Research.

World Trade Organization. 2007. WTO Database. Available at http://wto.org/Home/WTDBHome.aspx.

Comment   J. David Richardson

Headlines are not Bob Lipsey's strength. But I know of no better contemporary reporter of quantitative trends in globalization. Deep, definitive, discerning discourses are his hallmarks. And Bob is well into his third generation of "contemporary" professional reporting!

Headlines—memorable take-away points—are the first focus of my comments. As a two-generation devotee of Bob's underappreciated work, I am privileged to try to highlight and contextualize it. Someone needs to, because many of Bob's modestly and chronically understated findings fly in the face of widespread impression and intuition.

For example:

Nothing to the Hype

- It is *not true,* as sometimes alleged, that services are the growing frontier of global trade. There is little trend in any of the various measures of services trade relative to goods trade—the ratios of one to the other oscillate between 20 and 30 percent over the past thirty-five (or more) years.

Something to the High Tech

- It is *no longer true* that global services trade is dominantly travel and transportation. In 2003, their share was barely half, compared to two-thirds in 1983.
- "High-technology" services shares *soared* in the decade between 1983 and 2003, from 7 percent of total services trade (exports plus imports) to 18 percent. (I am identifying high technology services with finance and insurance, communications, and intellectual property [royalties and fees]).
- Other business services, contrary to breathless commentary about out-of-control offshoring, have seen a slight *decline* in their global share (roughly one quarter).

Anglo-Americans at it Again

- *It is principally* the United Kingdom and the United States (and only possibly France) that seem to possess strong and secularly increasing mea-

J. David Richardson is a professor of economics and international relations at the Maxwell School of Citizenship and Public Affairs, Syracuse University, and a research associate of the National Bureau of Economic Research.

sures of revealed comparative advantage in services trade, unlike almost every one of the other twenty-plus countries in this chapter's data sample.

Phantoms of the Corporate Operations

- *"Phantom" transactions*—economically meaningless attributions—increasingly *pollute* services-trade data, as services from intangible capital and intellectual property become more important inputs to all sorts of corporate operations worldwide. Where companies locate such inputs geographically is purely discretionary, and often motivated by minimization of taxes and regulations. The measured global asset position of U.S. multinational corporate affiliates would *shrink* to *one-eighth* of its recorded size if only tangible assets (plant, equipment, inventory) were counted! A supplementary set of corporate-ownership-based accounts would help identify and distill out such phantoms, and would raise a spate of new research questions.[1]

But so what? Headlines and capsules for articles on page 24B of the local paper hold distinctly low interest.

But *I* think these are *page-one* headlines!

They deserve page-one coverage because so much of services trade involves inputs of various kinds, with the fastest-growing trade in high-tech input services. Input trade generates gains from trade in much-vaunted national productivity, not merely in consumer purchasing power. Growth in trade in high-tech input services may contribute importantly to the holy grail of stronger national productivity *growth*. Finally, input trade affects national income distributions strongly when traded inputs substitute and complement differently for workers of differing skills and mobility.

But there is more to do here than headline hype.

My second focus is to describe two important gaps in Bob's path-breaking chapter; he is responsible for neither. One is services price measurement. The other is human-capital services measurement.

Services Prices Scattered, Primitive, Untrustworthy . . . Inferring Trends is Fraught

- Whether *any* of the interesting trends capsulized previously are *also* true of the *volumes* of services and goods traded (i.e., whether they are "real" in inflation-adjusted data) will remain an enormous unanswerable question for many years. Services price data are woefully primitive and patchy, as Bob and other chapters in this volume discuss, especially for traded services.

1. See Baldwin, Lipsey, and Richardson (1998), another Conference on Research in Income and Wealth (CRIW) volume, for discussion and examples.

- If prices of *traded* services could be approximately tracked by U.S. *domestic* implicit price indexes for services, then the threefold rise in services prices relative to goods prices over the past seventy-five years would seriously deflate the measured growth of services trade. In that case, the real volume of services traded would have grown very slowly compared to real goods trade, contrary to the first bullet point.

- And without refined price measurement for traded services by sector, it is anybody's guess how closely the *value*-based trends track the fundamental *real* trends in sectoral composition and comparative advantage in the previous bullet points.

- Bob understands this. In response, he builds an implicit speculative case for secularly *declining* traded services prices—even relative to goods prices—by emphasizing (as the norm) the long decline of international ocean-freight costs since the early 1950s, when they represented one-third of all services trade. If Bob's faith were to be accurate (and it may be accurate for the rapidly growing values and qualities of high-tech services), then *real* trends in services trade would be *sharper and larger* than the values trends in the chapter. Faith, however, is all that supports Bob's conjecture, and faith is in this case a very slender reed—freight transportation represented only 9 percent of overall services trade by 2003; high-tech services only 18 percent (table 1.6); and the soaring domestic relative prices of services is a strong counter-trend.

Below the Radar, Almost Completely: Human-Capital Services Trade

- Only in his section on rapidly growing educational services trade does Bob pay much attention to human-capital services, and there to point out important *nonmeasurement;* for example, imported human skill when foreign students become legal residents. I think he should have made more of this measurement gap in today's allegedly growing knowledge economy, and not only in education.

- In management and higher-skill occupations, temporary-worker mobility (dubbed officially "movement of natural persons") has mushroomed, and has been legally embedded in bilateral and regional trade treaties worldwide. Mere measurement of compensation fundamentals for such workers is rife with anomalies, arbitrariness, and incomparability. And that says nothing (nor does Bob) of more interesting measurement issues concerning remittances, contributions to properly-measured capital formation, native-input value added, and so on.[2]

---

2. Bob has worked intelligently on how to conceive exactly such measurements in an older series of jointly-authored, below-the-radar papers: Kirova and Lipsey (1998a, 1998b), Lipsey and Kravis (1987a, 1987b). Measurement authorities and their official supporters have not followed up.

- Trade negotiations in conventional services, both at the global and regional level, will likely stagnate unless richer countries extend temporary-worker concessions to designated mid-skill and nonmanagerial occupations, as advocated by India, the Philippines, South Africa, Special Commissions, and others.[3] So-called Mode 4 services (trade in temporary-worker services) currently represents only roughly 2 percent of conventional services trade in the other three Modes,[4] in all of which richer countries are generally thought to have comparative advantage. Measurement of cross-border trade in skills and worker services will finally become a priority when rich countries need to sit down to calculate the value and costs of their reciprocally negotiated services gains and concessions.

Bob Lipsey has for generations been a world leader at plugging the measurement gaps in economic globalization. It is a privilege to be plugging his plugging.

References

Baldwin, R. E., R. E. Lipsey, and J. D. Richardson, eds. 1998. *Geography and ownership as bases for economic accounting,* NBER studies in income and wealth, vol. 59. Chicago: University of Chicago Press.
Global Commission on International Migration. 2005. *Migration in an interconnected world: New directions for action.* Geneva: Global Commission on International Migration, October.
Kirova, M. S., and R. E. Lipsey. 1998a. *Measuring real investment trends in the United States and international comparisons.* NBER Working Paper no. 6404. Cambridge, MA: National Bureau of Economic Research, February.
———. 1998b. *Measuring real investment trends in the United States and international comparisons. Federal Reserve Bank of St. Louis Review* 80 (1): 3–18.
Lipsey, R. E., and I. B. Kravis. 1987a. *Is the U.S. a spendthrift nation?* NBER Working Paper no. 2274. Cambridge, MA: National Bureau of Economic Research, June.
———. 1987b. *Saving and economic growth: Is the United States really falling behind?* New York: Conference Board Research Report no. 901.
Pritchett, L. 2006. *Let their people come: Breaking the gridlock on global labor mobility.* Washington, D.C.: Center for Global Development.
World Bank. 2004. *Global economic prospects for developing countries, 2004.* Washington, D.C.: World Bank.

3. See Global Commission on International Migration (2005). See Pritchett (2006) for one recent example among many in the development-research community.
4. World Bank (2004, 168), for 2001.

2

Improved Measures of U.S. International Services

The Cases of Insurance, Wholesale and Retail Trade, and Financial Services

Maria Borga

The U.S. Bureau of Economic Analysis (BEA) compiles the official government statistics on U.S. international sales and purchases of private services. These estimates take a broad perspective by covering the two major channels of delivery—cross-border trade in services and sales of services through locally established direct investment enterprises, or affiliates. This broad perspective recognizes the key role in the delivery of services internationally played by affiliates that are located in—but are owned outside of—the markets they serve. It is also consistent with the view many firms take of their worldwide operations.

The bureau has undertaken a long-term improvement program for international services. The estimates of cross-border trade in private services have been upgraded by improving existing surveys, by initiating new surveys, and by identifying outside information that could be used to develop new estimates. The estimates of sales of services through affiliates have been developed by adding questions to the existing surveys on the operations of multinational companies.

These ongoing efforts to improve the data on U.S. international sales and purchases of services are partly in response to the increasing importance of these transactions in the world economy. To study the impact that the globalization of services is having on the U.S. economy, it is necessary to have complete and economically meaningful measures of international

Maria Borga is an economist at the U.S. Bureau of Economic Analysis.

The views expressed in this chapter are those of the author and do not necessarily reflect those of the Bureau of Economic Analysis. The author wishes to thank her colleagues at the U.S. Bureau of Economic Analysis, the organizers and participants of the NBER-CRIW Conference on International Services Flows, and two anonymous referees for their valuable suggestions and comments.

sales and purchases of services. The Bureau of Economic Analysis produces measures of the nominal value of exports and imports by type of service, which, when combined with estimates of prices for traded services, are essential for analyzing the impact that this growing trade in services has had, and will likely have, on growth in wages, in employment, and in productivity for the U.S. economy. In addition, international guidelines covering these transactions have become more detailed and specific in recent years.[1] Finally, the addition of services to the agenda in trade negotiations has required improved statistics to support the negotiations and assist in monitoring the resulting agreements, which, for services, cover sales through affiliates as well as cross-border trade.

The improvements to international services statistics discussed in this chapter pertain to three important services: insurance, wholesale and retail trade, and financial services. In a June 2002 article, BEA identified issues affecting the estimation of these services, including important data gaps and some estimates that were of limited usefulness to data users (Whichard and Borga 2002).[2] An example of a data gap is that the estimates of services sold through affiliates did not cover bank affiliates, because these affiliates were not required to report data on their sales of services to BEA. An example of a measure with limited usefulness is insurance services—cross-border trade in insurance services was measured as the difference between premiums and claims, which in a given period may bear little or no relationship to the value of services provided and can even be negative.

The new measure of cross-border trade in insurance services better represents the output of insurance companies by recognizing the services they provide that are funded by investment income instead of explicit fees, and by using a new measure of losses paid by insurers based on the long-run relationship between premiums and losses. This latter change will prevent anomalous results that could occur under the previous measure of premiums less actual claims, such as the trade deficit decreasing after a catastrophe's occurrence in the United States, as foreign insurers paid claims to their U.S. policyholders. The improved measure better captures the long-term trends in trade in insurance services, including the increased reliance on imports of reinsurance by U.S. insurance companies since 2001. In that year, imports of reinsurance services were $14.5 billion, which climbed to

1. Guidance for compiling statistics on trade in services for the international transactions accounts is provided in *Balance of Payments Manual,* 5th edition (BPM5). More detailed guidance is provided in the *Manual on Statistics of International Trade in Services* (MSITS), which provides guidance for compiling data on both cross-border trade in services and services delivered through affiliates. For cross-border trade, MSITS is consistent with BPM5 but more detailed. For sales through affiliates, MSITS' recommendations draw on the 1993 *System of National Accounts.*
2. This article also discussed measurement issues concerning two other services not covered in this chapter: utilities and construction.

$30.4 billion in 2006. By more accurately gauging the levels of and trends in imports and exports of insurance services, the new measure can be used to analyze the factors that are driving globalization in the insurance industry. It can be helpful in identifying the factors that determine where firms choose to reinsure their policies, in determining whether increased trade in insurance impacts the availability and the cost of insurance in the United States, and in examining the implications globalization has for regulating this industry.

In the International Transactions Accounts, the services of wholesalers and retailers in facilitating international trade in goods are embedded in the values of exports and imports of goods in accordance with the international guidelines. However, separate estimates of the value of distributive services for merchandise trade could be of interest because of the importance of these services to the U.S. economy. In 2005, wholesale and retail trade accounted for almost 13 percent of GDP; retail trade contributed more than 10 percent to real GDP growth, and wholesale trade almost 3 percent (Howell, Barefoot, and Lindberg 2006). These industries have also played a major role in the post-1995 acceleration in U.S. productivity growth. For example, Triplett and Bosworth found that between 1995 and 2001, the average annual multifactor productivity (MFP) growth in wholesale and retail trade, at 3.1 percent and 2.9 percent respectively, was more than double that for the private, nonfarm business sector, at 1.4 percent (Triplett and Bosworth 2004b).[3] Because the margins wholesalers and retailers earn are greater for some types of goods than for others, innovations that impact these margins could lead to changes in the amount of merchandise trade and in the mix of products that are traded. In addition, some innovations, such as reductions in the costs of identifying new suppliers, could increase the responsiveness of imports and exports of goods to changes in prices.

The improved measures of insurance, wholesale and retail trade, and financial services sold through affiliates will be comparable to the measures used in BEA's national and industry accounts. This point is particularly important because one of the uses of these statistics is to assess the share of U.S. services output produced by foreign-owned U.S. affiliates for negotiating and monitoring international agreements on trade in services. With the old measures, such shares could not be computed, either because the measure of sales through affiliates was not comparable to the corresponding national totals, as in the cases of insurance and wholesale and retail trade, or because of gaps in the coverage of the sales through affiliates statistics, as was the case for banks. In addition, for U.S. multinational cor-

---

3. Triplett and Bosworth attribute 24 percent of the MFP growth over this time period to wholesale trade and 32 percent to retail trade. However, as they state, some productivity growth may be incorrectly attributed to these industries due to technical reasons (Triplett and Bosworth 2004a).

porations (MNCs), the new measures will allow their total output of these services to be estimated, as well as the shares accounted for by the U.S. parent and its foreign affiliates. Thus, it will be possible to observe shifts in the MNCs' production of these services between U.S. and foreign locations, and to relate these shifts to changes in factors that influence the location of production, such as changes in relative labor costs. Finally, the improved measures will also increase the comparability between the measures of cross-border trade in services and of sales of services through affiliates, which could shed light on firms' choices to serve foreign markets through exports or through establishing affiliates in those markets.

To address these issues, BEA has developed new methodologies, initiated new data collections, and drawn on additional data from outside sources. These actions have closed some data gaps and resulted in improved estimates of some services. Some of these changes have already been implemented; others are still being developed.

This chapter begins with an overview of the data BEA provides on international services. It then considers the issues relevant to the measurement of insurance services, wholesale and retail trade services, and financial services.

2.1   Overview of BEA's Data on International Services

The Bureau of Economic Analysis' data on international services cover the two distinct channels by which services are sold in international markets: cross-border trade and sales through affiliates. Cross-border exports and imports represent trade in the conventional sense and cover transactions between residents of the United States and residents of foreign countries. They include both transactions between unaffiliated parties and trade within multinational companies (intrafirm trade). These estimates are included in the International Transactions Accounts (ITAs). Most of the data used to produce these estimates are derived from BEA surveys.

Sales of services through affiliates represent services sold through the channel of direct investment. The data on sales of services through affiliates cover majority-owned affiliates and are derived from benchmark and annual surveys of direct investment that require affiliates' sales or gross operating revenues to be distributed among sales of goods, sales of services, and investment income. The estimates include sales to foreign residents through the foreign affiliates of U.S. MNCs and sales to U.S. residents through the U.S. affiliates of foreign MNCs. These sales are not considered U.S. international transactions because, under the residency principle of balance-of-payments accounting, affiliates of multinational companies are regarded as residents of the countries where they are located rather than of the countries of their owners. Thus, sales abroad by the foreign affiliates of U.S. MNCs are transactions between foreign residents, and sales in the

Table 2.1   Private services trade: average annual growth rates, 1992 to 2006, and values, 2006

	Exports		Imports	
	Average annual growth rate (%)	Value in 2006 (billions of dollars)	Average annual growth rate (%)	Value in 2006 (billions of dollars)
Total private services	6.7	404.3	8.1	307.8
Travel	3.3	85.7	4.6	72.0
Passenger fares	2.1	22.2	7.0	27.5
Other transportation	5.6	46.3	7.5	65.3
Royalties and license fees	8.1	62.4	12.4	26.4
Other private services	9.9	187.8	11.5	116.5

Note: For purposes of comparison, U.S. exports of goods grew at an average annual rate of 6.2 percent between 1992 and 2006, and U.S. imports of goods grew at an average annual rate of 9.3 percent.

United States by the U.S. affiliates of foreign MNCs are transactions between U.S. residents.[4] However, the direct investors' shares of the profits earned on these sales are recorded as direct investment income under the income component of the ITAs.[5] The proposed measures of services sold through affiliates discussed in this paper will not affect the measure of direct investment income that appears in the ITAs.

In recognizing the important role that locally established affiliates play in supplying services to foreign markets, the General Agreement on Trade in Services (GATS) included this as one of the modes by which services are delivered in international markets—through a commercial presence (Mode 3). The *Manual on Statistics of International Trade in Services* (MSITS) recommends sales through affiliates as a basic indicator of Mode 3 transactions. However, it recognizes that for industries involving trade or financial intermediation, sales are not closely related to the value of services provided. The measures proposed in this paper provide a better measure than sales of the services provided by affiliates in three industry groups—insurance, wholesale and retail trade, and financial services.

In 2006, U.S. exports of private services were $404.3 billion, and U.S. imports of private services were $307.8 billion. In comparison, U.S. exports of goods were $1,023.1 billion, and U.S. imports of goods were $1,861.4 billion. Table 2.1 presents average annual growth rates between 1992 and 2006 and levels of imports and exports of services for 2006 for the five ma-

---

4. Data are collected on affiliates' sales of services to all destinations, but the estimates of international services focus on sales abroad by foreign affiliates of U.S. companies and sales in the United States by U.S. affiliates of foreign companies—that is, on the sales that are not included in U.S. cross-border exports or imports.

5. The Bureau of Economic Analysis produces an annual, ownership-based supplement to the current account portion of the U.S. International Transactions Accounts that highlights the participation of MNCs in the international markets for goods and services through both cross-border trade and sales through affiliates. See the appendix for a discussion of this ownership-based supplement.

jor categories of private services shown in the ITAs: travel (which includes purchases of goods and services—such as food, lodging, and entertainment—by U.S. residents traveling abroad and by foreign travelers in the United States), passenger fares, other transportation (which includes freight and port services), royalties and license fees, and other private services (which include financial services, insurance, education, telecommunications, and an array of business, professional, and technical services). Other private services have been growing relatively fast and are the largest category for both exports and imports. Within other private services, financial and insurance services account for more than one-quarter of exports and two-fifths of imports. Despite relatively slow growth, travel is still the second-largest category for both imports and exports. Royalties and license fees are growing relatively fast.

Sales through affiliates is the larger channel of delivery for services and has been growing faster (figure 2.1). In 2005, the most recent year for which data are available, sales of services through the majority-owned foreign affiliates (MOFAs) were $528.5 billion, and sales through the majority-owned U.S. affiliates (MOUSAs) were $389.0 billion. As discussed in the following, there are differences in measurement and coverage that make comparisons of sales through affiliates to cross-border trade imprecise. However, the large gap between cross-border trade and sales through affiliates and the higher rates of growth—sales through MOFAs grew at an average annual rate of 10.7 percent between 1992 and 2005, and sales through MOUSAs grew at an average annual rate of 8.9 percent—indicate the importance of sales through affiliates as a channel through which companies sell services to foreign markets. This could be due to the fact that selling through locally established affiliates is the only practical method of delivery for many types of services because of the need for proximity in both time and space between the consumer and producer. In addition to measurement and coverage differences, precise comparisons of the relative size of the two modes of delivery cannot be made for specific types of services because the data on cross-border trade are classified by type of service, whereas the data on sales of services through affiliates are classified by the primary industry of the affiliate.

2.2   Insurance

The economics literature provides two main conceptual views of the output of insurance companies. The first is that the insurance company provides a service by assuming risk from its policyholders; the second is that the insurance company serves to pool the risks of its policyholders. As Sherwood (1999) explains, a gross premiums approach to measuring output is consistent with the first concept (that of risk assumption). Under this approach, the goods and services purchased with the claims paid to poli-

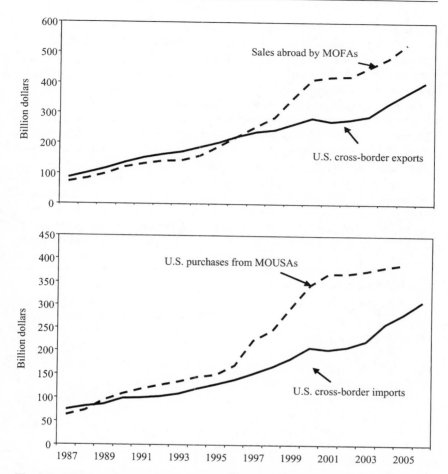

Fig. 2.1   U.S. international sales and purchases of private services, 1987–2006
Note: Sales through MOFAs and purchases from MOUSAs are shown through 2005, the latest year for which data are available.

cyholders are considered to be intermediate inputs purchased by the insurance company and passed on to its customers. A net premiums approach, in which a measure of claims is subtracted from premiums, is consistent with the second concept (that of risk pooling). Under this approach, the difference between premiums and the measure of claims paid is used to measure the costs of maintaining the risk pool. The Bureau of Economic Analysis has adopted a net premiums approach, which is consistent with international guidelines for the compilation of economic statistics.

The measure of insurance companies' output will consist of three components. First, insurers provide financial protection against the realization of specified risks faced by their policyholders. Second, they provide financial intermediation services; that is, insurers collect funds from policyholders, which are held as reserves, and invest these funds in financial or other assets. Third, insurers provide auxiliary insurance services, such as claims adjustment, actuarial services, and salvage services.

Economic models of the behavior of insurance companies assume that insurers maximize their profits by setting premiums given their expectations about future claims and investment income. The improved measure of insurance services will build on these models and will include estimates of all components of the services provided by insurers.

In the discussion that follows, the improved measure of insurance services will be discussed first for cross-border trade and then for sales through affiliates. Each section will begin with a description of the previous measures of insurance services, the shortcomings of these measures, and then a description of the changes that were made, or are being considered, to the measure of insurance services.

2.2.1   Cross-Border Trade

Prior to 2003, trade in insurance services was measured as premiums less actual losses (claims). The rationale behind this measurement of insurance services was that the portion of premiums remaining after provision had been made for losses could serve as a proxy for the operating expenses and profits—that is, the output—associated with this activity. The view of the insurance company that justified this measure was essentially that of a risk-pooling administrator, and premiums less losses provided a rough proxy for the administrative costs (and profits) associated with this activity. Under this view, only the portion of premiums not paid out in losses was treated as output of the insurance industry. The amount used for loss settlements simply reflected funds that, with the help of insurance companies, flowed from all policyholders to those policyholders who suffered losses.

A major shortcoming of the premiums-less-actual-losses measure is that losses can fluctuate from period to period in a way that bears little relation to the services provided. The fact that unusually large claims may be paid in a particular period does not reduce the value of services provided (or turn it negative), nor do unusually small claims raise the value of services provided. Hurricanes, floods, oil spills, and terrorist attacks are perils whose presence or absence may cause large fluctuations in claims that may not correspond to changes in the services provided or received. In the new measure, the relationship between claims and premiums over several years is used, which avoids these large fluctuations.[6] While the value of imports and exports in any given year under the new measure will be either higher

---

6. While normal losses are used in estimating the value of trade in insurance services, BEA continues to publish the actual losses in table 3 of the ITAs.

or lower than under the previous measure, the volume of transactions over several years will be roughly the same under the two measures. Measuring insurance services as premiums less claims also missed two important components of insurance output: investment income earned on technical reserves and auxiliary insurance services.

In 2006, U.S. imports of insurance services were $33.6 billion, and exports were $9.3 billion. United States residents paid foreign insurers $65.3 billion in premiums and recovered $29.3 billion in losses; foreign residents paid U.S. insurers $23.3 billion in premiums and recovered $10.9 billion in losses.

One distinguishing feature of cross-border trade in insurance services is the important role played by reinsurance. Reinsurance is the ceding of a portion of a premium to another insurer who then assumes a corresponding portion of the risk. It provides insurers with a tool for managing their risk exposure, including exposure to liability for events with such a high degree of risk or liability that a single insurer is unwilling or unable to underwrite insurance against their occurrence. In 2006, reinsurance premiums accounted for 96 percent of all U.S. payments of premiums and 76 percent of all U.S. receipts of premiums.

To measure the services provided by insurers more accurately and completely, three changes were made to BEA's estimate of U.S. trade in insurance. In the order they are discussed here, actual claims (which were deducted from premiums in calculating insurance services) were replaced by a measure that captures the long-term relationship between premiums and claims, which will be termed "normal" losses; a premium supplement, representing the investment income earned on reserves, was added to the measure, and the treatment of auxiliary insurance services was changed.

Premiums Less Normal Losses

To improve the estimates of imports and exports of insurance services (by reducing the large, random swings due solely to fluctuating losses), rather than measuring insurance services as premiums less actual losses, the new estimates are measured as premiums less normal losses, where normal losses are inferred from the relationship between actual losses and premiums averaged over several years (Bach 2003). One of the key factors for insurers when setting premiums is their expectations about the losses that will have to be paid. In a practical sense, a proxy for insurers' expectations must be used, because no information is available on what companies expect losses to be. A readily available indicator is the average of past actual losses in relation to premiums.

Normal losses comprise losses that occur regularly and a share of catastrophic losses that occur at infrequent intervals. Separate estimates are made for these two types of losses. For regularly occurring losses, a six-year arithmetic moving average of the ratio of actual losses to premiums is used. Data for the current period are not included in the average, in order to achieve an ex ante concept of regularly occurring losses. Because comprehensive source data for insurance begin in 1986, estimates based on a six-year average begin in 1992.

Insurance companies expect that catastrophes will occur occasionally and allow for this in setting premiums. However, because catastrophic losses occur much less frequently than regularly occurring losses, they are assumed to affect loss expectations over a much longer period. Under the new methodology, catastrophic losses are added in equal increments to the estimate of regularly occurring losses over the twenty years following their occurrence to derive an estimate of normal losses. Thus, only a small fraction of catastrophic losses is factored into each year's calculation of insurance services.

Separate estimates of normal losses are calculated for primary insurance and for reinsurance. The ratio of losses to premiums is lower for primary insurance than for reinsurance because administrative and financial intermediation services differ for these two types of insurance. Primary insurance is more retail in nature—selling and writing a large number of individual policies to customers—and, thus, may have higher administrative and other costs than reinsurance, which involves fewer, larger transactions between insurance companies.

Premium Supplements

Insurance premiums would be higher if insurance carriers were unable to earn income on funds held in reserves against future claims. In recognition of this fact, the international guidelines for national accounts in the 1993 *System of National Accounts* (SNA) included the income earned on technical reserves in its recommended measure of the output of the insurance industry. Technical reserves, which are regarded as assets of the policyholders, not of the insurance company, consist of prepaid premiums and reserves against outstanding losses. Investment income earned on the insurers' own funds is excluded from income on technical reserves. Insurers invest technical reserves, and the income earned on them is used to defray the expenses of providing insurance. The income is treated as accruing to the policyholders, who pay it back to insurers as supplements to cover the full cost of the insurance.

Similar to the use of normal losses in the new measure of trade in insurance services, estimates of the expected income on the technical reserves of insurance companies is used as a measure of premium supplements. The use of expected, rather than actual, investment income to measure premium supplements is intended to capture the ex ante concept of premium supplements; it is this expectation that insurance companies use in setting premiums to cover their expected losses and other costs.

Estimates of premium supplements for cross-border trade use the same data and similar methodology employed in the National Income and Product Accounts (NIPAs; Chen and Fixler 2003). Data on investment income are from *Best's Aggregates and Averages: Property-Casualty* by A. M. Best Company. A. M. Best provides data on investment gains that are attributable to insurance transactions, as opposed to investment gains attributable to the insurers' own funds. The estimate of premium supplements for a given year is the result of multiplying an expected investment gains-to-premiums ratio by the actual premiums observed for that year. The ratio is a weighted moving average of the previous five years of ratios of actual investment gains to premiums. In the cross-border trade data, the expected investment gains-to-premiums ratio is estimated separately for primary insurance and reinsurance, in recognition of the fact that reinsurers may have different ratios of net gains to premiums than primary insurers.[7] The different ratios may arise because reinsurers hold larger reserves than primary insurers or because they hold them for a longer time.

Once these ratios have been calculated, they are applied to the estimates of premium receipts for primary insurance and reinsurance, which are obtained from BEA surveys of international trade in services, to derive premium supplements receipts from foreigners. Because similar data on investment income of foreign insurance companies are not available for payments, the ratio used for receipts is applied to the estimates of premium payments to foreigners in order to estimate premium supplements payments to foreigners.[8]

Auxiliary Insurance Services

Auxiliary insurance services cover such items as agents' commissions, actuarial services, insurance brokering and agency services, and salvage administration services. Under the *Balance of Payments Manual,* 5th edition (BPM5), insurance services should include agent commissions, and under the *Manual on Statistics of International Trade in Services* (MSITS), auxiliary insurance services should be included in the measure of insurance services. Beginning in 2001, BEA's surveys collected a full range of auxiliary insurance services as a single, distinct category. Previously, these services had been covered in a fragmentary way as parts of other services. For example, data on claims adjustment services were collected as a part of legal services, and data on actuarial services were collected as part of a residual ("other") category that included other services as well. Also be-

---

7. For details on the estimation of the expected investment gains to premiums ratios, see Bach 2004, 60–62.

8. Because the balance of payments employs a double-entry accounting system, the value of the premium supplement transactions entered in the trade-in-services account must be offset elsewhere in the international transactions accounts. In this case, the offsetting entry is made by recording the value of supplements as income received by policyholders in the income accounts.

ginning in 2001, premiums were reported gross of commissions on BEA's surveys, and in the estimates, commissions were included in services auxiliary to insurance, rather than being subtracted from premiums, as was the case previously.

Comparison of the Previous Measure with the New Measure

Figure 2.2 compares the previous measure—premiums less actual losses—to the new measure—the sum of (a) premiums less normal losses, (b) premium supplements, and (c) auxiliary insurance services—for U.S. exports of insurance services from 1992 to 2006. Figure 2.3 compares these measures for U.S. imports of insurance services from 1992 to 2006. The new measures reflect the long-term increase in exports and imports of insurance services while avoiding the dramatic swings in the estimates of insurance services due to fluctuating losses. While premiums supplements are a significant addition to the estimates of insurance services, the majority of insurance services are accounted for by the premiums-less-normal-losses component of the new measure.

The improved measure of insurance services will improve BEA's overall measure of insurance services but does not specifically address the distortions caused by tax avoidance discussed in Robert Lipsey's paper "Measuring International Trade in Services," included in this volume, because the improved measure captures the actual financial flows between countries based on the residency-based principle recommended in the international guidelines. The distortions discussed by Lipsey result from financial transactions occurring within multinational firms that may result in the at-

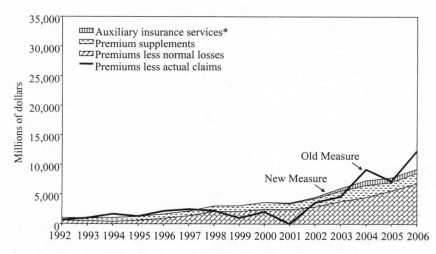

Fig. 2.2   The old and new measures of exports of insurance services
*Estimates of auxiliary insurance services are available only from 2001 forward.

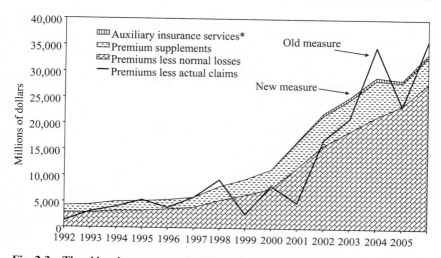

Fig. 2.3   The old and new measures of imports of insurance services
*Estimates of auxiliary insurance services are available only from 2001 forward.

tribution of output to foreign countries but in which little, if any, actual productive activity occurs abroad. Specifically, U.S. insurance companies may cede premiums to affiliated captive reinsurers abroad, resulting in U.S. imports of reinsurance services. However, most, or all, of the activity involved in the production of insurance services may occur in the United States.

2.2.2   Sales through Affiliates

This section discusses the current measure of insurance services sold through affiliates and planned changes to this measure. The proposed new measure is more economically meaningful and is more comparable to the measures of insurance services included in the estimates of cross-border trade in services and in the NIPAs. Experimental estimates are presented for sales through MOUSAs in 2002 and 2003; BEA plans to publish official estimates of sales of insurance services through affiliates in 2008.

One of the largest services sold through affiliates is insurance. In 2005, the MOUSAs of foreign MNCs classified in insurance sold $77.2 billion in services to U.S. residents, and the MOFAs of U.S. MNCs classified in insurance sold $94.4 billion of services to foreigners.

These estimates result from BEA's current methodology, which measures sales of insurance services through affiliates as services-related operating revenues. These revenues consist mostly of premium income, but they also include fees for auxiliary insurance services, such as claims adjustment or actuarial services. The current measure does not capture some important aspects of insurance services. First, it does not include a deduction for the losses paid out by insurers. In this regard, it differs from the measures of insurance output recommended for economic accounting purposes and the measures of insurance services in the ITAs and the NIPAs. Second, it does not include premium supplements.

A more economically meaningful measure of the insurance services supplied through affiliates would include premiums less *normal* losses and an estimate of premium supplements. There is no need to change the current reporting to capture services auxiliary to insurance because revenues reported on BEA's surveys include receipts earned from providing auxiliary insurance services.

To allow for the construction of this type of measure of insurance services, BEA collected data on the premiums earned and losses paid by MOUSAs with operations in insurance on the 2002 benchmark survey of foreign direct investment in the United States (FDIUS). These data items were subsequently added to the follow-on annual surveys of FDIUS and the surveys of U.S. direct investment abroad (USDIA), beginning with the 2004 benchmark survey of USDIA. At the time of this writing, estimates of insurance services are only available for FDIUS for 2002 and 2003. These new data will be combined here with data on the domestic insurance industry from A. M. Best to estimate the new measure of insurance services sold through MOUSAs.

One significant difference from the cross-border trade data is that the data on sales through affiliates are classified by the primary industry of the affiliate. The Bureau of Economic Analysis' industry codes for affiliates divide insurance providers into two broad types of insurance: non-life and life insurance. Non-life insurance covers all risks except for death: damage from accidents, fire, natural disasters, and so on. Sales of services by affiliates classified in insurance reflect sales of insurance services, but may also include sales of other types of services. Likewise, it is possible for affiliates in other industries to have secondary operations in insurance. The new measure of insurance services will apply to all affiliates with insurance operations, regardless of their industry classification.

Premiums Less Normal Losses

As for the estimates of cross-border trade in insurance, the estimates of sales of insurance services through affiliates will use a measure of normal losses as a proxy for insurers' expectations. Normal losses consist of two parts: regularly occurring losses and a share of catastrophic losses. Separate estimates are made for these two types of losses.

Regularly occurring losses will be measured as the average of past actual losses in relation to premiums earned from annual data over a six-year period, using an arithmetic moving average. This is identical to the measure of regularly occurring losses used in the cross-border trade estimates. To avoid having to wait until six years of data have been collected from

MOUSAs to produce the first estimates, and to improve correspondence with the NIPA measure of insurance services of which these are a subset, data on the entire domestic insurance industry are used to construct the estimates.

If it were determined that a catastrophe affected the insurance sold through MOUSAs in a particular year, the same procedures that are followed for cross-border trade could be followed for sales through affiliates: catastrophic losses would be spread, in equal increments, over the next twenty years.

Table 2.2 shows the premiums earned and actual losses paid for the property and casualty and life and health insurance industries as reported by A. M. Best for the years 1996 to 2002. Beginning in 2002, the table also shows data reported by MOUSAs.[9] Because no catastrophic losses are evident in the period covered, normal losses consist solely of regularly occurring losses. The six-year moving average of the ratio of losses to premiums, or the normal loss ratio, was 76.1 percent in 2002. The normal loss ratio is then applied to the estimate of premiums earned to derive the measure of normal losses. Applying the 76.1 percent normal loss ratio to the $63.3 billion in premiums earned yields normal losses of $48.2 billion in 2002.[10] Thus, in 2002, premiums earned less normal losses were $15.1 billion ($63.3 billion less $48.2 billion).

Premium Supplements

Because BEA does not collect data on the investment income earned on technical reserves separately from other investment income, its data on total investment income earned by affiliates will have to be combined with information on the domestic insurance industry to estimate the premium supplements for MOUSAs.

Premium supplements are the investment income earned from insurers investing policyholders' assets on their behalf and that are available to defray the insurers' expenses. While it is true that life insurers invest policyholders' assets on their behalf, the vast majority of the investment income earned on these assets is allocated to actuarial reserves to meet the capital sums guaranteed to individual policyholders under the life insurance policies and is, thus, unavailable to defray insurers' expenses (these sums must

---

9. On the 2002 benchmark survey of FDIUS, only MOUSAs filing the long form—those with total assets, sales or gross operating revenues, or net income exceeding $125 million for fiscal year 2002—were required to report the data on premiums earned and losses paid. The values in table 2.2 are reported data only and do not include any estimates for affiliates that were not required to report premiums and losses.

10. The difference of $3.8 billion between the estimate of $63.3 billion of premiums earned and the figure of $59.5 billion in table 2.2 is the estimate of premiums earned by affiliates not required to report the data on premiums and losses. The premiums were estimated by assuming that premiums accounted for the same share of sales in insurance as they did for those MOUSAs that had reported these data.

Table 2.2   Premiums earned and claims paid for U.S. insurance industry and MOUSAs, 1996 to 2003 (in millions of dollars)

| | U.S. insurance industry | | | | MOUSAs that reported the data on premiums and losses | | Ratio of actual claims to premiums (life and non-life insurance) | | Normal loss ratios (six-year moving average of previous years [%]) |
| | Property/casualty | | Life/health | | Life and non-life insurers | | | | |
Year	Premiums earned	Losses paid	Premiums earned	Losses paid	Premiums earned	Losses paid	U.S. insurance industry (%)	MOUSAs (%)	
1996	263,351	172,346	377,362	311,249	—	—	75.5	—	—
1997	271,502	163,775	405,612	343,061	—	—	74.9	—	—
1998	299,690	175,319	454,454	369,887	—	—	72.3	—	—
1999	282,791	184,609	494,285	430,351	—	—	79.1	—	—
2000	294,024	200,943	548,434	455,474	—	—	77.9	—	—
2001	311,529	234,518	472,730	369,801	—	—	77.1	—	—
2002	355,739	244,695	504,471	366,564	59,525	49,129	77.1	83.0	76.1
2003					57,805	38,359	—	68.7	77.4

Source for U.S. insurance industry data: A. M. Best's Aggregates and Averages: Property and Casualty Insurance 2001, 190, and A. M. Best's Aggregates and Averages: Life and Health 2002, 60.

eventually be paid to the policyholders or their beneficiaries).[11] In the NI-PAs, the investment income allocated to actuarial reserves is recorded as imputed interest paid by life insurance carriers in the period that it is earned. This investment income is, thus, not part of the services provided by life insurers. For U.S. affiliates, data are not available to apportion life insurers' investment income between earnings on technical reserves and their own funds, nor to further divide it into the investment income allocated to actuarial reserves and that used to defray their expenses. Accordingly, it was decided to omit the premium supplements from the measure of output for the life insurance operations of affiliates. Thus, the measure of life insurance services supplied through affiliates consists of premiums less normal losses plus any fees for auxiliary insurance services, which represents the funds available to life insurers to pay their operating expenses and earn a profit.[12]

The first step in estimating the premium supplements for non-life insurance is to determine the amount of investment income earned by MOUSAs that is attributable to non-life insurance activities. Majority-owned U.S. affiliates report total investment income for the consolidated U.S. enterprise, which may include operations in other industries, such as life insurance or finance industries, that generate investment income. So, for each MOUSA with operations in non-life insurance, the share of non-life insurance sales in its total sales in finance and insurance is calculated. This share is then multiplied by its reported total investment income to derive an estimate of its investment income from its operations in non-life insurance. For both 2002 and 2003, investment income of $11.8 billion was attributed to the non-life insurance activities of MOUSAs.

Once investment income attributable to non-life insurance activities has been estimated, then the share of that income earned on technical reserves must be estimated. This is done by using the ratio of investment income earned on technical reserves to total investment gains for the entire U.S. insurance industry, calculated from data in *Best's Aggregates and Averages—*

---

11. In addition, some life insurance policies include an explicit element of savings in which policyholders make payments to insurance companies that are held in personal accounts. The investment income credited to these accounts is excluded because it is paid directly to the individual account holders.

12. In the estimates of personal consumption expenditures (PCE) in the NIPAs, the output of life insurance companies is estimated as their "operating expenses for the package of services provided. These imputed fees, which include profits in the case of stock companies, appear as 'expense of handling life insurance' in PCE." U.S. Department of Commerce, Bureau of Economic Analysis, *Personal Consumption Expenditures* 1990, 12.

The expenses of handling life insurance equal value added plus purchased materials and services. The measure of value added can be constructed from the data reported to BEA, and it would be possible to estimate purchased materials and services by affiliates with life insurance operations by subtracting premiums earned, interest received, and value added from their gross operating revenues. However, these estimates would represent value added and purchased materials and services for the enterprise, and, for those affiliates with operations in multiple industries, it would be difficult to estimate the portion of their operating expenses attributable to their life insurance operations.

Table 2.3   **Derivation of new estimate of sales of services for MOUSAs with operations in insurance, 2002 and 2003 (in millions of dollars)**

		2002		2003	
		Worldwide sales of services	Sales to U.S. residents	Worldwide sales of services	Sales to U.S. residents
	Current estimates	92,665	88,162	93,715	91,501
LESS	Premiums earned*	63,321	60,244	70,693	69,024
EQUALS	Auxiliary insurance services or services from other industries	29,344	27,918	23,022	22,478
PLUS	Premiums less normal losses	15,119	14,385	16,000	15,622
PLUS	Premium supplements	5,719	5,441	5,864	5,725
EQUALS	New estimates of sales of services	50,182	47,744	44,885	43,825
	Difference from current measure	−42,483	−40,418	−48,829	−47,676

*To estimate the U.S. resident share of premiums earned, of premiums less normal losses, and of premium supplements, the share of sales to U.S. residents in worldwide sales is applied to the worldwide total for each of these items.

Property/Casualty Insurance, United States. This share is then multiplied by MOUSAs' investment income attributable to non-life insurance to derive the estimate of premium supplements. In both years, just under half of all investment income earned in the U.S. non-life insurance industry is attributable to earnings on technical reserves, so, in both years, just under half of the investment income attributable to the non-life insurance operations of MOUSAs is assumed to be earnings on their technical reserves. These earnings are the premium supplements. The estimate of premium supplements is $5.7 billion in 2002 and $5.9 billion in 2003 (table 2.3).

The premium supplements described here differ from those in the NIPAs and ITAs, both of which use a methodology that computes *expected* investment income. Estimation of this expectation depends on developing a relationship between investment income on technical reserves and premiums. That approach was not adopted here because the data for U.S. affiliates do not distinguish between premiums for non-life insurance and those for life insurance. The premium supplements for affiliates will be actual investment income, instead of expected investment income, which could make the estimates more volatile. However, between 1997 and 2003, the ratio of investment income to sales for non-life insurance carriers only varied between 14.0 percent and 17.8 percent, indicating that the use of the actual investment income may not increase the volatility greatly.

Incorporating the Changes into the Estimates of Sales of Services through Affiliates

This section explains how the new measure of insurance could be incorporated into the estimates of sales of services through affiliates; table 2.3 illustrates the steps. First, the premiums earned are subtracted from total sales of services by MOUSAs with operations in insurance. The remainder represents sales of services that are either auxiliary to insurance or for other services. Then, the two new elements of the measure of insurance services—premiums less normal losses and premium supplements for non-life insurance—are added to the remainder. These calculations are performed separately for worldwide sales of services and for sales to U.S. residents. In apportioning premiums earned and the new elements of the measure of insurance services between sales to U.S. residents and sales to the rest of the world, it is assumed that the share provided to U.S. residents is the same as the share of sales to U.S. residents in total sales of services by these affiliates. In 2002, 95.1 percent of sales of services were sold to U.S. residents, so it is assumed that 95.1 percent of premiums earned and of the two elements of the new measure of insurance services are supplied to U.S. residents. For 2002, the current estimate of sales of services to U.S. residents for these MOUSAs is $88.2 billion, of which $27.9 billion were sales of auxiliary insurance services or of services other than insurance. Under the proposed methodology, the two new elements of the measure of insurance services sum to $20.8 billion—$15.1 billion for premiums less normal losses and $5.7 billion for premium supplements—of which $19.8 billion are estimated to be supplied to U.S. residents. Adding this figure to the sales of other services yields a new estimate of sales of services to U.S. residents for these MOUSAs of $47.7 billion. The new estimate is $40.4 billion less than the current estimate. This reduction represents the net of the reduction for premiums devoted to the settlement of normal losses and the increase due to the inclusion of premium supplements.

2.3 Wholesale and Retail Trade

The wholesale and retail trade industries provide distributive services—that is, selling, or arranging for the sale of, goods to intermediate and final users. Wholesalers sell goods, or arrange for the sales of goods, to retailers, intermediate users, and final users (other than persons). Distributive services provided by wholesalers include merchandise handling, stocking, selling, and billing. Retailers sell goods primarily to persons. In the SNA and the NIPAs, distributive services are measured as trade margins—wholesale or retail sales of goods less the cost of the goods resold. In estimating the gross output of services provided by wholesalers and retailers, the goods for resale are excluded from the value of intermediate inputs consumed in production by wholesalers and retailers because these goods are subject to only minimal processing, such as cleaning or packaging.

These industries are important service industries in the U.S. economy; in 2005, they accounted for almost 13 percent of GDP (Howells, Barefoot, and Lindberg 2006). In contrast, the wholesale and retail trade industries are hardly noticeable in the estimate of U.S. international sales and purchases of private services. However, this does not indicate a lack of importance of these industries. Rather, it reflects the fact that the value of the distributive services they provide is embedded in the value of goods they sell through international channels, either in the value of exports and imports of goods or in the value of sales of goods through affiliates.

2.3.1   Cross-Border Trade

Cross-border trade in distributive services is not identified as such in the ITAs, but it could be said to occur when, for example, a wholesaler exports a good. Although a significant portion of U.S. exports and imports is arranged or facilitated by wholesalers and retailers, particularly the former, the estimates of cross-border trade in services do not include estimates of the distributive services provided by exporters because those services are included in the value of trade in goods. Exports of goods are valued at the f.a.s. (free alongside ship) value of the merchandise at the U.S. port of exportation, including inland freight, insurance, and other charges incurred in placing the merchandise alongside the carrier at the U.S. port. Imports of goods are valued at the price paid or payable for merchandise at the foreign port of exportation. Thus, any distributive services (as well as the value of other services that facilitate trade, such as transportation from the factory to the port), are included in the accounts for cross-border trade in goods and not those for cross-border trade in services.[13]

The inclusion of these services in the value of merchandise trade follows the treatment recommended in BPM5 and reflects the fact that data on cross-border trade are collected by product. In this case, the product is an exported good, and its value includes the distributive services used to arrange for its export. The Bureau of Economic Analysis has no intention of changing the basis on which merchandise trade is valued in the international accounts. However, as noted earlier, estimates of the services of wholesalers and retailers in facilitating international trade are important for understanding both the role of these distributive services industries in trade and the importance of trade for these industries. Here I use data from the 2002 Economic Census to construct rough estimates of the distributive services associated with merchandise trade.

According to the 2002 Economic Census (U.S. Census Bureau, *2002 Economic Census, Wholesale Trade* 2005), 3.3 percent of all sales by U.S. wholesalers were exports, or about $152.9 billion. In that year, wholesalers provided an average of 22.3 cents of distributive services for every one dollar in sales. Applying this average to their exports yields $34.1 billion in distributive services embodied in the value of goods exported by U.S. whole-

---

13. The transportation services involved in getting the goods from the port of exportation to the importing country are included in cross-border trade in services.

salers. Not surprisingly, exports accounted for a smaller share of total sales of retailers, at 0.1 percent (U.S. Census Bureau, *2002 Economic Census, Retail Trade* 2005). This corresponds to about $3.1 billion worth of exports. In 2002, retailers had an average of 28.7 cents of distributive services per dollar of sales, resulting in $0.9 billion of distributive services embodied in the value of goods exported by retailers. Summing the two estimates yields $35.0 billion in distributive services embodied in exports of goods (table 2.4).

The estimate of distributive services embodied in exports derived here can be compared to BEA's estimate of the wholesale trade margin on all exports, included in BEA's annual Input-Output (I-O) accounts. In 2002, this estimate was $65.4 billion. There are several factors that contribute to the discrepancy between the two estimates. Among them, the estimate de-

Table 2.4   **Impacts of changes in the measurement of insurance, wholesale and retail trade, and financial services on the estimates of cross-border trade and sales through affiliates, 2002 (in billions of dollars)**

	Cross-border trade in services			
	Exports of services	Imports of services	Exports of goods	Imports of goods
Current measure	279.2	209.0	682.4	1,167.4
Effects of new measures:				
Insurance services*	—	—	No change	No change
Distributive services	+35.0	+59.8	−35.0	−59.8
Financial services	+9.1	N.A.	No change	No change
Adjusted measure	323.7	N.A.	647.4	1,107.6

	Sales through MOUSAs		Sales through MOFAs	
	Sales of services to U.S. residents	Sales of goods to U.S. residents**	Sales of services to foreign residents	Sales of goods to foreign residents
Current measure	367.6	1,421.1	423.5	1,738.2
Effects of new measures:				
Insurance services	−40.4	No change	N.A.	N.A.
Distributive services	+134.9	−134.9	N.A.	N.A.
Services of bank affiliates	+30.5	No change	N.A.	N.A.
Adjusted measure	492.6	1,386.2	N.A.	N.A.

N.A. = No estimate is available.

*The new measure of insurance services has been incorporated in the current measure of exports and imports of services. Imports of insurance services are $0.8 billion higher in 2002 because of the new measure, and exports are $4.0 billion higher because of the new measure.

**The sales of goods to U.S. residents by MOUSAs have been estimated from data on exports of goods shipped by MOUSAs because the data on these sales are not disaggregated by destination.

rived here is based on the 2002 Economic Census, which has not yet been incorporated into the annual I-O accounts. In addition, the I-O accounts include manufacturers' sales offices and branches in the wholesale trade industry but the data used here on exports by wholesalers do not. Furthermore, margin rates vary by wholesale trade industry. The estimate derived here does not account for the possibility that wholesalers in industries with higher margin rates, such as some durable goods wholesalers, may account for a larger share of exports, while the estimate from the annual I-O accounts does take this into account. Finally, the estimates derived here only include the margin for the final sales from the exporting wholesaler to the purchaser, while the annual I-O accounts include any margins on sales from manufacturers or from other wholesalers to the exporting wholesaler.

U.S. imports of distributive services occur when a foreign wholesaler or retailer arranges for the export of a good to the United States. Data are not available on either the share of imports arranged by foreign wholesalers and retailers or on the margins earned by them. Therefore, it is assumed that foreign wholesalers accounted for the same share of U.S. imports as U.S. wholesalers did of U.S. exports. The $152.9 billion in exports by U.S. wholesalers accounted for 22.4 percent of all U.S. exports in 2002. Assuming that foreign wholesalers accounted for the same share of U.S. imports yields an estimate of imports facilitated by foreign wholesalers of $261.6 billion. Assuming that foreign wholesalers had the same average distributive services per dollar of sales as U.S. wholesalers (22.3 cents per dollar of sales) yields an estimate of distributive services embodied in imports from foreign wholesalers of $58.3 billion. The same assumptions and calculations for retail trade yield an estimate of distributive services embodied in imports from foreign retailers of $1.5 billion. Summing the two estimates yields $59.8 billion in distributive services embodied in imports of goods. The BEA's annual I-O accounts do not estimate wholesale trade margins on imports, and, so, the same comparison that was made for exports cannot be made for imports.

2.3.2   Sales through Affiliates

The estimates of sales of services through affiliates show that foreign-owned U.S. wholesalers and retailers accounted for less than 5 percent of all sales of services to U.S. residents in 2005, and U.S.-owned foreign wholesalers and retailers accounted for less than 5 percent of all sales of services to foreign persons in 2004.[14] However, as with the data on trade in services in the ITAs, this result is more of a reflection of the statistical conventions employed than a true indication of the importance of these industries in the delivery of services to international markets through the

---

14. The value of sales of services through the foreign wholesale and retail trade affiliates of U.S. MNCs is suppressed for 2005 to avoid the disclosure of company confidential data.

channel of affiliates' sales. In BEA's estimates, the total values of sales associated with wholesale and retail trade are treated as sales of goods. Thus, the estimates of services provided by wholesalers and retailers cover only secondary activities of these affiliates, not the distributive services that they provide. For example, the repair services provided by a car dealer are included in the estimates of sales of services, but the distributive services the dealer provides in selling cars are not. Instead, the value of the distributive services is included in the estimates of sales of goods. When the data collection system for sales of services through affiliates was instituted, BEA defined sales of services as those typical of a specified group of industries. The Bureau of Economic Analysis chose to treat sales in wholesale and retail trade as sales of goods because most of their value is attributable to the goods being sold, not to the distributive services. As a result, wholesale and retail trade affiliates are more important providers of services than the estimates suggest.

While the inclusion of distributive services in the value of goods sold is consistent with the treatment of cross-border trade, in which the value of distributive services is included in the value of trade in goods, an estimate of the distributive services supplied through affiliates would be valuable to data users. For example, it would allow for comparisons of the output of foreign-owned U.S. wholesalers and retailers with that of all U.S. wholesalers and retailers.

To allow estimates of the distributive services supplied through affiliates to be constructed, BEA collected data on the cost of goods sold and the beginning- and end-of-year inventories of the goods for resale on the 2002 benchmark survey of FDIUS. These data items have been included on the follow-on annual surveys of FDIUS, and they were introduced on the surveys of USDIA, beginning with the 2004 benchmark survey. These data are supplied by all affiliates with operations in wholesale or retail trade, not just those classified in these industries.

Preliminary estimates of the margin between sales and the cost of goods sold using the new data collected indicate that MOUSAs supplied $134.9 billion in distributive services to U.S. residents in 2002 and $135.1 billion in 2003. Including these estimates of distributive services in sales of services through affiliates would raise the estimates of sales of services through affiliates substantially—by 36.7 percent and 36.1 percent, respectively. These amounts are currently included in the estimates of sales of goods by MOUSAs in BEA's broader statistics on the activities of MOUSAs. As such, they are not an addition to the data on sales through affiliates, but, instead, are a reclassification within sales from goods to services. Majority-owned U.S. affiliates had sales of goods of $1,561.6 billion in 2002 and of $1,648.5 billion in 2003, which would fall by 8.6 percent and 8.2 percent respectively if distributive services were reclassified from sales of goods to sales of services (table 2.4).

2.4   Financial Services

In 2006, U.S. exports of financial services were $42.8 billion, and U.S. imports of financial services were $14.3 billion. Sales to U.S. residents by U.S. affiliates in finance were $24.9 billion in 2005, and sales to foreigners through foreign affiliates in finance were $42.9 billion. Despite the size of these flows, the coverage of financial services in BEA's data on international services is incomplete. While the data cover those services for which explicit fees or commissions are charged, they only partly capture the value of services for which payment is implicit—that is, reflected in differences between rates charged to borrowers and rates paid to lenders or in differences between buying and selling rates for financial assets. In addition, the data on cross-border trade include services provided by banks, but the data on sales through affiliates do not.

2.4.1   Cross-Border Trade

The Bureau of Economic Analysis' data on trade in financial services include explicit commissions and fees for a wide variety of services, including funds management, credit card services and other credit-related activities, and transactions in securities. The estimates of cross-border trade also include the value of two services that are measured only indirectly: implicit commissions and fees for bond trading and underwriting. For example, the services provided by an underwriter, who brings securities to market by buying them from the issuer at an agreed price and reselling them to investors, are remunerated by the margin generated from these transactions.

Other implicitly charged financial services are not included in BEA's estimates of cross-border trade in financial services. For example, one of the ways in which financial institutions charge implicitly for services is by paying lower interest rates on deposits than they charge to those who borrow from them. The resulting net receipts of interest are used to defray expenses and provide profits. Due to the lack of explicit charges, the value of services charged for implicitly must be imputed. The guidance for compiling statistics on trade in services offered by the SNA, BPM5, and the MSITS differs regarding the treatment of these unpriced financial services.

The SNA, which refers to these unpriced financial services as "financial intermediation services indirectly measured" (FISIM), recommends that FISIM be measured as the total property income receivable by financial intermediaries minus their total interest payable. It excludes any property income earned from the investment of their own funds because this income does not arise from financial intermediation. The SNA also recommends that FISIM purchased by depositors be measured as the difference between the average interest paid to depositors and a reference rate, or risk-free rate, and that FISIM purchased by borrowers be measured as the difference between the average rate paid by borrowers and the reference rate. In the SNA, production that is disposed of must be recorded in one or more of the following ways—as intermediate consumption by enterprises, as final consumption by households, or as exports to nonresidents. The allocation to nonresidents appears as exports of FISIM in the foreign transactions account of the SNA. Exports of FISIM occur when foreign residents borrow from U.S. banks or lend to them in the form of deposits. Likewise, imports of FISIM occur when U.S. residents borrow from or lend money to foreign banks.

In contrast to the SNA, BPM5 excludes the imputed value of financial intermediation services indirectly measured from exports and imports of financial services because of concerns that it would be impractical or difficult to collect the necessary data to impute a value for cross-border trade in these unpriced services. Instead, the values of these services are recorded indistinguishably under receipts and payments of interest.

To maintain consistency with BPM5, MSITS does not recommend including FISIM in trade in services. However, it does provide memorandum items for "services provided without payment by financial intermediaries" and for financial services including these unpriced services. These memorandum items were included both to allow for a measure that reflects implicit as well as explicit charges for services and because of concerns that, over time, financial institutions may change how they charge for some services. For example, if financial institutions begin to charge explicitly for services that had previously been charged implicitly, financial services excluding FISIM would show growth greater than if there had been no change in charging policies. However, this greater growth would be attributable to the change in charging policies and not to an actual increase in services provided. In addition, the memorandum items would facilitate international comparisons because financial institutions in some countries may charge explicitly for services that are usually charged implicitly by financial institutions in other countries.

In compiling the NIPAs, BEA allocates a portion of the imputed output of commercial banks to the rest of the world (Fixler, Reinsdorf, and Smith 2003). This imputation appears under exports of services, as "services furnished without payment by financial intermediaries except life insurance carriers and private noninsured pension plans," in the Foreign Transactions Account of the NIPAs. In 2002, "services furnished without payment by financial intermediaries except life insurance carriers" to the rest of the world were $9.1 billion, rising to $10.8 billion in 2006. It is not necessary to estimate imports of FISIM used for final consumption when estimating GDP because imports of FISIM are not included in the source data for consumption.[15] However, imports of FISIM for intermediate use by businesses should be estimated to avoid understating intermediate inputs.

---

15. Generally, when estimating GDP, it is necessary to remove the value of imports from the estimates of private and government consumption and investment because the source data of these components include purchases of imports.

Consistent with BPM5 recommendations, BEA currently excludes "services provided without payment by financial intermediaries" in its recording of cross-border trade in financial services in the ITAs. However, it is expected that the revision to BPM5, which is currently being written, will recommend including FISIM in cross-border trade in financial services.[16] Also, BEA considers it important to include unpriced services in its estimates, to accurately measure trade in financial services. Thus, BEA is examining the issues involved in estimating imports of "services provided without payment by financial intermediaries." Including imports and exports of unpriced financial services in the ITAs would raise the value of exports and imports of financial services and would result in offsetting entries in receipts and payments of interest.[17]

2.4.2   Sales through Affiliates

The coverage of sales through affiliates is incomplete because data for bank affiliates are excluded. Because most of the information on bank affiliates that is needed for policymaking purposes is already reported to other U.S. government agencies, BEA collected only limited data from bank affiliates. However, the absence of banks in the data causes a potentially large gap in the coverage of financial services sold through affiliates. As a first step toward closing this gap, BEA collected data on the 2002 benchmark survey of FDIUS that can be used as the basis for estimating bank affiliates' explicit and implicit fees for services. These same data items were added to the 2004 benchmark survey of USDIA.

Fixler and Zieschang (1999) develop a measure of the output of banks using the cost of money framework that covers all of the financial services provided by banks and that is consistent with national economic accounting principles. The measure consists of the value of explicitly charged services and, for implicitly charged services, of the bank's net interest adjusted for the fact that not all of a bank's assets and liabilities are associated with services. This measure was the basis for the revised treatment of the services provided by commercial banks introduced in the 2003 comprehensive revision of the NIPAs (Fixler, Reinsdorf, and Smith 2003). The measure of

16. See, *Revision of the Balance of Payments Manual, 5th Edition (Annotated Outline)* 2004, paragraph 9.51.

17. If FISIM could be estimated separately for borrowers and depositors, then purchases of these unpriced services by borrowers would result in some of the interest that nonresident borrowers pay on their loans being recharacterized as purchases of unpriced financial services. For purchases by depositors, it would be assumed that depositors receive, as interest, an amount equal to their purchases of these unpriced services. The imputed values for interest paid to depositors and their purchases of these unpriced services would raise the estimates of both receipts of interest and payments for financial services (or payments of interest and receipts for financial services) by equal amounts. The U.S. receipts of interest on bank claims were $22.7 billion in 2002, rising to $107.9 billion in 2006; U.S. payments of interest on bank liabilities were $22.5 billion in 2002, rising to $109.9 billion in 2006 (Bach 2005, 38, and Bach 2007, 37).

services supplied by U.S. bank affiliates discussed in the following is comparable to this measure.

For explicit charges for services, bank affiliates reported data on their total sales of services by destination, as nonbank affiliates do. In 2002, U.S. bank affiliates reported total sales of services of $17.0 billion, of which $14.1 billion, or 83 percent, was sold to U.S. residents.

For implicit charges for services, bank affiliates reported data on their total interest paid and total interest received. In 2002, they reported interest income of $100.6 billion and interest expense of $78.5 billion, for net interest income of $22.1 billion. In estimating FISIM, a part of FISIM on the banks' own funds is deducted to reflect the absence of a depositor. The amount deducted is equal to the reference interest rate[18] multiplied by the banks' own funds, which are defined as the difference between the banks' interest-bearing assets and liabilities (Fixler, Reinsdorf, and Smith 2003). Because bank affiliates report all assets and liabilities on BEA's direct investment surveys, the reported data must be adjusted to derive an estimate of their own funds. Applying the shares of interest-bearing assets and liabilities in total assets and liabilities for the domestic banking industry, calculated from the FDIC Historical Statistics on Banking, to the reported data produces an estimate of bank affiliates' own funds. Multiplying this estimate by the reference rate yields an estimate of $2.3 billion for interest earned on their own funds in 2002. Deducting this from their net interest income of $22.1 billion yields a value of FISIM of $19.8 billion. Assuming that the share of FISIM supplied to U.S. residents is the same as the share of explicit charges results in an estimate of $16.4 billion of FISIM supplied to U.S. residents. Total services supplied to U.S. residents by U.S. bank affiliates are estimated to be $30.5 billion in 2002 (table 2.4).

2.5 Conclusions

This paper has provided an update of BEA's efforts to improve its data on and measures of U.S. international sales and purchases of services. It has focused on changes in data collections and methodologies for three important services: insurance services, wholesale and retail trade services, and financial services. In some cases, the changes will improve the comparability of BEA's data on cross-border trade in services and sales through affiliates. In addition, some of the changes will improve the comparability of BEA's data on international services with the NIPAs. Table 2.4 shows the impact on the estimates for 2002; table 2.5 summarizes the changes and the impacts that they have had, or would have, on the accounts. For the esti-

---

18. The reference rate is computed by dividing the interest received from Treasury and Federal agency securities by the average book value of these securities over the period during which interest was received.

Table 2.5   Summary of changes in the measurement of insurance, wholesale and retail trade, and financial services

Channel of delivery	Issue	Action taken or proposed	Effect on the estimates
Cross-border trade		*Insurance*	
	Unusually large or small claims caused fluctuations in the measure of services (premiums less claims) unrelated to changes in the levels of services	Adopted a measure of claims that reflected the long-run relationship between claims and premiums, called *normal losses*	Reduced volatility in the measure of trade in services
	Omitted investment income earned on technical reserves	Developed estimates of premium supplements	Raised the estimates of trade in insurance services
	Data on premiums recorded net of commissions	Collected data on premiums gross of commissions	Raised exports and imports of services by equal amounts
	Estimates of insurance services excluded services auxiliary to insurance	Collected data in a new category for services auxiliary to insurance	Raised estimates of trade in insurance services, partly offset by reductions in other services
Sales through affiliates	No deduction for claims	Proposed adopting a measure that deducts normal losses from premiums earned	Would substantially reduce the estimates
	Omitted investment income earned on technical reserves	Proposed adding an estimate of premium supplements	Would raise the estimates

		Wholesale and retail trade	
Cross-border trade	Distributive services provided in connection with trade in goods are included indistinguishably in the value of goods	Construct rough estimates using data from the 2002 Economic Census	Estimates would not be deducted from trade in goods but would be provided as supplementary information
Sales through affiliates	Distributive services are included indistinguishably in the value of goods sold through affiliates	Collect data on the costs and inventories of goods for resale	Would substantially raise the estimates, offset by reductions in estimates of sales of goods through affiliates
		Financial services	
Cross-border trade	Estimates exclude the value of some financial services provided without explicit charge	Conduct research into estimating imports of these services	Would raise the estimate of trade in services, offset by changes in receipts and payments of interest
Sales through affiliates	Estimates exclude services supplied by bank affiliates	Collect data from bank affiliates on explicit fees and commissions and interest paid and received	Would raise substantially the value of services sold through affiliates

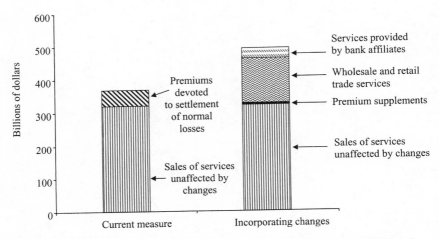

Fig. 2.4   Estimates of sales of services to U.S. persons through the MOUSAs of foreign MNCs, 2002

mates of sales of services through U.S. affiliates of foreign MNCs, removing the premiums devoted to the settlement of normal losses results in a reduction in the estimates of sales of services through U.S. affiliates, only partly offset by the addition of premium supplements for non-life insurance. Including the two services not currently included in the estimates—wholesale and retail trade services and services provided by bank affiliates—raise the estimates above the current measure (figure 2.4).

For cross-border trade in insurance services, a more meaningful measure of services was developed that avoids the large, random swings in the estimates due to fluctuations in losses by using a measure called *normal losses,* based on the long-run relationship between premiums and claims, as a proxy for insurers' expectations. In addition, it is a more complete estimate, because it includes premiums supplements, commissions, and other services auxiliary to insurance. For sales through affiliates, the proposed measure is more meaningful because it deducts a measure of claims paid out by insurers and is more complete because it includes premium supplements.

For wholesale and retail trade, estimates of the services supplied by affiliates with wholesale and retail trade operations will provide measures of services output that are comparable to those in the NIPAs and the industry accounts.

For cross-border trade in financial services, research to identify data sources and to develop a methodology to estimate imports of "services provided without payment by financial intermediaries" continues. For sales through affiliates, an important data gap has been closed by including estimates of explicit and implicit charges for services by bank affiliates in the estimates in benchmark years.

The Bureau of Economic Analysis's efforts to improve its estimates of international services continue. Future efforts will focus on providing greater detail on affiliated trade in services, on improving the quality of travel estimates, and on improving the coverage of BEA's surveys of international trade in services. Affiliated trade accounts for the majority of transactions in royalties and license fees and in business, professional, and technical services, yet little detail by type of service was collected for these transactions. The bureau began collecting data on affiliated and unaffiliated trade at the same level of detail on the same surveys with the 2006 Benchmark Survey of Transactions in Selected Services and Intangible Assets with Foreign Persons. Travel services are an important component of trade in services; BEA is exploring the use of data on credit card transactions to improve the quality of these estimates. Concerns about the coverage of BEA's surveys of trade in services have been raised by bilateral comparisons that sometimes show BEA's estimates of U.S. exports to and imports from a particular country are lower than that country's estimates of imports from and exports to the United States. While most of these discrepancies can be explained by differences in definitions, some of the discrepancies remain, raising the possibility that some firms trading services are not reporting on BEA's surveys. At BEA's request, the Census Bureau included a screening question on the 2006 Company Organization Survey to identify importers of services, and BEA funded an expansion in the number of firms sampled from 40,000 to 55,000. Any firms that report imported services and that are not already reporting on BEA's trade in services surveys would be included in future surveys.

Appendix

Ownership-Based Framework of the U.S. Current Account

In order to highlight the participation of MNCs in international markets for both goods and services, BEA produces an annual, ownership-based supplement to the current account portion of the ITAs. Table 2A.1 reproduces key lines of the ownership-based framework of the U.S. current account for exports for 2005 and 2006.[19] Line 1 of the ownership-based

---

19. For the complete ownership-based supplement to the current account portion of the U.S. International Transactions Accounts, see "An Ownership-Based Framework of the U.S. Current Account, 1997–2006," *Survey of Current Business,* January, 2007, 59–61.

Table 2A.1 **Selected entries from the ownership-based framework of the U.S. current account, 2005–2006 (in billions of dollars)**

Line		2005	2006*
1	Exports of goods and services and income receipts (ITA table 1, line 1)	1,788.6	2,096.2
2	Receipts resulting from exports of goods and services or sales by foreign affiliates	1,552.4	1,755.9
3	Exports of goods and services, total (ITA table 1, line 2)	1,283.1	1,455.7
3a	Goods, balance of payments basis (ITA table 1, line 3)	894.6	1,023.1
3b	Services (ITA table 1, line 4)	388.4	422.6
4	To unaffiliated foreigners	916.4	—
4a	Goods	621.9	—
4b	Services	294.4	—
5	To affiliated foreigners	366.7	—
5a	Goods	272.7	—
5b	Services	94.0	—
6	To foreign affiliates of U.S. parents	258.2	—
6a	Goods	188.6	—
6b	Services	69.6	—
7	To foreign parent groups of U.S. affiliates	108.6	—
7a	Goods	84.2	—
7b	Services	24.4	—
8	Net receipts by U.S. parents of direct investment income resulting from sales by their foreign affiliates (ITA table 1, line 14)	269.3	310.2
9	Nonbank affiliates	269.1	311.1
10	Sales by foreign affiliates	4,224.7	—
11	Less: Foreign affiliates' purchases of goods and services directly from the United States	287.8	—
12	Less: Costs and profits accruing to foreign persons	2,800.5	—
13	Compensation of employees of foreign affiliates	391.8	—
14	Other	2,408.7	—
15	Less: Sales by foreign affiliates to other foreign affiliates of the same parent	867.2	—
16	Bank affiliates	0.2	-0.8
17	Other income receipts	236.1	340.2
18	Other private receipts on U.S.-owned assets abroad (ITA table 1, line 15)	230.5	335.0
19	U.S. Government receipts (ITA table 1, line 16)	2.7	2.4
20	Compensation of employees (ITA table 1, line 17)	2.9	2.9

*The estimates in this column are from the international transactions accounts, which are published quarterly. Estimates are not yet available for the items from BEA's annual survey of U.S. direct investment abroad and of foreign direct investment in the United States, which are processed in the two years following the year of coverage. The detailed preliminary estimates for 2006 will be published in the second half of 2008.

framework matches the exports of goods and services and income receipts shown in the standard current account. Line 2 is the new item: U.S. exports are combined with the net receipts of U.S. parent companies from the sales of their foreign affiliates. Lines 3 through 7 highlight the important role of MNCs in cross-border trade by breaking out trade between affiliated parties (intrafirm trade) and between unaffiliated parties. Line 8 corresponds to direct investment income on U.S.-owned assets abroad, included in the income component of the standard current account. Lines 9 through 16 derive these net receipts as the sales of foreign affiliates less their purchases from the United States and costs and profits accruing to foreigners. Only the net receipts that accrue to the U.S. parent companies, not the gross value of sales by their foreign affiliates, are included because only the U.S. direct investors' shares in profits accrue to the United States; the other income, including compensation of employees, typically accrues to foreigners. The improvements to the sales of services through affiliates discussed in this paper will not affect the measure of direct investors' income that appears in the standard, or the ownership-based, current account. Lines 17 through 20 correspond to the items in the income component of the standard current account other than direct investment income. An identical framework is followed for imports of goods and services and income payments.

References

A. M. Best Company. 1940–2004. *Best's aggregates and averages: Property-casualty, United States.* Oldwick, NJ.
———. 1996–2004. *Best's aggregates and averages: Life/health, United States.* Oldwick, NJ.
Bach, C. L. 2003. Annual revision of the U.S. International Accounts, 1992–2002. *Survey of Current Business* 83 (July): 32–45.
———. 2004. Annual revision of the U.S. International Accounts, 1989–2003. *Survey of Current Business* 84 (July): 52–64.
———. 2007. U.S. international transactions in 2006. *Survey of Current Business* 87 (April): 22–73.
———. 2005. U.S. international transactions, 2004. *Survey of Current Business* 85 (April): 24–68.
Balance of payments manual, 5th ed., 1993. International Monetary Fund. Washington, D.C.
Balance of payments and international investment position manual, 6th ed. 2007. Washington, D.C.: International Monetary Fund. Available at http://www.imf.org/external/pubs/ft/bop/2007/pdf/BPM6.pdf.
Chen, B., and D. J. Fixler. 2003. Measuring the services of property-casualty insurance in the NIPAs: Changes in concepts and methods. *Survey of Current Business* 83 (October): 10–26.
Fixler, D., M. B. Reinsdorf, and G. M. Smith. 2003. Measuring the services of com-

mercial banks in the NIPAs: Changes in concepts and methods. *Survey of Current Business* 83 (September): 33–44.

Fixler, D., and K. Zieschang. 1999. The productivity of the banking sector: Integrating financial and production approaches to measuring financial service output. *The Canadian Journal of Economics* 32 (2): 547–69.

Howells III, T. F., and K. B. Barefoot. 2006. Annual industry accounts: Advance estimates for 2005. *Survey of Current Business* 86 (May): 11–24.

Howells III, T. F., K. B. Barefoot, and B. M. Lindberg. 2006. Annual industry accounts: Revised estimates for 2003–2005. *Survey of Current Business* 86 (December): 45–87.

Manual on Statistics of International Trade in Services. 2002. Commission of European Communities, International Monetary Fund, Organisation for Economic Co-operation and Development, United Nations, United Nations Conference on Trade and Development, and World Trade Organization: Geneva, Luxembourg, New York, Paris, and Washington, D.C.

Sherwood, M. 1999. Output of the property and casualty insurance industry. *The Canadian Journal of Economics* 32 (2): 518–46.

System of National Accounts. 1993. Commission of the European Communities, International Monetary Fund, Organisation for Economic Co-operation and Development, United Nations, and World Bank: Brussels/Luxembourg, New York, Paris, and Washington, D.C.

Triplett, J. E., and B. P. Bosworth. 2004a. Output and productivity in retail trade. In *Productivity in the services sector: New sources of economic growth,* 233–55. Washington, D.C.: Brookings Institution.

———. 2004b. Overview: Industry productivity trends. In *Productivity in the services sector: New sources of economic growth,* 6–40. Washington, D.C.: Brookings Institution.

U.S. Census Bureau. 2005. 2002 Economic Census, Series EC02-44-SX-SB. *Retail trade: Miscellaneous subjects 2002.* Washington, D.C.: U.S. Government Printing Office.

U.S. Census Bureau. 2005. 2002 Economic Census, Series EC02-42-SX-SB. *Wholesale trade: Miscellaneous subjects 2002.* Washington, D.C.: U.S. Government Printing Office.

U.S. Census Bureau. 2005. Current business reports, series BR/04A. *Annual benchmark report for retail trade and food services: January 1992 through February 2005.* Washington, D.C.: U.S. Government Printing Office.

U.S. Department of Commerce, Bureau of Economic Analysis. 2006. An ownership-based framework of the U.S. Current Account, 1993–2004. *Survey of Current Business* 86 (January) 2006:43–45.

———. 1990. *Personal consumption expenditures.* Methodology paper series MP-6. Washington, D.C.: GPO.

Whichard, O. G., and M. Borga. 2002. Selected issues in the measurement of U.S. international services. *Survey of Current Business* 82 (June): 36–56.

II

R&D and Intellectual Property

The Effect of Taxes on Royalties and the Migration of Intangible Assets Abroad

John Mutti and Harry Grubert

3.1 Introduction

A front page article of the *Wall Street Journal* in November 2005 describes the way that Microsoft's four-year-old Irish subsidiary, Round Island One Ltd., allows the parent company to save at least $500 million in taxes each year (Simpson 2005). By licensing its software for use in Europe, the Middle East, and Africa through the Irish subsidiary, Microsoft receives royalty payments that are deductible in high-tax locations and subject to a low rate of corporate income taxation in Ireland. Because the earnings are retained abroad, they are not subject to a residual U.S. tax. According to company filings with the Securities and Exchange Commission, Simpson reports that other technology companies are following a similar strategy to reduce their overall tax burden.

Such reports are an indication of major changes over the past ten years in the tax planning strategies of U.S. multinational corporations (MNCs). These changes have affected the likelihood that a U.S. parent will receive royalties from its foreign affiliates or that the parent will be able to increase its earnings abroad from exploiting intangible assets that it develops in the United States. Additionally, U.S. parents have found new ways to accomplish the relocation or migration of intangible assets abroad. These new strategies have implications for the way the return to U.S. research and development (R&D) is reported to the Internal Revenue Service (IRS), as well as any incentive to relocate innovative activity outside of the United

John Mutti is the Sidney Meyer Professor of Economics at Grinnell College. Harry Grubert is an economist in the Office of Tax Policy in the U.S. Treasury Department.

The authors thank Mihir Desai, the editors, reviewers, and conference participants for helpful comments.

States. This chapter demonstrates how firms have interpreted two important tax regulations to create these new strategies, and it examines how they appear to have influenced measures of MNC activity reported by the U.S. Department of the Treasury, the Bureau of Economic Analysis, and the National Science Foundation.

One important tax planning development was the issuance of the "check-the-box" regulations by the IRS in 1997, which greatly simplified the use of hybrid entities. These are operations that are classified as incorporated subsidiaries by one country and transparent branches by another. As explained in section 3.2, this distinction allows U.S. MNCs to avoid immediate taxation of intersubsidiary payments that otherwise would occur under the antiabuse Controlled Foreign Corporation (CFC) provisions of subpart F of the Internal Revenue Code. Hybrids can make such intersubsidiary payments invisible to the U.S. Treasury. As a result, MNCs can retain earnings abroad in low-tax locations.

A second element of the successful tax-saving strategies that accomplish the transfer of intellectual property abroad is that an affiliate can acquire the rights to a valuable intellectual property at a favorable price. A tax haven entity can engage in a cost-sharing agreement with the parent in which it shares in the cost of an R&D project in exchange for the right to exploit the technology abroad. Once the technology is developed the tax haven company can license an operating sibling in a high-tax location, but with a hybrid structure the deductible royalty paid to the tax haven will not be subject to immediate U.S. tax. Companies have apparently been able to arrange favorable cost-sharing agreements that permit them to leave abroad in a low-tax location a greater share of the return to the U.S. R&D.

If this strategy is widely adopted, the growth in royalties received by U.S. parents can be expected to decline, and earnings retained in the tax haven company will grow. The popularity of cost-sharing agreements combined with hybrid structures also suggests that there will be an increase in payments for technical services by U.S. subsidiaries to their parents relative to royalties. In the long run, however, the sum of these service payments should decline relative to foreign direct investment income abroad as more of the return to U.S. intangible assets is in the form of net income deferred abroad in low-tax locations.

The chapter assesses these predictions empirically at two levels, one using data aggregated to the country or worldwide level, and one examining firm-specific practices. Verifying whether the determinants of affiliate royalty payments have been affected by this new tax-saving strategy also is relevant in addressing a potential policy issue in tax reform. In November 2005, the President's Advisory Panel on Federal Tax Reform recommended two possible reform plans. One was termed the Simplified Income Tax, whose provisions in the international area would exempt from U.S. tax any dividends received from active business income abroad. The foreign tax would be the final tax imposed on that income. Because that dividend income would never be subject to U.S. tax, such a change would be likely to reduce royalty payments made to U.S. parents; royalties would continue to be fully taxed under the rationale that they are a deductible expense abroad.

The remainder of the chapter proceeds by first providing a fuller explanation of hybrid structures and cost-sharing agreements. It then examines evidence from IRS and Bureau of Economic Analysis (BEA) data to determine whether the strategies suggested previously can be detected either in data aggregated to the country level or in firm-specific data. For both levels of empirical analysis several measures are quite consistent with the predictions already described.

3.2 Alternative Ways of Utilizing a Hybrid Structure to Affect Payments for Technology

The United States taxes the worldwide income of its residents, but allows a credit for foreign income taxes paid on income received from abroad. Although any residual U.S. tax is deferred until active business income is repatriated to the United States, for some types of income a U.S. tax is due immediately. Hybrids are a business structure that allows U.S. firms to avoid having income treated in that latter category. To understand the significance of hybrids, first consider the role of the CFC rules that otherwise would apply to transactions between related parties. A recent Treasury document (2000, xii) states the following:

> The subpart F rules attempt to prevent (or negate the tax advantage from) deflection of income, either from the United States or from the foreign country in which earned, into another jurisdiction which is a tax haven or which has a preferential tax regime for certain types of income. Thus, subpart F generally targets passive income and income that is split off from the activities that produced the value in the goods or services generating the income. Conversely, subpart F generally does not require current taxation of active business income except when the income is of a type that is easily deflected to a tax haven, such as shipping income, or income earned in certain transactions between related parties. In related party transaction, deflection of income is much easier because a unified group of corporations can direct the flow of income between entities in different jurisdictions.
>
> [. . .]Generally, rents and royalties earned by a CFC in an active business are excluded from Foreign Personal Holding Company Income (FPHCI). This exception does not apply, however, if the CFC's rents or royalties are received from a related person. Accordingly, rents and royalties received from a related person are generally treated as FPHCI, without regard to the nature of the business activities of the CFC that give rise to the rents and royalties.

This statement distinguishes payments to related parties from other transactions that affiliates might make, because of the belief that the former can be more easily manipulated to shift income from one jurisdiction to another. The CFC rules might be regarded as a backstop to transfer pricing regulations that attempt to limit income shifting practices. If payments between related parties cannot be observed by the U.S. Treasury, however, an MNC can avoid this subpart F treatment. Note that this residual tax is important to U.S. MNCs whose foreign tax payments are less than the U.S. tax liability on that foreign income. For companies that have substantial excess foreign tax credits, there is little incentive to create a hybrid to avoid U.S. taxation of royalty income, because that income already would have been shielded from any additional U.S. tax.

To illustrate the potential benefit from a hybrid arrangement, consider an example where a parent capitalizes a hybrid entity in a tax haven with equity, and then has it lend to an operation in a high-tax location. The MNC reports to the high-tax jurisdiction that the tax haven affiliate is a corporation, but it tells the U.S. Treasury that the tax haven affiliate is an unincorporated branch of the high-tax subsidiary. The high-tax subsidiary receives a deduction for the interest paid to the tax haven affiliate, but from the U.S. Treasury's perspective the two affiliates are treated as one consolidated company. The interest income received in the tax haven is not reported to the U.S. Treasury and can therefore be deferred from current U.S. tax. Without the hybrid, a payment to a tax haven finance subsidiary would be subject to current U.S. tax under the CFC rules.[1] Altshuler and Grubert (2005) calculate that these types of structures allowed U.S. multinational companies to lower their foreign taxes by $7.0 billion per year in 2002 compared to 1997.

Figure 3.1 shows a hybrid structure applicable in the technology setting considered here, which allows the low-tax affiliate to strip out income from the high-tax affiliate through royalty payments that are a deductible expense in the high-tax country. From the perspective of the high-tax country, less income will be declared by the affiliate that operates there, and the host government will have collected less tax revenue. The royalty income is not recognized by the U.S. Treasury and can be retained in the low-tax country where it escapes a current U.S. tax.

Similar benefits may arise under other hybrid structures, although the way such benefits will be reported to the U.S. Treasury changes. For example, an affiliate in a high-tax country A may claim for U.S. tax purposes

---

1. A tax law change in 2006 makes it possible for a firm under certain circumstances to achieve this same tax-saving result without a hybrid structure. Under the Tax Increase Prevention and Reconciliation Act signed into law on May 17, 2006, which is scheduled to apply through 2008, CFCs can avoid the subpart F treatment explained previously if the intersubsidiary payments of dividends, interest, rents, and royalties are attributable to active business income, in contrast to passive income.

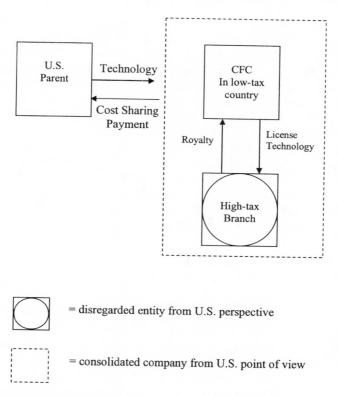

Fig. 3.1   A possible hybrid structure

that a related affiliate in a low-tax country B is its branch, and therefore the latter entity becomes invisible to the U.S. Treasury. If the high-tax affiliate in country A pays a royalty to the low-tax affiliate in B, it is not recognized by the U.S. Treasury. The consolidated net income of the high-tax affiliate rises because the royalty is deducted against a high tax rate, but the higher income now earned by the low-tax affiliate can be retained in B and need not face the higher tax rate in A. The country A affiliate appears more profitable because the tax burden on a given dollar of income is now lower.

In the case of R&D cost-sharing agreements, a key issue is the basis on which the affiliate is allowed to buy in to successful research carried out by the parent. If a parent's latest innovation builds on several previous generations of research, but the affiliate is able to pay a favorable price that places little value on those past expenditures, the strategy is particularly successful in allowing a migration of the intangible asset to the location abroad. New proposed regulations under the cost-sharing provisions of Section 482.7 of the Internal Revenue Code (Reg-144615-02, announced for public comment on August 29, 2005) are intended to address the "inappropriate migration of intangibles." These proposed regulations have been revised in response to comments, but as of January 2008, they still are not finalized. Initial reactions to them suggest that they represent a major revision, which is more likely to require that such agreements reflect a price that would be offered in an arms-length transaction to an investor who bore none of the risk of the earlier product developments. Under the less explicit current regulations, U.S. parents have been able to achieve the outcome that a smaller ownership share of successful technological innovations is retained in the United States, and fewer royalties will be received by the parent in the future. While payments from the affiliate for technical services under the cost-sharing agreement will result in an initial increase in parent receipts, over the longer run the parent will receive fewer payments for the utilization of its intangible assets abroad either in the form of royalties or in the form of cost-sharing payments.

3.3   Indications of the Changing Importance of Royalty Payments at the Aggregate Level

3.3.1   U.S. Treasury Data

As previously indicated, the U.S. Treasury receives tax returns from U.S.-controlled foreign corporations, which provide information about royalty payments, payments for technical services, and CFC earnings. Table 3.1 is based on compilations of information from the Form 5471, which is filed with the basic corporate return and reports on each controlled foreign corporation's transactions with its related parties. The table compares the values reported in 1996, before the check-the-box regime was adopted, and 2002. The latter year is the latest one for which these data are available. Because some of the hybrid arrangements and cost-sharing agreements already described may take time to design and implement, a longer time frame generally is desirable to allow more complete adjustment to these new tax-saving opportunities. Over a longer time frame, however, the actual response observed may be affected by other policy changes or by changes in the business cycle. For example, due to the economic downturn that occurred in many parts of the world in 2002, the likely shift in affiliate earnings relative to royalty payments may be less pronounced than in years that represent comparable stages of the business cycle.

The summary measures in the top portion of table 3.1 indicate how income for all affiliates has changed relative to the income declared in seven major low-tax countries. The share of earnings in the latter group grew much more rapidly than total earnings and profits of all U.S. subsidiaries, as shown on lines 1 and 2. Although part of the increase in low-tax countries is due to the growth in dividends received from other CFCs (not hybrids), shown on line 3, the remaining portion shown on line 4 reflects in-

Table 3.1   **Tabulations from the 1996 and 2002 Form 5471 files (in billions of dollars)**

	1996	2002	Growth as %
All CFCs			
1. Total pretax earning and profits	$160.8	$228.7	42
2. Earnings and profits in seven major low-tax countries (Ireland, Singapore, Bermuda, Cayman Islands, Netherlands, Luxembourg, and Switzerland.)	36.5	82.5	126
3. Dividends received in the seven major low-tax countries	6.4	25.7	302
4. Earnings and profits in the seven major low-tax countries, less dividends received	30.1	56.8	89
5. Total tangible capital (net plant and equipment plus inventories)	767.5	1,119.5	46
6. Tangible capital in five major holding company low-tax countries (Bermuda, Cayman Islands, Netherlands, Luxembourg, and Switzerland)	51.7	205.0	296
Top 7,500 CFCs			
7. Earnings and profits	139.8	196.8	41
8. Compensation for technical and management services (cost-sharing)	13.2	27.4	108
9. Royalties paid to parents	22.4	37.6	68

Source: Treasury tax files.

creased real activity and the effect of tax planning structures that leave the visible affiliate in a low-tax country. That figure increases at double the rate of the overall growth in affiliate income, an outcome consistent with the tax-saving strategies previously outlined.[2]

Lines 5 and 6 show further evidence of hybrid structures in which the high-tax company disappears from the perspective of the U.S. Treasury. The rate of growth in tangible capital in five low-tax countries that serve as attractive locations for holding companies is over six times as great as for the total of all CFCs. Tangible capital reported in these five countries represents about 18 percent of the total in 2002. However, the tangible capital need not be physically present in those countries, because it instead can be located in the invisible branch in a high-tax country.

The bottom three lines of the table are based on transactions among related parties reported by the 7,500 largest CFCs. Of the three measures shown, payments to U.S. parents for technical and management services grew most rapidly (by 108 percent), a likely indication of the rising importance of cost-sharing agreements. Earnings and profits grew less than royalties paid to the parent, 41 percent compared to 68 percent. That result is

2. This outcome applies to the case where the remaining entity seen by the U.S. Treasury is located in the tax haven country. If the remaining entity were located in a high-tax country instead, the contrast cited in table 3.1 would not be as great. Evidence for that latter strategy would appear as a lower effective tax rate in the high-tax country, a situation examined by Altshuler and Grubert (2005).

somewhat unexpected, if the combination of a hybrid and a cost-sharing agreement makes royalty payments from high-tax affiliates invisible to the U.S. Treasury.

To put this observation in perspective, however, consider two factors that are more supportive of the hybrid strategy's importance. First, the relative ranking of royalties and profits for 2002 may result because earnings are more cyclically volatile than royalties, and 2002 was a year in which earnings and profits declined from their 2000 peak. By way of contrast, royalties grew less rapidly than earnings over the period 1996 to 2000.[3] Second, between 2000 and 2002 the Treasury data show that royalties received by U.S. parents increased 29 percent, whereas the BEA's international transactions figures indicate that royalties received by U.S. parents only grew by 5 percent between those same years. Such ambiguities suggest the importance of considering multiple data sources to indicate MNC responses to the changing tax incentives.[4]

3.3.2   Bureau of Economic Analysis Data

The Bureau of Economic Analysis publishes two important sources of data on affiliate operations. One is the Annual and Benchmark Surveys of Direct Investment Abroad, which presents financial and operating data of foreign affiliates. Greater detail is available in the case of majority-owned affiliates (MOFAs). A second important source of information comes from the U.S. international transactions accounts. These data lie behind the calculation of the direct investment position. However, they only consider the transactions of foreign affiliates with their U.S. parents and do not provide any basis for analyzing transactions among affiliates.

The surveys of financial and operating data offer the advantage that information is collected for each affiliate, regardless of whether it operates as a branch or is incorporated in the foreign country. In contrast to the Treasury data, the disappearance of affiliates under a hybrid arrangement should not occur in the BEA data. Nevertheless, care is warranted in interpreting these data, too, because certain measures of affiliate activity,

---

3. Changing composition of this group also may influence these comparisons. Because the largest 7,500 affiliates are selected based on their reported assets, this set includes more capital-intensive operations, such as finance, insurance, and real estate. Based on income or receipts, manufacturing, wholesale and retail trade, and construction would play a larger role. Throughout the 1990s these latter industries have declined in relative importance (Nutter 2001).

4. A further example of the difference between Treasury tax data and BEA data comes from looking at total royalty payments reported by U.S. corporations on Form 1118, the basis for claiming a foreign tax credit. In 2000, firms claimed royalties of $75 billion. In the BEA international transactions data, total royalties received by all U.S. residents was $43 billion. The MNCs may have a bigger tax incentive to characterize payments received from abroad as royalties, because that increases the foreign source income they receive and thereby increases the foreign tax credits they can claim (see Mutti and Grubert [1998] for discussion of the effects of different source rules).

such as net income, may appear overstated due to double counting.[5] If net income is likely to be overstated, but royalties are not, then comparing the percentage changes in each of these items will not be a valid test of the firm's response to the tax incentives previously identified.

For example, if a MOFA in country A receives a dividend from a MOFA in country B, the U.S. parent will report the affiliate's earnings in country B and also the remitted dividend as part of the income of the affiliate in country A. The sum of income across all MOFAs will appear larger because of this double counting. As holding company operations expand, and fulfill the role of the country A MOFA in the previous example, the potential double counting becomes larger. While the trend toward greater use of holding companies can be observed from the 1980s onward, the shift from 1996 to 2004 is particularly large. As reported by Koncz and Yorgason (2005), the portion of the U.S. direct investment position abroad that they account for has roughly doubled, from 17 percent to 34 percent.[6]

In contrast, the direct investment income figure from the international transactions account does not include the double counting that can occur with the financial and operating data. Because it only records transactions between a U.S. parent and its foreign subsidiaries, it is not affected by transactions among affiliates.

Those observations serve as useful background to interpret alternative measures of the operations of foreign affiliates reported in table 3.2. The table shows relevant data by which to assess changes in earnings and royalties from benchmark surveys from 1989, 1994, and 1999. Annual survey data are available for 2003, but those data do not provide a complete representation of transactions among affiliates. The royalty payments and other private direct investment service payments for that year are taken from the international transaction accounts.

First consider the implications of the changes observed from 1994 to 1999, the benchmark years that span the introduction of the check-the-box opportunity. Then examine whether those trends are reinforced by additional responses to those incentives in the subsequent 1999 to 2003 period or whether other factors that operate over that period offset the initial responses observed. Also, consider how these patterns differ from those observed in the earlier benchmark intervals from 1982 to 1989 and 1989 to 1994.

---

5. See Borga and Mataloni (2001), and Altshuler and Grubert (2005) for presentation of this issue. Altshuler and Grubert were interested in how much tax saving was possible through the growth of payments that presumably were deductible in high-tax locations, in contrast to payments of dividends from one affiliate to another.

6. Luxembourg has been a particularly attractive location, because it exempts from corporate tax the dividends, interest, and royalties received from a foreign source by the holding company. Exemption systems more typically do not tax dividends received from abroad, because they have born a corporate tax in the host country, but do not exempt payments that were deductible abroad.

Table 3.2   Aspects of affiliate activity from BEA benchmark survey measures (1989–1994, 1994–1999) and financial and operating data /international transactions accounts (2003)

Measure	1989	1994	1999	2003	Growth, 1989–1994 (%)	Growth, 1994–1999 (%)	Growth, 1999–2003 (%)
1. Affiliate net income before tax	105.4	110.4	207.8	396.9	5	88	91
2. Before-tax direct inv. income	86.6	87.6	145.2	247.8	1	66	71
3. Property, Plant and Equipment	248	350	593	730	41	69	23
4. R&D	7.0	11.9	18.1	22.3	70	52	23
5. Gross product	320	404	566	705	26	40	25
6. Employees	5,114	5,924	7,766	8,364	16	31	8
7. Sales	1,020	1,436	2,219	2,906	41	55	31
8. Royalties paid	12.5	22.0	35.8	—	76	63	—
9. Royalties to U.S. parent	9.8	16.7	25.0	30.9	70	50	18[a]
10. Royalties to other foreign affiliate	1.5	2.6	6.0	—	73	131	—
11. Other direct investment services to parent	7.1	11.8	20.6	27.0	66	75	22[a]
12. Income/sales (line2/line 7)	8.5	6.1	6.5	8.5	—	—	—
13. Royalties/(royalties + income) line 9/(line 9 + line 2)	10.2	16.0	14.7	11.1	—	—	—

[a]Based on change in international transactions accounts entries for 1999 and 2003.

The BEA data indicate that over the 1994 to 1999 period, royalties paid by affiliates to U.S. parents grew by 50 percent, a rate faster than some indicators of MNC activity (such as sales, gross product, employment, and R&D) but not as fast as several other measures such as income, property, plant and equipment, and payments to the parent for other private direct investment services. Comparing royalty payments to affiliate income requires careful attention to the distinctions raised previously, and therefore two measures for income are included in the table. The first is based on the sum of before-tax income reported by all MOFAs (which can include double counting described previously). The second is based on the direct investment return to U.S. parents (which should be free from the double counting) adjusted upward by the amount of foreign income tax paid. The increase in the former figure is particularly large, probably a reflection of the growth of holding company operations. The increase in the latter figure still is greater than that of royalty payments to the parent over the 1994 to 1999 period that spans the introduction of check-the-box regulations.

To give greater insight into the conflicting forces that influence the royalty figure, note that in the earlier 1989 to 1994 period royalties grew quite rapidly at a time when the growth in income was very slight. As explained, the opportunity to receive royalties free of any residual U.S. tax occurs when the U.S. parent has excess foreign tax credits. While the U.S. Tax Reform Act of 1986 reduced the U.S. corporate tax rate from 46 percent to 34 percent, and caused an initial increase in the share of U.S. parents that were in excess credit positions, that initial consequence was not a permanent change. Companies adjusted the types of payments they made and host countries reduced their corporate tax rates (Grubert, Randolph, and Rousslang 1996). Nevertheless, the incentive to pay additional royalties continued to operate into the 1990s. There was substantial public commentary over various iterations of proposed regulations that would specify what royalty methods could be used under the provisions of 1986 act, and the standard that emerged when those regulations were finalized in 1994 was more stringent than existed prior to 1986. Companies likely adjusted their practices before 1994 in anticipation of such a change. Also, in 1993 penalty regulations were adopted, which applied if royalties were understated. In short, there were several policy changes that could be expected to create increasing pressure to raise royalty payments over the 1989 to 1994 period.

While the rate of increase of royalty payments by affiliates to parents was slower in the 1994 to 1999 period, the growth rate of payments to other affiliates increased sharply by 131 percent, the largest increase shown in table 3.2. Relative to the royalties paid to the parent, the proportion paid to other affiliates rose from 15 percent to 24 percent. This pattern is consistent with the rising role of hybrid structures and the payment of royalties from high-tax affiliates to low-tax affiliates. Finally, parent receipts of other direct investment service payments rose faster than royalties, 75 percent versus 50 percent from 1994 to 1999. The larger increase in direct investment service payments is a pattern consistent with the rise of cost-sharing agreements in the Treasury data.

A particular advantage of the BEA data is that they show distinctions by country of origin of these payments by affiliates. The summary figures in tables 3.3, 3.4, and 3.5 demonstrate that the pattern of royalty payments is sensitive to tax incentives. From 1994 to 1999 a particularly large increase occurred in royalty payments to U.S. parents from affiliates in Ireland and Singapore, as shown in table 3.3. In the case of Ireland, over the earlier five-year period (1989 to 1994), its share of all royalties received by U.S. parents from their MOFAs rose from 2.2 percent to 5.1 percent, but in the more recent period (1994 to 1999) that proportion increased to 15.0 percent. In the case of Singapore, the corresponding changes were from 1.6 percent to 3.2 percent and then to 4.6 percent.

This pattern of payments suggests that U.S. parents have found it profitable to locate intellectual property in low-tax countries, and from the additional revenue received there to pay additional royalties to the U.S. parent. This strategy will be particularly attractive if only a portion of the additional revenue is paid to the U.S. parent, and the rest is retained in the low-tax country. In the case of Ireland, royalties as a share of net income

Table 3.3   U.S. parent transactions with majority-owned affiliates

	1989 Benchmark III.X.1	1994 Benchmark III.Z.1	1999 Benchmark III.AA.1	2003 International transactions data
Royalties, received from affiliate	9,839	16,744	25,045	30,876
Europe	6,373	10,627	d	16,784
France	993	1,428	1,777	1,639
Germany	1,166	2,019	1,950	1,873
Ireland	216	859	3,761	4,065
Netherlands	652	1,397	d	1,566
Switzerland	259	446	d	1,614
United Kingdom	1,487	1,873	2,270	2,739
Asia	2,287	3,991	5,732	8,099
Japan	1,435	2,242	2,864	3,061
Singapore	158	542	1,150	2,385
Canada	1,011	1,123	1,746	2,584
Latin America and other Western Hemisphere	138	929	d	3,167
All other	30	74	296	242
Royalties, paid to affiliate	54	368	2,200	2,550
Europe	43	270	d	1,365
France	9	26	70	193
Germany	6	43	25	d
Ireland	d	4	16	21
Netherlands	0	20	d	d
United Kingdom	25	56	151	176
Asia	7	58	170	d
Japan	1	25	73	92
Singapore	1	2	19	d
Canada	4	—	113	153
Latin America and other Western Hemisphere	0	0	d	d
All other	0	0	6	36

Sources: U.S. Department of Commerce (1998, table III.X.1; 1994, table III.Z.1; 2004, table III.AA.1).
Note: d denotes suppressed for disclosure reasons.

more than doubled from 1989 to 1994, but then only increased slightly from 1994 to 1999. In 1994 before-tax income per dollar of sales, net of earnings from equity investments in other foreign affiliates was more than three times higher for Irish affiliates than for the average across all affiliates. Before the advent of check-the-box, U.S. parents already had found it attractive to shift profits to Ireland. Although that differential did not increase between 1994 and 1999, a substantial increase in the absolute amount of profits occurred. For Irish affiliates, there was a threefold increase in before-tax equity income, whereas the increase for all other affiliates was 73 percent. For evidence of the operation of hybrids, note that royalty receipts from high-tax countries such as France, Germany, or Japan have either declined or grown at rates much slower than the average. Those affiliates may still be paying royalties commensurate with their expanding sales, but they are not paying them to the U.S. parent, a consequence of hybrid structures being created.

In the case of royalty payments from one MOFA to another, disclosure limitations mean that the large increase in payments to other MOFAs shown in table 3.4 generally cannot be assigned to specific countries. More rapid growth in payments from high-tax countries might be expected on average. Disclosure limitations also make it impossible to show whether the largest increases in royalties received occurred for affiliates in low-tax countries.[7]

Consider an alternative standard to apply in assessing how MNC royalty receipts have changed over time: compare those received by MNCs as a share of all royalties received in the United States.[8] For the two benchmark years that span the 1986 tax reform, which resulted in many more MNCs having excess foreign tax credits and the opportunity to receive royalties free of any residual U.S. tax, the share of royalties received from related parties jumped from 67 percent in 1982 to 77 percent in 1989. From that peak, however, the ratio decreased to 72 percent in 1994, and it continued to decrease to 69 percent in 2003 and 63 percent in 2006. The continuation of the downward trend, long after the share of MNCs in an excess credit position had returned to earlier values, is consistent with later tax policy changes such as check-the-box.

Regarding the rapid increase in payments for other direct investment services (such as cost-sharing agreements), the receipts by U.S. parents do not show the same dominant position for Ireland and Singapore as appeared in the case of royalties received by U.S. parents. Payments from those countries did grow at an above-average rate from 1994 to 1999, but the current values still represent a small share of the total. Note, however, that the combination of cost-sharing agreements and hybrids means that a location where real production occurs, such as Ireland or Singapore, is no longer necessary to relocate intangible assets. A cost-sharing agreement with an affiliate in the Cayman Islands, for example, which then licenses a branch in Germany to produce using the technology acquired, will accomplish the desired migration of the intangible to a low-tax location. Consistent with that new opportunity, payments from holding country destinations such as the Netherlands and Switzerland hardly rose at all. Of particular significance is the table 3.5 entry for the "Other Western Hemisphere," which includes Bermuda and the Cayman Islands. For these coun-

---

7. The fact that such disclosure problems are reported for Ireland does seem surprising, given the anecdotal evidence cited at the outset over the large number of companies establishing affiliates there.
8. We thank Mihir Desai for suggesting this comparison.

Table 3.4   Royalties received and paid by affiliates

	1989 III.I.7	1994 III.J.7	1999 III.J.7
Royalties received			
Total	1,461	2,581	9,241
From affiliated persons	710	1,464	6,456
from U.S. parent	54	368	2,200
from other foreign affiliates	656	1,096	4,256
Europe	462	799	d
France	31	45	173
Germany	44	314	725
Ireland	d	d	d
Netherlands	66	76	105
Switzerland	87	87	106
UK	117	234	928
Asia	127	254	251
Japan	d	d	65
Singapore	d	d	8
From unaffiliated	750	1,116	2,785
Royalties paid			
Total	12,472	22,039	35,846
by Europe	7,871	14,708	19,949
by Ireland	469	1,496	4,640
by Asia	2,574	4,641	8,889
by Singapore	76	555	2,844
To affiliated persons	11,327	19,358	31,073
to U.S. parent	9,839	16,744	25,045
to other for affiliates	1,488	2,615	6,029
by Europe	938	2,153	d
France	188	118	242
Germany	130	d	725
Ireland	251	d	395
Netherlands	82	537	d
UK	127	187	578
by Asia	157	249	2,216
Japan	68	105	205
Singapore	d	75	d
To unaffiliated	1,145	2,681	4,773

Sources: U.S. Department of Commerce (1992, table III.J.7; 1998, table III.J.7; 2004, table III.I.7).

Note: d denotes suppressed for disclosure reasons.

tries there is a fourfold increase in payments to U.S. parents between 1994 and 1999, while the overall rate of increase is only 75 percent.

Cost-sharing agreements take time to design and implement, and the 1994 to 1999 observation period may simply not allow enough time for this influence to be more significant than the other determinants of such activity. Extending the observation period, however, may introduce other con-

Table 3.5   U.S Parent transactions with majority-owned affiliates

	1989 Benchmark III.X.4	1994 Benchmark III.Z.4	1999 Benchmark III.AA.3	2003 International transactions data
Other direct investment services, received	7,101	11,780	20,600	26,960
Europe	3,981	6,133	10,143	14,016
France	235	737	1,000	1,470
Germany	431	673	1,589	1,811
Ireland	121	316	738	1,299
Netherlands	412	1,236	1,246	1,473
Switzerland	166	510	506	872
United Kingdom	1,733	1,681	3,187	4,773
Asia and Pacific	902	2,167	4,369	5,641
Japan	246	554	1,220	1,893
Singapore	d	490	1,103	734
Canada	1,590	2,455	3,507	3,691
Latin America and other Western Hemisphere	347	763	2,222	2,577
All other	281	372	359	1,035
Other direct investment services, paid	3,810	6,477	14,939	18,605
Europe	1,938	3,521	8,472	11,234
France	290	529	715	826
Germany	479	644	767	1,153
Ireland	d	48	335	336
Netherlands	197	186	269	536
Switzerland	74	155	233	324
United Kingdom	600	1,514	4,915	6,263
Asia and Pacific	1,085	1,753	3,262	4,065
Japan	881	1,119	765	1,301
Singapore	d	152	1,025	458
Canada	267	473	942	1,149
Latin America and other Western Hemisphere	292	457	1,129	1,811
All other	228	273	480	346

Sources: U.S. Department of Commerce (1992, table III.X.4; 1998, table III.Z.4; 2004, table III.AA.3).
Note: d denotes suppressed for disclosure reasons.

founding factors, beyond the question of cyclical performance mentioned previously. In the table 3.2 observations for 1999 to 2003, the item that stands out most sharply is the growth of direct investment income. Over that same period, the share of foreign earnings distributed to U.S. owners steadily fell, from 49 percent in 1999 to 30 percent in 2003 and 22 percent in 2004. While such a strategy is consistent with the incentives previously explained, the trend undoubtedly was influenced by expectations of a change in U.S. tax law that would treat such retained earnings more favorably. Such an opportunity arose in 2004 when the U.S. Congress phased out the Extraterritorial Income Regime for taxing export income, given unfavorable rulings against it by the dispute resolution panels of the World Trade Organization. Congress passed the American Jobs Creation Act, which also reduced the U.S. tax rate on qualifying dividends from MNC operations abroad for a period of one year from the statutory rate of 35 percent to 5.25 percent. Figures for 2005 indicate that firms repatriated $33 billion more than the entire direct investment earnings for that year, resulting in a reduction in the amount of retained earnings abroad. At the same time, payments to U.S. parents in the form of royalties and other direct investment services both rose less rapidly than other measures of affiliate activity, such as gross output, sales, or property, plant and equipment. These large changes in MNC behavior demonstrate why there is a limited window over which aggregate responses can be expected to reflect a dominant role for cost-sharing agreements and hybrids alone.

3.3.3   BEA and NSF Measures of Research and Development

A final issue to address at the aggregate level is the possible role of tax considerations in the location of R&D. Although the U.S. transition to a knowledge-based economy accelerated over the latter half of the 1990s, in terms of the operations of affiliates abroad, table 3.2 shows that the increase in R&D performed abroad did not keep up with the growth in property, plant and equipment. The tax incentives for shifting R&D abroad are not straightforward. In a high-tax location the R&D would receive a valuable current deduction, as in the United States, but any income, including royalties, would be subject to the same high tax. If the company had reason to believe that the R&D project was likely to be very profitable, it might locate it in a tax haven because the value of the current deduction would become less important. This could be combined with a hybrid structure to facilitate the payment of royalties to the tax haven. On the other hand, the cost-sharing structure described may make the actual shift of R&D unnecessary.

The BEA measures of R&D performed by affiliates and by parents are reported in tables 3.6 and 3.7. The ratio of these two values is shown for two different measures, one on line 3 based on the published figures measured in U.S. dollars at current exchange rates, and one on line 4 based on an adjustment of the numerator to take account of changes in the real exchange rate that may affect the amount of research that can be performed for a given dollar expenditure. (See, e.g., National Science Foundation [2005] for a discussion of this issue.) The first set of figures suggests a small increase in the proportion of research activity carried out by affiliates. The adjustment for purchasing power parity (PPP) indicates that this increase has been somewhat larger, because the dollar was undervalued in 1994 compared to 1999. In that situation a given foreign currency expenditure in 1994 translated into more dollars and a higher ratio of affiliate effort on

Table 3.6   **BEA measures of R&D performed by parent and majority-owned affiliates, 1994–2003**

Line	1994	1999	2003
1. Parent	90,913	126,291	140,103
2. Affiliate	11,877	18,144	22,328
3. Ratio, line 2/line 1	0.131	0.144	0.159
4. Ratio, adjusted for PPP	0.114	0.131	0.152
5. Six low-tax countries	1,170	1,287	1,752
6. Ratio, line 5/line 2	.099	.071	.078
7. Four major countries	7,509	10,352	11,168
8. Ratio, line 7/line 2	.632	.571	.500

Sources: U.S. Department of Commerce (1998, table III.L.1 and III.J.1; 2004, table III.M.1 and III.J.1); Mataloni (2005).

Notes: Low-tax countries are Ireland, the Netherlands, Switzerland, Singapore, Bermuda, and the Cayman Islands. Major countries are France, Germany, the United Kingdom, and Japan.

Table 3.7   **Performance of R&D outside the United States by U.S. companies and their foreign affiliates**

Location	1995	1999	2001
Total	13,052	16,765	17,869
Four major countries	5,367	7,260	5,809
Ratio, line 2/line 1	.411	.433	.325

Source: NSF, Research and Development in Industry (table A-12, various issues).

line 3, even though the real amount of R&D work accomplished was not correspondingly larger.

The BEA data allow some breakdown of these figures by country. Two groupings are shown in table 3.6, one that reports R&D performed by affiliates in the four most important sites (France, Germany, Japan, and the United Kingdom), and one that reports R&D performed in six low-tax countries (Luxembourg is excluded from the group used in table 3.2, because in most years this entry cannot be disclosed). The share accounted for by the top four countries shown on line 6 has dropped, as R&D efforts of U.S. firms have been dispersed more broadly across the globe. At the same time line 8 shows that there is no marked increase in the share of R&D performed in low-tax countries, which would have been more likely if U.S. firms found that was the best way to ensure that future innovation of highly profitable ideas could be attributed to affiliates in such low-tax countries. The absence of such a response suggests that U.S. firms have found other ways to shift intangibles to those countries, such as the combination of hybrids and favorable cost-sharing agreements, which are more effective than carrying out R&D in countries that lack appropriate infrastructure or have limited personnel available to carry out such work.

The annual National Science Foundation (NSF) surveys give the share of total industrial R&D performed abroad by U.S. companies. The value for R&D abroad is smaller than the BEA number previously reported, and the value for R&D performed domestically is higher, given that it is not restricted to the value performed by U.S. corporations that have foreign affiliates. Therefore, the ratios calculated here are lower than those from the BEA calculated previously. Figure 3.2 shows the comparable ratios for unadjusted and PPP-adjusted R&D effort by affiliates abroad relative to domestic R&D based on these data. The unadjusted series is quite volatile and exhibits no clear trend. The adjusted series is much more regular, and the trend line suggests that if the initial value of the series is 8.6 percent, the annual increase in this value will be slightly less than a tenth of a percentage point.

The NSF data offer a limited breakdown by the country where the R&D is performed. Although no geographic detail was provided in 1994, information is given in 1995, which can be compared to similar information in 1999 to examine whether the patterns in this compilation mirror the trends shown in the BEA data. A somewhat different picture emerges, because for the same four large countries, their share of the total actually rises over the time that check-the-box was introduced, from 41 percent to 43 percent.

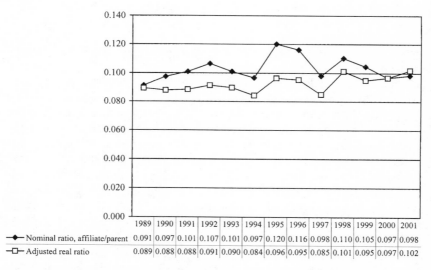

	1989	1990	1991	1992	1993	1994	1995	1996	1997	1998	1999	2000	2001
Nominal ratio, affiliate/parent	0.091	0.097	0.101	0.107	0.101	0.097	0.120	0.116	0.098	0.110	0.105	0.097	0.098
Adjusted real ratio		0.089	0.088	0.088	0.091	0.090	0.084	0.096	0.095	0.085	0.101	0.095	0.097	0.102

Fig. 3.2   NSF measures of R&D performed abroad relative to domestic R&D, nominal and adjusted for purchasing power parity

Source: NSF, Research and Development in Industry, various issues, and IMF, real effective exchange rate for the United States, based on unit labor costs.

Such a pattern again indicates that other strategies to promote the migration of intangibles must be more attractive.

The lack of a significant response by U.S. MNCs to perform more R&D in low-tax locations may suggest that the combined strategy of a hybrid and a favorable cost-sharing agreement have kept more R&D activity at home. Because the lack of response also could reflect a situation where decisions on the location of real R&D activities are not very sensitive to tax factors, the evidence here does not have an unambiguous interpretation. Studies by Hines (1993) and by Bloom, Griffith, and Van Reenen (2002) do report significant response internationally in the way firms locate their R&D activities, especially in the long run. To the extent that their findings can be generalized, the higher return to domestic R&D possible with the strategies outlined previously does make domestic locations more attractive and increase R&D activity in the United States.

3.4   Returns to Intangibles and Affiliate Payments at the Firm Level

Prior research at the country level indicates that the location of property, plant and equipment became more sensitive to host country tax rates in the 1990s than it was in the 1980s (Altshuler, Grubert, and Newlon 2001). Does a similar result hold for intangible capital in the more recent decade? Unfortunately, measuring intangible capital is not straightforward.[9] This chapter attempts to infer its migration through the examination of affiliate royalties, cost-sharing payments, and earnings and profits, based on firm-level, tax return data accessed at the U.S. Treasury Department. A cross-section of all foreign manufacturing affiliates in 1996 and 2002 provides the basis for comparing how the determinants of these payments have changed across years when a major change in tax policy occurred. This analysis does not suggest new theoretical approaches in explaining affiliate earnings and repatriations. Rather, standard models in the literature are applied to the data available for the two years previously identified.[10] The focus is not on the absolute size of the coefficients obtained, but instead on the *relative* importance of variables that determine affiliate earnings and payments to parents for royalties and for technical services.

In contrast to the country aggregates already presented, a particular advantage of the firm-specific data is that it is possible to control for characteristics of the parent firm and the affiliate when observing the affiliate's transactions. Additionally, because parent firms report the earnings and

---

9. Examples of more comprehensive attempts to measure intangibles are analyses by Hall (2001) through stock market valuations and by Cummins (2005) from analysts' profit projections. For approaches that create a stock measure of R&D from annual flow measures, see Fraumeni and Okubo (2005) and the paper by McNeil (2006), both of which must assume an appropriate rate of depreciation of intellectual property.

10. See, for example, Grubert (1998, 2001, 2003).

profits (E&P) of each affiliate—and the E&P calculation is based on income as defined in the U.S. tax code, not the host country—making comparisons across countries is more straightforward in this data set. Aside from the benefits of consistency, the E&P measure is an approximation of financial book income. The Form 5471s filed for each affiliate and the related parent corporate tax return, Form 1120, are the basis for the firm-level analysis.

With respect to important parent characteristics, a prime goal is to accurately represent the intangible assets that a parent has developed. Expenditures for advertising and R&D are two potentially important measures. The R&D measure comes from the research and experimentation tax credit claimed by the U.S. parent. This credit is restricted to research expenditures made within the United States, and the tax code specifies the ways in which such expenditures must differ from routine product maintenance and production. The parent's R&D intensity, measured as a share of sales, indicates its ability to contribute valuable technology to the affiliate.[11] This ratio, which is based on parent sales rather than assets, is generally more appropriate because it avoids errors in measurement caused by the valuation of assets at their historical book value.

In addition to the two parent characteristics that indicate the likely magnitude of intangible assets, two dummy variables represent the age of the affiliate. Younger affiliates might be expected to show a lower rate of return than those that are better established, although this influence of age may be offset by more recent aggressive strategies to locate intangibles in attractive tax locations.

3.4.1 Empirical Results

Table 3.8 presents estimates based on such data from 1996. A key point to observe is that in 1996 the return abroad to the exploitation of U.S. R&D appears to favor the U.S. parent, because the coefficient for the parent R&D per dollar of parent sales variable is 25 percent greater in the equation estimated to explain royalties per dollar of affiliate sales than in the equation to explain earnings and profits per dollar of affiliate sales (0.70 compared to 0.56). In the 2002 data the comparable coefficient in the royalty equation is now less than 60 percent of the value obtained in the earnings and profits equation (0.24 compared to 0.45). A larger share of the gain from parent technology appears to be received abroad, where it can be retained free of U.S. tax, rather then being remitted to the U.S. parent.

Also noteworthy is the importance of the parent R&D variable in the regression for technical service payments, an indicator of cost-sharing agreements. If those payments are compared to royalties, the coefficients in the

---

11. Current R&D expenditures serve as a proxy for the parent's stock of R&D or intellectual property (IP) from which higher affiliate earnings might be expected.

Table 3.8   **Determinants of CFCs profits, royalties, and technical service payments from Form 5471, U.S. Treasury data**

	1996			2002		
	Profit/ sales	Royalty/ sales	Cost share/ sales	Profit/ sales	Royalty/ sales	Cost share/ sales
Age < 5 years	0.0197	−0.0163	0.0042	−0.0004	−0.0015	0.0304
	(2.27)	(−4.23)	(1.41)	(−0.03)	(−0.32)	(6.17)
Age 5–15 years	0.0215	−0.0041	−0.0015	0.0455	−0.0007	−0.0036
	(3.77)	(−1.60)	(−0.78)	(4.21)	(−0.17)	(−0.86)
Parent R&D/sales	0.556	0.697	0.346	0.4510	.236	.4100
	(3.45)	(9.77)	(6.25)	(3.06)	(4.36)	(7.24)
Parent Advertising/sales	0.599	0.0581	0.0613	1.5530	−0.0637	−.0654
	(9.06)	(1.99)	(2.71)	(9.84)	(−1.10)	(−1.08)
Constant	.0585	0.0088	0.0015	0.0488	0.0151	−0.0055
	(14.44)	(4.92)	(1.07)	(5.87)	(4.96)	(−1.71)
Adjusted R^2	0.062	.062	0.028	0.150	0.018	0.096
Number observations	1,640	1,640	1,640	861	861	861

Note: t-statistics shown in parentheses.

1996 estimates indicate twice as great a role in determining royalty payments (0.70 compared to 0.35), whereas in 2002 those proportions had nearly reversed, with the coefficient in the cost-sharing equation now appearing much larger (0.24 compared to 0.41). While that comparison may appear exaggerated because of the major change in importance of parent R&D in the case of royalty payments, a similar comparison with the estimated coefficient from the equation for affiliate earnings and profits shows the rising importance across these two years of cost-sharing payments to compensate a parent for its contribution of valuable intellectual property.

These results are consistent with what the hybrid plus cost-sharing strategy suggests. A potential concern may be that the simplified model used to estimate the relevant coefficients for the three different dependent variables may be distorted by omitted variable bias.[12] To address important aspects of that concern, consider the additional estimates reported in table 3.9.

The royalty equation shown in column 2 includes two additional variables important in tax-planning strategies, the host country's statutory tax rate, and the parent's overall foreign tax rate on all dividend income re-

12. Another concern may be the fact that many affiliates make no royalty payments, and these zero values may make ordinary least squares (OLS) estimates less desirable than alternative approaches, such as tobit estimation or the Heckman two-step procedure. Because the proportion of affiliates that pay royalties to the U.S. parent is roughly the same in each year, (42 percent in 1996 and 45 percent in 2002), the extent of the bias from this truncation is likely to be comparable for the two years. The effect of the shrinkage from 1996 to 2002 in the number of manufacturing affiliates included in the sample is not clear.

Table 3.9   **Additional evidence of manufacturing CFCs' royalties and technical service payments from Form 5471, U.S. Treasury data, 2002**

	Royalties/ sales	Royalty/ sales	Cost share/ sales	Cost share/ sales[a]	Cost share/ sales
Age < 5 years	−0.0023	−0.0075	0.0310	−0.0002	0.0072
	(−0.47)	(−1.62)	(6.27)	(−0.07)	(1.47)
Age 5–15 years	−0.0013	−0.00009	−0.0044	−.0058	−0.0058
	(−0.32)	(−0.02)	(−1.07)	(−2.05)	(−1.49)
Parent R&D/sales	.241	.249	.4238	0.4130	0.365
	(4.66)	(4.66)	(7.51)	(10.64)	(6.75)
Parent advertising/sales	−0.0685	−0.095	−.0660	−0.0017	−0.0836
	(−1.17)	(−1.71)	(−1.09)	(−0.03)	(−1.29)
Affiliate assets/sales	0.0011	—	−0.0034	—	—
	(0.95)	—	(−1.11)	—	—
Local statutory tax rate	—	−0.127	—	—	—
	—	(−6.86)	—	—	—
Foreign tax rate on dividends	—	0.093	—	—	—
	—	(6.65)	—	—	—
Ireland	—	—	—	0.0461	0.068
	—	—	—	(5.73)	(5.55)
Singapore	—	—	—	0.0044	0.0030
	—	—	—	(0.59)	(0.22)
Pure tax havens	—	—	—	0.0424	0.143
	—	—	—	(9.31)	(15.71)
Manufacturing	—	—	—	0.0018	—
	—	—	—	(0.72)	—
Constant	0.0139	0.0316	−0.0043	−0.0059	−0.0058
	(4.24)	(3.81)	(−1.28)	(−2.62)	(−1.95)
Adjusted R^2	0.019	0.120	0.103	0.164	0.345
Number observations	849	848	848	1,393	756

Note: t-statistics shown in parentheses.
[a]Includes all sectors except financial affiliates.

ceived (as calculated from its Form 1118 to claim a foreign tax credit). The role of the statutory rate is ambiguous. To review the comments made earlier in the chapter, a parent may have an incentive to pay high royalties from a high-tax host country to benefit from the fact that they are a deductible expense. Yet a parent may choose to locate valuable intangibles in low-tax countries in order to benefit from the low taxation of its profits. Even if the affiliate pays less than an arm's-length royalty, total royalty payments from a low-tax country may be higher. The importance of such an effect in Ireland and Singapore, where actual production might occur, was shown in the aggregated BEA data reported in table 3.3. Due to the existence of hybrids, the effect also can occur in other low-tax locations, where an affiliate owns a portion of the intellectual property that it licenses for use elsewhere.

The outcome that more royalties will be paid from low-tax countries is confirmed in the firm-specific data, too, because the coefficient on the statutory tax rate is negative.

Firms are more likely to pay royalties when they can be shielded from taxation in the United States. The foreign tax rate paid or deemed paid on dividends received from all foreign affiliates is a potential indicator of a parent's likelihood of having excess foreign tax credits that would eliminate a residual tax due on repatriated royalties. Royalties, which are deductible abroad and only bear a (usually low) withholding tax in the host country, can absorb excess credits originating with highly taxed dividends. In 2000, 67 percent of royalties were shielded by credits. The positive coefficient on this variable is consistent with tax optimizing behavior of U.S. firms, as a higher tax rate applied on foreign dividends creates a larger shield to receive royalties.[13] These tax-planning variables are of interest in their own right, but the key point to observe is that while adding them to this regression does raise its overall explanatory power, the coefficient for parent R&D is hardly affected at all.

In the case of payments for technical services, a particularly noteworthy extension is to consider whether certain host countries have been more likely to attract such activity. Country dummies are included to represent low-tax countries where future product development could take place (Ireland and Singapore), as well as tax havens where the most important motive would appear to be the migration of existing intangibles (Bermuda, the Cayman Islands, and Luxembourg). While such dummies were not significant in 1996, in 2002 the coefficients for Ireland and for Bermuda, the Cayman Islands, and Luxembourg (the pure tax havens) both were quite significant and quantitatively very large. The importance of Ireland substantiates the anecdotal evidence cited in the introduction to the chapter. The importance of the pure tax havens suggests that the amount of real activity expected in the host country need not be great, and a shift of R&D activity out of the United States need not be made in order to accomplish the migration of intangibles. Those patterns appear both in the column 4 results based on all affiliates (not just those in manufacturing) and in the column 5 results based on just those affiliates in manufacturing. In the latter case, however, the role of activity in the pure tax havens is particularly large. Again, including the dummies adds to the explanatory power of the estimated equation, but it has little effect on the importance of the parent R&D variable.

13. While the tax rate on foreign dividends may not be predetermined entirely independently of a firm's planned royalty payments, it generally is the source of any excess foreign tax credits, and it is not affected by other adjustments a firm may make in determining its foreign tax credit position. Therefore, it is a better exogenous variable than the ex post excess credit position of the parent.

3.4.2   Possible Implications

The strategies identified in this chapter have already altered and are likely to continue to alter the way returns to U.S. intellectual property are reported in the future. Relative to previous practice, royalties received by U.S. parents will be smaller and income from direct investment abroad will be larger, but more of that income will be retained abroad to take advantage of the deferral of any U.S. tax liability. In addition, the way that income is allocated across countries can be expected to change more than the physical location of production.

A very rough characterization of the potential shift can be calculated from the royalties received by U.S. parent MNCs. Suppose royalties were to continue to account for the same share of direct investment income (plus royalties) that was observed prior to check-the-box regulations, which was 16 percent in the BEA data for 1994 and also for the Treasury data in 1996. Applied to the data for 2003 reported in table 3.2, that ratio implies royalties would have been $44.6 billion, rather than $30.9 billion, or an understatement of $14 billion. If that number were inflated by the continued growth of royalties reported in the balance of payments through 2006, that understatement could have risen to $20 billion. If the firms taking advantage of this strategy indeed were the ones who would have owed a residual tax in the United States, then this practice has tax revenue implications. From the standpoint of interpreting changes in the profitability of U.S. technology, measured as direct investment income per dollar of sales, a portion of the rising profit rate may represent merely a shift in how the return to technology is being reported. In the 2003 figures reported in table 3.2, that adjustment would reduce the line 12 profit rate from 8.5 percent to 8.1 percent.

While these adjustments are not inconsequential, the greatest difference occurs in considering the impact across host countries. When most of this adjustment is concentrated in a small number of small countries, the consequent impact on GDP attributed to those countries can be much larger. The BEA reports the value added of U.S. MOFAs as a percentage of GDP for host countries such as Ireland (18.5 percent) and Singapore (15.0 percent), but not for the Cayman Islands or other pure tax havens. Several billion dollars attributed to those countries, if similarly recorded by their national income accountants, would raise skepticism over the reported growth in GDP and lead economists to pay more attention instead to gross national income (GNI).

With respect to the location of real activity, the strategy results in less incentive to relocate R&D activity outside the United States, because the intangible assets created can emigrate. Production that utilizes the technology made possible by U.S. R&D will more likely occur outside of the United States and in high-tax host countries. For example, if an affiliate previously produced in Germany and paid a royalty to the U.S. parent, then a residual U.S. tax would have been paid, a disincentive to produce in Germany. If the German affiliate becomes a branch of an affiliate in the Cayman Islands, then production in Germany becomes more attractive, because the tax burden in Germany is reduced by the payment of a royalty, but there is no additional tax on that royalty in the Cayman Islands. To the extent that affiliates in low-tax countries pay a smaller share of their total returns as royalties, they gain less from this strategy.

3.5   Conclusions

Substantial migration of intangible assets from the United States to foreign countries appears to have occurred over the last decade. That trend has been facilitated by the ability of U.S. firms to create hybrid entities in their affiliates abroad and to reach favorable cost-sharing agreements with them. This strategy was particularly encouraged by the U.S. adoption of check-the-box regulations in 1997, which resulted in intersubsidiary payments between affiliates incorporated in one foreign country and their branches operating in another foreign country becoming invisible to the IRS.

An expected result is that there will be more rapid growth of earning and profits in foreign affiliates relative to the royalties they pay to U.S. parents, as companies have an incentive to retain profits abroad in low-tax countries where they can avoid any residual U.S. tax. Although that pattern was observed in aggregate Treasury data over the 1996 to 2000 period, for the longer 1996 to 2002 period royalties grew more rapidly than affiliate earnings and profits, a possible reflection of the cyclical nature of earnings and profits. Payments by affiliates to U.S. parents for technical services, as would be called for under cost-sharing agreements, have increased rapidly even through the longer 2002 observation period. In the process of certain affiliates becoming invisible to the U.S. Treasury, affiliates in low-tax countries with little potential to produce goods and services now claim major increases in their plant and equipment, presumably an indication of the capital held by their branches in high-tax countries.

The BEA data, which retain the identity of individual establishments even if they are part of a hybrid structure, show more than double the growth of royalty payments from one affiliate to another compared to the growth in royalty payments to the U.S. parent. Such a trend might not be so surprising if there had been a major shift in R&D out of the United States to low-tax locations abroad, but evidence from the BEA and from the NSF especially suggest that this has not occurred. In fact, over the 1995 to 1999 period the NSF data show the traditional importance of high-tax OECD locations has increased.

Analysis of firm-specific data from the U.S. Treasury demonstrates how changes in the returns to parent R&D have shifted when years before check-the-box was adopted are compared to subsequent years. In regression analysis with 1996 tax returns, parent R&D contributed more to royalty payments to U.S. parents than it did to affiliate earnings and profits. In 2002, however, the importance of parent R&D had switched in these two regressions, with it now playing a larger role in earnings and profits relative to royalties. That outcome is consistent with the tax avoidance strategies explained in section 3.2. Also, the relative importance of cost-sharing payments rose over this period, relative to both royalties and earnings and profits. Cost-sharing payments from affiliates in Ireland and from pure tax havens (Bermuda, the Cayman Islands, and Luxembourg) are particularly significant, both economically and statistically. Thus, the ability to carry out research and development in the affiliate does not appear to be a key prerequisite for the successful pursuit of this strategy, and alleged pressures to relocate research and development activity abroad for tax reasons have not been so compelling.

References

Altshuler, R., and H. Grubert. 2005. The three parties in the race to the bottom: Host countries, home countries, and multinational companies. CESifo Working Paper Series no. 1613, December.

Altshuler, R., H. Grubert, and S. Newlon. 2001. Has U.S. investment abroad become more sensitive to tax rates? In *International taxation and multinational activity,* ed., James Hines, 9–32. Chicago: University of Chicago Press.

Bloom, N., R. Griffith, and J. Van Reenen. 2002. Do R&D tax credits work? Evidence from a panel of countries 1979–1997. *Journal of Public Economics* 85 (1): 1–31.

Borga, M., and R. Mataloni. 2001. Direct investment positions for 2000. *Survey of Current Business* 81 (July): 16–29.

Cummins, J. 2005. A new approach to the valuation of intangible capital. In *Measuring capital in the new economy,* ed. C. Corrado, J. Haltiwanger, and D. Sichel, 47–73. Chicago: University of Chicago Press.

Fraumeni, B., and S. Okubo. 2005. R&D in the national income and product accounts. In *Measuring capital in the new economy,* ed. C. Corrado, J. Haltiwanger, and D. Sichel, 275–316. Chicago: University of Chicago Press.

Grubert, H. 1998. Taxes and the division of foreign operating earnings among royalties, interest, dividends and retained earnings. *Journal of Public Economics* 68 (2): 269–90.

———. 2001. Enacting dividend exemption and tax revenue. *National Tax Journal* 54 (4).

———. 2003. Intangible income, intercompany transactions, income shifting and the choice of location. *National Tax Journal* 56 (1, Part 2)

Grubert, H., W. Randolph, and D. Rousslang. 1996. Country and multinational company responses to the tax reform act of 1986. *National Tax Journal* 49 (3): 341–58.

Hall, R. 2001. The stock market and capital accumulation. *American Economic Review* 91 (5): 1185–1200.

Hines, J. 1993. On the sensitivity of R&D to delicate tax changes: The tax behavior of U.S. multinationals in the 1980s. In *Studies in international taxation,* ed. A. Giovannini, G. Hubbard, and J. Slemrod, 149–87. Chicago: University of Chicago Press.

Internal Revenue Code. 2005. Reg-144615-02. *Internal Revenue Bulletin* (August).

Koncz, J., and D. Yorgason. 2005. Direct investment positions for 2004. *Survey of Current Business* July: 40–53.

Mataloni, R. 2005. U.S. Multinational companies operations in 2003. *Survey of Current Business* 85 (7):22.

McNeil, L. 2006. International trade and economic growth: A methodology for estimating cross-border R&D spillovers. Paper presented at CRIW Conference on International Service Flows. 28–29 April, Bethesda, MD.

Mutti, J., and H. Grubert. 1998. The significance of international tax rules for sourcing income: The relationship between income taxes and trade taxes. In *Geography and ownership as bases for economic accounting,* ed., R .E. Baldwin, R. E. Lipsey, and J. D. Richardson, 259–80. Chicago: University of Chicago Press.

National Science Foundation, Division of Science Resources Statistics. 2005. *National patterns of research and development resources: 2003,* NSF 05-308. Arlington, VA: Brandon Shackelford.

Nutter, S. 2001. Controlled foreign corporations, 1996. *Statistics of income bulletin* 20 (4): 134–73.

Office of Tax Policy, U.S. Treasury Department. 2000. *The deferral of income earned through U.S. controlled foreign corporations.* Policy Study 36, December.

Simpson, G. R. 2005. Irish subsidiary lets microsoft slash taxes in U.S. and Europe. *Wall Street Journal,* November 7.

U.S. Department of Commerce, Bureau of Economic Analysis. 1992. *U.S. direct investment abroad: 1989 benchmark survey, final results.* Washinton, D.C.: GPO.

———. 1998. *U.S. direct investment abroad: 1994 benchmark survey, final results.* Washington, D.C.: GPO.

———.2004. *U.S. direct investment abroad: 1999 benchmark survey, final results.* Washington, D.C.: GPO.

Measuring Payments for the Supply and Use of Intellectual Property

Carol A. Robbins

4.1 Introduction

A clear set of metrics is critical for economists and policymakers interested in understanding the role of intangibles, intellectual property, and innovation in international trade and the domestic economy. In an influential paper, Corrado, Hulten, and Sichel (2005) estimate that business investment in intangible capital is as large as business investment in tangible capital—approximately $1 trillion dollars per year, or about 10 percent of gross domestic product (GDP). Despite this substantial magnitude, comprehensive data about these investments and the incomes they generate are scarce.

Renewed interest in economic measurement of intangibles and intellectual property (IP) comes from multiple directions. Knowledge-intensive businesses are increasingly interested in developing external markets for their intellectual property, and these markets will depend on consistent valuation measures.[1] Policymakers are interested in metrics to evaluate the impact of intangibles, intellectual property, and innovation on economic

Carol A. Robbins is an economist at the U.S. Bureau of Economic Analysis.

The views expressed in this paper are those of the author and do not necessarily reflect those of the Bureau of Economic Analysis. Thanks to Steve Landefeld, Fritz Foley, Amy Jo Glass, Ned Howenstine, Ralph Kozlow, Maria Borga, Marshall Reinsdorf, Sue Okubo, and two anonymous referees for helpful comments.

1. See, for example, the *Global Innovation Outlook 2.0 Report, Building a New IP Marketplace* (http://domino.research.ibm.com/comm/www_innovate.nsf/images/gio-ip/$FILE/building_a _new_ip_marketplace-report.pdf) and *The Intellectual Property Marketplace, Emerging Transactions and Investment Vehicles* (2007), by J. E. Malackowski, K. Cardoza, C. Gray, and R. Conroy, in *The Licensing Journal*, 27 (2): 1–11.

growth and competitiveness.[2] The upcoming revision of the System of National Accounts, which provides guidelines for internationally comparable measures of national economic activity, will change the treatment R&D expenditures to recognize these expenditures as the acquisition of an intangible asset. In preparation for this change, the Bureau of Economic Analysis (BEA) and national accountants in other countries are developing methodologies to incorporate R&D activity as an intangible asset into their accounts. Thus market-based information on the value of intangible assets and the measurement of payments and receipts for their use becomes increasingly important. However, existing survey data are sparse, and these data limitations will have a greater impact on the accounts than in the past.

This chapter provides the first detailed estimation of U.S. corporate income from the use of intellectual property, commonly called royalties and licensing fees. The existing Federal data sources for this income are described and U.S. corporate receipts for the use of this intellectual property component of intangibles are organized into licensing commodities and decomposed by industrial sector. Data are presented for 2002, the most recent year that Economic Census industry receipts are available.

The income received by owners of intellectual property assets in these licensing or leasing-type transactions is on a par with the income received by owners of a large component of tangible assets in similar transactions. After adjusting U.S. corporate royalty income in 2002 for natural resource royalties and income earned by foreign sources, domestic income from licensing intellectual property is estimated to be approximately $92 billion dollars; this compares with rental and leasing receipts for automobiles, machinery, computers, and other equipment of $95.1 billion dollars in 2002.

Based on available evidence, payments and receipts for the use of IP through royalties and licensing fees are growing rapidly. Internal Revenue Service data from corporate income tax returns indicate that U.S. corporations received $115.9 billion dollars in gross royalty receipts in 2002 (IRS 2005b). Figure 4.1 shows this royalty income for the years 1994 to 2004; the growth has been an average rate of 11 percent per year since 1994. This compares with an average growth rate of 6 percent per year for gross output of all private services producing industries over the same time period.[3]

The contribution to economic measurement that this chapter makes is a set of preliminary estimates for a series of IP-licensing transactions that are not separately reported in existing statistical data for large parts of the domestic economy. This income comes from four types of service commodi-

2. See, for example, the January 2008 *Report to the Secretary of Commerce's Advisory Committee on Measuring Innovation in the 21st Century,* available at http://www.innovationmetrics.gov/Innovation%20Measurement%2001-08.pdf.
3. Based on BEA GDP-by-industry data.

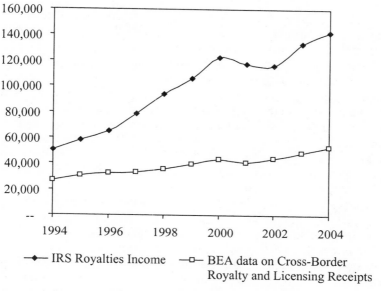

Fig. 4.1   U.S. Corporate royalties income and cross-border royalty and licensing receipts (in millions of dollars)

Sources: BEA: U.S. international services: Cross-border trade 1986–2005, royalties and license fees, Table 4. IRS: Statistics of income, "Returns of Active Corporations 1994–2004, Table 6—Balance sheet, income statement, tax, and selected other items, by major industry."

ties—the use of IP protected as (a) industrial property by patents and trade secrets, (b) trademarks, (c) copyrights, and (d) business format franchises. Order-of-magnitude estimates of domestically earned corporate income for these commodities in 2002 are approximately $50 billion dollars for licensing of industrial property, $20 billion for licensing of trademarks, and $10 billion each for the licensing of copyrights and franchises.

In the past, this lack of data had little impact on GDP because domestic business spending on intangibles as well as spending for its use or rental through royalties and licensing fees has been considered intermediate services. When the acquisition of intangibles is treated as investment instead of as intermediate services, these business expenditures become part of the investment component of GDP. The Bureau of Economic recognized computer software as investment in 1999 and currently plans to change the treatment of R&D activity to investment in the national accounts around 2012.

While some long-term data improvements are already underway, recognizing R&D as investment in the national accounts will require improved data sources. Because many intangibles are not sold in market transactions, there is limited opportunity to develop market-based price data to value these intangibles directly. With the exception of the comprehensive expenditure data on R&D available from the National Science Foundation, information is also limited on expenditures for the creation of intangibles. In U.S. Census-reported data, most of these costs of creation and purchase are bundled together with other business expenses. However, royalties and licensing fees provide data on direct transactions for the use of technology, patents, trade secrets, trademarks, copyrights, and franchises. Because of the scarcity of information to consistently value intangibles, royalties and licensing transactions are important indicators. Expanded data collection of royalties and licensing fees for the domestic economy would provide quantitative measures of innovation and the value of intangibles, as well as improve the accuracy of the national economic accounts.

This chapter proceeds from here in the following way. Section 4.2 provides background information and defines the measurement concepts used in the paper. Section 4.3 outlines the kind of information about transactions for the use of IP that would be valuable for economic measurement and describes the issues that complicate this measurement. Section 4.4 describes the Federal statistical and administrative data that measure income from these transactions, and discusses the specific limitations of these data. The tables described in this section compare three Federal data sources on royalties income, BEA international services transaction data, Economic Census data, and IRS Statistics of Income data. This section also provides previously unreleased tables showing an industry sector distribution of royalties and licensing fees in unaffiliated transactions for 2002. Section 4.5 presents order-of-magnitude estimates that show corporate receipts by industrial sector for the use of IP by type—an area where current data are incomplete. Section 4.6 discusses the limitations of these estimates and the direction for future work in measurement. An appendix details the estimation methodology.

4.2 Background

4.2.1 Intangibles and Intangible Assets

For our purposes, *intangibles* are the useful result of productive activity that exists separately from any material object.[4] These products include literary, artistic, and entertainment creations, scientific and engineering innovations, as well as ideas for new products. Specific examples include a musical score, a collection of poetry, the plans for new machinery or structures, computer programs, and formulas for new chemical or pharmaceutical products.

---

4. This separate existence qualification is similar to the definition of intangibles in Hill (1999). Hill's paper also includes a thoughtful discussion of the economic distinctions between goods and services and their relationship to intangibles.

For other analytical purposes, intangibles are sometimes defined more broadly. For example, in the Brookings Task Force Report on Intangibles, *Unseen Wealth,* the scope of intangibles includes qualities that are inseparable from the people who work with them. For firms, intangibles can include human capital, core competencies, organizational capital, and relationship capital (Blair and Wallman 2001). Since these important qualities cannot be separately rented or licensed, they are outside the scope of this chapter.

4.2.2   Intangible Assets, Intellectual Property, and Types of Protection

When intangibles meet the additional qualification that they produce *future* economic benefits, some economists identify these intangibles as assets (Corrado, Hulten, and Sichel 2005). However, both financial accounting standards and national economic accounting standards require a further qualification for assets: that the owner has the power to control the asset and obtain the economic benefits.[5] It is this more restrictive accounting concept of an asset that is used here.

The term *intellectual property* in this paper refers to intangible assets that are protected by a legal right to exclude others from their use. Types of intellectual property protection include copyrights, patents, trademarks, trade secrets, and sui generis rights. These protections are briefly described:

Copyrights

Copyrights are legal rights that protect original works of authorship. In the United States, these rights are granted by registering the original work with the Copyright Office of the Library of Congress. The types of works protected are (a) literary works; (b) performing art works, such as musical works, dramatic works, motion pictures, pantomimes, and choreographic works; (c) periodicals and magazines; (d) visual artworks; (e) sound recordings; (f) architectural works; and (g) computer programs (United States Copyright Office 2004).

Patents

Patents protect useful inventions and designs of three types: utility patents, design patents, and plant patents. Most U.S. patents are utility patents, which provide for a limited time the exclusive right to a nonobvious invention with a practical application. These inventions can be processes, machines, manufactures, and compositions of matter. In addition to utility patents, the United States grants patents on designs and on newly invented or developed species of living plants. In each case, the character-

---

5. System of National Accounts 1993, Paragraph 13.12. The International Accounting Standards paragraph 38.8 definition is cited in Lev 2001, 151.

istic quality of a patent is novelty. Patents are granted by the U.S. Patent and Trademark Office in the Department of Commerce (USPTO 2005).

Trade Secrets

A trade secret is any valuable and not generally known information that is kept secret by its owner and has economic value attached to its secrecy. The secret may be a formula, pattern, compilation, program, device, method, or technique. Protection is granted by the Uniform Trade Secrets Act, and is fundamentally different from that of a patent or copyright in that the secret information need never enter the domain of public knowledge (NCCUSL 1985).

Trademarks

Trademarks are brand names and the symbols associated with them. Like patents, trademarks are granted by the U.S. Patent and Trademark Office of the Department of Commerce. The characteristic quality of a trademarked good is distinctiveness; trademarked goods or services must be able to be distinguished from those of another producer. While the right to exclusive use of the symbol does not expire, trademarks that become a generic term lose their right to protection.

Sui Generis Rights

These are laws that provide legal protection to industrial designs. In the United States, protection for the layout of microelectronic circuitry on a semiconductor chip mask is established by the Semiconductor Chip Protection Act (SCPA) of 1984, which grants the owner exclusive use for ten years. Similarly, the Vessel Hull Design Protection Act (VHDPA) of 1998 provides legal protection for the design of ship hulls (United States Copyright Office 2004).

4.2.3   Service Commodities That Correspond to Types of IP Protection

When a firm receives royalty income for the use of intangibles protected as intellectual property, what economic activity has taken place? While the purchase of all the rights of ownership of intellectual property is the purchase of an intangible asset rather than a service transaction, the purchase of only the right to use these assets for a limited time is considered here to be the purchase of a service commodity. Because intangibles provide inputs to the production process in much the same way that labor, tangible capital assets, and computer software provide service flows, this service commodity is the rental of an intangible asset that is protected as intellectual property.

How can these service commodities be identified? The method described here is based on type of intellectual property protection and the way the IP

Table 4.1   **Examples of receipts for different types of IP-related commodities**

Commodity type	Patent or trade secret protection of industrial property	Copyright protection for artistic or literary expression
IP-protected intangible assets	Trade secret or patented industrial process and all future rights	Copyrighted song, including all future rights
IP-derived products	Industrial products produced with protected technology—for example, chemicals	Purchase of a recording of the soundtrack
Licensing of IP assets	Licensing a patented or secret industrial process for use in production	Licensing the right to use a musical score in commercial advertising

is used in production. This framework is proposed by Mohr and Murphy (2002) for product classification. The following example for two types of IP, a patented industrial process innovation and a copyrighted musical composition, shows the relationship of these service commodities to other IP-related commodities. For each type, separate commodities can be produced: (a) the IP assets, (b) goods with IP embedded in them, and (c) leasing and subleasing of the assets for economic use.

In table 4.1, the first commodity, IP-protected intangible assets, is purchased in a transaction where the purchaser gains all future rights to the IP. In contrast, when IP-derived products are purchased, the right to reproduce the product for further sale is not part of the transaction. The third commodity, licensing or leasing of intellectual property, allows the IP to be used in production without conveying ownership.

Transactions for computer software can fall into any of these categories. When software is mass produced and shrink-wrapped, BEA considers it a good; otherwise, it is a service. Payment for the right to use software with a useful life of a year or more without the additional right to reproduce is considered the purchase of a fixed capital asset. However, end-user software licenses are not generally the same type of licensing transaction as the IP-licensing commodity described previously because these end-user licenses do not allow for the software to be reproduced.

This set of examples uses the type of intellectual property protection to distinguish different types of commodities. This approach works well to separate industrial processes and formulas from artistic and literary originals, and it corresponds to the way that existing data are collected. Additionally, although this commodity framework is consistent with the treatment of royalties in the System of National Accounts, it is not the only way royalty transactions could be treated. Other ways to classify these IP-licensing commodities are plausible, such as based on the technology involved.

4.3   Uses of Data on IP-Related Income and Some Measurement Issues

4.3.1   What Would We Like to Know about Intellectual Property
Income and IP-Licensing Commodities?

This section describes the questions we are interested in.

1. For international transactions, which countries are earning income from trade in intangibles and their use, and which countries are paying? Are these transactions predominantly within multinational corporations, or between unrelated companies?

2. What type of intellectual property do these transactions cover? Can transactions for the purchase of IP be separated from transactions for the use of IP and transactions for IP-embedded products?

3. What industries are most heavily engaged in these transactions?

4. Within the domestic economy, which industries produce intellectual property and intangible assets as part of their output, and how much do they produce? Which industries earn incomes from the licensing of these assets, and how much do they earn?

5. Which industries purchase or pay to use intellectual property and intangible assets produced by other industries, and how much do they pay?

6. In order to understand the impact of intangibles and their use on output and productivity, can we specify a unit of output and a price index for deflation?

Existing statistical data provide information about the first question, and a partial answer to the second and third questions. When the transactions are components of international trade, they are reported in BEA's international services trade data. For the domestic economy, data are available for royalty and licensing receipts for some industries, but no information is available about industry expenditures. The IRS statistics of income provide industry data on total royalty income, but these data include income from foreign sources and lack a breakdown by type of IP. The result is an incomplete picture of this activity for the domestic economy.

4.3.2   What Is the Relevant Unit of Output
for IP-Licensing Commodities?

One of the most basic questions for economic measurement is to specify a unit of output that can be priced over time in order to create measures of real output. The difficulties with pricing intangibles—for example, R&D output—are well known. Many intangibles are by their nature unique, and a patented innovation can represent a marginal improvement in the quality of an existing product, or can create an entirely different category of products.

The unit of output associated with the rental or licensing of intellectual property is similarly difficult to specify. Licensing of industrial processes can range from precommercial designs to the right to duplicate a fully developed device, system, or service (Razgaitus 2003). Accordingly, the degree of risk will vary, as will the structure of the payments. These royalty payments often have two parts—a lump sum payment made up front, and a running royalty that is calculated as a percent of receipts. Further, technology licensing is often a bundled commodity, consisting of both the rights to use the intellectual property as well as proprietary technical information and access to technical support on how to use the licensed technology. Similarly, business format franchises often combine the right to use a trademark together with manuals and other forms of instruction on how to operate the business.

Royalty rates for musical performance vary based on whether the royalty is for performance or recording, and on the negotiating strength or market power of the artist. Royalty rates for trademarks vary by type of product and the market power of the brand; a range of 3 percent to 10 percent is reported in Razgaitus (2003).

What price index should be used, then, for these transactions? Neither the Bureau of Labor Statistics nor the BEA has yet developed price indexes for these commodities. Khatchadourian and Wiesner (2006) note that the heterogeneity of the transactions categorized as royalties and license fees complicate the development of a price index. The BEA currently deflates the output of the intangible assets rental industry (Lessors of Nonfinancial Intangible Assets [except Copyrighted Works]) with a much broader deflator, the implicit price deflator for personal consumption expenditures.

4.3.3   Transfer Prices and Intra-Firm Transactions for Intellectual Property

Given the complexity of identifying and pricing intellectual property licensing transactions, it is not surprising that most intellectual property is used within a firm. Within a firm the benefits of integration, lower transactions costs, and the avoidance of monopoly rents in input markets can be realized. In most cases, these internal transactions are unobserved, and pricing information is closely held.

Transfer prices are used to allocate costs and profits within the firm. These estimated prices for intrafirm transactions are also needed for taxation and economic accounting purposes when commodities cross international borders. The general rule of transfer pricing is to estimate the price that would be observed if the transaction was an arms-length transaction between unrelated parties. Three different approaches are frequently used: estimating the cost of production or acquisition of the products, estimating the price that would obtain if the product were purchased in external market based on comparable products, and estimating the net present value of the income the product will earn.

Although the external market-based approach is preferred as the most objective, for intellectual property it is difficult and sometimes impossible to identify comparable products. The cost approach and the income approach may yield very different estimates from each other, depending on the time horizon applied to the benefits, the discounting for uncertainty, and the extent to which the benefits of intangibles can be separately estimated. For products that have been in development for a long time and are part of a family of related products, it may also be difficult to separately identify the costs of a particular intellectual property commodity. Finally, the historical cost of creating the commodity may be quite different from what it would cost to recreate the product in current dollars with current technology. For more discussion of these transfer pricing issues for intangibles, see Bos (2003).

When the transferred commodity is a private good (nonjoint in consumption and excludable), the optimal transfer price is found by setting the marginal benefit the affiliated firm receives from using the input to the parent firm's marginal cost in producing the transferred commodity. However, the public-goods characteristics of intangibles and intellectual property also make them more subject to ambiguity in the setting of transfer prices than would be the case for tangible goods, and thus more vulnerable to manipulation based on disparities in international tax regimes. In an example that is directly relevant to royalty payments for the use of intellectual property between multinational parents and their foreign affiliates, Bos (2003) shows that when the commodity being transferred has public-goods characteristics (joint in consumption and nonexcludable), multinationals can set the royalty payments independently of revenue, cost, technology, or market conditions. Since the transferred commodity is a public good that can be used in more than one location simultaneously, the marginal cost of the intangible is set equal to the sum of the marginal benefits for the entire firm, and the profit-maximizing royalty payment from the affiliate is indeterminate.

The implications of transfer pricing issues and differences in tax regimes for international trade data are further discussed in this volume by both Lipsey (2006) and by Mutti and Grubert (2006). Mutti and Grubert describe the use of hybrid entities by multinational corporations to move their intellectual property to other countries in order to lower their overall tax liabilities. A firm that anticipates future royalties from an R&D activity can set up a cost-sharing agreement with a foreign subsidiary, whereby the foreign subsidiary buys a stake in a patent before it generates income. The subsidiary earns profits from the use of intellectual property in a low-tax location, while royalties and licensing fees, which are deductible from the firm's tax liabilities, are paid in a high tax location. As Lipsey points out, the location of intangibles is particularly susceptible to the kinds of manipulation that lead to distortions in service trade data. Lipsey illustrates the very high ratio of capital income to labor for the low-tax location Bermuda (13.007), compared to an average for Europe of 0.439.

4.3.4   Cross-Licensing and Measurement of Income from the Use of Intellectual Property

In order to understand the full magnitude of the flows of IP-licensing commodities in the economy, data on the gross values of licensing transactions would clearly be preferred. However, reported cash income from licensing and other royalties is an underestimate of the gross value of the transactions to each firm and an underestimate of the magnitude of the flows of IP between firms and industries because of the prevalence of cross-licensing agreements. In cross-licensing agreements, firms exchange access to other's patent portfolios. Where the estimated value of the patent portfolios differ, a net royalty is paid by the owner of the lesser-valued portfolio. If the value of each party's relevant intellectual property is considered to be equivalent, then the cross-licensing agreement involves no direct exchange of payment.

Although cross-licensing agreements reflect exchanges of economic value that should, in concept, be incorporated into BEA's measures of industry and commodity output, their full extent is unknown. Cross-licensing agreements are particularly important in industries like electronics, semiconductors, aircraft, and automobiles (Grindley and Teece 1997).

The general rule for income that is subject to taxation by the Internal Revenue Code is that gross income includes income from whatever source derived, and that barter income is subject to taxation. However, the practice of IRS has been to value as income only the net amount of cross-licensing transactions. After asking for comments on the treatment of cross-licensing arrangements, a 2007 revenue procedure rules that for unrelated parties, qualified patent cross-licensing arrangements are to be valued for income purposes as by a "net consideration method." That is to say, reported income from the agreement should be the cash received net of the license rights and intangible property from the other party. The revenue procedure goes on to say that this treatment is consistent with the way that generally accepted accounting principles treat income from cross licenses (IRS 2008).

With respect to BEA's international service transactions data, the two-way (gross) value of the transactions rather than the net value is what is both intended to be measured (Ascher and Whichard 1999) and what is specified in the survey instructions (BEA 2006). Although no specific instructions are provided to respondents on the treatment of cross-licensing agreements for patents, companies are instructed in the BEA's survey forms to value reciprocal exchanges at market rates and report them as a receipt and an offsetting payment. Since this treatment as a gross measure is different from the way that many firms report cross-licensing receipts on their income tax forms, it is possible that the values reported to BEA from cross-licensing agreements are net rather than gross measures and thus underestimate the value of the transaction. Economic Census data reflect actual cash receipts, and thus also reflect a net concept of licensing income. All of this suggests that the existing measures of income from IP-licensing underestimate the full extent of this activity.

4.3.5   Industry Classification Based on Enterprise or Establishment

Although royalty and licensing income is received by many industries, for one industry the North American Industrial Classification system (NAICS) characterizes this activity as primary—Lessors of Nonfinancial Intangible Assets (except Copyrighted Works)—NAICS 533. This industry rents intangibles and intellectual property such as patents, trademarks, brand names, and business formats used under franchise agreements.

One example of a firm in this intangible asset rental industry comes from a review of publicly available Securities and Exchange Commission filings. Competitive Technologies of Fairfield, Connecticut describes itself as a full service technology transfer and licensing provider, representing technologies invented by corporations, individuals, and universities. Although its income is mainly derived from license and royalty fees, the firm also gains some of its income as shares of royalty legal awards that result from litigation (Competitive Technologies SEC Filing, 2007). It is this latter activity that has earned some firms in this industry their characterization as "patent trolls." Both IRS data from corporate income tax returns and BEA international services trade data are collected at the unit of the firm or enterprise (BEA, 1998).

Other data, for example Economic Census data on royalty receipts, are classified by industry based on the activity of individual establishments. These separate establishments are single-unit companies as well as separate workplaces that comprise a multi-unit company. When industry classification is assigned based on establishment activity, the establishments in the intangible asset rental industry may be attached to any industry but perform the economic activity of leasing the firm's intangibles and managing its intellectual property portfolio. Economic Census data currently identifies a small number of establishment types as receiving IP-licensing income.

4.4   Existing Statistical and Administrative Data

Existing data from BEA, Census, and the IRS Statistics of Income program can be used to estimate income from the use of intellectual property and IP-licensing commodities. These three data sources are compared in table 4.2. Reported receipts differ greatly. While BEA data report $44.5 billion dollars in receipts by U.S. firms from foreigners, in both affiliated and unaffiliated transactions, Census data, which include both receipts for exports and for domestic transactions, report just $24 billion dollars. A third source, administrative records data from the IRS based on corporate income tax returns, reports royalty income of $115.9 billion dollars for U.S. firms.

While each source covers many of the same types of IP-licensing trans-

Table 4.2   **Summary of data sources for royalty-related receipts and income**

Data source	Receipts or income for 2002 (in billions of dollars)	Coverage	Scope of royalty and licensing rights
BEA international services transactions, receipts for royalties and licensing fees	44.5	U.S. receipts in international transactions from both affiliated and unaffiliated entities. Data are also available on payments	Industrial processes, including patents and trade secrets; books, records, tapes; broadcasting and recording of live events; franchises; trademarks; general use computer software; other intangibles; includes purchase as well as use of these intangibles
Economic Census royalty receipts	24.0	U.S. establishments with paid employees, Census data only available for selected industries	Content published on the Internet; musical compositions; master recordings; television program rights; oil and petroleum; patent leasing and licensing; franchise leasing and licensing; software, music, motion picture, and other intellectual property; literary works, musical recordings, filmed entertainment, and other cultural works
IRS royalty income	115.9	Gross royalty income for U.S. corporations, including income from foreign sources	Books, stories, and plays; copyrights; trademarks, formulas, and patents; exploitation of natural resources

Sources: BEA: U.S. International Services: Cross-Border Trade 1986–2005, Royalties and License Fees, Table. 4.

Census: 2002 Economic Census, "Subject Series," Table 1, Product Lines

IRS: Statistics of Income, "Returns of Active Corporations 1994–2004, Table 6–Balance Sheet, Income Statement, Tax, and Selected Other Items, by Major Industry."

actions, the IRS data covers royalty income from all enterprises with tax liability, while the BEA data covers only the portion of licensing income earned in transactions with foreign residents. In contrast, the Economic Census data separately reports income for the sale of licensing commodities for only a limited number of establishment types. Licensing income received by other establishments may be included in Census-reported total receipts for other industries, but is not separately identified.

4.4.1 BEA International Royalties Data

For the United States, international transactions in royalties and license fees are an important part of technology trade in services. In 2002, royalties and licensing fees made up about 16 percent of the value of exports for total private services, and about 9 percent of the imports. However, for affiliated trade, these ratios are higher; 44 percent for exports and 33 percent for imports. In BEA data, these royalties and licensing fees are combined with payments and receipts for the purchase of intangible assets and thus present undifferentiated income for the IP-licensing commodities along with income from the sale of assets. For this combination of transactions, BEA collects data separately on affiliated transactions, those conducted between multinational parent firms and their subsidiaries in a different country, and on unaffiliated transactions, those conducted between unrelated parties in different countries.

The largest share of service trade reflected by royalties and license fees is between the U.S. and other developed countries; this is true for both affiliated and unaffiliated trade (table 4.3). Tax-related effects on the trade flows in affiliated trade data are suggested by the presence of low-tax locations Bermuda and the Netherlands as top-five recipients of large shares of royalties and licensing fees.

Table 4.4 shows the magnitudes of transactions in three broad categories: between unaffiliated parties, transactions between U.S. parents from their foreign affiliates, and transactions between U.S. affiliates and their foreign parents. The majority of royalty and licensing transactions by dollar value are between multinational corporations and their affiliates. These royalties and licensing fees are paid for the use of several types of intangibles, but only the smaller component of the transactions—trade between unaffiliated parties—is currently collected and can be analyzed by type.[6]

---

6. In 2008 BEA released data on royalties and licensing fees by type of IP for affiliated transactions covering the years 2006 and 2007. While the breakdown by type of IP is not available for affiliated transactions for years prior to 2006, BEA's 1989 Benchmark Survey of U.S. Direct Investment Abroad does provide a breakdown for receipts and payments between U.S. parents and their foreign affiliates (Table I.X.I). These measures are not directly comparable to current data because the large category of general use computer software was not part of the estimates in 1989. In 1989, 88.5 percent of the receipts from foreign affiliates to U.S. parents were for the use of industrial processes (patents, formulas, and trade secrets). In that same year the share for receipts for the same categories from unaffiliated transactions was substantially lower, 68.1 percent.

Table 4.3   Royalties and license fees, between the U.S. and top five countries, 2002 (in millions of dollars)

Receipts				Payments			
Affiliated		Unaffiliated		Affiliated		Unaffiliated	
Total	32,770	Total	11,738	Total	15,134	Total	4,219
Top five		Top five		Top five		Top five	
United Kingdom	3,402	Japan	3,236	Japan	4,566	France	688
Japan	3,102	Germany	1,073	Germany	1,710	United Kingdom	512
Canada	2,407	Korea, Republic of	939	Switzerland	1,701	Switzerland	472
Singapore	2,337	United Kingdom	906	Netherlands	1,443	Japan	440
Germany	2,052	Canada	707	Bermuda	1,357	Other European countries*	409

*European countries other than Belgium-Luxembourg, France, Germany, Italy, Netherlands, Norway, Spain, Sweden, Switzerland, United Kingdom.

Source: BEA: U.S. International Services: Cross-Border Trade 1986–2005, Royalties and License Fees, Table 4. http://www.bea.gov/bea/di/1006serv/tab4.xls.

Table 4.4   Cross-border royalties and license fees, 2002 (in millions of dollars)

	Total	Industrial processes[a]	Books, records, and tapes[b]	Broadcasting and recording of live events[c]	Business format franchise fees[d]	Trademarks[e]	General use computer software[f]	Other intangibles[g]
Receipts								
Between unaffiliated parties	11,738	4,039	516	296	542	1,284	4,408	651
By U.S. parents from their foreign affiliates	29,656							
By U.S. affiliates from their foreign parents	3,114							
Receipts total	44,508							
Payments								
Unaffiliated payments	4,219	2,049	301	906	3	283	487	190
By U.S. parents to their foreign affiliates	2,925							
By U.S. affiliates to their foreign parents	12,209							
Payments total	19,353							

Source: Data are from BEA's International Investment Division and are available on the BEA website as U.S. International Services: Cross-border Trade, 1986–2005; Table 4, Royalties and License Fees 1986–2005. These data are collected on BE-577 for transactions between U.S. parents and their foreign affiliates and the BE-605 for transactions between U.S. affiliates and their foreign parents.

Note: In 2002, royalties and licensing fees made up about 16 percent of the value of exports for total private services, and about 9 percent of the imports.

[a]This includes the use, sale, or purchase of intangibles that are used in connection to the production of goods as well as technology licensing fees, royalties, and payments for the use of patents, trade secrets, and other proprietary rights used in the production of goods. The category includes payments to foreign governments for the maintenance of patent rights.

[b]This includes the rights to perform, broadcast, reproduce, and sell copyrighted material and other intellectual property in the form of books, compact discs, and audiotapes.

[c]This includes the rights to record or broadcast live artistic performances, sports events, and other live events.

[d]Business-format franchising is an ongoing business relationship between a franchisor and franchisee that includes not only the product, service, or trademark, but also the business format.

[e]This includes rights to sell under a trademark, brand name, or signature, including Internet domain name registration.

[f]This includes rights to distribute general-use software and rights to reproduce or use general-use computer software electronically produced from a master copy. It includes licensing fees for reproducing copies of general-use software for local area network computer systems and excludes prepackaged software as well as custom software and programming services.

[g]Intangibles not elsewhere classified, including rights to secure capacity for communications carriers.

Table 4.5   **Receipts of royalties and license fees from unaffiliated foreigners, by industry sector and type of intangible, 2002 (in millions of dollars)**

	Total	Industrial processes	Other[a]
All industries	11,738	4,039	7,699
Manufacturing	3,585	2,809	777
Distributive services[b]	271	29	242
Information[c]	(D)	(D)	4,368
Professional, scientific, and technical industries[d]	1,159	342	818
Other industries[e]	(D)	(D)	(D)

Source: Special tabulation by BEA's International Investment Division.

Note: (D) Suppressed to avoid disclosure of data of individual companies.

[a]Other consists of payments for rights related to books, records, and tapes; broadcasting and recording of live events; franchise fees; trademarks; general-use computer software; and other intangibles.

[b]Includes wholesale and retail trade and transportation.

[c]Includes publishing, software publishing, motion picture, and sound recording, broadcasting, telecommunications, and Internet services.

[d]Includes computer system design and related services, and scientific research and development services.

[e]Other industries include unallocated payments.

The BEA data on transactions between unaffiliated parties are collected by industry classification as well as by type of intangible. For these measures, the industry assignment is the industry of the consolidated enterprise, which may consist of more than one establishment. Tables 4.5 and 4.6 provide a previously unpublished summary of the industry distributions of unaffiliated payments and receipts prepared by BEA's International Investment Division for 2002, which shows the magnitude of receipts and payments for IP for industrial processes protected by patents and trades secrets in the manufacturing sector.

The underlying confidential data used for these tables were analyzed by the author under an agreement with BEA's International Investment Division not to disclose respondent-specific information. The following observations are based on analysis of this underlying data.[7] In 2002 the manufacturing sector received $2.8 billion in unaffiliated international receipts for use of IP for industrial processes protected by patents and trades secrets; this accounted for about three quarters of the sector's $3.6 billion receipts. Within professional, scientific, and technical industries, a little less than half of the $1.2 billion dollars of receipts are for general-use software, and more than a quarter are for IP for industrial processes protected by

7. Annual Survey of Royalties, License Fees, and Other Receipts and Payments for Intangible Rights between U.S. and Unaffiliated Foreign Persons (BE-93).

Table 4.6   Payments of royalties and license fees to unaffiliated foreigners, by industry sector and type of intangible, 2002 (in millions of dollars)

	Total	Industrial processes	Other[a]
All industries	4,219	2,049	2,170
Manufacturing	2,933	1,776	1,157
Distributive services[b]	66	(D)	(D)
Information[c]	596	2	594
Professional, scientific, and technical industries[d]	(D)	(D)	85
Other industries[e]	332	59	273

Source: Special tabulation by BEA's International Investment Division.

Note: (D) Suppressed to avoid disclosure of data of individual companies.

[a]Other consists of payments for rights related to books, records, and tapes; broadcasting and recording of live events; franchise fees; trademarks; general-use computer software; and other intangibles.

[b]Includes wholesale and retail trade and transportation.

[c]Includes publishing, software publishing, motion picture, and sound recording, broadcasting, telecommunications, and Internet services.

[d]Includes computer system design and related services, and scientific research and development services.

[e]Other industries include unallocated payments.

patents and trades secrets. The industry within the sector receiving the largest share of industrial process royalties is the Scientific Research and Development industry (NAICS 5417), followed by Architectural, Engineering, and Related Services (NAICS 5413).

Table 4.6 shows the corresponding data for industry payments of royalties and licensing fees by industry sector. This is the only information from the Federal statistical system about which industry sectors are *using* intellectual property through licensing and royalty transactions, and only international transactions are reported. In 2002, manufacturing industries paid out $2.9 billion of the total of $4.2 billion, with 61 percent of that going for IP for industrial processes protected by patents and trade secrets. The majority of these payments are reported by firms in the pharmaceutical industry. Although the data show overall that U.S. firms receive substantially higher royalty receipts from foreign parties than they pay out in unaffiliated transactions, for the pharmaceutical industry this pattern is reversed. U.S. pharmaceutical firms make substantially higher payments to foreign parties for industrial processes than they receive.

4.4.2   Economic Census Data on Payments for the Use of IP

For the domestic economy, data on the industry structure and types of transactions for intellectual property are relatively limited. Receipts for IP-licensing service commodities, such as licensing and leasing of patents,

Table 4.7   **Economic Census Data on royalty receipts, 2002 (in millions of dollars)**

Industry		Total royalties
1. Publishing industries except Internet (511)		24,039
Sale or licensing of rights to content	460	460
2. Motion picture and sound recording industries (512)		2,408
Royalties, license fees, and other payments for authorizing the use of musical compositions	1,665	
Receipts for sales, leasing, and licensing fees for master recordings	743	
3. Telecommunications (517)		5,207
Television program rights	5,207	
4. Internet service providers, web search portals, data processing services (518)		71
Sale or licensing of rights to content	71	
5. Other information services (519)		80
Sale or licensing of rights to content	80	
6. Lessors of nonfinancial intangible assets (533)		15,959
Oil and petroleum	366	
Patent leasing/licensing	7,761	
Franchise leasing/licensing	5,960	
Copyright leasing/licensing	1,490	
All other	382	
7. Management of companies and enterprises (551)		5,055
Sales, license fees, royalties, and other payments from the marketing of intangible property such as software, music, motion pictures, and other intellectual property	3,788	
Franchise sales and fees	1,267	
8. Performing arts, spectator sports, and other related works (711)		2,686
Amounts received from royalties, licensing fees, and residual fees from literary works, musical recordings and compositions, filmed entertainment, and other cultural works	2,686	
9. Museums, historical sites, and similar institutions (712)		46
Amounts received from royalties, licensing fees, and residual fees from literary works, musical recordings and compositions, filmed entertainment, and other cultural works	46	

Source: These royalty receipts are found in the 2002 Economic Census publications titled "Subject Series," and are drawn in each case from Table 1, Product Lines.

copyrights, and franchises, are only reported for a relatively small number of industries. For most industries, IP-licensing receipts are not separately reported in Census receipts.

Economic Census data are classified by industries based on the activity of the establishments rather than the activity of the enterprise; Census collects licensing receipts from the types of establishments considered most likely to receive them. These royalty receipts are shown in table 4.7 for

2002. The $24 billion in Census-measured royalty receipts are received by establishments in four areas of the economy: information (51),[8] real estate and rental leasing (53), management of companies and enterprises (551), and arts, entertainment, and recreation (71). Census data identify the IP-licensing service commodities at varying levels of aggregation. For the establishment-based industry with the most royalty receipts, the intangible asset rental industry (533), product lines are identified based on type of intangible. Establishments in this industry collected $7.8 billion dollars in receipts for the leasing and licensing of patents, $6.0 billion dollars for the leasing and licensing of franchises, and $1.5 billion for the leasing and licensing of copyrights.

Compared to the BEA international services trade data, Economic Census data show $20 billion dollars *less* in royalties and licensing receipts, yet the scope of these transactions includes both domestic sales and exports. Several factors are responsible for this. In the Economic Census data, IP licensing receipts are separately reported for fewer types of IP. Data on these transactions in the Census data are only collected for a few industries and the establishments that actually collect royalties within large firms may not be receiving Census forms with these questions. Additionally, because Census data reflect measures of receipts, cross-licensing payments would be reported as net payments, while some cross-licensing may be reported as gross within the BEA trade data.

4.4.3   Royalty Receipts from Corporate Tax Returns

Although Census provides royalty receipts for information and service industries, for statistical purposes that require a more comprehensive estimate of royalty income, the Internal Revenue Service's Statistics of Income (SOI) data from corporate income tax returns are sometimes used because they cover all industries. One place where this occurs is in BEA's Input-Output accounts, to measure the commodity output for the leasing of non-financial intangible assets.

Royalties are one component of income reported in U.S. Corporation Income Tax Return Form 1120, and SOI data for active corporations are estimated from a sample of these corporate income tax returns. For 2002 the returns of active corporations reported gross royalty receipts of $115.9 billion dollars. Table 4.8 presents royalty income by industry sector and then sorted by magnitude of industry royalty receipts. All manufacturing industries together receive $72.7 billion dollars in royalty income and three manufacturing industries make up 46 percent of the $115.9 billion total, or $53.3 billion dollars. These industries are computer and electronic product manufacturing, chemical manufacturing, and transportation equipment manufacturing.

---

8. The two-digit number in parentheses is the NAICS industry sector.

Table 4.8   **IRS royalties by industry and percent of total receipts from royalties, 2002 (in millions of dollars)**

Sector		
Manufacturing		72,767
Distributive services[a]		13,112
Information[b]		13,463
Finance and insurance		2,362
Professional and business services[c]		6,654
Total royalty income from all industries		115,860
Average percentage of total receipts from royalties	0.59%	

Industry	Royalty receipts	Percentage of receipts from royalties (%)
Computer and electronic product manufacturing	23,317	4.3
Chemical manufacturing, including pharmaceuticals	20,482	3.1
Transportation equipment manufacturing	9,406	1.1
Publishing industries	4,755	2.2
Professional, scientific, and technical services	4,692	0.7
Beverage and tobacco product manufacturing	4,305	2.0
Food services and drinking places	3,564	1.3
Wholesale trade, nondurable goods	3,190	0.3
Machinery manufacturing	2,516	0.8
Motion picture and sound recording industries	2,422	2.8
Broadcasting, radio and television, cable networks, and program distribution	2,308	3.2
Electrical equipment, appliance, and component manufacturing	2,246	0.9
Building materials and garden equipment and supplies dealers	2,226	1.2
Fabricated metal product manufacturing	2,168	0.8
Miscellaneous manufacturing	1,996	1.1
Internet service providers, web search portals, and data processing services	1,952	2.4
Telecommunications	1,922	0.5
Food manufacturing	1,864	0.5
Accommodation	1,456	1.2
Food, beverage, and liquor stores	1,434	0.3
Administrative and support services	1,370	0.5
Wholesale trade, durable goods	1,365	0.1
General merchandise stores	1,350	0.3

(continued)

This IRS royalty income reported on the corporate income tax returns include foreign sources of royalties income, and for manufacturing industries, this foreign income is substantial. While data are not collected for the royalty and licensing component alone, SOI data reported for firms that report foreign tax credits indicate that the chemical manufacturing industry, for example, report $9.1 billion dollars in combined foreign income for rents,

Table 4.8   (continued)

Industry	Royalty receipts	Percentage of receipts from royalties (%)
Other royalty-intensive industries		
Paper manufacturing	923	0.6
Mining	923	0.6
Other transportation and support activities	805	0.6
Apparel manufacturing	641	0.9
Sporting goods, hobby, book, and music stores	482	0.6
Printing and related support services	481	0.5
Lessors of nonfinancial intangible assets	384	34.1
Educational services	215	0.8
Other information services	87	0.4
Leather and allied product manufacturing	68	0.7
Internet publishing and broadcasting	17	0.5
All other industries	8,526	

Source: Internal Revenue Service (2005), Statistics of Income—2002, Corporation Income Tax Returns, Table 6—Balance Sheet, Income Statement, Tax, and Selected Other Items, by Major Industry.

[a]Includes wholesale and retail trade and transportation.

[b]Includes publishing, software publishing, motion picture and sound recording, broadcasting, telecommunications, and Internet services.

[c]Includes computer system design and related services and scientific research and development services.

royalties, and licensing fees in 2002.[9] This income from foreign sources represents royalty income that is not in scope for either the Economic Census data or the BEA data on U.S. receipts of royalties and licensing fees, but the royalty component is not separable from the rents in the IRS data.

The right-hand column of table 4.8 presents the share of total U.S. corporate income tax receipts that are comprised of royalties. This gives an indication of the role of licensing of intangibles and intellectual property as a source of direct income. For all industries the average is 0.6 percent, with most of the higher shares coming from industries in the manufacturing and information sectors. The industry in the IRS data that receives the largest share of receipts from royalties is Lessors of Nonfinancial Intangible Assets (the intangibles rental industry). In 2002, according to the SOI data, this industry received 34 percent of its IRS reported income from royalties.

In the 2002 Economic Census data, establishments classified in this industry have receipts totaling $16 billion dollars, while the IRS-based receipts total just $384 million dollars. The IRS royalty income data, like the BEA service trade data, are collected on the basis of consolidated operations of the firm rather than by type of establishment; thus they only include *firms* classified in the Lessors of Nonfinancial Intangible Assets in-

9. IRS Table 2. U.S. Corporation Returns with a Foreign Tax Credit, 2002

dustry. The IRS-based receipts for this industry reflect receipts from corporations that identify their primary source of receipts as leasing of nonfinancial intangible assets; for example, the technology transfer firms discussed earlier. The $16 billion dollars in the Census data represent establishments that may be attached to any industry but perform the economic activity of leasing the firm's intangibles and managing its intellectual property portfolio. This suggests that most of the Census receipts in the intangible asset rental industry (533) are collected in establishments that are part of other industries and exist to license the industry's intangibles, rather than in firms classified as in the intangible asset rental industry.

4.5   Order-of-Magnitude Estimates

Piecing together information from each of these three Federal data sources, we can develop a composite picture of industry income from IP-licensing commodities. Both IRS data and BEA international services trade data are organized into industries based on the aggregated activity of the firm rather than establishments. The IRS data provide a broad total for each industry, and the unaffiliated component of international trade data provide information for an industry-based distribution of income across IP-licensing commodity types for international transactions alone.

The use of the industry-based distribution of income for unaffiliated transactions assumes that while differences in tax policies can affect the *volume* of royalties' transactions for particular countries' transactions, the distribution of these transactions across *types* of IP income from foreign residents is the similar to the distribution of domestic income across types of IP. In this case, the BEA data described earlier by type of intangible can be used to create a proxy distribution for royalties for each industry.

Although the arms-length nature of unaffiliated royalty transactions renders them less susceptible than affiliated transactions to tax-related distortions, unrelated firms have more at risk from a foreign licensee in terms of misappropriation of intellectual property than entities within the same multinational corporation. Substantively different institutional environments with respect to intellectual property could make the distribution of international royalties from unaffiliated transactions unsuitable for distributing domestic income into types of I-O licensing commodities.

The economics literature has produced mixed results on the relationship between international licensing and the strength of international property rights regimes.[10] Nevertheless, data show that the bulk of the international licensing transactions are not with countries with very different intellectual property rights regimes compared to the United States. Table 4.9 shows a five-point scale index on a set of minimum international standards for patenting rights from Park and Wagh for 2000, where the United States re-

10. See Park and Lippoldt (2004) for a review.

Table 4.9   Patent rights index and the distribution of receipts for royalties and licensing fees from unaffiliated entities, 2002

Countries	Index of patent rights**	Industrial processes receipts (in millions)	Distribution of receipts*				
			Use of industrial processes (%)	Books, records, and tapes, broadcasting and recording of live events (%)	Franchise fees (%)	Trademarks (%)	Other intangibles (%)
All countries		4039	55.1	11.1	7.4	17.5	8.9
Countries with index of 3.9 or above		3293	62.6	11.8	6.2	19.0	0.5
Japan	4.19	1273	69.4	5.3	2.0	22.9	0.4
Korea, Republic of	4.2	613	87.9	2.2	4.2	5.0	0.7
Germany	4.52	389	71.1	14.8	5.7	8.4	near 0
Taiwan	NA	336	89.8	2.9	3.2	4.0	0
United Kingdom	4.19	236	47.6	21.2	10.7	20.6	0
Other Europe	NA	199	51.8	14.6	10.9	20.3	2.3
France	4.05	193	61.3	18.1	4.1	16.5	0
Canada	3.9	138	34.5	19.0	15.0	31.5	0
Switzerland	4.05	123	83.7	7.5	1.4	7.5	near 0
Italy	4.33	101	45.9	21.8	8.6	21.4	2.3
Belgium-Luxembourg	4.04	49	59.0	8.4	7.2	25.3	0
Mexico	2.86	40	30.3	21.2	13.6	34.8	0
Sweden	4.38	40	38.8	15.5	7.8	37.9	0
Australia	4.19	37	32.7	22.1	12.4	32.7	0
China	2.48	33	47.1	8.6	5.7	30.0	8.6
Singapore	4.05	28	63.6	4.5	15.9	11.4	4.5

Netherlands	4.38	26	40.6	32.8	6.3	20.3	0
Other Western hemisphere	NA	19	35.8	13.2	35.8	15.1	near 0
Indonesia	2.27	19	57.6	6.1	27.3	9.1	near 0
Hong Kong	2.9	18	29.5	8.2	26.2	36.1	0
Israel	4.05	16	35.6	22.2	15.6	13.3	13.3
Other Asia and Pacific, except Taiwan	NA	13	25.0	7.7	46.2	21.2	0
South Africa	4.05	13	43.3	23.3	13.3	20.0	0
Thailand	2.24	13	50.0	7.7	19.2	23.1	near 0
India	2.18	13	61.9	4.8	4.8	28.6	near 0
Other Middle East	NA	12	23.5	5.9	51.0	9.8	9.8
Spain	4.05	11	13.4	36.6	20.7	29.3	0
Brazil	3.05	10	23.3	46.5	4.7	25.6	0
Other Latin America	NA	6	9.1	22.7	28.8	39.4	0
Saudi Arabia	NA	5	13.2	5.3	26.3	7.9	47.4
Venezuela	2.9	5	15.2	42.4	12.1	30.3	0
New Zealand	4	4	20.0	45.0	20.0	30.3	0
Norway	3.9	3	14.3	19.0	42.9	15.0	0
Other Africa	NA	3	21.4	7.1	50.0	23.8	0
Chile	3.41	2	10.5	36.8	15.8	21.4	0
Argentina	3.33	1	10.0	40.0	10.0	36.8	0

*This distribution reflects the use of the data for allocating IRS receipts, and excludes the receipts for general-use software because the IRS royalties are assumed to reflect passive income. Data are from BEA's International Investment Division, available on the BEA website as U.S. International Services: Cross Border Trade, 1986–2004; Table 4, Royalties and License Fees 1986–2004, collected on BE-577 for transactions between U.S. parents and their foreign affiliates and the BE-605 for transactions between U.S. affiliates and their foreign parents. **Index of Patent Rights for 2000, from Park and Wagh.

ceives five points. The table is sorted from highest to lowest by the value of IP-licensing receipts for the use of industrial processes protected by patents and trade secrets; countries with an index ranking of 3.9 or above provided 80 to 90 percent of these receipts. This suggests that the potential for distortion in the distribution of types of IP based on differences in IP regimes is minimal.

Under the working assumption that international demand for IP-licensing commodities is similar to domestic demand, table 4.10 presents order-of-magnitude estimates by industry sector and IP type that show the supply of four IP-related service commodities, based on the totals from IRS corporate royalty receipts. The industry totals are directly from the IRS data on U.S. corporate royalty income. The distributions across types of intangible are based on the available Census data, the distribution of BEA royalty and licensing receipts from unpublished data aggregated to match the IRS industries, and estimates based on franchise industry data. Greater detail on the estimation procedure is provided in the Appendix.

Table 4.10 shows that the manufacturing sector receives the vast majority of all licensing receipts for the right to use IP for industrial processes protected by patents and trade secrets. The largest recipients are the chemical manufacturing industry and the computer and electronic product manufacturing industry. Industries in manufacturing also receive substantial receipts for the use of both trademarks and franchises. Both of these are in large part received in the beverage manufacturing industry. For the distributive services sector, the largest share of IP-licensing service commodity receipts are from the use of trademarks and franchises. Within distributive services, retail trade receipts are divided between trademarks and franchise receipts, and wholesale trade receipts are predominantly trademark related and are earned by apparel wholesalers and grocery wholesalers. Within professional and business services, the scientific research and development services industry receives a large share of the licensing receipts for the use of IP protected as industrial property. Within the "other industries" category, franchise-licensing receipts are particularly substantial for accommodation and food service industries.

How reasonable are these order-of-magnitude estimates? Arora, Fosfuri, and Gambardella (2002) estimate the average value of the global market for technology licensing and related transactions at $36 billion dollars a year in the 1990s, a value they suggest is likely an underestimate. They note that available estimates for the late 1990s, including Degnan (1998), are in the range of $35 to $50 billion dollars. The method used in this paper for 2002 produces estimates for U.S. corporate supply of IP-licensing of industrial processes at $27.4 billion dollars for 1995, $29.4 billion dollars for 1996, and $31.8 billion dollars for 1997.

While these estimates are in the range of others, to account for the foreign component of the IRS corporate income, the estimates should be ad-

Table 4.10 Order-of-magnitude distribution of IRS receipts for types of IP-licensing service commodities across industry sectors, 2002 (in billions of dollars)

Sector	Licensing of rights to use IP protected as industrial property	Licensing of rights to use IP protected by trademarks	Licensing of rights to use IP protected by copyright	Licensing of rights to use a business format under a franchise	Payments for rights to use natural resources and other intangibles	IRS royalties total
Manufacturing	59.5	9.4	1.0	2.9	—	72.8
Distributive services (wholesale, retail, and transportation)	1.0	6.9	0.1	5.1	—	13.1
Information	1.9	4.9	6.6	0.0	0.1	13.5
Finance and insurance	0.2	0.7	0.0	1.4	0.0	2.4
Professional and business services	3.0	0.2	1.6	1.5	0.4	6.7
Other industries	1.0	0.7	0.1	4.8	0.8	7.5
Total	66.6	22.8	9.4	15.7	1.3	115.9

justed downward to reflect income earned domestically. Because the only available information for the adjustment, data on firms reporting foreign tax credits, combines royalty incomes with rents, the exact proportion due to royalties is not estimable. An order-of-magnitude adjustment is made using the ratio of royalties to rents in the total U.S. corporate income; roughly 20 percent of U.S. royalty income is attributed to foreign sources. This twenty percent adjustment leaves order-of-magnitude estimates for domestically earned corporate income of approximately $50 billion dollars for licensing of industrial property, $20 billion for licensing of trademarks, and $10 billion each for the licensing of copyrights, and franchises.

In terms of the distributions, the results from one of the questions on a 2003 survey of intellectual property managers by Cockburn and Henderson (CH 2004) can also be used for comparison purposes, and suggest that the distribution of the order-of-magnitude estimates are also in the right range. The IP managers were asked to estimate the fractions of total monetary value represented by their different IP assets, and the distribution was as follows: patents, 44.5 percent; trade secrets, 15.7 percent; copyrights, 8.8 percent; trademarks, 18.2 percent; know-how, 13.9 percent.[11] The approximations in table 4.10 of IP-licensing receipts (excluding payments for natural resources and other intangibles) are distributed similarly. The share represented by industrial process licensing (patents and trade secrets) represents 58.1 percent of the total, compared to 60.2 percent in the CH survey for patents and trade secrets; copyrights represent 8.2 percent of the total, compared to 8.8 percent in the CH survey. The comparison for trademarks is 19.9 percent compared to 18.2 percent in the CH survey. On the whole this evidence suggests that the IP-licensing commodity distributions are in the right order of magnitude.

4.6   Summary and Conclusion

Using a variety of sources, broad estimates of IP-licensing transactions have been presented for 2002 using a product classification for IP-licensing commodities. The allocation method is simple and relies on the assumption that industries sell the same bundle of IP-licensing commodities domestically that they sell internationally. The analysis shows that manufacturing firms are important suppliers of IP-licensing commodities.

In the year 2002, U.S. corporations reported $115.9 billion dollars in royalty income to the IRS, and about $67 billion dollars of this was earned for the use of industrial property protected by patents and trade secrets.

---

11. They had eighty-one usable surveys from managers of intellectual property and reported that 44 percent of these identified their corporations as IT and communications, 22 percent from the chemical industry, 14 percent from life sciences, 16 percent from mechanical sectors, and less than 7 percent from financial and service sectors. This total slightly exceeds 100 percent, as do the shares of IP assets, likely due to rounding and some respondents not claiming all types of IP assets.

Existing data sources do not allow the domestic component of this royalty income to be separately measured by industry, either at the firm or the establishment level. Using simple allocation methods we estimate that the domestic component of this corporate income is approximately $50 billion dollars for licensing of industrial property, $20 billion for licensing of trademarks, $9 billion for the licensing of copyrights, and $10 billion for franchises.

These order-of-magnitude estimates provide a preliminary indication of the role of market transactions for IP licensing in the economy. The estimates were created using broad distribution ratios to allocate royalty and licensing income into the categories of information that would be analytically useful, but are no substitute for comprehensive survey data. The sector and commodity presentation indicate the kinds of information that would provide quantitative measures of innovation and the value of intangibles, as well as improve the accuracy of the national economic accounts.

Data improvements in many areas will be needed in order to develop more precise estimates and to more fully measure the role of intangible investments in the economy. For expenditures on scientific R&D and some additional information on industrial process-related transactions, a substantial redesign is underway at the National Science Foundation for business R&D activity. For other intangibles, such as artistic and entertainment creations, comprehensive data are not yet available to estimate the scope of this investment.

By improving the collection of data for the observable, market transactions in the domestic economy for the use of intangibles that are protected as intellectual property and thus earn royalties and licensing fees, we can get a much clearer picture of the role of intangibles in economic growth. The taxonomy used in this chapter parses intangibles by type of IP protection and allows for improved estimates of industry output.

What else is needed?

- A clear separation of receipts for the purchase of intangibles and intellectual property from receipts for the use of these assets.
- Broader measurement of receipts for the use of IP by industry within the domestic economy.
- Separate accounting of industry expenses for the use of IP from other business expenses.
- Data on the estimated value of cross-licensing agreements and greater transparency about whether reported licensing receipts reflect net or gross flows.
- Better identification of copyright and patent royalties and licensing fees that are for the right to reproduce computer software programs.
- Improved price indexes for IP-licensing commodities.

More accurate accounting will likely require enterprise-based surveys that focus directly on the creation of IP assets and transactions for their use, including cross-licensing. This kind of information would resolve a great deal of the ambiguity surrounding the estimates of unmeasured components of economic activity and provide a means to trace technology flows across industries. For economists and policymakers interested in understanding the impact of intangibles on the economy, improved measurement is the essential next step.

Appendix
Methodology for the Order-of-Magnitude Estimates

Internal Revenue Service reported royalties are assumed to be a combination of (a) licensing of rights to use IP protected as industrial property by patents and trade secrets, (b) licensing of rights to use IP protected by trademarks, (c) licensing of rights to use IP protected by copyright, (d) licensing of rights to use a business format under a franchise, and (e) royalties for the use of natural resources. The BEA data on international royalty transactions for unaffiliated entities cover a somewhat different spectrum of intangibles and are adjusted before being used to infer the distribution of IP-licensing commodities. Six of the seven types of intangibles covered in the BEA data match the available definition of scope of the IRS royalties. The IRS royalties are assumed to be primarily passive income rather than payments for a service or a good, and are assumed to exclude electronically transmitted software as well as end-user license fees for shrink-wrapped software. The BEA international transactions data for royalties and licensing fees category includes a category for both the rights to reproduce software and for the general use of electronically transmitted software. While the rights to reproduce software are clearly within the scope of the IP-related service commodities, the latter use is more closely aligned to the licensing of software for end use as a final expenditure and more likely to be the majority of the payments and receipts. Excluding computer software licensing, receipts for royalties and licensing fees for the use of industrial processes makes up 55.1 percent of the unaffiliated royalty receipts for 2002 (calculated from data shown in table 4.4).

The distribution of IP-licensing commodities by industry is based on Census data where it was available, franchise royalty estimates, and the distribution of the BEA international receipts. The IRS-based royalties were allocated by type of IP, using BEA international receipts for the purchase and use of intangibles.[12] For industries without international transactions,

---

12. In a related exercise, Degnan (1998) used the IRS industry distribution of royalties to parse out the likely industry distribution of unaffiliated receipts. This paper estimates types of IP-licensing commodity by industry.

mostly in the service industries, royalties were evenly split between trademarks and franchise royalties. Payments for the right to use natural resources are combined with "Other Intangibles," a category that includes spectrum rights for broadcasting. This category represents payments for the use of non-IP intangibles. All IRS royalties in agriculture and utilities were attributed to natural resources as were a large share of mining royalties.

Estimating Franchise Licensing Fees

Royalties for the use of business format franchises are estimated for this chapter with data on total industry receipts, the share of total industry receipts represented by franchisee-operated establishments, and average annual royalty payments. Where data are not available from Federal statistical sources, data from the franchise industry are used.[13]

For Food Service and Drinking Places, the franchisee share of the industry is available in the 2002 Economic Census. Using the franchisee share of industry receipts for full and limited service restaurants and industry association royalty rates yields an estimate of $3.2 billion for 2002.[14] This estimate is relatively close to the IRS reported royalties for this industry—$3.6 billion, and suggests that most of the IRS royalties for this industry can be attributed to domestic franchise royalties.

For the Accommodation industry, using franchise industry estimates of the share of the industry represented by franchisee-owned businesses and the average royalty rate, the Accommodation industry (NAICS 721) received franchise royalties of about $1.2 billion in 2002.[15] This compares to an IRS royalty receipts total of $1.6 billion for NAICS 721, Accommodation.

13. A summary of royalty fees developed from the Uniform Franchise Offering Circulars that twelve states require for business format franchise offerings is combined with information on the share of industry payroll in establishments that pay franchise royalties. Because the published level of industry aggregation of the data is not particularly detailed, this information is most useful for Food Service and Drinking Places and Accommodation, the two industries with very large royalty receipts.

14. 2002 Economic Census, Sector 72, Accommodation and Food Service, Miscellaneous Subject Series Table 7. Frandata Corporation (2000) provides annual royalty rate estimates of 4.2 percent for full service restaurants and 4.7 percent for limited service restaurants as part of its royalty analysis in the Profile of Franchising. For more information on franchise royalty structure, see pages 122–51. Because the initial study was created for 1998, Frandata provided the author with updated royalty rates for 2004, and the rates were averaged to create a usable royalty rate for 2002.

15. Economic Impact of Franchised Businesses (EIFB), Price WaterhouseCoopers (2004), these data were created for 2001. A reality check for Full and Limited Service Restaurants suggests that the EIFB numbers are in the right range; EIFB suggests that 10.8 percent of payroll for full service restaurants was in franchise-operated establishments. The Census ratio based on receipts is 12.4 percent. For limited service restaurants the EIFB ratio is 44.3 percent and the Census ratio is 43.9 percent. These EIFB estimates are based on three sources: U.S. Census's County Business Patterns, Nonemployer Statistics, and the IMPLAN model.

References

Arora, A., A. Fosfuri, and A. Gambardella. 2001. Specialized technology suppliers, international spillovers and investment: Evidence from the chemical industry. *Journal of Development Economics* 65 (1):31–54.

———. 2002. *Markets for technology.* Cambridge, MA: The MIT Press.

Ascher, B., and O. G. Whichard. 1991. Developing a Data system for international sales of services: Progress, problems, and prospects. In *International economic transactions, issues in measurement and empirical research,* 203–236. ed. P. Hooper and J. D. Richardson. Chicago: University of Chicago Press.

Blair, M. M., and S. M. H. Wallman. 2001. *Unseen wealth.* Washington, D.C.: Brookings Institution.

Bos, M. 2003. *International transfer pricing: The valuation of intangible assets.* Kluwer Law International, The Hague, The Netherlands.

Cockburn, I. M., and R. Henderson. 2004. Survey results from the 2003 Intellectual Property Owners Association survey on strategic management of intellectual property. Available at http://www.ipo.org/articles.

Competitive Technologies, Inc. 2007. 10-Q Report filed for the quarter ending October 31, 2007: http://www.sec.gov/edgar/searchedgar/companysearch.html.

Corrado, C., C. Hulten, and D. Sichel. 2005. Measuring capital and technology: An expanded framework. In *Measuring capital in the new economy,* ed. C. Corrado, J. Haltiwanger, and D. Sichel, 11–41. Chicago: University of Chicago Press.

Degnan, S. A. 1998. *Macro view of R&D, licensing. Les Nouvelles,* Journal of the Licensing Executives Society (December) 144–47.

Frandata Corporation. 2000. *A profile of franchising.* Arlington, VA: Frandata.

Grindley, P. C., and D. J. Teece. 1997. Managing intellectual capital: Licensing and cross-licensing in semiconductors and electronics. *California Management Review* 39 (2) 8–41.

Hill, P. 1999. Tangibles, intangibles, and services: a new taxonomy for the classification of output. *Canadian Journal of Economics* 32 (2): 426–37.

Internal Revenue Service. 2005a. Statistics of Income, Returns of active corporations, table 6—Balance sheet, income statement, tax, and selected other items, by major industry. Available at http://www.irs.gov/taxstats/article/0,,id=170692,00 .html.

———. 2005b. Statistics of income, table 2—U.S. corporation returns with a foreign tax credit, 2002: Foreign income, deductions, and taxes, by industrial sector and by type of foreign income for which separate credit was computed. Available at http://www.irs.gov/pub/irs-soi/02it02fi.xls.

———. 2007. *Code of Federal Regulations. Title 26, Chapter 1.* Washington, D.C.: GPO.

———. 2008a. Bulletin 2007-10, March 5, 2007. Revenue Procedure 2007-23. Washington, D.C.: GPO.

Lev, B. 2001. *Intangibles, management, measurement, and reporting.* Washington, D.C.: Brookings Institution.

Lipsey, R. E. 2006. Measuring international trade in services. Prepared for the NBER/CRIW Conference on International Service Flows, Washington, D.C., April 28, 2006.

Khatchadourian, K., and A. Wiesner. 2006. International price program's (IPP's) services price indexes." Prepared for the NBER/CRIW Conference on International Service Flows, Washington, D.C., April 28, 2006.

Malackowski, J., K. Cardoza, C. Gray, and R. Conroy. 2007. The intellectual property marketplace, emerging transactions and investment vehicles. *The Licensing Journal* 27 (2), posted 8/17/2007 at www.aspenpublishers.com.

Mohr, M. F., and J. B. Murphy. 2002. NAPCS discussion paper: An approach for identifying and defining intellectual property (IP) and related products in product classification systems. Presented at the 17th Annual Meeting of the Voorburg Group on Service Statistics, Nantes, France.

Mutti, J., and H. Grubert. 2006. New developments in the effect of taxes on royalties and the migration of intangible assets abroad. Prepared for the NBER/CRIW Conference on International Service Flows, Washington, D.C., April 28, 2006.

National Conference of Commissioners on Uniform State Laws (NCCUSL). 1985. Uniform Trade Secrets Act with 1985 Amendments. August.

Office of Management and Budget (2002). NAICS Manual 2002. Washington, D.C.: GPO.

PriceWaterhouseCoopers (2004), "The Economic Impact of Franchised Businesses." Created for the International Franchise Association Education Foundation.

Park, W., and D. Lippoldt. 2004. International licensing and the strengthening of intellectual property rights in developing countries. OECD Trade Policy Working Paper no. 10. Paris.

Park, W., and S. Wagh. 2002. Index of patent rights, in *Economic freedom of the world, 2002 annual report*. Vancouver, B.C.: The Fraser Institute.

Razgaitis, R. 2003. *Valuation and pricing of technology-based intellectual property*. Hoboken, NJ: Wiley.

———. 2005. U.S.-Canadian licensing in 2004: survey results. *Les Nouvelles,* Journal of the Licensing Executives Society (Dec.):145–55.

United States Copyright Office. (2004). Copyright basics. Revised December. Available at http://www.copyright.gov/circs/circ1.html. Accessed October 20, 2005.

United States Patent Office (USPTO). 2005. General information concerning patents. Available at http://www.uspto.gov/web/offices/pac/doc/general/index.html. Accessed October 20, 2005.

U.S. Department of Commerce, Bureau of Economic Analysis. 1992. *U.S. direct investment abroad. 1989 Benchmark Survey, final results.* Washington, D.C.: GPO.

———. 1998. *United States international transactions in private services. A guide to the surveys conducted by the Bureau of Economic Analysis.* Washington, D.C.: GPO.

———. 2006. *Benchmark survey of transactions in selected services and intangibles.* (BE-120). Washington, D.C.: GPO.

Comment   C. Fritz Foley

Understanding the functioning of the U.S. and global economy increasingly requires understanding how intellectual property (IP) is developed and deployed. Industries that intensively use intangible assets make up a large and growing share of U.S. industrial activity. These types of assets also play a significant role in determining the productivity of U.S. firms and

C. Fritz Foley is an associate professor of finance at Harvard Business School, and a faculty research fellow of the National Bureau of Economic Research.

their international competitiveness. However, measuring the value of intellectual property and how it flows throughout the economy is fraught with difficulties. Existing studies attempt to track investments in intangible assets by studying R&D or advertising expenses, but it is difficult to determine if these expenditures are effective. Researchers have attempted to value the stock of intangibles by subtracting the value of tangible assets from the market capitalization of public firms, but these residuals could capture many sources of value. Patent citations and patterns in productivity changes provide only some traces of the path of flows of intellectual property. As a consequence, there is plenty of room for improvement in measuring the value and use of intangible assets.

This paper takes a valuable step in providing a framework for measuring payments for the supply and use of intellectual property. This framework distinguishes between four types of payments for the use of intangible assets, or "service commodities." These are (a) licensing of rights to use IP protected as industrial property, (b) licensing of rights to use IP protected by trademarks, (c) licensing of rights to use IP protected by copyright, and (d) licensing of rights to use a business format under a franchise agreement. One advantage of the taxonomy of service commodities is that it ties to an academic literature that examines what types of intellectual property protections are used to protect intangibles in different industries. Cohen, Nelson, and Walsh (2000), and Cockburn and Henderson (2004) present results of surveys of the relative use of different types of IP protections.

With this categorization in hand, Robbins exploits existing data sources to estimate the value of payments for these different service commodities, by industry, for the United States. Developing estimates illustrates how data collected by distinct parts of the U.S. Department of Commerce can be combined to provide a new look at important issues. First, the results of the 2002 Annual Survey of Royalties, License Fees, and Other Receipts and Payments for Intangible Rights between the U.S. and Unaffiliated Foreign Persons provides a breakout of payments from unaffiliated persons to U.S. firms for each type of service commodity. This breakout is valuable because the most extensive source of data on payments for the use of intangible assets by U.S. firms is the Internal Revenue Service's Statistics of Income, and these data only capture aggregate payments. The distribution of payments provides a way of splitting aggregate payments into distinct service commodities by industry. These figures are augmented with data captured in the 2002 Economic Census covering franchise licensing fees and licensing fees collected for a few other segments of the economy.

Table 4.9 of the paper displays the author's estimates of the value of payments for intangibles, classified by type of service commodity and industry. A few patterns emerge from these estimates. About half of licensing fees are licensing fees for intangibles that are protected as industrial property. Receipts of licensing fees are largest in the manufacturing sector.

While IP protected as industrial property receives the largest share of receipts in manufacturing, IP protected by trademarks earns substantial receipts in the distributive services and information industries, and franchise fees are a source of significant receipts in the distributive services and finance and insurance industries.

Two limitations of this paper are worth noting. First, as duly noted by the author, it may not be appropriate to use the distribution of international licensing payments made by unaffiliated foreign persons to U.S. persons to determine the distribution of domestic licensing payments. Antràs, Desai, and Foley (forthcoming) show that flows of intangible assets to unaffiliated foreign persons are determined by many characteristics of the foreign country, including the development of the foreign country's capital markets. As a consequence, patterns in the international payments for intangibles may not reflect patterns in domestic payments.

Second, the measures developed in the paper are best suited to capture the licensing of intangible assets between firms, but this is only one aspect of intellectual property that one would like to measure. More generally, one would like to have estimates for the value of intangible assets held by firms, the value of flows within different parts of the firm, the value of flows between firms, and the value of flows between industries.

The data sources described in the paper do not capture the development and deployment of intellectual property that takes place within firms. The IRS data do not include measurements of the value of IP employed within firms, and the Census data would only capture the use of IP employed within firms if it triggered payments between establishments of the same firm. Table 4.1 of the paper provides some indication of the relative importance of IP that is deployed within firms. International licensing payments made by affiliated foreign persons to U.S. persons are about three times as large as those payments made by unaffiliated foreign persons.[1]

Because the estimates in the paper only capture one type of income generated by IP, they cannot be used to value intangibles in aggregate or to inform how effective investments in intangibles are. They also probably are not sufficient to measure the flow of intangibles across industries, given that cross-industry flows could occur within firms. For example, IP probably flows across industries within General Electric, but these flows are probably not completely captured by the data sources the paper uses.

In conclusion, this paper makes a valuable contribution to our understanding of the extent and nature of licensing of intellectual property across firms in the U.S. economy. It develops a framework for classifying types of licensing payments that is clearly defined and relates to academic work. It makes extensive use of existing data sources to develop estimates that provide a new look at the receipts of licensing payments by U.S. firms.

---

1. Branstetter, Fisman, and Foley (2006) analyze affiliated royalty payments in detail.

These estimates confirm that receipts of licensing fees are most pronounced in the manufacturing sector, and that these receipts mostly relate to intellectual property that is protected by patents and trade secrets.

Future work that aims at improving estimates of the value of intellectual property and the value of flows of intellectual property other than flows between firms must address a number of significant challenges. In many situations, intangible assets do not trade in an efficient marketplace, making them very hard to value. In addition, even if these types of assets could be valued, it would be difficult to collect data on their value. Identifying which person within a firm would be best positioned to respond to a survey on the value of IP by service commodity and industry would be hard. Intangible assets and intellectual property clearly play an essential and increasing role in the U.S. economy, but much more work is required to obtain precise measurements of how much value they have and how they flow throughout the economy.

References

Antràs, P., M. Desai, and C. F. Foley. Forthcoming. Multinational firms, FDI flows and imperfect capital markets. *Quarterly Journal of Economics* 124 (3).

Branstetter, L., R. Fisman, and C. F. Foley. 2006. Do stronger intellectual property rights increase international technology transfer? Empirical evidence from U.S. firm-level panel data. *Quarterly Journal of Economics* 121 (1) 321–49.

Cockburn, I. M., and R. Henderson. 2004. Survey results from the 2003 Intellectual Property Owners Association survey on strategic management of intellectual property. Available at http://www.ipo.org/articles.

Cohen, W. M., R. R. Nelson, and J. P. Walsh. 2000. Protecting their intellectual assets: Appropriability conditions and why U.S. manufacturing firms patent (or not). NBER Working Paper no. 7552. Cambridge, MA: National Bureau of Economic Research.

R&D Exports and Imports
New Data and
Methodological Issues

Francisco Moris

5.1 Introduction

Innovation—the introduction of new goods, services, or processes in the marketplace—builds on new knowledge as it flows from its originators to its eventual users. This knowledge may or may not result from scientific research and development (R&D), where R&D is defined as "creative work undertaken on a systematic basis to increase the stock of knowledge and [its] . . . use . . ." (OECD 2002,30). In the words of Rosenberg, "a high degree of scientific originality [has] been neither necessary nor sufficient condition for technological dynamism" (Rosenberg, 1982 13–14). Nevertheless, the importance of R&D in economic growth and productivity is well-established at the aggregate level (Griliches 2000, and references therein).

At the same time, the intangible nature of knowledge and its public good characteristics have long presented measurement challenges.[1] Thus, for example, the impact of knowledge is largely captured residually in total fac-

Francisco Moris is a senior analyst in the Division of Science Resources Statistics at the U.S. National Science Foundation.

The author would like to thank John Jankowski (National Science Foundation), Ned Howenstine, Maria Borga, Carol Robbins, Brian Sliker, and Dan Yorgason (U.S. Bureau of Economic Analysis), Wolfgang Keller (University of Colorado), Charlie Aspden (OECD), and participants of the 2006 NBER/CRIW Conference on International Service Flows in Bethesda, MD and the 2007 Joint OECD/NESTI—Canberra II Session on R&D Capitalisation in Paris for valuable feedback. Any remaining errors are the author's responsibility. Note: Views expressed are those of the author and do not necessarily do not reflect those of the National Science Foundation.

1. For studies on continuing data needs on the creation, diffusion, and impact of knowledge in the context of theoretical, measurement, and policy-making challenges see Corrado, Hulten, and Sichel (2005), Gault and Earl (2006), Griliches (2000), and Hulten (2007). For ongoing work on innovation-related metrics in the United States see NSF (2007) and Moris, Jankowski, and Perrolle (2008) and references therein.

tor productivity measures, even when some intangibles are capitalized or otherwise considered endogenously. Further, the strategic value and high specificity of knowledge creation implies the prevalence of internal production, minimizing opportunity for arms-length transactions. More recently, however, open or collaborative innovation, outsourcing, and global supply chains (Arora, Fosfuri, and Gambardella 2001; Chesbrough, Vanhaverbeke, and West 2006; Howells 2006; OECD 2006b) imply increased flows of knowledge and technology.

The statistics introduced in this chapter represent a new measure of market-based R&D flows compared with uncompensated knowledge flows studied by the spillovers literature (e.g., Branstetter 2004; Coe and Helpman 1995; Jaffe and Trajtenberg 1998; Xu and Wang 1999). However, given the invisibility of ideas, market-based transactions are bound to capture only a small part of the flows suggested by the economics of intangibles. Further, even in the context of market transactions, cross-border exchanges within MNCs may suffer from coverage or measurement issues such as transfer prices (reported payments that diverge from market prices for similar goods or services), as discussed elsewhere (Grubert and Mutti, chapter 3 in this volume; Hines 1996).

Nevertheless, the new R&D services statistics presented here complement other fee-based knowledge flows such as international royalties and license fees (see Robbins, chapter 4 in this volume), by covering transactions earlier in the innovation process. Secondly, R&D services trade data reflect transactions for knowledge that may not be formally captured by IP protection. Thirdly, R&D services trade bring new insights on the international distribution of R&D, which may inform further studies on the role of trade and FDI in growth. For example, even though R&D services exports represent less than 5 percent of U.S. R&D industrial performance in the early 2000s, the ratio is at least four times larger for foreign-owned companies in the U.S. (as presented in table 5.3). Lastly, to the extent that these data are ultimately embedded in the Bureau of Economic Analysis/National Science Foundation (BEA/NSF) R&D Satellite Account (Jorgenson and Landefeld 2005; Robbins and Moylan 2007; Yorgason 2007), they enhance the international components of the account.[2]

In short, this chapter has two major objectives. It introduces data on affiliated international trade in R&D-related services from Bureau of Economic Analysis (BEA) surveys on international transactions.[3] The affili-

2. Satellite accounts are supplementary estimates of GDP and other National Income and Product Accounts (NIPA), allowing for greater detail or alternative measurement concepts. The R&D satellite account considers R&D as an economic investment, consistent with ongoing revision of the 1993 System of National Accounts (SNA) manual. For information on the SNA update see http://unstats.un.org/unsd/sna1993/snarev1.asp.

3. Data refer to international transactions in private services involving all kind of companies, not just companies classified in services industries. In particular, the R&D services trade data presented in this chapter refer to exports and imports by all companies regardless of industry classification, not just to activities of companies or establishments classified in NAICS 5417.

ated trade data, available since 2001, allows estimating total U.S. trade in these private services. The second objective is methodological. In particular, the R&D services trade data are compared with well-known statistics on industrial R&D from NSF by assessing their underlying accounting concepts. The analysis leads to an integrated characterization of R&D performance (production), funding, and transactions consistent with both trade and R&D statistics terminology. The proposed framework allows identifying data gaps and methodological differences across different sources, and illustrates the potential for data integration.

The next two sections of this chapter discuss issues of globalization statistics and R&D accounting as defined in several international statistical manuals (section 5.2) and presents U.S. data on R&D-related trade and trade-expenditure ratios (section 5.3). Section 5.4 develops an integrated characterization of R&D expenditures and transactions, and applies it to existing data. Section 5.5 concludes. An appendix covers data notes.

5.2   R&D Transactions and R&D Expenditures

Research and development services exports imply R&D performance, whereas R&D imports highlights the need to track external sources of knowledge regardless of whether the buyer is an R&D performer. These activities are tracked by different official surveys subject to several international statistical manuals. Across Organization for Economic Cooperation and Development (OECD) member countries, R&D expenditures are collected on a performance and funding basis by national statistical offices based on definitions and prescriptions of the OECD's *Frascati Manual: Proposed Standard Practice for Surveys on Research and Experimental Development* (hereafter Frascati or FM).[4] On the other hand, the OECD's OSLO Manual (OECD 2005b) provides guidance on technological innovation statistics, including external sources of knowledge (see especially paragraphs 265–277).[5] However, R&D exports and imports are not explicitly defined in these manuals, nor in the *Technology Balance of Payments*

---

4. For example, in the United States national R&D expenditures are measured as the aggregate of R&D performed in industry, colleges and universities, Federal agencies, and other organizations based on NSF surveys targeted to these sectors (NSF 2003). These surveys use common definitions but have their own statistical methodologies appropriate for their respective populations. Respondent burden issues, respondent recordkeeping procedures, and institutional context vary considerably across these sectors, resulting in several unmeasured activities or units. For example, to reduce cost and respondent burden, estimates from the NSF/Census U.S. Survey of Industrial R&D currently exclude companies with less than five employees. Social science R&D is also excluded from this survey. I use industrial R&D data from both the NSF/Census Survey of Industrial R&D and from BEA FDI surveys. See data notes in appendix. For a compilation of official definitions of R&D across U.S. agencies see NSF (2006a).

5. The OSLO Manual serves as the basis for the EU Community Innovation Surveys (CIS). For a recent study on productivity growth, spillovers, and external sources of knowledge using CIS and economic data see Crespi et al. (2007).

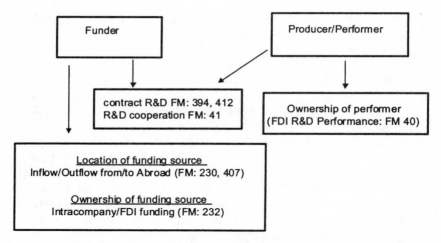

Fig. 5.1   R&D globalization in the Frascati Manual: Ownership and location of funding or performance

Manual (OECD 1990), the *Systems of National Accounts* (CEC et al. 1993 [SNA manual], paragraphs 8.27–8.33), or the *Handbook on Economic Globalisation Indicators* (OECD 2005a).

5.2.1   Globalization and R&D Accounting in the Frascati Manual

The Frascati manual (2002) is devoted to measuring R&D inputs (FM 14). The basic measure is "intramural expenditures," that is, all expenditures for R&D performed within a statistical unit or sector of the economy (FM 34). The manual recognizes that "R&D is an activity for which there are significant transfers of resources among units, organisations, and sectors, especially between government and other performers. . . . [thus] it is important . . . to know who finances R&D and who performs it" (FM 35). Further, Frascati takes "the globalization process into account by suggesting more detailed breakdowns of sources of funds for R&D and extramural R&D for transactions with units abroad" (FM 40), including R&D by multinational corporations (MNCs) through foreign direct investment (FDI), or FDI R&D.[6] See figure 5.1.

The focus by FM on R&D performed and used internally follows the history of R&D activities in industrial economies, along with the received wisdom of the economics of R&D. That is, R&D, and more generally, knowledge and information, exhibit public goods characteristics (e.g., nonrivalry and appropriability issues). These characteristics limit open market transactions and often the full exploitation of technological inno-

---

6. Within a national territory, this includes R&D by parent companies of MNCs and by affiliates of foreign MNCs.

vation (Teece 1986). However, even though the vast majority of R&D is still performed at home by developed-country MNCs, R&D is increasingly performed globally and collaboratively, driven by market, costs, and technological factors. Increased and more dispersed FDI in R&D-intensive industries (NSB 2008; OECD 2006b; UNCTAD 2005) and emerging global R&D management strategies (Le Bas and Sierra 2002; Niosi 1999; von Zedtwitz and Gassmann 2002) imply the need to complement information on international R&D production and funding with international transactions statistics.

5.2.2   International Transactions and R&D Exports/Imports

Both the *Manual on Statistics of International Trade in Services* (*MSITS*) (UN et al. 2002) and the IMF's *Balance of Payments Manual* (*BPM5*) (IMF 1993) define international trade as transactions between residents and nonresidents of an economy (UN et al. 2002, Box 1).[7] "A transaction itself is defined as an economic flow that reflects the creation, transformation, exchange, transfer or extinction of economic value and involves changes in ownership of goods and/or financial assets, the provision of services or the provision of labour or capital" (UN et al. 2002, 2.31). For its part, residency requires both having a center of interest (i.e., participation in economic activities) and residing in the country for one year or more. This "concept of residence . . . is identical to that used in BPM5 and the 1993 SNA [and] . . . it is not based on nationality or legal criteria . . ." (UN et al. 2002, 3.3).[8] (Note that considerations on ownership of the transaction parties or financing of the exchanged product [good or service] are outside the scope of these definitions.)

The MSITS also recognizes four modes of international delivery of services (UN et al. 2002, 2.14–2.21). Two of them are particularly relevant for business technical services such as R&D. The first mode refers to transactions between residents and nonresidents—international trade in the conventional sense as defined previously. The other mode of interest is the provision of services through foreign affiliates (Mode 3). Notably, the manual indicates that *only* Mode 1 transactions (between residents and nonresidents) should be labeled exports and imports. Separately, the manual recognizes that statistics based on Mode 1 definitions may be disaggregated in terms of transactions between related parties and transactions between unrelated parties (in this chapter, affiliated and unaffiliated trade, respectively) (UN et al. 2002, 3.36).

For a full account of cross-border flows, transfers are also of interest. The SNA defines transfers as "transaction[s] in which one institutional

---

7. Both manuals are also under revision; however, definitions used in this paragraph are unlikely to be affected.
8. See "The rest of the world account (external transactions account)," in the 1993 SNA, especially paragraphs 14.7 to 14.14.

unit provides a good, service or asset to another unit without receiving from the latter any good, service or asset in return as counterpart." Transfers may arise, for example, across geographically dispersed units of the same company or between public and private organizations. They can be classified as in cash or in kind transfers and as current or capital transfers (where the latter reflects or is linked to change in asset ownership) (CEC et al. 1993 [SNA manual], paragraphs 8.27–8.33). Thus, transfers are one-way or unrequited flows[9] and should be valued as if they were sold or purchased. Note, however, that for the purposes of R&D exports and imports as defined in this chapter, only in-kind transfers of R&D (properly valued) are of interest. Transfers of cash (grants) or other resources targeted for the performance of R&D do not result in cross-border flow of R&D regardless of the context.[10]

This discussion suggests that *R&D exports and imports* should be defined in terms of cross-border exchanges or transactions between residents and nonresidents. The next section introduces available data on international transactions in R&D services. The subsequent section develops a taxonomy that incorporates production, funding, and use/exchange concepts allowing a systematic characterization of exports and imports of R&D. The proposed framework may be useful to identify data gaps and illustrates the potential for integration across different data sources.

5.3   U.S. Trade in Research, Development, and Testing Services

Data on international transactions in R&D services are becoming available in several advanced economies, including the United States.[11] In addition to their potential as new flow indicators for further research and for national accounting development discussed in the introduction, these data may be also useful in studies on services offshoring (Graham 2007; van Welsum 2004).[12] Further, international trade in research, development, and testing (RDT) services is contributing to the U.S. trade surplus in business services overall, based on BEA data (NSF 2006b). Research, development, and testing services are defined as commercial and noncommercial research, product development services, and testing services. In general,

9. Also called transactions without a quid pro quo in the SNA (3.19–3.20).
10. Obviously, transfers in the forms of grants (public or private) are important when the objective is to measure R&D financing/funding flows between countries or within MNCs.
11. According to the IMF Committee on Balance of Payments Statistics, the proportion of IMF countries reporting international transactions in research and development services more than doubled between 1997 and 2003 (IMF 2004). See also OECD (2007).
12. Offshoring refers to the sourcing of production inputs through companies located outside of the home country. Offshoring may be done internally through controlled subsidiaries or affiliates, which involves foreign direct investment (FDI) (leading to affiliated trade within MNCs), or through external providers (leading to unaffiliated trade with independent entities). The latter is part of outsourcing activities that in general involve either domestic or overseas external suppliers.

however, data on R&D services trade include development activities or testing beyond the R&D boundary established by the Frascati Manual.[13] Research, development, and testing services are a category within business, professional, and technical services (BPT). Examples of other categories within BPT are computer and information services and management and consulting services. Business, professional, and technical, in turn, is a major category of private services. Other categories within private services include financial services, travel services, telecommunications, and royalties and licensing fees.

Trade in RDT services can be disaggregated into affiliated (intracompany) and unaffiliated (cross-company) trade. There have been trade surpluses in RDT services since 2001, when these data started to be collected separately from BPT for affiliated companies. Further, U.S. trade surpluses in RDT services have been driven more by U.S. affiliates of foreign MNCs and their relatively large exports of services than by parent companies of U.S. MNCs. This finding is consistent with the growing share these affiliates have in U.S. industrial R&D. In contrast, the unaffiliated trade surplus in RDT services has been down since 2001, due to the faster growth in imports than in exports of these services.

5.3.1   Trade Flows in Private, Business, and RDT Services

The United States has had annual trade surpluses in overall private services of at least $60 billion since the early 1990s, including a surplus of $79.9 billion in 2005.[14] Business, professional, and technical, together with royalties and license fees, accounted for most of the trade surplus within private services in 2005 ($33.1 billion and $32.9 billion, respectively).

In 2005, total exports (affiliated and unaffiliated) of RDT services reached a record $10.1 billion, compared with record imports of $6.7 billion, resulting in a trade surplus of $3.4 billion (table 5.1). This trade surplus is little changed from $3.7 billion in 2004 but smaller than trade surpluses around $5 billion in both 2002 and 2003. As discussed more fully following, this shift reflects gradual increases in trade deficits in unaffiliated trade for these R&D-related services.

5.3.2   Comparison of Affiliated and Unaffiliated Trade in RDT Services

For private services overall, the unaffiliated portion of exports and imports has been larger than the affiliated portion since at least 1992. The reverse has been true for BPT services and its subcomponent, RDT ser-

---

13. We will return to this point later. At the same time, this disadvantage turns into a plus for studies that focus on innovation activities. In either scenario, however, separating out R&D and non-R&D testing services is still desirable.

14. See Koncz and Flatness (2007) for updated data from BEA. For studies on the measurement of transactions and investment in overall services see Hoekman and Stern (1991) and Baldwin and Kamura (1998).

Table 5.1   U.S. trade in research, development, and testing services: 2001–2005 (millions of U.S. current dollars)

	Exports			Imports			Trade balance		
	Total	Affiliated	Unaffiliated	Total	Affiliated	Unaffiliated	Total	Affiliated	Unaffiliated
2001	6,746	5,700	1,046	2,425	1,700	725	4,321	4,000	321
2002	8,142	7,000	1,142	3,028	2,000	1,028	5,114	5,000	114
2003	9,376	8,200	1,176	4,410	3,100	1,310	4,966	5,100	−134
2004	8,760	7,500	1,260	4,993	3,100	1,893	3,767	4,400	−633
2005	10,095	8,800	1,295	6,717	4,400	2,317	3,378	4,400	−1,022

Source: Bureau of Economic Analysis, U.S. International Services. Available at http://www.bea.gov/international/intlserv.htm. Data accessed December 2006.

vices—affiliated exports and imports have been larger than unaffiliated exports and imports—since data have been available (1997 and 2001, respectively). Further, affiliated trade has recorded trade surpluses between $4 billion and $5 billion since 2001. However, unaffiliated trade moved from relatively small surpluses (< $500 million) in the 1990s (NSF 2006b), to small deficits in the early 2000s, reaching a deficit of just over a billion dollars in 2005.

The prominence of affiliated trade in business services, particularly R&D-related services, reflects advantages of internally managing, exploiting, and protecting complex or strategic transactions involving proprietary technical information (Caves 1996; McEvily, Eisenhardt, and Prescott 2004). For the United States, the large size of affiliated relative to unaffiliated trade in RDT services is consistent with strong U.S. FDI activity, which increases the number of potential affiliated trading partners. It is also consistent with expanded R&D by MNCs (NSB 2008).

5.3.3   Affiliated RDT Trade within U.S. and Foreign MNCs

Table 5.2 shows U.S. affiliated trade in RDT services in terms of the identity of the U.S.-located trading partner (parent company of U.S. MNC or U.S. affiliate of a foreign MNC) and the foreign trading partner (foreign affiliate of a U.S. parent or foreign parent of a U.S. affiliate), thus making possible an examination of intra-MNC trade.

From 2001 to 2005, annual exports of RDT services from U.S. parents to their foreign affiliates fluctuated narrowly around $2 billion, compared with around $1 billion in annual imports from their foreign affiliates, resulting in trade surpluses within U.S. MNCs of between one and two billion over this period (table 5.2). Over the same period, RDT services exports by affiliates of foreign MNCs in the United States to their foreign parents (and other foreign members of the company) were larger and increasing, reaching $6.8 billion in 2005. Annual imports under $3.2 billion over this period generated trade surpluses of up to $4.1 billion.

Table 5.2   U.S. affiliated trade in research, development, and testing services: 2001–2005 (billions of U.S. current dollars)

	U.S. affiliated trade			Within U.S. MNCs			Within foreign MNCs		
	Exports	Imports	Trade balance	Exports from U.S. parents to foreign affiliates	Imports from foreign affiliates to U.S. parents	Trade balance	Exports from U.S. affiliates to foreign parents[a]	Imports from foreign parents to U.S. affiliates[a]	Trade balance
2001	5.7	1.7	4.0	2.2	0.6	1.6	3.5	1.1	2.4
2002	7.0	2.0	5.0	1.9	0.8	1.1	5.1	1.3	3.8
2003	8.2	3.1	5.1	2.0	1.0	1.0	6.2	2.1	4.1
2004	7.5	3.1	4.4	1.8	1.2	0.6	5.6	1.9	3.7
2005	8.8	4.4	4.4	2.0	1.4	0.6	6.8	3.1	3.7

Source: Bureau of Economic Analysis, U.S. International Services.

[a]Data include transactions with other foreign members of the MNC.

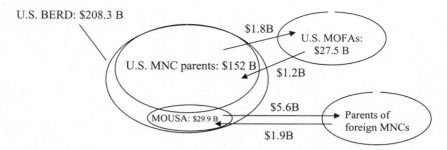

Fig. 5.2   U.S. affiliated RDT services trade flows (*data along arrows*) and industrial R&D expenditures (*U.S. BERD and data inside circles*): 2004

Notes: B = Billions of current U.S. dollars; BERD = Business Enterprise Expenditures on R&D; MOFAs = majority-owned affiliates of U.S. parent companies; MNCs = multinational corporations; MOUSA = majority-owned U.S. affiliates of foreign MNCs. Some companies are both parents of U.S. MNCs and also owned by foreign parent companies. Direction of arrows indicates flow of R&D services.

Sources: NSF Survey of Industry R&D (SIRD); BEA international investment surveys; BEA international transaction surveys.

The preceding analysis suggests that U.S. trade surplus in RDT services is driven by the relatively large exports by U.S. affiliates of foreign MNCs. This is consistent with their growing share in U.S. R&D (NSB 2008), although they still perform under 15 percent of U.S. industrial R&D, according to NSF and BEA data. Further, a substantial share of R&D-related activities is apparently aimed at services for their foreign parents (and other foreign members of the company). In particular, RDT services exports of $5.6 billion from U.S. affiliates of foreign MNCs to their foreign parents in 2004 was the equivalent of 19 percent of their $29.9 billion in R&D expenditures (fig. 5.2 and table 5.3).

For their part, parents of U.S. MNCs performed about three-fourths of U.S. industrial R&D. However, parents' $1.8 billion in RDT services exports to their overseas affiliates was the equivalent of only 1.2 percent of their R&D expenditures (table 5.3).

Note that R&D trade-expenditure ratios combine market-based data with cost-based expenditures that do not include operating surplus.[15] Further, the ratios presented in table 5.3 should be treated with caution. For one, the ratios are overstated since RDT trade includes *non-R&D* testing services. In addition, the ratios for affiliates are further overstated since affiliate's trade data are for all affiliates, not for majority-owned affiliates as the corresponding R&D figures. Nevertheless, they provide one indication

---

15. In practice, data from these different sources may be closer to each other: some R&D surveys include items on contract R&D while intra-MNC exchanges may not fully reflect arm's-length market values due to transfer pricing issues, as noted earlier.

Table 5.3   R&D trade/expenditure ratios for selected sectors of U.S. industrial
R&D: 2001–2005 (billions of U.S. current dollars, except as noted)

	R&D performance	RDT exports	(%)	R&D performance	RDT exports	(%)
	All companies located in U.S.	All companies located in U.S.		MOFAs	From foreign affiliates of US MNCs to their US parents[a]	
2001	202.0	6.7	3.3	19.7	0.6	3.0
2002	193.9	8.1	4.2	21.1	0.8	3.8
2003	200.7	9.4	4.7	22.8	1.0	4.4
2004	208.3	8.8	4.2	27.5	1.2	4.4
2005	226.2	10.1	4.5	n.a.	1.4	n.a.
	U.S.-MNC parents	From U.S. parents to their foreign affiliates		MOUSAs	From U.S. affiliates of foreign MNCs to their foreign parents[b]	
2001	143.0	2.2	1.5	26.5	3.5	13.2
2002	137.0	1.9	1.4	27.5	5.1	18.5
2003	139.9	2.0	1.4	29.8	6.2	20.8
2004	152.4	1.8	1.2	29.9	5.6	18.7
2005	n.a.	2.0	n.a.	n.a.	6.8	n.a.

Sources: Based on data from NSF Survey of Industry R&D and BEA surveys on international investment and international services.
Notes: n.a. = not available; MOFAs = majority-owned foreign affiliates; MOUSAs = majority-owned U.S. affiliates; RDT = research, development, and testing services.
[a]This is equal to imports of U.S. MNC-parents.
[b]Data include transactions with other foreign members of the MNC.

of the global distribution of R&D-related services within U.S. MNCs and for MNCs with operations in the U.S.

5.4   R&D Accounting in an Integrated Expenditures-Transactions Framework

The following proposed framework is based on a little-noticed insight in the Frascati Manual on the separate identities of performer, funder, and user of R&D. According to Frascati, for a given R&D project, the performer, funder, and user fulfill different economic functions, possibly performed by three different organizations:

"The [Frascati] Manual distinguishes between performers and funders of R&D. The SNA distinguishes between the producers and users of

Table 5.4   An integrated expenditures-transactions framework for business R&D

	R&D functions		
R&D profiles	FM Funder	SNA, FM producer/ performer	SNA user
1 Performer of company-funded own account R&D	yes	yes	yes
2 Custom R&D contractor (sale of externally-funded R&D)	no	yes	no
3 Speculative R&D producer	yes	yes	no
3a Sale of speculative R&D (captive or open market sale)			
3b Donation of speculative R&D			
4 Purchaser of custom R&D (funder of contract R&D)	yes	no	yes
5 Recipient of speculative R&D (not R&D funder)	no	no	yes
5a Purchase of speculative R&D			
5b Reception of donated speculative R&D			
6 Grants recipient (externally funded own account R&D)	no	yes	yes
7 Grants source	yes	no	no
8 Outside R&D statistics	no	no	no

R&D services (expenditure account). The unit which 'performs' the R&D also 'produces' it. The 'funder' unit is usually, but not always, the SNA 'user.'" (*OECD* 2002, annex 3, paragraph 28).

By acknowledging the SNA user, Frascati effectively recognizes three distinct approaches for the collection and analysis of R&D data.[16] R&D performance reflects technological capabilities of companies, whereas R&D funding reflects financial capabilities or policy priorities. Data based on R&D performers avoid potential double counting of the same activity when funds flow across several sectors. Lastly, R&D users subsequently produce new or improved products or processes, realizing profits through commercialization (*OSLO Manual,* OECD 2005b).[17]

R&D performance underlines the statistical aggregates of gross domestic expenditures on R&D (GERD) and business enterprise expenditures on R&D (BERD), whereas funding is used to compile gross national expenditures on R&D (NGERD). (See appendix, Terms in Official R&D Statistics.)

Table 5.4 summarizes all possible combinations of these R&D functions

16. As noted earlier, acquisition, diffusion, and use of R&D also figure prominently in the OSLO Manual (101, 265–76, 351) (OECD 2005b).

17. For its part, the 1993 SNA states that "goods and services are used when institutional units make use of them in a process of production or for the direct satisfaction of human needs or wants" (SNA 9.35). In practice, for services "the distinction between acquisition and use may not be relevant" (SNA 9.37). Indeed, the definition of services implies that for many services production, delivery, and use may be indistinguishable (SNA 6.8). The SNA terminology is also used to define market and nonmarket R&D and own account R&D.

(and corresponding accounting perspectives), resulting in eight nonoverlapping R&D profiles (rows). This template could be populated with quantitative indicators at a given aggregation level (e.g., country, region, industry, company).

These R&D profiles can also be depicted as an n-Venn diagram where n = 3 intersecting sets or curves correspond to dollar amounts associated with performance, funding, and user activities (fig. 5.3). With 3 curves there are exactly $2^n = 8$ regions that partitions the space of expenditures, one for each R&D profile in table 5.4. The eighth region corresponds to the area surrounding the three circles. The regions formed by the intersections are nonempty. Following is a list of R&D profiles and examples of organizations (numbers indicate rows in table 5.4 and sectors in the Venn diagram of figure 5.3):

[1] Own account, company-funded, R&D: high-tech manufacturers
[2] Custom R&D services supplier: defense contractors
[3] Provider of speculative R&D: companies (or units within companies) specialized in R&D services
[4] Purchaser of custom R&D: defense ministries
[5] Recipient of speculative R&D: financial services companies
[6] Grants recipient: government grantees
[7] Grants supplier: government agencies
[8] Non-R&D-players (the vast majority of economic agents)

The proposed taxonomy identifies different types of R&D producers and users, juxtaposed with different financing schemes. Own account R&D (R&D produced and consumed internally) can either be self-funded (profile 1) or funded externally (e.g., grants) (profile 6). Custom R&D is performed on behalf of an outside buyer under contract. Speculative

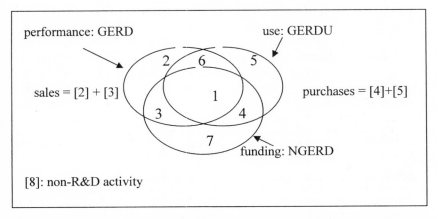

Fig. 5.3   The relationship among R&D functions underlying official R&D accounting

R&D[18] [3] refers to self-funded production not intended for internal use and with no advanced, secured buyer.[19] This is exemplified by commercial R&D service providers (of course, the latter also perform custom R&D). The immediate result of speculative R&D would be an increase in inventories, whereas its eventual disposition is either a sale or transfer. Research and development transfers, as defined earlier, are not generally collected in R&D or services transaction surveys. Thus, most of the remainder of this chapter abstracts from transfers [3b, 5b] and refer to [3] and [5] as a whole as part of sales and purchases, respectively.[20]

R&D transactions comprise profiles [2] through [5], where R&D sales (domestic sales + exports) = [2] + [3] and R&D purchases (domestic purchases + imports) = [5] + [4].

5.4.1   Discussion

R&D in a closed economy: In a closed economy, each "pie" in figure 5.3 is a different representation of the same total R&D in a given period:

- Performance: Gross domestic expenditure on R&D (GERD): total R&D performed in country: [1] + [6] + [2] + [3]
- Funding: Gross national expenditure on R&D (NGERD): total R&D funded by country: [1] + [3] + [4] + [7]
- Use: "Gross domestic expenditures on R&D used": [1] + [6] + [4] + [5]

where GERD = NGERD = "Gross domestic expenditures on R&D used."[21]

The last accounting equality is applicable to a closed economy, assuming no inventories or unused R&D. Further, in this closed economy: [2] = [4]; [3] = [5]; and [6] = [7], assuming R&D grants are used only for own account R&D. This is consistent with intra-country equilibrium, which requires: domestic R&D sales ([2] + [3]) = domestic R&D purchases ([5] + [4]).

R&D transactions in a two-country system: Figure 5.4 shows international R&D exchanges involving R&D services and transfer funds by adding a second country with a similar 3-Venn diagram whose sectors are indicated by ('). Abstracting from intra-country transactions, international trade implies:

18. The label for this profile is due to Charlie Aspden, OECD.
19. The 1993 SNA recognizes speculative production of assets (see, e.g., paragraph 10.75). Mohr and Murphy (2002: 5) consider speculative IP production in the context of product classification systems.
20. The legal form of the underlying IP (e.g., patent rights assignments) is outside the scope of table 5.4. Also note that the framework is static and it is focused on current-period R&D production and exchange. Thus, licensing and sales of R&D-based patents are not considered in the present work.
21. The last term is a new aggregate discussed later.

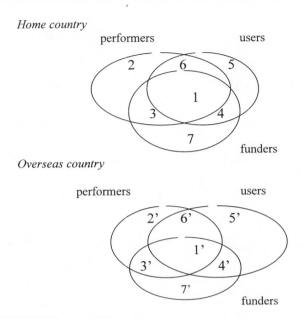

Fig. 5.4   R&D flows in an open economy

Notes: R&D exchanges in a two-country system: As drawn, the home country has larger R&D producer and funding sectors, whereas the overseas country has a larger R&D user sector. Also, the sector that simultaneously produces, funds, and uses its own R&D is larger in the home country: [1] > [1'].

$5 + 4 = 2' + 3'$ (R&D imports in the base country = R&D exports of overseas country) and $2 + 3 = 5' + 4'$ (R&D exports in the base country = R&D imports of overseas country).

Sectors 7 and 7' in figure 5.4 are R&D grant sources (e.g., nonprofits, public organizations, parent companies). These sectors may direct funds either to domestic or overseas grant recipients (sectors 6 and 6').

Research and development exports and imports can then be defined as transactions of R&D services between residents and nonresidents. This definition corresponds with Mode 1 of delivery of services (UN et al. 2002, 2.16), namely, "cross border supply [which] takes place when the consumer remains in [the] home territory while the service crosses national borders." In terms of table 5.4, R&D exports are the cross-border components of [2] and [3]. For both [2] and [3], R&D is being performed but not used by the performer. The difference between them is the financing scheme. In [2] the R&D was funded by a customer, whereas in [3] it was funded internally. In turn, the latter can either be sold [3a] or transferred in kind [3b]. Similarly, R&D imports are the cross-border components of [4] and [5], both showing a user of R&D that source it from an external provider. In the case of

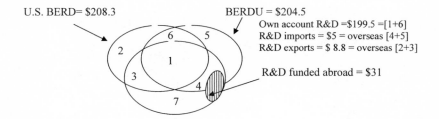

BERD: Business enterprise expenditures on R&D;

BERDU: Business enterprise expenditures on R&D use

Fig. 5.5   A profile of U.S. industrial R&D expenditures and flows (billions of current U.S. dollars): 2004

Notes: BERD: Business enterprise expenditures on R&D; BERDU: Business enterprise expenditures on R&D use. Figure does not reflect necessarily the relative size of associated data.
Sources: NSF Survey of Industry R&D (SIRD) and BEA international transactions surveys.

[4], the user paid for the R&D in advance whereas in [5] it acquired existing R&D for a fee [5a] or as a recipient of an in-kind transfer [5b]. Excluded from R&D trade are self-funded own account R&D [1] and R&D grants (cash transfers) [6,7]. Cross-border grants are outside the scope of R&D exports and imports (since they do not involve flow of R&D), although they are obviously important when the objective is to measure financing/funding flows between countries or within MNCs.

In addition to GERD and NGERD defined earlier, the taxonomy suggests a new aggregate: "gross domestic expenditures on R&D use" (GERDU), depicted by the user pie previously, defined more formally as:

$$GERDU \equiv GERD - R\&D \text{ exports} + R\&D \text{ imports.}[22]$$

The corresponding term for the business sector would be "business enterprise expenditures on R&D use" (BERDU): BERDU $\equiv$ BERD – industrial R&D exports + industrial R&D imports.

The definition for GERDU corresponds to "apparent consumption" in the trade literature. Of course, by combining data from different sources, GERDU has similar shortcomings as the trade-expenditures ratios introduced earlier.

An illustration with 2004 U.S. data: (see fig. 5.5).

---

22. By using the fact that GERD is also equal to own account R&D plus R&D exports (Frascati Manual OECD 1993: Annex 11, paragraph 58) we also have: GERDU = own account R&D + R&D imports.

- BERD (= aggregate of [1] + [6] + [2] + [3]) = \$208.3 billion (NSF SIRD)
- R&D exports (= overseas portion of [2] + [3]) = \$8.8 billion (BEA)
- R&D imports (= overseas portion of [4] + [5]) = \$5.0 billion (BEA)
- BERDU ≡ BERD – industrial R&D exports + industrial R&D imports = ([1] + [6] + [2] + [3]) – ([2] + [3]) + ([4] + [5]) = \$208.3 – \$8.8 + \$5.0 = \$204.5 billion = aggregate of ([1] + [6] + [4] + [5])
- Business own account R&D (= [1] + [6]) = BERD – industrial R&D exports (= BERDU – industrial R&D imports) = \$208.3 – \$8.8 = \$199.5 billion
- Industrial R&D funding from abroad: Not available.
- Industrial R&D funded abroad = \$31 billion (NSF SIRD)[23]

5.5 Conclusion

The importance of R&D in economic growth and productivity is well-established at the aggregate level. However, the intangible nature of knowledge and its public good characteristics have long presented problems for the measurements of its outputs, impacts, and associated transactions. In this regard, trade in RDT services constitute a welcome addition to the menu of indicators on knowledge flows, even if market-based transactions are bound to capture only part of the flows of interest. One advantage of services trade data presented in this chapter is that they cover both affiliated (MNCs) and unaffiliated trade, as well as transactions by companies that do not perform R&D (especially important for R&D imports). Even though the size of the trade flows examined here are modest relative to U.S. industrial R&D performance, the data already reveal new insights on the international distribution of FDI R&D. In turn, this may inform further studies on the role of trade and FDI in innovation, productivity, and growth. These exchanges may also be sizable for specific industries,[24] smaller developed economies, and emerging markets.

Further, the new statistics complement other fee-based knowledge flows by covering transactions earlier in the innovation process (compared, for example, with patent fees). The data also capture flows that may not be formally protected by IP (exploited, for example, in the patent citations approach). In addition, by focusing on R&D services across all companies the transaction surveys capture exports beyond stand-alone

23. As collected by NSF, and in the language of this chapter, industrial R&D funded abroad by (R&D-performing) for-profit U.S. residents is the aggregate of overseas purchases of custom and open market R&D, plus cross-border grants. Recipients of the funds include overseas affiliates and independent contractors. Thus, R&D funded abroad straddles the regions corresponding to "custom R&D" imports [4] and grants source [7]. This statistic is not available for U.S. non-R&D performers that may fund or buy R&D abroad.

24. Data limitations on U.S. RDT trade at the industry level precluded further analysis.

R&D labs or captive establishments classified in North American Industry Classification System (NAICS) 5417.[25] However, statistics on R&D services trade may include non-R&D testing services and do not provide additional R&D details (e.g., research vs. development, technology area, product vs. process focus). Some of this information may be obtained without increasing respondent burden, however, by linking data from the relevant surveys.

Lastly, the methodological approach followed in this chapter illustrates potential benefits and challenges of leveraging different official accounting perspectives and existing survey instruments to measure the varied dimensions of global R&D sourcing, deployment, and exploitation. In particular, table 5.4 allows a systematic account of R&D production (own account, speculative, and custom), exports and imports, apparent consumption, and cross-border transfers and grants flows. The application of the proposed framework to existing statistics points out the need not only for continued data development and integration but also to further enhancements in official statistical guidance by more systematically recognizing trade-based measures in Frascati-related manuals, as well as Frascati-based R&D terminology in services statistics, balance of payments, and other SNA-related manuals.

Appendix A

Data Sources

R&D Expenditures

Data for U.S. industrial R&D (BERD) were obtained from the NSF Survey of Industrial R&D (SIRD), a nationally representative sample of all for-profit companies in the fifty U.S. states and the District of Columbia, regardless of ownership status. Estimates are subject to sampling and non-sampling errors. See http://www.nsf.gov/sbe/srs/sird/start.htm for a description of the survey and its methodology.

Estimates on affiliates' and U.S. parents' R&D performance are collected by BEA FDI surveys (along with and other operations data): Survey of Foreign Direct Investment in the United States (FDIUS) and Survey of U.S. Direct Investment Abroad (USDIA). For more information see http://www.bea.gov/bea/surveys/diasurv.htm (USDIA) and http://www.bea.gov/bea/surveys/fdiusurv.htm (FDIUS).

---

25. For export revenues by NAICS 5417 establishments based on Census Bureau data see "Technology Linkages" section in NSB (2008).

International Transactions

Statistics on affiliated services trade were collected by BEA's quarterly balance of payments surveys on affiliates: Transaction of U.S. Affiliates, Except U.S. Banking Affiliates, with Foreign Parent (survey form BE-605) covers affiliates of foreign MNCs in the U.S.; Direct Transactions of U.S. Reporter with Foreign Affiliate (survey form BE-577) covers U.S. MNCs. In these affiliates' surveys, RDT services are defined as "[c]ommercial and noncommercial research, product development services, and testing services." Affiliated trade data in RDT services, a component of business, professional, and technical services (BPT), have been available since 2001. Business, professional, and technical affiliated trade data have been available since 1997. Previously, these components were included in the overall trade figures but were not separately available.

Data on unaffiliated trade in RDT services were collected by BEA's surveys on transactions with unaffiliated foreign persons, along with other business, professional, and technical services (Benchmark Survey of Selected Services Transactions With Unaffiliated Foreign Persons [survey form BE-20], conducted every five years, and the Quarterly Survey of Transactions Between U.S. and Unaffiliated Foreign Persons in Selected Services and in Intangible Assets [survey form BE-25] for nonbenchmark years). Surveys for unaffiliated transactions define RDT services as "[c]ommercial and noncommercial research, product development services, and testing services. Includes fees for the conduct of experiments or performance of research and development activities aboard spacecrafts. Excludes medical and dental laboratory services." For more information see http://www.bea.gov/bea/surveys/iussurv.htm.

Starting with 2006 benchmark data, new survey forms BE-120 (benchmark) and BE-125 (quarterly) will collect services transactions for both affiliated and unaffiliated trade.[26] For full historical tables on international transactions in private services see http://www.bea.gov/bea/di/1001serv/intlserv.htm.

Services sold to, or purchased from, unaffiliated foreign persons are reported regardless of whether the services were performed in the United States or abroad. Transactions for RDT services are reported on an accrual basis, gross of U.S. or foreign taxes.[27] Purchases of services are included without regard to whether they are charged as an expense on the income statement, capitalized, or charged to inventories. Data is on consolidated enterprise basis for all U.S. reporters. The fully consolidated U.S. domestic

---

26. The BE-120 replaces BE-20 and adds affiliated services transactions formerly covered by BE-605 and BE-577. Similarly, BE-125 replaces BE-25 and adds affiliated transactions.

27. Accounting data on an accrual basis refer to revenues and expenses recognized in the period in which they are earned (products are delivered or services provided). Cash may or may not be received or paid during this period.

enterprise excludes foreign branches and other foreign affiliates. The classification of services is based on the IMF's Balance of Payments Manual (BPM5), the United Nations' Manual on Statistics of International Trade in Services (MSITS) (which in turn draws guidance from the SNA), and the International Surveys Industry classifications developed by BEA.

Appendix B

Terms in Official R&D Statistics

FM-Based Terms

Business Enterprise Expenditures on R&D (BERD): Portion of GERD performed by the business or industrial sector. This is the same as industrial R&D in this chapter.

Gross domestic expenditure on R&D (GERD): Total intramural expenditures on R&D performed on the national territory during a given period (FM 423). Includes R&D performed within a country and funded from abroad but excludes payments for R&D performed abroad (FM 424).

Gross national expenditure on R&D (NGERD): Total expenditures on R&D financed by a country's institutions during a given period. It includes R&D performed abroad but financed by national institutions or residents; it excludes R&D performed within a country but funded from abroad (NGERD $\equiv$ GERD – funding from abroad + funding funded abroad) (FM 426).

R&D funder: Organization that is source of funding for R&D. R&D funding is the basis for NGERD (defined previously).

R&D performer: Organization that engages in R&D. This is the same as R&D producer in SNA terms. The R&D performance is the basis for GERD and BERD (defined previously).

FDI R&D: R&D performed by multinational corporations (MNCs). Within a national territory, this includes R&D by MNC-parent companies and by affiliates of foreign MNCs.

SNA-Based Terms

Market R&D: R&D produced for sale at an economically significant price (Robbins 2005).

Nonmarket R&D: R&D distributed for free or at noneconomically significant prices (Robbins 2005).

Own account R&D: R&D both performed and used internally, regardless of funding source (also in OECD Frascati Manual 1993: Annex 11, paragraph 58). Own account R&D in the business sector of advanced economies is funded mostly internally.

R&D producer: Same as R&D performer.

R&D user: Organization that exploits results or knowledge from R&D. The R&D used could be produced internally or acquired from an external provider.

References

Arora, A., A. Fosfuri, and A. Gambardella. 2001. *Markets for technology—the economics of innovation and corporate strategy.* Cambridge, MA: MIT Press.

Baldwin, R. E., and F. Kamura. 1998. Measuring U.S. international goods and services transactions. In *Geography and ownership as bases of economic accounting,* National Bureau of Economic Research, Studies in income and wealth, vol. 59, ed. R. E. Baldwin, R. E. Lipsey, and J. D. Richardson, 9–48. Chicago: University of Chicago: Press.

Branstetter, L. 2004. Is foreign direct investment a channel of knowledge spillovers? Evidence from Japan's FDI in the United States. Discussion Paper no. 30, APEC Study Center. New York: Columbia Business School.

Caves, R. E. 1996. *Multinational enterprise and economic analysis,* 2nd ed. London: Cambridge University Press.

Chesbrough, H., W. Vanhaverbeke, and J. West. 2006 *Open innovation—Researching a new paradigm.* Oxford: Oxford University Press.

Coe, D. T., and E. Helpman. 1995. International R&D spillovers. *European Economic Review* 39 (5): 859–87.

Commission of the European Communities (CEC), International Monetary Fund, Organisation for Economic Cooperation and Development, United Nations, and World Bank. 1993. *System of national accounts 1993* [SNA 1993]. Brussels/Luxembourg, New York, Paris, Washington, DC. Available at http://unstats.un.org/unsd/sna1993/toctop.asp.

Corrado, C. A., C. R. Hulten, and D. E. Sichel. 2005. Measuring capital and technology: An expanded framework. In *Measuring capital in the new economy,* National Bureau of Economic Research, Studies in income and wealth, vol. 65, ed. C. Corrado, J. Haltiwanger and D. Sichel, 11–46. Chicago: University of Chicago Press.

Crespi, G., C. Criscuolo, J. Haskel, and M. Slaughter. 2007. Productivity growth, knowledge flows and spillovers. CEP Discussion Paper dp0785. Centre for Economic Performance, London School of Economics.

Gault, F., and L. Earl. 2006. Insights into innovation, indicators, and policy. In *National Innovation, Indicators, and Policy,* ed. L. Earl and F. Gault, 221–232. Cheltenham, UK: Edward Elgar Policy Publishing.

Graham, J. M. 2007. *The measure of a nation: Quantifying innovative strength through improved service sector metrics.* National Bureau of Asian Research (NBR), in consultation with the NBR Commission on Measuring Services in the U.S. Economy, Seattle. Available at http://www.nbr.org/publications/issue.aspx?ID=401.

Griliches, Z. 2000. *R&D, education, and productivity—A retrospective.* Cambridge: Harvard University Press.

Hines, J. R. 1996. *Tax policy and the activities of multinational corporations.* NBER Working Paper no. 5589. Cambridge, MA: National Bureau of Economic Research, May.

Howells, J. 2006. Intermediation and the role of intermediaries in innovation. *Research Policy* 35 (5): 715–28.

Hoekman, B. M., and R. M. Stern. 1991. Evolving patterns of trade and investment in services. In *International economic transactions, issues in measurement and empirical research,* National Bureau of Economic Research, Studies in income and wealth, vol. 55, ed. P. Hopper and J. D. Richardson, 237–292. Chicago: University of Chicago Press.

Hulten, C. R. 2007. Theory and measurement, an essay in honor of Zvi Griliches. In *Hard-to-measure goods and services, essays in honor of Zvi Griliches,* National Bureau of Economic Research, studies in income and wealth, vol. 67, E. R. Berndt and C. Hulten, 15–30. Chicago: University of Chicago Press.

International Monetary Fund (IMF). 1993. *Balance of payments manual (BMP5),* 5th ed. Washington, D.C.: International Monetary Fund.

———. 2004. *International trade in services statistics—Monitoring progress on implementation of the manual and assessing data quality.* Paper presented at the Seventeenth Meeting of the IMF Committee on Balance of Payments Statistics, BOPCOM-04/13. 26–29 October, Pretoria, South Africa.

Jaffe, A. B., and M. Trajtenberg. 1998. International knowledge flows: Evidence from patent citations. NBER Working Paper no. 6507. Cambridge, MA: National Bureau of Economic Research, April.

Jorgenson, D. W., and J. S. Landefeld. 2005. Blueprint for expanded and integrated U.S. accounts: Review, assessment, and next steps. In *A new architecture for the U.S. national accounts,* National Bureau of Economic Research, Studies in income and wealth, vol. 66, ed. D. W. Jorgenson, J. S. Landefeld, and W. D. Nordhaus, 13–112. Chicago: University of Chicago Press.

Koncz, J., and A. Flatness. 2007. U.S. international services cross-border trade in 2006 and sales through affiliates in 2005. *Survey of Current Business* 87: (10) 94–113.

Le Bas, C., and C. Sierra. 2002. Location versus home country advantages in R&D activities: Some further results on multinationals' locational strategies. *Research Policy* 31 (4): 589–609.

McEvily, S. K., K. M. Eisenhardt, J. E. Prescott. 2004. The global acquisition, leverage, and protection of technological competencies. *Strategic Management Journal* 25 (8–9): 713–22.

Mohr, M. F., and J. B. Murphy. 2002. *An approach for identifying and defining intellectual property (IP) and related products in product classification systems.* NAPCS Discussion Paper. Paper presented at 17th Annual Meeting of the Voorburg Group on Service Statistics. 23–27 September, Nantes, France.

Moris, F., J. Jankowski, and P. Perolle. 2008. Advancing measures of innovation in the United States. *Journal of Technology Transfer—Special Issue on Advancing Measures of Innovation: Knowledge Flows, Business Metrics, and Measurement Strategies* 33:123–30.

National Science Board (NSB). 2008. Research and development: National trends and international linkages. In *Science and engineering indicators 2008.* Available at http://www.nsf.gov/statistics/indicators/.

National Science Foundation (NSF), Science Resources Statistics (SRS). 2003. *National patterns of R&D resources: 2003.* Available at http://www.nsf.gov/statistics/natlpatterns/.

———. 2006a. *Definitions of research and development: An annotated compilation of official sources.* Available at http://www.nsf.gov/statistics/randdef/.

————. 2006b. *Trade in R&D-related services: A new indicator of industrial knowledge flows* (NSF 06-326). Available at http://www.nsf.gov/statistics/infbrief/nsf 06326/.

————. 2007. *Workshop report: Advancing measures of innovation knowledge flows, business metrics, and measurement strategies, 6–7 June 2006.* Available at http://www.nsf.gov/statistics/workshop/innovation06/.

Niosi, J. 1999. The internationalization of industrial R&D: From technology transfer to the learning organization. *Research Policy* 28 (2–3): 107–17.

Organization for Economic Cooperation and Development (OECD). 1990. *Technology Balance of Payments Manual.* Paris: OECD.

————. 1993. *Frascati manual: Proposed standard practice for surveys on research and experimental development.* Paris: OECD.

————. 2002. Frascati Manual: Proposed Standard practice for surveys on research and experimental development. Paris: OECD.

————. 2005a. *OECD Handbook on economic globalization indicators.* Paris: OECD.

————. 2005b. *Oslo manual: Proposed guidelines for collecting and interpreting technological innovation data.* Paris: OECD.

————. 2006a. *OECD science, technology, and industry outlook 2006.* Paris: OECD.

————. 2006b. *Recent trends in internationalization of R&D in the enterprise sector.* Special session on globalisation. 16–17 November, Paris.

————. 2007. *Trade involving multinational corporations: Conceptual measurement issues.* Directorate for Science, Technology, and Industry, Committee on Industry, Innovation, and Entrepreneurship, Working Party on Statistics, Special Session on Globalisation. March, Paris.

Robbins, C. A. 2005. *Linking Frascati-based R&D spending to the system of national accounts.* Washington, D.C.: Bureau of Economic Analysis.

Robbins, C. A., and C. E. Moylan. 2007. Research and development satellite account update estimates for 1959–2004—New estimates for industry, regional, and international accounts. *Survey of Current Business* 87 (10): 49–64.

Rosenberg, N. 1982. *Inside the black box: Technology and economics.* Cambridge: Cambridge University Press.

Teece, D. J. 1986. Profiting from technological innovation: Implications for integration, collaboration, licensing, and public policy. *Research Policy* 15 (6): 285–305.

United Nations, European Commission, International Monetary Fund, Organization for Economic Cooperation and Development, United Nations Conference on Trade and Development, and World Trade Organization. 2002. *Manual on statistics of international trade in services* (MSITS). Geneva.

United Nations Conference on Trade and Development (UNCTAD). 2005. *World investment report—Transnational corporations and the internationalization of R&D.* Geneva.

van Welsum, D. 2004. In search of 'off shoring': Evidence from U.S. imports of services. Birbeck Working Papers in Economics and Finance, BWPEF 0402. London: Birkbeck College.

von Zedtwitz, M., and O. Gassmann. 2002. Market versus technology drive in R&D internationalization: Four different patterns of managing research and development. *Research Policy* 31 (4): 569–88.

Xu, B., and J. Wang. 1999. Capital goods trade and R&D spillovers in the OECD. *Canadian Journal of Economics* 32 (5): 1258–74.

Yorgason, D. R. 2007. Treatment of international research and development as investment, issues and estimates. BEA/NSF R&D Satellite Account Background Paper. Washington, D.C.: Bureau of Economic Analysis.

Comment   Wolfgang Keller

High per capita output is primarily achieved by using a given bundle of factors more efficiently—not by changing the bundle (Hall and Jones 1999). What is the source of these efficiency gains? They are driven by firms' technology investment and adoption decisions. Moreover, investments in technology lead to complementary capital accumulation, further increasing per capita output (Howitt 2000). In his chapter, Francisco Moris describes recent efforts to get a better grasp on technology investments and diffusion in the era of globalization by focusing on international trade in R&D services. Does this significantly improve the ability of economists to explain these activities? There are good reasons to believe that, no, it does not, but there are even better reasons to believe that yes, it does. Why? In my comments, I will start with the former before turning to the latter.

Not Even Close!

The case that this is an exercise in futility can be made by noting, first, that many technology investments are not showing up in R&D tables according to the standard conventions. For example, financial service firms derive most of their profit flows from financial products and types of transactions that did not exist fifteen years ago. Financial firms hold patents codifying and protecting their products and methodologies, but finance firms spend nothing on R&D, according to the usual accounting conventions. Or take Southwest Airlines as another example. It is widely regarded as having introduced many frontier innovations, such as boarding passengers by broad group without assigned seats. One will not find an R&D figure that led to this strategy in Southwest's books, but it still has driven Southwest's success. Thus, formal R&D figures, according to the Organization for Economic Cooperation and Development (OECD's) *Frascati* definition, grossly underestimate technology investments.

Second, even if most of technology investments were captured in R&D figures, R&D service trade would still capture only a small fraction of technology flows between countries. This is because the majority of international technology transfers are not market transactions, but externalities, or spillovers. Such spillovers are often unintentional and hence no contract where buyer and seller agree on the price of the transaction exists. According to McNeil's (2006) estimate, I compute that U.S. R&D and Testing Service exports in 2001 of $40.7 billion are less than 5 percent of the technology spillovers the United States has provided in that year.[1]

Wolfgang Keller is professor of economics at the University of Colorado, and a research associate of the National Bureau of Economic Research.

Then what can we learn from these R&D service trade figures? This is where the case for this agenda begins.

Way to Go!

First, consider the possibility that technology investments are nothing but a proximate cause for growth—the fundamental drivers are differences in institutions across countries (Acemoglu, Johnson, and Robinson 2005). If so, then surely differences in economic and political institutions should have a strong effect on firms' technology investment and adoption decisions. Or consider the influential view that productivity differences across countries are in large part due to barriers to technology adoption (Parente and Prescott 2000). In both cases, research in support of the argument using observable counterparts of technology investment and adoption is extremely scarce.

At a less aggregate level, research often includes specific technology variables. Griffith, Harrison, and van Reenen (2006), for example, provide evidence on technology flows from the United States to the United Kingdom: high technology growth in the U.S. is associated with relatively high U.K. firm productivity growth if the U.K. firms locate a relatively high share of their innovative activity in the United States. Similarly, Keller (2002) shows that the productivity benefits from R&D spending in the largest industrialized countries are smaller, the more geographically distant a recipient country is from these countries. At the same time, these studies are typical in that they rely on indirect or proxy variables—they do not employ direct information on the monetary value of technology transfers.

The information on trade in R&D services that Moris describes in this chapter is a big step forward in this respect. While clearly only a part of all international technology transfer, in principle these data have the information that is of interest. In particular, the R&D service trade figures capture the value, not the cost, of international technology flows. Moreover, the technology sender and recipient are identifiable as the buyer and seller. Therefore, this information provides an important angle to tackle the issue.

Multinational enterprises (MNEs) play the key role in international R&D service trade (see table 5.1). This is not surprising given that MNEs account for most of the R&D conducted in the world. In the United States, for example, U.S. multinational parents, together with U.S. affiliates of foreign-owned multinationals, account for more than 90 percent of R&D in the United States. The breakdown is about 83 percent for U.S. multinational parents and about 9 percent for U.S. affiliates of foreign-owned

---

1. McNeil's (2006) figures are based on the framework of Coe and Helpman (1995), Keller (1998), and Xu and Wang (1999).

multinationals.[2] The technological "footprint" of MNEs is indeed very large. This is a major reason of why it is promising to start studying technology transfer by looking at MNEs.

A second reason for a focus on MNEs, at least initially, is the fact that much of the observable part of international technology transfer today consists of transfers within the parent and affiliates of the same multinational enterprise. United States statistics at the Bureau of Economic Analysis (BEA) paint a rich picture of parent and affiliate activity, as well as their relationships in terms of trade in goods and services. Recent efforts to link the (BEA) MNE data to detailed company-level R&D data from U.S. surveys has the potential of greatly improving our understanding of international technology flows (see NSF 2005). For example, we need to learn more about the headquarter services provided by MNE parents for their affiliates: what exactly is their nature, and how do the services provided vary by industry and by MNE host country?

One important question is how similar the within-MNE trade patterns are to trade at arm's length between unaffiliated parties. For example, how important are transfer pricing issues? Second, how representative international R&D transfers are for all international knowledge flows. Extending the analysis to include patent royalty and licensing payments of MNEs should help in this respect. While royalties are only observed whenever a firm has patented, which is a strategic choice, R&D trade and royalty flows together will provide a better picture of international technology flows than either by itself. It will also be useful to combine the analysis of R&D with results from surveys that define innovation more broadly, such as the Community Innovation Surveys of the European Union; see Criscuolo, Haskel, and Slaughter (2005) for a recent analysis that relies on this survey.

To sum up, information on international R&D service trade begins to open up new avenues for quantitative work on international technology flows. This should yield important insights for productivity growth and convergence versus divergence in the world. A better understanding of domestic and international dimensions of technological activity will also inform the policy debate on whether international technological transfers should be encouraged or rather reduced: what is the impact of a relatively open versus closed technological knowledge regime? Getting this right has major implications for economic welfare.

References

Acemoglu, D., S. Johnson, and J. Robinson. 2005. Institutions as the fundamental cause of long-run growth. In *Handbook of economic growth,* ed. S. Durlauf and P. Aghion, 385–472. North-Holland: Elsevier.

2. See NSF (2005, appendix table 1). This figure is for the manufacturing sector around the year 1998. If one looks at all industrial R&D, not only manufacturing, MNEs still account for more than 80 percent of R&D inside the United States (NSF 2005).

Coe, D., and E. Helpman. 1995. International R&D spillovers. *European Economic Review* 39 (5): 859–87.

Criscuolo, C., J. E. Haskel, and M. J. Slaughter. 2005. Global engagement and the innovation activities of firms. NBER Working Paper no. 11479. Cambridge, MA: National Bureau of Economic Research, July.

Griffith, R., R. Harrison, and J. Van Reenen. 2006. How special is the special relationship? Using the impact of U.S. R&D spillovers on UK firms as a test of technology sourcing. *American Economic Review* 96 (5): 1859–79.

Hall, R., and C. Jones. 1999. Why do some countries produce so much more output per worker than others? *Quarterly Journal of Economics* 114 (1): 83–116.

Howitt, P. 2000. Endogenous growth and cross-country income differences. *American Economic Review* 90 (4): 829–46.

Keller, W. 1998. Are international R&D spillovers trade-related? Analyzing spillovers among randomly matched trade partners. *European Economic Review* 42 (8): 1469–81.

———. 2002. Geographic localization of international technology diffusion. *American Economic Review* 92 (1): 120–42.

McNeil, L. 2006. International trade and economic growth: A methodology for estimating cross-border R&D spillovers. U.S. Bureau of Economic Analysis, April.

National Science Foundation (NSF). 2005. Research and development data link project. Final report. Census Bureau, Bureau of Economic Analysis, and National Science Foundation. Washington, D.C., June.

Parente, S. L., and E. C. Prescott. 2000. *Barriers to riches.* Cambridge, MA: MIT Press.

Xu, B., and J. Wang. 1999. Capital goods trade and R&D spillovers in the OECD. *Canadian Journal of Economics* 32 (5): 1258–74.

6

International Trade in Motion Picture Services

Gordon H. Hanson and Chong Xiang

6.1 Introduction

In the last dozen years, empirical research in international trade has blossomed. There are now extensive bodies of work on testing the Heckscher-Ohlin trade model (Davis and Weinstein 2002), examining the impact of globalization on wages and productivity (Feenstra and Hanson 2002; Tybout 2002), and estimating how trade flows respond to trade costs (Anderson and van Wincoop 2004), among other topics. These strands of literature, however, are almost entirely about international trade in manufactures. Due in part to a paucity of data on service trade flows, relatively few papers address international trade in services (e.g., Freund and Weinhold 2002, Amiti and Wei 2005, and Marvasti and Canterberry 2005). Indicatively, Feenstra's (2004) recent graduate text on international trade includes no references to research on trade involving service industries.

Yet, for the United States and other advanced countries it is services in which their export strength increasingly lies. The 2004 *Economic Report of the President* touts information services (Internet publishing and service provision, motion pictures, printed media, radio and TV programming, software, sound recordings, telecommunications) and professional services (accounting, advertising, architecture, consulting, engineering, law, R&D services) as sectors with the highest recent growth in U.S. net exports. In 2002, U.S. exports and foreign sales of information services were $90 billion, relative to total service exports of $295 billion and manufacturing exports of $627 billion (Siwek 2004). In 2003, information services were 5

Gordon H. Hanson is a professor of economics at the University of California, San Diego, and a research associate of the National Bureau of Economic Research. Chong Xiang is an assistant professor of economics at Purdue University.

percent of U.S. GDP (relative to 14 percent for manufacturing), and exports of U.S. motion pictures accounted for 73 percent of box office revenues in Europe (Siwek 2005).

Why are services such an important part of the U.S. tradables production? One possibility is that the United States has a comparative advantage in tradable services, due to the country's abundant supply of workers (either native or foreign born) with advanced degrees (computer scientists, engineers, lawyers, MBAs) or specialized skills (actors, musicians, recording technicians, screenwriters), which information and professional services use intensively. Reductions in trade costs—associated with improvements in information technology or falling cultural barriers to trade—may have accentuated the U.S. comparative advantage in services. A second possibility is that scale economies may give service providers an incentive to locate in the large U.S. market (Rauch and Trindade 2006). For many information services, average costs decline sharply in output. Where these services are provided in a specific language or cultural context, large markets may be the optimal site for global production (Krugman 1980; Helpman and Krugman 1985). So far, empirical literature has found evidence that large markets affect trade only in manufacturing (Feenstra, Markusen, and Rose 1998; Davis and Weinstein 1999 and 2003; Head and Ries 2001; Hanson and Xiang 2004).

In this paper, we present data on U.S. trade in motion pictures and examine the determinants of U.S. motion picture exports using a modified version of the gravity model. Our focus on motion pictures is warranted by the importance of information services to the U.S. economy and their role in current debates about trade policy. Information services embody large amounts of intellectual property, whose accumulation appears to be important for economic growth but whose ownership rights are often difficult to enforce across national borders (McCalman 2004). Beyond the threat of piracy, many governments aggressively restrict imports of motion pictures and sound recordings, ostensibly to preserve domestic production of cultural goods (Janeba 2004).

In section 6.2, we derive a gravity model of trade in which a country's imports of U.S. motion picture services relative to its expenditure on domestically produced motion picture services depends on the country's size relative to the United States, proximity to the United States in terms of geography and culture, and other trade costs. We measure cultural trade costs using indicators of linguistic distance between countries in Dyen, Kruskal, and Black (1992), Melitz (2002), and Chiswick and Miller (2004), and policy trade barriers using data on the motion picture industry collected in Marvasti and Canterberry (2005).

Given limited public data, empirical research on trade in services requires one to assemble information from private sources. In section 6.3, we describe available data on U.S. exports of motion pictures. The publicly available data on motion picture trade flows appear to be of dubious quality.[1] The U.N. Comtrade database reports trade in motion pictures in terms of the value of *cinematographic film exposed or developed,* which is a commodity rather than a service. Importers appear to have considerable discretion in reporting the value of physical film prints, as Comtrade trade flows are up to two orders of magnitude smaller than foreign box office revenues for U.S. films compiled by Screendigest.com, a private industry source. What makes motion pictures an attractive case to study is that bilateral trade in the industry is easily measured at the point of consumption (movie cinemas, video rental stores, pay TV operators), which facilitates their collection by private consultancies. We use data from Screendigest.com, as reported in Hancock and Jones (2003), to estimate a gravity model of trade for the motion picture industry, the results for which we report in section 6.4. The estimates indicate how market size and trade costs affect trade in motion pictures.

Though information services are among the most dynamic sectors in the U.S. economy, they have been the subject of little research by international economists. Key to new research efforts will be the collection of data on service trade flows. Since service trade rarely passes through ports, airports, or land borders, it is difficult to detect using standard government methods for measuring imports and exports. A further problem is that the channels through which firms export or import services change continually over time. In the early 1990s, most foreign revenue on U.S. motion pictures was generated at the box office. By the late 1990s, videos, DVDs, and pay TV had become important sources of foreign film distribution. Going forward, the Internet may become the dominant mode for film distribution. Given rapid change in the distribution of services, and the slow speed with which government data collection strategies tend to change, private industry sources are likely to be the most useful data source for research on trade in services in the near term.

6.2 Trade Theory and Trade in Information Services

We base our model of information services on Hanson and Xiang (2004), which extends the monopolistic-competition model of trade (e.g., Helpman and Krugman 1985) to a continuum of industries. The setup has a large country and a small country, each with one production factor, labor (though the extension to a many-factor setting is straightforward). There are many industries, some of which are information services (movies, music) and others of which are manufactures (cars, clothes). Production of each good or service is subject to increasing returns to scale. Consumers have identical Cobb-Douglas preferences. Each industry consists of many

---

1. The difficulty of measuring economic activity in services has been studied in much other work. On measurement issues related to services, see Hooper and Richardson (1991), Griliches (1992), Baldwin, Lipsey, and Richardson (1998), and Berndt and Hulten (2007).

Dixit-Stiglitz-type varieties (action movies, comedies), the number of which is endogenous. For industry m, let n_m denote the number of varieties and σ_m denote the elasticity of substitution between varieties, where $\sigma_m > 1$. Each manufacturing industry is subject to an iceberg transport cost, $\tau_m > 1$.

Information services are subject to a cultural discount and perhaps a policy trade barrier (in the form of a tariff or quantity restriction). For a consumer, one unit of a domestic service brings as much satisfaction as $1/\delta$ units of a foreign service, where $0 < \delta < 1$. We expect δ to be higher the more similar are two countries' culture and language. Domestic and foreign varieties of an information service are symmetric in consumption. For each information service i, $\sigma_i > 1$ is the elasticity of substitution between varieties.

Given increasing returns to scale and constant elasticity of substitution (CES) preferences, in equilibrium each service firm and each manufacturing firm is monopolistically competitive and sets a price that is a constant markup over marginal cost. Prices for a given variety of a good or service produced in a given country vary across destination markets according to trade costs.

Based on this framework, let S_{iuk} and S_{ikk} be total sales of information service i by country u (the United States) to country k and by country k to itself. Exploiting the CES structure of preferences, we obtain the following expression for relative sales:

$$(1) \quad \frac{S_{iuk}}{S_{ikk}} = \frac{E_{ik}n_{iu}(\delta_{iuk})^{1-\sigma_i}(p_{iuk}/P_{ik})^{1-\sigma_i}}{E_{ik}n_{ik}(p_{ikk}/P_{ik})^{1-\sigma_i}} = \frac{n_{iu}}{n_{ik}}\left(\frac{w_{iu}}{w_{ik}}\right)^{1-\sigma_i}(\delta_{iuk})^{1-\sigma_i}(t_{iuk})^{1-\sigma_i},$$

where E_{ik} is expenditure by country k on service i, P_{ik} the CES price index in country k for service i, and p_{iuk} is the delivered price (including customs, insurance, and freight charges) in country k of service i produced by country u, w_{iu} is marginal production cost in service i and country u, and t_{iuk} is the ad valorem trade cost on exports from country u to country k. The second equality follows from solving for price in terms of marginal cost. Expressing sales in relative terms removes the CES price index and domestic expenditure from the expression, as shown in the second equality. In the estimation, we will associate the cultural discount (δ_{iuk}) with linguistic distance and ad valorem trade costs (t_{iuk}) with geographic distance, import tariffs, and other policy trade barriers.

One can implement equation (1) empirically by taking a first-order Taylor approximation of the equation that determines the relative number of product varieties produced in the two countries, the derivation of which we do not show in the informal discussion in this paper. For information services, the relative number of product varieties is increasing in relative country size, given certain assumptions. Thus, we can replace the relative number of varieties in (1) with a measure of relative country size, Y_u/Y_k.

The main empirical exercise is to estimate the effect of market size and the effects of trade costs on information services, using the following specification:

$$(2) \quad \ln \frac{S_{luk}}{S_{lkk}} = \beta_0 + \beta_1 \ln \frac{Y_u}{Y_k} + \beta_2 \ln GD_{uk} + \beta_3 \ln LD_{uk} + \beta_4 \ln T_{luk}$$

$$+ \beta_5 \ln \frac{W_u}{W_k} + \varepsilon_{iuk},$$

where u is the United States, k is the importing country, Y_u/Y_k is the relative size of countries u and k, GD_{uk} is geographic distance between u and k, LD_{uk} is linguistic distance between u and k, T_{luk} is k's ad valorem tariff on imports of product i from country u, W_u/W_k is relative production costs in countries u and k, and ε_{iuk} is a disturbance term associated with unobserved trade costs between country pair uk. Again, by examining relative sales of United States and domestic films, we remove expenditure on motion pictures as a determinant of trade flows in equation (2). In theory, the only role that relative country size plays in determining relative sales is through its impact on the relative size of the motion picture industry in the two countries. A positive coefficient on relative income would indicate that large countries are a relatively attractive site for motion picture production.

In estimating equation (2), we confront several important econometric and measurement issues. These include measuring cultural trade costs and policy trade barriers, allowing for the endogeneity of policy trade barriers, and incorporating the threat of piracy as a source of trade frictions. Each of these is an important issue. In this paper, we will focus on the first problem of measuring trade costs and leave accounting for their endogeneity to future work. The empirical exercise in this paper should be seen as a preliminary exploration of whether trade in information services obeys the laws of gravity.

6.3 Data and Empirical Application

In this section, we present data on international trade on motion pictures. We begin by discussing relevant previous research on the motion picture industry, proceed to examine data sources on international trade in motion picture services and on trade costs that may be relevant for motion pictures, and conclude by using data from private industry sources to describe U.S. exports of motion pictures to Europe.

6.3.1   Previous Literature on Trade in Motion Pictures

What has previous research discovered about trade in motion pictures? There appears to be tremendous heterogeneity in the performance of movies. De Vany and Walls (1999, 2004) and Walls (2005) find that the distributions of production cost, box office revenue, and profits (box office revenue minus production cost) have heavy right tails. For example, the mean of production costs is the 62nd percentile of the distribution, the mean of box office revenues is the 71st percentile, and 78 percent of movies lose money while 6 percent of movies account for 80 percent of total profits. Perhaps in response to the uncertainty in movie revenues, Goettler and Leslie (2005) find that studios are more likely to cofinance movies that account for a large fraction of their total annual production budget. De Vany and Eckert (1991) and De Vany and Walls (1996) emphasize that the difficulties with forecasting movie demand necessitate the use of short-term, contingent contracts between distributors and exhibitors. Filson, Switzer, and Besocke (2005) argue that these contracts have evolved to help distributors and exhibitors share risks and overcome measurement problems, rather than to resolve information problems.

The attraction of individual films to consumers appears to be short-lived. De Vany and Walls (1999) show that movies earn 66 percent of their box office revenues during their first three weeks of showing. De Vany and Walls (1997) show that a movie has less than a 25 percent chance of lasting seven weeks or more in the top fifty chart and less than a 15 percent chance of lasting ten weeks or more. In a similar vein, Elberse and Eliashberg (2003) find that the U.S. movies with stronger domestic market performance tend to have higher opening week box office revenues when they are released in the foreign markets (where this correlation becomes weaker the longer the time lag between the movies' U.S. releases and foreign releases).

There is increasing interest in the protection of intellectual property in motion pictures, either domestically or internationally. Byers et al. (2004) study successful movie downloads from peer-to-peer file sharing networks. Of the successful downloads, 60 percent appeared on the peer-to-peer networks prior to the movies' DVD release dates. Of the movies that had been released on DVD as of the time of their study, only 5 percent first appeared after their DVD release date on a network. Together, these facts suggest consumer DVD copying is minor compared with insider leaks of DVDs. Turning to trade, McCalman (2004) finds that while Hollywood studios are more likely to use licensing in countries with moderate protection of intellectual property rights (IPR), they tend to use more integrated governance structures in countries with both high and low IPR protection. McCalman (2005) finds that while moderate IPR protection encourages the spread of U.S. movies, either very weak or very strong IPR protections decrease the speed with which U.S. movies are released abroad.

6.3.2   Data on Trade in Motion Picture Services

Data on international trade in motion pictures or other information services are very difficult to obtain. The U.S. Bureau of Economic Analysis (BEA) publishes limited bilateral trade flows for the film industry. The

BEA surveys of U.S. multinational firms provide some industry data on service trade flows (Kozlow and Borga 2004), but only for U.S. parent firms that own subsidiaries located abroad. The BEA Quarterly Survey of Transactions in Selected Services and Intangible Assets with Foreign Persons does give data on foreign receipts from film and television tape rentals, but does not list data on foreign box office revenues earned by U.S. motion pictures.

The U.N.'s Comtrade lists motion picture trade as a *commodity,* Cinematographic Film Exposed or Developed (SITC 883), which is the reported value of *physical* shipments of exposed film across borders. The value of physical film shipments appears to vastly understate film revenues. For instance, Comtrade reports 2000 U.S. exposed film exports of $0.5 million to France, $0.5 million to Germany, and $6.5 million to the United Kingdom, while Screendigest.com reports 2000 box office revenues for U.S. films of $513 million in France, $615 million in Germany, and $429 million in the United Kingdom (Hancock and Jones 2003).

We evaluate the demand for U.S. films, other foreign films, and domestically made films using data on box office revenues by country and year. Box office revenues are equivalent to the c.i.f. (customs, insurance, freight) value of motion picture services consumed in cinemas, plus retail markups. These revenues include import duties, transport costs, and other trade costs incurred in delivering the service to the consumer, as well as sales taxes and exhibition fees collected by cinemas. Box office revenues are consistent with the trade-cost-inclusive measure of sales in equation (1). Individuals may consume motion picture services through cinemas (for new movie releases) or through video rentals, video purchases, or pay TV (for previous movie releases).[2] Distributors tend to release movies to cinemas first and to retail outlets and pay TV operators later in time, suggesting for a given film these services do not compete contemporaneously. Recently, studios have experimented with releasing films in the U.S. market in cinemas and in video format simultaneously, but this practice appears to be rare in foreign markets. As of yet, the provision of motion picture services through the Internet accounts for a very small share of global film revenues. In this paper, we limit our analysis to motion picture revenues earned through cinema exhibition (box office revenues).

Data on box office revenues for the period 1995 to 2004 are available from Screendigest.com. For this paper, we use data on cinema exhibition and distribution in nineteen European countries from Hancock and Jones (2003). In each country and year, Screendigest.com reports the number of films screened, total film attendance, and total box office revenues for films

---

2. Data on DVD/video sales and rentals are very difficult to get. For example, Screendigest .com charges £5,000 for access to its Video and DVD Global Intelligence database. We are still in the process of acquiring such data.

imported from the United States, films imported from other major producing countries, and films produced domestically. The company also reports attendance and revenue for each of the ten top-grossing films by country and year and other national market data. Screendigest.com compiles these data from government agencies, national film bodies, film exhibitor and distributor associations, and company spokespeople.

An important issue in using data on box office revenues is how to classify the nationality of a motion picture. Screendigest.com defines the origin country for a film by the location of the company that produces the film. Production companies (e.g., 20th Century Fox in the United States) oversee the writing or purchase of screenplays and musical scores, casting, costume and set design, animation, filming, sound recording, and editing, marketing, distribution, and financing.[3]

To consider how data on trade in motion pictures from Comtrade and Screendigest.com compare, figure 6.1, panel A plots the value of total film imports reported by Comtrade and box office revenues for foreign films reported by Screendigest.com for nineteen European countries for the period 1992 to 2002; figure 6.1, panel B shows a similar plot for film imports from the United States and box office revenues for U.S. films in Europe. For either total imports or imports from the United States, box office revenues greatly exceed film imports reported by Comtrade. The magnitude of the differences are perhaps more apparent in table 6.1, which shows the Comtrade value of film imports and the Screendigest.com value of box office revenues for foreign films, by year, for Europe. Over the sample period, the average ratio of the former to the latter is 46.2. Table 6.2 shows averages over 1992 to 2002 by country for Comtrade film imports and Screendigest.com foreign film box office revenues. There appears to be little systematic relationship between the two series. Over the sample period, the average ratio of box office revenues to film imports varies from a low of 20.7 in Austria to a high of 155.8 in Italy. It appears that Comtrade data on film imports (at least for Europe) give no meaningful indication of foreign sales of motion picture services.

6.3.3   U.S. Exports of Motion Pictures

⌠ The data we use for our analysis is from Hancock and Jones (2003), which gives information on U.S. exports of motion pictures to Europe. While the United States is by far and away the dominant player in the European film industry, there is substantial variation across countries in the share of the market held by U.S. studios. It is this variation that we exploit in the gravity estimation in the following section.

Figure 6.2 shows total box office revenues and average ticket prices in the

3. Independent exhibition companies tend to oversee the screening of movies to consumers in destination markets.

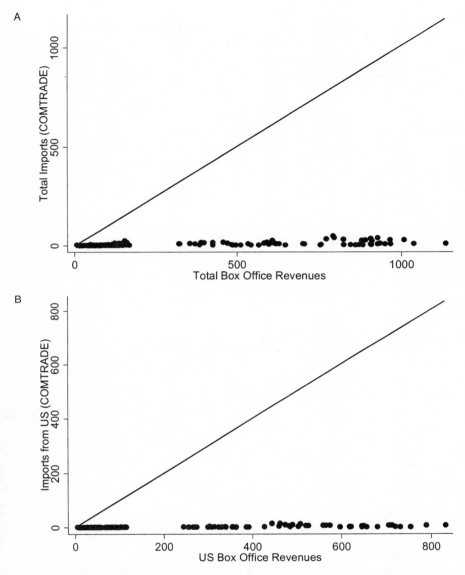

Fig. 6.1 Film imports from comtrade versus box office revenues of foreign films in Europe: *A*, total imports and total box office revenues; *B*, imports from the United States and U.S. box office revenues

Table 6.1   **Imports of motion pictures in europe (in millions of U.S. dollars)**

Year	Total film imports (Comtrade)	Total box office revenues for foreign films (Screendigest.com)
1992	140.9	3,756.2
1993	99.9	3,520.3
1994	96.0	3,902.5
1995	103.1	4,226.9
1996	109.8	4,502.5
1997	92.5	4,612.5
1998	90.5	5,062.5
1999	93.3	4,891.5
2000	91.2	4,409.3
2001	78.0	4,868.7
2002	95.8	5,245.2

Notes: Column 2 reports total imports of SITC 8830 from Comtrade for nineteen countries in Europe; Column 3 reports total box office revenues for foreign films in these countries (as reported by Hancock and Jones 2003). The nineteen countries are Austria, Belgium, Czech Republic, Denmark, Finland, France, Germany, Greece, Hungary, Ireland, Italy, Netherlands, Norway, Poland, Portugal, Spain Sweden, Switzerland, and the United Kingdom.

Table 6.2   **Imports of motion pictures by country (in millions of U.S. dollars)**

Country	Mean film imports (Comtrade)	Mean box office revenues for foreign films (Screendigest.com)
Austria	4.1	85.5
Belgium	2.4	110.8
Czech Republic	0.6	15.5
Denmark	1.0	70.8
Finland	1.2	42.2
France	34.1	880.3
Germany	6.4	812.3
Greece	1.3	50.3
Hungary	1.0	23.5
Ireland	0.4	51.7
Italy	3.3	518.9
Netherlands	1.5	118.5
Norway	2.4	70.9
Poland	1.8	51.9
Portugal	1.9	49.5
Spain	13.9	425.7
Sweden	1.9	119.8
Switzerland	11.9	141.7
United Kingdom	9.7	822.9

Notes: Column 2 reports the average value of imports for SITC 8830 from Comtrade across the years 1992–2002; Column 3 reports average box office revenue for foreign films from Screendigest.com across the years 1992–2002.

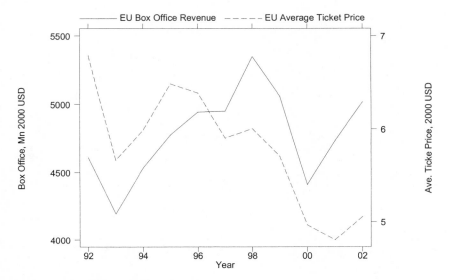

Fig. 6.2   Box office revenues in Europe

nineteen European countries. Revenues grow modestly over the sample period, showing considerable volatility. The surge in revenues in 1998 is associated with the movie, *Titanic,* which at the time was the highest-grossing movie in history. Ticket prices fall over the sample period, due in part to a rising share in European film revenues of lower-priced markets in central and eastern Europe. The importance of high-grossing films is further evident in figure 6.3, which shows the share of the top ten films in total box office revenues. The top ten share fluctuates considerably, reaching its height in 1998 with *Titanic,* with an average of the period of 0.48.

For Europe as a whole, the United States is the most important source of motion pictures. Figure 6.4 shows the share of box office revenues of U.S. films, domestically made films, and other foreign films. Over the sample period, the U.S. revenue share averages 0.69 and is quite stable. Revenue shares for domestic films and films from third countries are roughly equal. The dominance of U.S. studios is due largely to a relatively small number of high-grossing films. This is seen in figure 6.5, which shows the average number of films released in Europe by origin country or region. While the U.S. share of box office revenues is over twice that for domestic and non-U.S. foreign films combined, the number of U.S. film releases is slightly smaller than the sum of domestic and non-U.S. foreign releases. Domestic and non-U.S. foreign releases tend to have small gross revenues.

Countries in Europe vary in the size of their domestic motion picture industries. Figure 6.6 shows the ratio of local box office revenues for U.S. films to local box office revenues for domestically produced films by Euro-

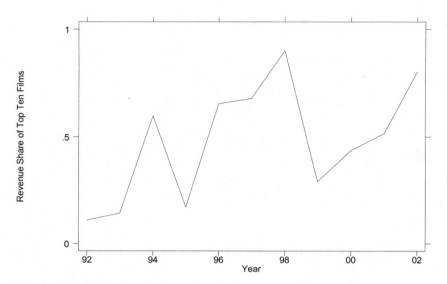

Fig. 6.3 **Share of high-grossing films in European box office revenues**

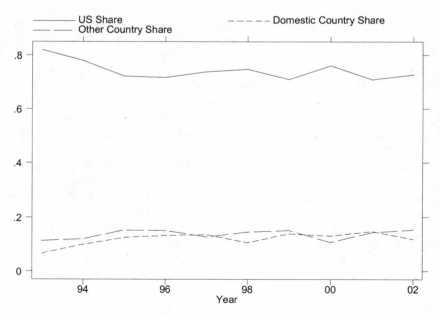

Fig. 6.4 **U.S. share of box office revenues in Europe**

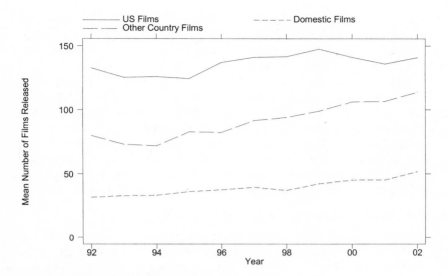

Fig. 6.5   Number of films released in Europe

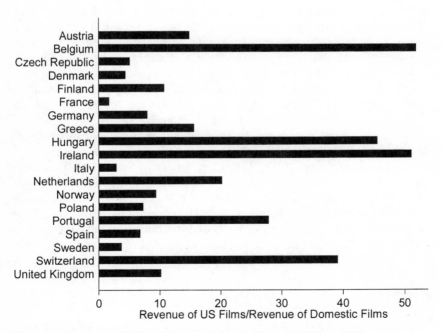

Fig. 6.6   Revenues of U.S. and domestic films in Europe, 1995 to 2002

pean country averaged over 1995 to 2002, which is the period for which data on every country is available. The log of this ratio is the dependent variable in equation (2). Relative U.S. film revenues range from over fifty times domestic film revenues in Belgium and Ireland to less than five times in France. Differences in the size of national movie industries in part reflect differences in country size. Relative U.S. film revenues are strongly positively correlated with the ratio of U.S. GDP to national GDP, with the log correlation between relative film revenues and relative GDP a highly significant 0.45. Differences in trade costs vis-à-vis the United States may also affect the size of national movie industries. As we discuss next, countries in Europe vary both in their cultural proximity to the United States and in the protection they afford their domestic motion picture industries.

6.3.4 Trade Costs in Motion Pictures

Before turning to the estimation, we need to identify data on trade costs relevant to motion pictures. We measure cultural trade costs between the United States and its trading partners using indicators of the linguistic distance between English and other countries' primary languages.[4] Distances between languages capture the extent to which two countries share a common linguistic heritage, which may indicate how easily cultural ideas flow between them. Linguists group languages according to family trees. English belongs to the Indo-European language family, whose speech varieties have been examined extensively. In a classic study, Dyen, Kruskal, and Black (1992) measure the similarity between ninety-five Indo-European speech varieties. They create a percentage cognate matrix, which identifies for each pair of languages the fraction of words for 200 basic meanings (e.g., all, and, father, ice) that can be traced back to a common ancestral word. In Europe, the Dyen index for English ranges from a high of 0.60 for Dutch (indicating that 60 percent of English and Dutch words for the 200 basic meanings share a common ancestral word) to 0.23 for Czech.[5]

As an additional indicator of linguistic distance, we use the relative ease with which U.S. citizens learn foreign languages. After receiving a foreign job posting, employees of the U.S. Department of State (DOS) undergo twenty-four weeks of foreign language training, at the end of which they are tested on their proficiency. Chiswick and Miller (2004) use the average scores of DOS test takers by language in the early 1990s as a metric of the distance between English and forty-three other languages. The DOS index encapsulates both linguistic differences between English and other lan-

4. Two countries in our sample, Belgium and Switzerland, do not have a single dominant language. For these countries, we calculate linguistic distance as the weighted average of the distance between English and their primary languages, using data in Melitz (2002) and Gordon (2005) to calculate language weights.
5. For other work on trade using the Dyen index, see Ginsburgh, Ortuno-Ortin, and Weber (2005).

guages and the exposure of U.S. citizens to other cultures. United States citizens have an easier time learning Spanish (average score of 2.25) than Japanese (average score of 1) in part because Spanish is more similar to English and in part because U.S. citizens have been more exposed to Spanish.[6] A disadvantage of the DOS measure is that language tests are not randomly assigned. Department of State employees may be posted to particular countries based in part on their perceived ability to learn a language. Thus, test takers may be selected into a specific exam based on their unobserved ability, which could compress variation in DOS exam scores. The correlation between the Dyen and DOS indices is 0.65.

To measure policy barriers on motion-picture trade, we use a country-level trade barrier index (TBI) constructed by Marvasti and Canterberry (2005) for thirty-three countries in the early 1990s. Their index is the average across six dummy variables for trade barriers in motion pictures. These dummies capture the presence of tariffs on film imports, quantitative restrictions on film imports, levies on imported video sales, subsidies to domestic film producers, overall trade barriers on service imports, and obstacles in enforcing property rights. In Europe, France and Italy have the most restrictive barriers on motion pictures, followed closely by Spain. The Netherlands, Norway and Sweden have the least restrictive barriers. Belgium, Germany, Switzerland, and the United Kingdom have intermediate levels of trade barriers. Marvasti and Canterberry (2005) find that their trade barrier index is *positively* correlated with imports of U.S. motion pictures. However, they use a gravity specification that does not control for multilateral resistance, contrary to the estimation strategy suggested by Anderson and van Wincoop (2004). Using a theoretically grounded gravity specification, as in equation (2), we find a negative correlation between trade levels and trade costs in motion pictures.

6.4   Gravity Estimation Results

Table 6.3 reports estimates of equation (2). The dependent variable is the log ratio of box office revenues of U.S. films to box office revenues of domestic films, by country. The independent variables are the log ratio of U.S. to domestic GDP; the log ratio of U.S. to domestic average annual earnings for skilled labor in manufacturing (from the UNIDO Industrial Database); log geographic distance to the United States; the log trade barrier index from Marvasti and Canterbury (2005) and a dummy variable for whether the country has no TBI data; the log Dyen index and a dummy variable for whether a country's primary language is non-Indo-European (for which the Dyen index is undefined); and the log Department of State language exam index from Chiswick and Miller (2004) and a dummy variable for

6. The highest average score is 3, for both Afrikaans and Swedish.

Table 6.3   Gravity model estimation results for U.S. exports of motion picture services

	(1)	(2)	(3)	(4)	(5)	(6)
ln Y_{us}/Y_k	0.450	0.552	0.456	0.483	0.790	0.812
	(0.073)	(0.114)	(0.092)	(0.072)	(0.132)	(0.110)
ln W_{us}/W_k	−0.324	−0.175	−0.23	−0.480	−0.007	−0.452
	(0.128)	(0.133)	(0.139)	(0.157)	(0.140)	(0.144)
ln Distance	−1.526	−0.523	−0.412	−2.077	1.202	−2.119
	(0.893)	(1.161)	(1.037)	(0.988)	(1.448)	(1.207)
ln TBI		−0.268			0.774	−0.878
		(0.360)			(0.435)	(0.289)
No TBI		−1.123			0.336	−3.458
		(0.7020)			(0.7700)	(0.6860)
ln Dyen			−0.493		−0.882	
			(0.162)		(0.234)	
Non-Indo-European			−0.634		−1.106	
			(0.256)		(0.281)	
ln DOS				−1.309		−5.534
				(0.662)		(0.880)
English				−0.799		−4.515
				(0.691)		(0.829)
R^2	0.235	0.271	0.271	0.261	0.337	0.423
N	171	171	171	171	171	171

Notes: The dependent variable is the log ratio of box office revenues of U.S. films to box office revenues of domestic films. The independent variables are the log ratio of U.S. to domestic GDP (ln Y_{us}/Y_k); the log ratio of U.S. to domestic average annual earnings for skilled labor in manufacturing (ln W_{us}/W_k); log geographic distance to the United States (ln Distance); the log trade barrier index from Marvasti and Canterbury (2005) and a dummy variable for whether the country has no TBI data (ln TBI, No TBI); the log Dyen index and a dummy variable for whether a country's primary language is non-Indo-European (ln Dyen, Non Indo-Euro); the log Department of State language exam index from Chiswick and Miller (2004) and a dummy variable for whether a country's primary language is English (ln DOS, English). The specification also includes year dummies, which are unreported. The sample is the nineteen European countries (see table 6.1) over the period 1992 to 2002.

whether a country's primary language is English (for which the DOS index is undefined). The specification also includes year dummies, which are unreported. The sample is the nineteen European countries included in Hancock and Jones (2003) over the period 1992 to 2002. Since there are only nineteen countries and the six trade-cost variables do not vary across time, it is not feasible to include all trade cost measures in the same regression. For some trade cost measures, the results are sensitive to which other trade costs are included as regressors.

Relative U.S. film revenues are increasing in relative U.S. GDP.[7] The

---

7. The coefficients on GDP are not directly comparable to standard gravity model estimates (which are closer to 1), since our dependent variable is not log trade but log trade relative to log domestic consumption.

United States has a more dominant position in the motion picture industries of smaller countries. These results suggest that larger countries have an advantage as a production location in motion pictures, consistent with results on market-size effects in the theoretical models in Krugman (1980) and Helpman and Krugman (1985) and gravity results for differentiated manufacturing industries in Feenstra, Markusen, and Rose (1998) and Hanson and Xiang (2004). Given fixed costs in producing motion pictures and trade costs (associated with language, culture, and trade policy) in delivering motion picture services, studios appear to have an incentive to situate production in large countries. As a result, the dominance of U.S. studios is weakest in the larger European markets, including France, Germany, Italy, Spain, and the United Kingdom, which is apparent in figure 6.6.

Exports of U.S. films are smaller in countries where U.S. wages are relatively high. This is consistent with higher production costs deterring U.S. exports. Trade costs appear to affect the ability of U.S. studios to penetrate foreign markets. Relative U.S. film revenues are decreasing in each of the trade cost measures.

The estimated coefficient on the trade barrier index is negative in two specifications, as expected, but precisely estimated in only one case. There is an obvious concern about the endogeneity of policy trade barriers. Countries whose unobserved characteristics are associated with weaker domestic film industries may be more likely to impose import protection for motion pictures, which would tend to introduce positive bias in the coefficient estimate on the trade barrier index. A further problem is that we do not observe trade barriers for all countries in the sample. Controlling for the endogeneity of trade barriers and expanding the coverage of this measure to include additional countries are important tasks for further research.

The coefficient on the Dyen index, which is the most precisely estimated trade-cost parameter, indicates that, all else equal, moving from an English-speaking country (Dyen index of 1) to a Czeck-speaking country (Dyen index of 0.23) would reduce U.S. film revenues relative to domestic film revenues by 72 log points, based on results in column (3), which is a large effect. Relative U.S. film revenues are also substantially lower in non-Indo-European-language countries, which in our sample include Finland, Hungary, and Norway. Languages that belong to the same family share common ancestral origins in their speech varieties. Countries whose languages belong to different language families may have relatively few historical links between their cultures, which could tend to dampen trade in cultural goods such as motion pictures.

The coefficient on the DOS language index is negative, again indicating that trade is lower between countries that are more linguistically distant from the United States, but is quite sensitive to which other regressors are included in the estimation.

6.5   Summary

In this project, we develop a theoretical framework to examine international trade in information services and apply this framework to an empirical study of trade in motion pictures. Despite the growing importance of services, in general, and information services, in particular, for U.S. trade, the export performance of these sectors has been the subject of little empirical research.

The intellectual merit of our research comes from identifying the extent to which the size of the U.S. market has contributed to the global concentration of the motion picture industry in the U.S. and using newly available measures of linguistic distance to estimate the impact of cultural trade barriers on trade in motion pictures. Market size, language, and trade are each important determinants of U.S. motion picture exports.

To date, the poor quality of published data on trade in services has hampered research on the sector's role in the global economy. However, poor data quality does not mean the U.S. current account is mismeasured. Foreign revenues earned by U.S. motion pictures still appear in the current account, either as exports or as investment income (resulting from license agreements, royalties, or foreign sales by affiliates of U.S. multinationals).

References

Amiti, M., and S.-J. Wei. 2005. Fear of service outsourcing: Is it justified? *Economic Policy* 20:308–47.

Anderson, J. E., and E. van Wincoop. 2004. Trade costs. *Journal of Economic Literature* 42 (3):691–751.

Baldwin, R. E., R. E. Lipsey, and D. Richardson. 1998. *Geography and ownership as bases for economic accounting.* Chicago: University of Chicago Press.

Berndt, E., and C. R. Hulten. 2007. *Hard-to-measure goods and services: Essays in honor of Zvi Griliches.* Chicago: University of Chicago Press.

Byers, S., L. F. Cranor, E. Cronin, D. Korman, and P. McDaniel. 2004. An analysis of security vulnerabilities in the movie production and distribution process. *Telecommunications Policy.* Special Issue, 28 (7–8):619–44.

Chiswick, B., and P. Miller. 2004. Linguistic distance: A quantitative measure of distance between English and other Languages. IZA Discussion Paper no. 1246.

Council of Economic Advisors. 2004. *Economic Report of the President.* Washington, D.C.: GPO.

Davis, D. R., and D. E. Weinstein. 1999. Economic geography and regional production structure. *European Economic Review* 43:379–407.

———. 2002. The factor content of trade. In *Handbook of international trade,* ed. E. K. Choi and J. Harrigan, 119–46. London: Blackwell.

———. 2003. Market access, economic geography and comparative advantage: An empirical assessment. *Journal of International Economics* 59 (1):1–24.

De Vany, A. S., and R. D. Eckert. 1991. Motion pictures antitrust: The paramount cases revisited. *Research in Law and Economics* 14:51–112.

De Vany, A. S., and W. D. Walls. 1996. Bose-Einstein dynamics and adaptive contracting in the motion pictures industry. *Economic Journal* 1493–1514.
———. 1997. The market for motion pictures: Rank, revenue, and survival. *Economic Inquiry* 35 (4):783–97.
———. 1999. Uncertainty in the movie industry. *Journal of Cultural Economics* 23 (4):285–318.
———. 2004. Motion picture profit, the stable Paretian hypothesis, and the curse of the superstar. *Journal of Economic Dynamics and Control* 28 (6):1035–57.
Dyen, I., J. B. Kruskal, and P. Black. 1992. An Indoeuropean classification: A lexicostatistical experiment. *Transactions of the American Philosophical Society* 82 (5):1–132.
Elberse, A., and J. Eliashberg. 2003. Demand and supply dynamics for sequentially released products in international markets: The case of motion pictures. *Marketing Science* 22 (3):329–54.
Feenstra, R. C. 2004. *Advanced international trade: Theory and evidence.* Princeton, NJ: Princeton University Press.
Feenstra, R. C., and G. H. Hanson. 2002. Global production and inequality: A survey of trade and wages. In *Handbook of international trade,* ed. E. K. Choi and J. Harrigan, 146–85. London: Blackwell.
Feenstra, R. C., J. R. Markusen, and A. Rose. 1998. Understanding the home market effect and the gravity equation: The role of differentiating goods. NBER Working Paper no. 6804. Cambridge, MA: National Bureau of Economic Research.
Filson, D., D. Switzer, and P. Besocke. 2005. At the movies: The economics of exhibition contracts. *Economic Inquiry* 43 (2):354–69.
Freund, C., and D. Weinhold. 2002. The Internet and international trade in services. *American Economic Review* 92 (2):236–40.
Ginsburgh, V., I. Ortuno-Ortin, and S. Weber. 2005. Disenfranchisement in linguistically diverse societies: The case of the European Union. *Journal of the European Economic Association* 3 (4):946–65.
Goettler, R. L., and P. Leslie. 2005. Cofinancing to manage risk in the motion picture industry. *Journal of Economics and Management Strategy* 14 (2):231–61.
Gordon, R. G., Jr., ed. 2005. *Ethnologue: Languages of the world,* 15th ed. Dallas, TX: SIL International.
Griliches, Z. 1992. *Output measurement in the service sectors.* Chicago: University of Chicago Press.
Hancock, D., and C. Jones. 2003. *Cinema distribution and exhibition in Europe,* 2nd ed. London: Screendigest.
Hanson, G. H., and C. Xiang. 2004. The home market effect and bilateral trade patterns. *American Economic Review* 94:1108–29.
Head, K., and J. Ries. 2001. Increasing returns versus national product differentiation as an explanation for the pattern of US-Canada trade. *American Economic Review* 91 (4):858–76.
Helpman, E., and P. Krugman. 1985. *Market structure and foreign trade.* Cambridge, MA: The MIT Press.
Holmes, T. J., and J. J. Stevens. 2002. The home market and the pattern of trade: Round three. Federal Reserve Bank of Minneapolis Staff Report no. 304.
Hooper, P., and D. Richardson. 1991. *International economic transactions: Issues in measurement and empirical research.* Chicago: University of Chicago Press.
Hoskins, C., S. McFadyen, and A. Finn. 1997. *Global television and film.* Oxford: Clarendon.
Janeba, E. 2004. International trade and cultural identity. NBER Working Paper no. 10426. Cambridge, MA: National Bureau of Economic Research.

Johnson, N. L., S. Kotz, and N. Balakrishnan. 1994. *Continuous univariate distributions.* New York: Wiley.

Kozlow, R., and M. Borga. 2004. Offshoring and the U.S. balance of payments. U.S. Bureau of Economic Analysis Working Paper 2004-05.

Krugman, P. 1980. Scale economies, product differentiation, and the pattern of trade. *American Economic Review* 70:950–59.

Marvasti, A., and E. R. Canterberry. 2005. Cultural and other barriers to motion pictures trade. *Economic Inquiry* 43 (1):39–54.

McCalman, P. 2004. Foreign direct investment and intellectual property rights: Evidence from Hollywood's global distribution of movies and videos. *Journal of International Economics* 62 (1):107–23.

———. 2005. International diffusion and intellectual property rights: An empirical analysis. *Journal of International Economics* 67:353–72.

Melitz, M. J. 2002. Language and foreign trade. CEPR Discussion Paper no. 3590.

———. 2003. The impact of trade on intra-industry reallocations and aggregate industry productivity. *Econometrica* 71 (6):1695–1725.

Rauch, J. E., and V. Trindade. 2006. Neckties in the tropics: A model of international trade and cultural diversity. University of Missouri Working Paper no. 0517.

Siwek, S. E. 2004. Copyright industries in the U.S. economy: The 2004 report. Economists Incorporated for the International Intellectual Property Alliance. Washington, D.C.: IIPA.

———. 2005. Engines of growth: Economic contributions of U.S. intellectual property industries. Economists Incorporated for NBC Universal. Washington, D.C.: IIPA.

Tybout, J. R. 2002. Plant and firm-level evidence on 'new' trade theories. In *Handbook of international trade,* ed. E. K. Choi and J. Harrigan, 388–415. London: Blackwell.

Walls, W. D. 2005. Demand stochastics, supply adaptation, and the distribution of film earnings. *Applied Economics Letters* 12 (10):619–23.

Comment   Phillip McCalman

International trade studies the exchange of goods and services between countries. However, for the most part, empirical research has focused on the former—goods, and neglected the latter—services. While the historical reasons for this concentration are relatively clear—goods are generally thought of as traded, while services (haircuts, physician consultation) are naturally thought of as nontraded—the pronounced shift in the structure of most economies toward services, along with technological change, has dramatically changed this notion. Consequently, in contemporary discussions of globalization, reference is not only made to the integration of goods markets but also increasingly to the integration of services markets, with service outsourcing receiving particular attention. With this change

Phillip McCalman is an associate professor of economics at the University of California, Santa Cruz.

in emphasis naturally comes the question of whether the standard theories need to be modified, and if so, in what way? To make any progress on these questions, evidence of the capacity of existing theories to provide answers is required. This is the challenge that Gordon and Chong take up in their paper with respect to arguably one of the most important service exports of the United States, motion pictures.

The analysis of motion picture trade provides a particularly neat template for the study of trade in other services. Like most services, it is very skill intensive and has a very high ratio of fixed costs to total costs. So on the cost side, it is generally relatively straightforward to measure the cost of factors used in the production process. However, the difficulty generally comes when measuring the amount and value of service that is exchanged in any transaction. This is especially the case in relation to motion pictures, since customs officials are typically interested in the value of the physical property that is either leaving or entering a country. If a canister of film is shipped from the United States to Europe, what is the value recorded by U.S. customs service? If the question is answered exclusively in terms of the replacement cost of the film in the canister, then this is of the order of a couple of thousand dollars. However, if the answer is based on the estimated revenue from the services that film generates in European cinemas, then the answer could well be millions of dollars. The key point is that the value of the physical asset that crosses the border is typically not a true reflection of the value of the service. This point is neatly illustrated by the difference between the European box office for foreign films and the official trade data, with the former approximately fifty times larger than the latter. The message here is clear—if we are to use official statistics to track the most dynamic sector of the economy, then the way in which these statistics are collected needs to be fundamentally reformed.

To overcome this handicap, Gordon and Chong turn to commercial sources to get an understanding of how well standard theories predict the pattern of trade in motion picture services. The key measurement issue they focus on is the relative performance of American movies in foreign markets. While aspects of this data are publicly available, since box office revenues are published, it is the compilation of this data for a large number of countries that is harder to come by. Somewhat surprisingly, this straightforward data collection exercise turns out to be extremely expensive to purchase, creating a major and essentially unnecessary barrier to research in this area. Having paid this cost, Hanson and Xiang ask a relatively standard goods trade style question; does domestic market size influence the scale of local production? In models of product differentiation and transport costs the answer to this question is yes—a larger local market is associated with a disproportionately larger share of varieties produced in the larger market. This result is known as the *home market effect.*

Since movies are differentiated products, the parallel to the analysis with goods trade is relatively clear. However, the transport costs associated with shipping a movie from the United States to Europe at first seem trivial. Can a very small trade friction be responsible for Hollywood? Clearly not. To complete the analogy to trade in goods they employ the neat trick of thinking of things in terms of cultural distance rather than physical distance. Under this notion of distance the question is how much of a film's message/concept can be translated into another culture? This concept is clearly multidimensional, but to make it operational in an econometric sense they focus on measures of linguistic distance—how similar a language is to English. Here the idea is that languages that are more similar to English also reflect cultures that are also relatively similar. With this measure in hand, the notion of trade friction is well defined. To provide a point of contrast, the empirical analysis also includes physical distance along with more standard measures of barriers to market access, such as quotas.

The empirical analysis concentrates on U.S. penetration into nineteen European markets over the period 1992 through 2002. The dependent variable is the log of the box office for U.S. films relative to the log of a country's box office. In general, they find that relative size does matter, with the U.S. box office share being large in smaller markets. This result is consistent with the home market effect and the associated advantages of size. However, the home market effect depends critically on trade frictions, and this is the more innovative aspect of the paper. Here the standard measures of physical distance or trade barriers tended not to have a robust relationship, but the measures of cultural distance perform much better. While not confirming the theory, the results are certainly consistent with its main predictions. This suggests that standard models do have a role to play in analyzing the rapidly growing services trade. Nevertheless, it would be nice to get a sense of the relative size of the home market effect and whether it is more or less pronounced than in goods trade. While data limitations are a barrier to such analysis, it would provide a natural measure of how similar the determinants of services trade are to those of goods trade.

III

Offshoring of Services

Does Service Offshoring Lead to Job Losses?
Evidence from the United States

Mary Amiti and Shang-Jin Wei

7.1 Introduction

A relatively new dimension of economic globalization is exports and imports of services, which used to be quintessential nontradables in a typical textbook on international economics. One of the authors once wanted to change his United Airlines flight while in Paris, but ended up talking to a service representative in Ireland after dialing a Parisian phone number. An American company may also find it most cost-efficient to farm out a computer programming task to a firm in India instead of doing it in-house or buying it from another firm in the United States. This phenomenon, known as either "service offshoring" or "international outsourcing of services," has gathered enormous attention in news media and political circles, especially in times leading up to national elections in industrialized countries. For example, in a recent presidential election year in the United States, from January 1 to November 2, 2004 (the day of the election), there

Mary Amiti is a Senior Economist in the International Research Function of the Federal Reserve Bank of New York. Shang-Jin Wei is a professor of finance and economics and the N.T. Wang Chair in Chinese Business and Economy at Columbia University, and a research associate of the National Bureau of Economic Research.

International Research, Federal Reserve Bank of New York, 33 Liberty Street, New York, NY 20431, email mary.amiti@ny.frb.org; Columbia Business School, 3022 Broadway, Uris Hall Room 619, New York, NY 10027. We would like to thank John Romalis, Robert Feenstra, Caroline Freud, Gordon Hanson, Simon Johnson, Jozef Konings, Aart Kraay, Anna Maria Mayda, Christopher Pissarides, Raghu Rajan, Tony Venables, the editors and two reviewers, participants at the NBER-CRIW and EIIE conferences, and seminar participants at the IMF, Georgetown University, and the U.S. International Trade Commission for helpful comments. We thank Yuanyuan Chen, Jungjin Lee, and Evelina Mengova for excellent research assistance. The views expressed in this Working Paper are those of the authors and do not necessarily represent those of the IMF or IMF policy, or those of the Federal Reserve Bank of New York or the Federal Reserve System.

were 2,850 news reports on service offshoring that used the term "offshoring." The interest in the subject has not disappeared and is likely to grow again in future national elections. In the first five months of 2006, there were 876 news reports in the United States that used the term "offshoring."[1] In fact, there were many more news reports on the subject, but perhaps they used the word "outsourcing" instead of "offshoring."

With rapid technological progress in computers, telecommunication, and other areas, more information and other business services can now be relocated from rich countries to lower-cost overseas sites and imported back. The amount of media and political attention in rich countries presumably has to do with the fear that service offshoring may lead to job losses at home. The newspapers are full of estimates on the effects of offshoring on jobs, which primarily come from management consultants. For example, management consultants at McKinsey forecast offshoring to grow at the rate of 30 to 40 percent a year over the next five years. They report that a leading IT analyst, Forrester, projects that the number of U.S. jobs that will be offshored will grow from 400,000 jobs to 3.3 million jobs by 2015, accounting for $136 billion in wages. Of this total, 8 percent of current IT jobs will go offshore over the next twelve years. The report goes on to say that fears of job losses are being overplayed, but it is unclear how their numbers are derived. Blinder (2006) provides a sector-by-sector guess on which types of service jobs may move offshore based on whether they can be delivered electronically. While the gross job loss is likely to be bigger than the Forrester estimate, he asserts that the net loss is likely to be small. Krugman (1995) argues that foreign trade in general is unlikely to have contributed significantly to the rising skill premium in the United States, although Krugman (2008) conjectures that this might have changed in more recent years. A rigorous study of job market effects in the United States is by Feenstra and Hanson (1996, 1999) but their focus is on material offshoring and its effects on the skill wage premium. They do not consider the effects of service offshoring, nor do they consider the effects on employment. Feenstra and Hanson (1996, 1999) found that material offshoring explained over 40 percent of the increase in nonproduction wages in the 1980s. Jensen and Kletzer (2005) find that a significant number of service industries are tradable, and displaced service sector workers tend to have higher skills and better predisplacement pays than displaced manufacturing workers.[2]

In this chapter, we study the employment effect of service offshoring for

1. Authors' calculation based on FACTIVA, an eletronic news database.
2. More recently, a number of studies have analyzed employment effects of offshoring in Europe. For example, Ekholm and Hakkala (2005) disentangle the employment effects by skill, using Swedish data; and Lorentowicz, Marin, and Raubold (2005) analyze the wage skill premium in Austria and Poland.

the United States during the period 1992 to 2000.[3] The results show that service offshoring has no significant effect on employment when manufacturing industries are aggregated to ninety-six industries. However, at a more disaggregated division of the manufacturing sector of 450 industries, we were able to detect a statistically significant negative effect. Service offshoring reduced manufacturing employment by around 0.4 of a percent. So, to examine whether service offshoring leads to net job losses, the level of aggregation is important. Because the U.S. labor market is reasonably flexible, one does not need to aggregate sectors very much to find that this employment effect washes out.

The rest of the chapter is organized as follows. Section 7.2 sets out the model and estimation strategy. Section 7.3 describes the data. Section 7.4 presents the results and section 7.5 concludes.

7.2   Model and Estimating Framework

This section describes a conceptual framework that motivates the empirical specification.

7.2.1   Model

The production function for an industry i is given by:

$$(1) \qquad Y_i = A_i(oss_i, osm_i) \, F(L_i, K_i, M_i, S_i),$$

where output, Y_i; is a function of labor, L_i; capital, K_i; materials, M_i; and service inputs, S_i. The technology shifter, A_i, is a function of offshoring of services (oss_i), and offshoring of material inputs (osm_i).[4]

We assume that a firm chooses the total amount of each input in the first stage and chooses what proportion of material and service inputs will be imported in the second stage. The fixed cost of importing material inputs, F_k^M, and the fixed cost of importing service inputs, F_k^S, vary by industry k. This assumption reflects that the type of services or materials required are different for each industry, and hence importing will involve different amounts of search costs depending on the level of the sophistication of the inputs.

Cost minimization leads to the optimal demand for inputs for a given level of output, Y_i. The conditional labor demand is given by:

---

3. A crucial part of the data, the input-output tables from the Bureau of Labor Statistics, is available only up to year 2000. Therefore, it is not straightforward to extend the measure of offshored services beyond 2000 on a consistent basis.

4. Mann (2004) provides a back-of-envelope calcuation suggesting that offshoring in the IT industry led to an annual increase in productivity of 0.3 percentage points for the period 1995 to 2002. For the entire U.S. manufacturing sectors, Amiti and Wei (2006) show that offshoring increased productivity between 1992 and 2000.

(2) $L_i = g(w_i, r_i, q^m, q^s, Y_i)/A_i(oss_i, osm_i).$

It is a function of wages, w_i; rental, r_i; material input prices, q_i^m; service input prices, q_i^s; and output. Offshoring can affect the labor demand through three channels. First, there is a substitution effect through the input price of materials or services. A fall in the price of imported services would lead to a fall in the demand for labor if labor and services are substitutes. Second, if offshoring leads to a productivity improvement then firms can produce the same amount of output with less inputs. Hence, conditional on a given level of output, offshoring is expected to reduce the demand for labor. Third, offshoring can affect labor demand through a scale effect. An increase in offshoring can make the firm more efficient and competitive, increasing demand of its output and hence labor. To allow for the scale effect, we substitute in for the profit-maximizing level of output, which is also a function of offshoring, then the labor demand function is given by

(3) $L_i = g(w_i, r_i, q^m, q^s, p_i, oss_i, osm_i)/A_i(oss_i, osm_i),$

where p_i is the price of the final output, which is also a function of factor prices. Thus, offshoring may have a positive or negative effect on employment depending on whether the scale effect outweighs the negative substitution and productivity effects.

7.2.2   Estimation

The conditional labor demand, equation (2), will also be estimated in first differences as a log-log specification as is common in the empirical literature (see Hamermesh 1993; and Hanson, Mataloni, and Slaughter 2003) as follows:

(4) $\Delta \ln l_{it} = \gamma_0 + \gamma_1 \Delta oss_{it} + \gamma_2 \Delta osm_{it} + \gamma_3 \ln \Delta w_{it} + \gamma_4 \Delta \ln Y_{it} + \delta_t D_t$
        $+ \delta_i D_i + \varepsilon_{it}.$

The source of identification of employment in these type of industry labor demand studies is the assumption that the wage is exogenous to the industry. This would be the case if labor were mobile across industries. However, if labor were not perfectly mobile and there were industry-specific rents then wages would not be exogenous. Provided these rents are unchanged over time, they would be absorbed in the industry fixed effects and the results would be unbiased.

In general, an increase in output would be expected to have a positive effect on employment and an increase in wages a negative effect; whereas an increase in the price of other inputs would have a positive effect if the inputs are gross substitutes.

The question arises as to which input prices to use for imported inputs. If the firm is a multinational firm deciding on how much labor to employ at home and abroad then it should be the foreign wage. But not all offshoring takes place within multinational firms, and also with imported inputs sourced from many countries it is unclear which foreign wage to include, if any. Firms that import inputs at arm's length do not care about the foreign wage per se but instead are concerned about the price of the imported service. We assume that all firms face the same price for inputs, such as imported inputs and the rental on capital, which we assume is some function of time, $r = f(t)$.[5] In this time-differenced equation, these input prices will be captured by the time fixed effects, δ_t. In a conditional demand function, we expect that if offshoring increases productivity, then this will have a negative effect on the demand for labor since less inputs are needed to produce the same amount of output.

Substituting in the price of output for the quantity of output, we allow for scale effects:

$$(5) \quad \Delta \ln l_{it} = \gamma_0 + \gamma_1 \Delta oss_{it} + \gamma_2 \Delta osm_{it} + \gamma_3 \ln \Delta w_{it} + \gamma_5 \Delta \ln p_{it} + \delta_t D_t$$
$$+ \delta_i D_i + \varepsilon_{it}.$$

In this specification it is unclear what the net effect of offshoring is on labor demand (see equation [3]) as it will depend on whether the scale effects are large enough to outweigh the substitution and productivity effects. In some specifications we will estimate a more reduced form of equation (5), omitting p_{it}, which is a function of input prices.

This first difference specification controls for any time-invariant industry-specific effects such as industry technology differences. In this time-differenced specification, we also include year fixed effects, to control for unobserved time-varying effects common across all industries that affect employment growth, and in some specifications we also include industry fixed effects. Some industries may be pioneering industries that are high-growth industries and hence more likely to offshore inputs, and some industries might be subject to higher technical progress than others. Adding industry fixed effects to a time differenced equation takes account of these factors, provided the growth or technical progress is fairly constant over time. We estimate this equation using ordinary least squares (OLS), with robust standard errors corrected for clustering. We also include one period lags of the offshoring variables to take into account that productivity effects may not be instantaneous.

There may also be a problem of potential endogeneity of offshoring. A firm that is shedding jobs in response to declining demand may also choose to import business services to save cost. In this example, service offshoring

---

5. Note that in Amiti and Wei (2005), which estimates a labor demand equation for the United Kingdom, the offshoring intensity is interpreted as an inverse proxy of the price of imported service inputs (i.e., the lower the price of imported service inputs, the higher the offshoring intensity). Similarly, in this specification, the offshoring intensity may be picking up the productivity effect and/or the substitution effect.

does not cause the change in employment even if there is a correlation between the two. We also use the Arellano-Bond GMM estimator, which uses lags as instruments, to address the potential endogeneity of offshoring.

7.3   Data and Measurement of Offshoring

We estimate the effects of offshoring on employment for the period 1992 to 2000. Service offshoring ($oss_{i,t}$) for each industry i at time t is defined as the share of imported service inputs and is calculated analogously to the material offshoring measure in Feenstra and Hanson (1996, 1999) as follows:

$$(6) \quad oss_{it} = \sum_{j} \left(\frac{\text{input purchases of service } j \text{ by industry } i, \text{ at time } t}{\text{total non-energy inputs used by industry } i, \text{ at time } t} \right)$$
$$\cdot \left(\frac{\text{imports of service } j, \text{ at time } t}{\text{production}_j + \text{imports}_j - \text{exports}_j \text{ at time } t} \right).$$

The first term in parenthesis is calculated using annual input/output (I/O) tables from 1992 to 2000 constructed by the Bureau of Labor Statistics (BLS), based on the Bureau of Economic Analysis (BEA) 1992 benchmark tables. The BEA uses standard industrial classification (SIC) 1987 industry disaggregation, which consists of roughly 450 manufacturing industries. These are aggregated up to ninety-six input/output manufacturing codes by the BLS.[6] We include the following five service industries as inputs to the manufacturing industries: telecommunications, insurance, finance, business services, and computing and information.[7] Business services is the largest component of service inputs, with an average share of 12 percent in 2000, then finance (2.4 percent), telecommunications (1.3 percent), insurance (0.5 percent), and the lowest share is computing and information (0.4 percent).

The second term in parenthesis is calculated using international trade data from the IMF Balance of Payments yearbooks. Unfortunately, imports and exports of each input by industry are unavailable and so an economy-wide import share is applied to each industry. As an example, the U.S. economy imported 2.2 percent of business services in 2000—we then assume that each manufacturing industry imports 2.2 percent of its business service that year. Thus, on average, the offshoring of business services is

6. We were unable to use the more disaggregated BEA I/O tables because the next available year is 1997 and this is under a different classification system, called North American Industry Classification System (NAICS). Unfortunately, the concordance between SIC and NAICS is not straightforward, thus there would be a high risk that changes in the input coefficients would reflect reclassification rather than changes in input intensities. In contrast, the BLS I/O tables use the same classification throughout the sample period.

7. The service categories were more disaggregated in the input/output tables but we aggregated them up to match the service categories in the IMF Balance of Payments statistics.

Table 7.1   **Material and service offshoring 1992–2000**

Year	Material offshoring—OSM		Service offshoring—OSS	
	%	%Δ	%	%Δ
1992	11.72	—	0.18	—
1993	12.68	5.25	0.18	4.88
1994	13.41	5.06	0.20	6.39
1995	14.18	4.65	0.20	4.10
1996	14.32	1.75	0.21	6.64
1997	14.55	1.75	0.23	6.97
1998	14.94	2.97	0.24	6.57
1999	15.55	3.49	0.29	16.73
2000	17.33	10.12	0.29	−2.23
1992–2000		4.38		6.26

equal to $0.12 * 0.022 = 0.3$ percent. We aggregate across the five service inputs to get service offshoring measure for each industry, oss_{it}. An analogous measure is constructed for material offshoring, denoted by osm_{it}.

Table 7.1 presents average material and service offshoring, weighted by industry output. The average service offshoring in 2000 is only 0.3 percent, whereas the average materials offshoring is 17.4 percent. Both types of offshoring have been increasing over the sample period, with higher growth rates for service offshoring at an annual average of 6.3 percent, compared to an average growth rate of 4.4 percent for material offshoring.

The breakdown of the two components of the service offshoring for each service category is provided for 1992 and 2000 in table 7.2. The first column shows the average share of each service category (the first term in equation [6]), and the last column gives the average import share of each service category (the second term in equation [6]). We see from column (1) that business services is the largest service category used across manufacturing industries, and this has grown from an average of 9.7 percent in 1992 to 12 percent in 2000. There is also much variation between industries. For example, in the household audio and video equipment industry, business services only accounted for 2 percent of total inputs in the year 2000 whereas in the greeting cards industry it was 45 percent. From the last column, we see that the import share of all service categories, except communications, increased over the period.

There are a number of potential problems with these offshoring measures that should be noted. First, they are likely to underestimate the real value of offshoring because the cost of importing services is likely to be lower than the cost of purchasing them domestically. While it would be preferable to have quantity data rather than current values, this is unavailable for the United States. Second, applying the same import share to all

Table 7.2   **Service inputs, by type: 1992 and 2000**

Services	Share of service inputs (%)				Import of services (%)
	Mean	Standard deviation	Min	Max	
(1992)					
Communication	1.16	0.79	0.25	4.82	2.47
Financial	1.91	0.63	0.93	4.72	0.25
Insurance	0.43	0.18	0.16	1.39	1.82
Other business service	9.69	7.16	1.87	37.93	1.47
Computer and information	0.55	0.44	0.02	2.53	0.16
(2000)					
Communication	1.27	0.94	0.28	5.45	1.18
Financial	2.37	0.86	0.71	5.28	0.51
Insurance	0.47	0.22	0.10	1.36	2.84
Other business service	12.02	8.55	1.89	44.99	2.23
Computer and information	0.38	0.31	0.01	2.01	0.62

Source: BLS, Input-Output Tables, and IMF, *Balance of Payments Statistics Yearbook.*

industries is not ideal, but given the unavailability of imports by industry this is our "best guess." The same strategy was used by Feenstra and Hanson (1996, 1999) to construct measures of material offshoring. This approach apportions a higher value of imported inputs to the industries that are the biggest users of those inputs. Although this seems reasonable, without access to actual import data by industry it is impossible to say how accurate it is. Despite these limitations, we believe that combining the input use information with trade data provides a reasonable proxy of the proportion of imported inputs by industry.

The employment equations are estimated at two different levels of aggregation: (a) BLS I/O categories comprising ninety-six manufacturing industries; and (b) SIC categories comprising 450 industries. In order to aid comparison between these different levels of aggregation, the employment equations all use data from the NBER Productivity Database (Bartelsman and Gray 1996), which provides input and output data at the 4-digit SIC level up to the year 1996. We extend this data to 2000 using the same sources as they do, which include the BEA and Annual Surveys of Manufacturers (ASM), and the same methodology wherever possible. See the appendix for details of the data sources. All the summary statistics are provided in table 7.3.

7.4   Results

We estimate equations (4) and (5) at the industry level for the period 1992 to 2000. All variables are entered in log first differences, except those vari-

Table 7.3   **Summary statistics**

Variable	Observations	Mean	Standard deviation	Min	Max
BLS I/O classifications					
$oss_{i,t}$	864	0.239	0.162	0.040	1.071
$\Delta oss_{i,t}$	768	0.016	0.032	−0.145	0.411
$osm_{i,t}$	864	14.949	9.808	1.220	69.255
$\Delta osm_{i,t}$	768	0.694	1.950	−16.173	21.220
ln(value-added per worker)$_{i,t}$	864	−2.591	0.480	−4.034	−0.526
Δln(value-added per worker)$_{i,t}$	768	0.043	0.070	−0.231	0.364
ln(real output)$_{i,t}$	864	10.112	0.953	6.549	12.979
Δln(real output)$_{i,t}$	768	0.036	0.074	−0.256	0.443
ln(materials)$_{i,t}$	864	9.032	1.034	5.577	12.498
Δln(materials)$_{i,t}$	768	0.031	0.103	−0.567	0.544
ln(services)$_{i,t}$	864	7.060	1.025	3.892	9.875
Δln(services)$_{i,t}$	768	0.045	0.075	−0.316	0.418
ln(labor)$_{i,t}$	864	11.834	0.847	8.618	13.836
Δln(labor)$_{i,t}$	768	−0.001	0.038	−0.165	0.139
ln(capital stock)$_{i,t}$	844	9.175	1.030	5.979	11.701
Δln(capital stock)$_{i,t}$	748	0.029	0.043	−0.809	0.301
htech (ex post)$_{i,t}$	864	10.070	6.302	2.574	24.112
Δhtech (ex post)$_{i,t}$	768	0.265	0.959	−2.899	4.410
htech (ex ante)$_{i,t}$	860	9.738	5.961	2.508	23.149
Δhtech (ex ante)$_{i,t}$	764	0.107	0.338	−0.729	1.512
import share$_{i,t}$	855	0.257	0.486	0.000	3.408
Δ(import share)$_{i,t}$	760	0.014	0.050	−0.375	0.579
(SIC aggregated to BLS I/O)					
employment	823	181,824	158,096	4,936	838,385
Δln(employment)	728	−0.00005	0.048	−0.2496	0.2541
wage	823	32,581	8,068	14,709	56,506
Δln(wage)	728	0.0299	0.0235	−0.0796	0.1464
real output, $1M	823	39,023	49,277	785	495,348
Δln(real output)	728	0.0322	0.069	−0.323	0.4424
price (1987 = 1.00)	823	0.983	0.096	0.37	1.99
Δln(price)	728	0.010	0.047	0.34	0.28
(SIC 4-digit level)					
employment	4,018	37,548	54,458	100	555,063
Δln(employment)	3,565	−0.0077	0.0937	−0.803	0.7368
wage	4,018	31,115	8,947	12,350	72,157
Δln(wage)	3,566	0.0307	0.0476	−0.2826	0.6219
real output, $1M	4,018	8,613	52,802	24	2,292,522
Δln(real output)	3,566	0.0222	0.1086	−1.100	0.84
price (1987 = 1.000)	4,018	1.2218	0.1682	0.0407	2.012
Δln(price)	3,567	0.0113	0.0469	−0.4854	0.405

Note: "htech" is defined as high-tech capital services/total capital services.

ables that are constructed as ratios (such as offshoring) are entered as differences in the ratios. All estimations include year fixed effects and some specifications also include industry fixed effects. The errors have been corrected for clustering at the I/O industry level, which is the aggregation level of the offshoring variables.

The results show that service offshoring has no significant effect on manufacturing employment when the manufacturing sector is divided into ninety-six industries.[8] In columns (1) to (3) of table 7.4, we present results from estimating the conditional employment equation, and allow for scale effects, with one period differences using OLS. All of these specifications show that the contemporaneous and the lagged service offshoring variables are individually and jointly insignificant. Material offshoring has a positive effect on employment, but this is only significant in column (3), which allows for scale effects. In some specifications, import share (defined as the ratio of total imports to total output in that industry i) is negative and significant, showing that increasing imports displaces employment in that industry.

Robustness checks for potential endogeneity using the GMM estimator are presented in columns (4) and (5) of table 7.4. These specifications also show that service offshoring has an insignificant effect on employment, and that material offshoring has a significant positive employment effect. This finding is consistent with Hanson, Mataloni, and Slaughter (2003), who find that expansion in the scale of activities by foreign affiliates appears to raise demand for labor in U.S. parents.[9]

7.4.1   More Disaggregated Effects

It is possible that any negative effects from offshoring could be washed away within broadly defined industry classifications. To explore this possibility, we reestimate equations (4) and (5) using the more disaggregated 4-digit SIC categories of 450 manufacturing industries. Note that it was only possible to construct the offshoring measures at the BLS I/O classification comprising ninety-six industries, hence we cluster standard errors at the BLS I/O industry category.

In fact, we do see a negative effect from service offshoring on employment in table 7.5 using the more disaggregated industry classifications, with OLS in columns (1) to (3) and GMM in columns (4) and (5). Service offshoring has a significant negative effect in all specifications in table 7.5, and there are no offsetting scale effects. That is, the size of the negative coefficients on service offshoring are of similar magnitude in all columns,

---

8. All of the employment specifications exclude the tobacco industry; and all include year and industry fixed effects.

9. Harrison and McMillan (2005) report correlations between U.S. multinational employment at home and abroad. Their preliminary findings also suggest a positive correlation between jobs at home and abroad.

Table 7.4   Offshoring and employment

Dependent variable: Δln(employment)_t	OLS			GMM	
	(1)	(2)	(3)	(4)	(5)
$\Delta oss_{i,t}$	0.015	−0.123	−0.129	−0.040	−0.123
	(0.106)	(0.131)	(0.134)	(0.094)	(0.121)
$\Delta oss_{i,t-1}$	−0.035	0.079	0.055	−0.104	0.024
	(0.077)	(0.094)	(0.090)	(0.072)	(0.086)
$\Delta osm_{i,t}$	0.002	0.003	0.003*	0.003**	0.005***
	(0.001)	(0.002)	(0.002)	(0.002)	(0.001)
$\Delta osm_{i,t-1}$	0.001	0.001	0.001	0.001	0.001
	(0.001)	(0.001)	(0.001)	(0.001)	(0.001)
$\Delta\ln(\text{wage})_{i,t}$	−0.498***	−0.327***	−0.325***	−0.425***	−0.28***
	(0.092)	(0.109)	(0.109)	(0.084)	(0.108)
$\Delta\ln(\text{wage})_{i,t-1}$	0.071	0.161*	0.163*	0.128	0.185*
	(0.077)	(0.093)	(0.093)	(0.095)	(0.110)
$\Delta\ln(\text{real output})_{i,t}$	0.489***	—	—	0.509***	—
	(0.060)			(0.054)	
$\Delta\ln(\text{real output})_{i,t-1}$	0.066	—	—	0.046	—
	(0.042)			(0.062)	
$\Delta\ln(\text{price})_{i,t}$	—	0.060	—	—	−0.002
		(0.042)			(0.053)
$\Delta\ln(\text{price})_{i,t-1}$	—	0.089	—	—	0.066
		(0.056)			(0.063)
$\Delta(\text{htech})_{i,t}$ (ex post rental prices)	−0.002	−0.004	−0.004	0.000	−0.002
	(0.002)	(0.003)	(0.003)	(0.002)	(0.003)
$\Delta(\text{htech})_{i,t-1}$ (ex post rental prices)	−0.004	−0.003	−0.004	−0.001	−0.001
	(0.002)	(0.003)	(0.003)	(0.002)	(0.003)
$\Delta(\text{impshare})_{i,t}$	0.000	−0.002***	−0.002***	0.000	−0.002***
	(0.000)	(0.001)	(0.001)	(0.000)	(0.001)

(continued)

Table 7.4   (continued)

	OLS			GMM	
Dependent variable: $\Delta\ln(\text{employment})_t$	(1)	(2)	(3)	(4)	(5)
$\Delta(\text{impshare})_{i,t}$	0.000	−0.000	−0.000	0.001	0.000
	(0.001)	(0.001)	(0.001)	(0.001)	(0.001)
$\Delta\ln(\text{employment})_{i,t-1}$				0.063	0.152**
				(0.051)	(0.066)
Joint significance tests					
$\Delta oss_{i,t} + \Delta oss_{i,t-1} = 0$	$F(1,93) = 0.02$	$F(1,93) = 0.05$	$F(1,93) = 0.15$	$\chi^2(1) = 1.18$	$\chi^2(1) = 0.34$
	$p\text{-value} = 0.89$	$p\text{-value} = 0.82$	$p\text{-value} = 0.69$	$p\text{-value} = 0.28$	$p\text{-value} = 0.56$
$\Delta osm_{i,t} + \Delta osm_{i,t-1} = 0$	$F(1,93) = 1.98$	$F(1,93) = 2.87$	$F(1,93) = 2.47$	$\chi^2(1) = 2.74$	$\chi^2(1) = 8.8$
	$p\text{-value} = 0.16$	$p\text{-value} = 0.09$	$p\text{-value} = 0.12$	$p\text{-value} = 0.10$	$p\text{-value} = 0.00$
$\Delta(\text{htech})_{i,t} + \Delta(\text{htech})_{i,t-1} = 0$ (ex post rental prices)	$F(1,93) = 1.57$	$F(1,93) = 1.73$	$F(1,93) = 2.50$		
	$p\text{-value} = 0.21$	$p\text{-value} = 0.19$	$p\text{-value} = 0.12$		
$\Delta(\text{impshare})_{i,t} +$ $\Delta(\text{impshare})_{i,t-1} = 0$	$F(1,93) = 0.71$	$F(1,93) = 8.17$	$F(1,93) = 8.02$		
	$p\text{-value} = 0.40$	$p\text{-value} = 0.01$	$p\text{-value} = 0.01$		
H_0: no 2nd order autocorrelation				$z = -0.35$	$z = -0.21$
				$p\text{-value} = 0.72$	$p\text{-value} = 0.83$
Sargan test					
				$\chi^2(20) = 29.8$	$\chi^2(20) = 32.3$
				$p\text{-value} = 0.07$	$p\text{-value} = 0.01$
Observations	626	626	626	529	529
R^2	0.63	0.44	0.44		

Notes: Robust standard errors in parentheses. Import shares for metal coating and engraving (I/O code 36) are missing. All columns have year and industry fixed effects.

OLS = ordinary least squares; GMM = generalized method of moments.

***Significant at the 1 percent level.

**Significant at the 5 percent level.

*Significant at the 10 percent level.

Table 7.5   Offshoring and employment: more disaggregated manufacturing industries (450 industries– SIC)

		OLS			GMM	
Dependent variable: $\Delta \ln(\text{employment})_t$	(1)	(2)	(3)	(4)	(5)
$\Delta oss_{i,t}$	-0.069	-0.253**	-0.278**	-0.224	-0.392*
	(0.084)	(0.119)	(0.111)	(0.147)	(0.179)
$\Delta oss_{i,t-1}$	-0.175*	-0.007	-0.047	-0.341***	-0.159
	(0.105)	(0.114)	(0.106)	(0.121)	(0.149)
$\Delta osm_{i,t}$	0.002	0.000	0.000	0.003	0.002
	(0.001)	(0.002)	(0.001)	(0.002)	(0.002)
$\Delta osm_{i,t-1}$	0.001	-0.001	-0.001	0.001	0.003
	(0.001)	(0.001)	(0.001)	(0.001)	(0.001)
$\Delta \ln(\text{wage})_{i,t}$	-0.646***	-0.531***	-0.527***	0.662***	-0.557***
	(0.083)	(0.090)	(0.090)	(0.073)	(0.08)
$\Delta \ln(\text{wage})_{i,t-1}$	0.039	0.075**	0.077**	0.018	0.042
	(0.039)	(0.033)	(0.034)	(0.06)	(0.065)
$\Delta \ln(\text{real output})_{i,t}$	0.523***	—	—	0.517***	—
	(0.029)			(0.034)	
$\Delta \ln(\text{real output})_{i,t-1}$	0.050***	—	—	0.052	—
	(0.017)			(0.032)	
$\Delta \ln(\text{price})_{i,t}$	—	0.113**	—	—	0.136**
		(0.045)			(0.053)
$\Delta \ln(\text{price})_{i,t-1}$	—	0.072	—	—	0.095
		(0.063)			(0.090)
$\Delta(\text{htech})_{i,t}$ (ex post rental prices)	-0.003	-0.006*	-0.006**	-0.002	-0.005*
	(0.002)	(0.003)	(0.003)	(0.002)	(0.003)
$\Delta(\text{htech})_{i,t-1}$ (ex post rental prices)	-0.006**	-0.007**	-0.007**	-0.004	-0.004
	(0.003)	(0.003)	(0.003)	(0.003)	(0.004)
$\Delta(\text{impshare})_{i,t}$	-0.000	-0.001**	-0.001***	-0.0002**	-0.0009***
	(0.000)	(0.000)	(0.000)	(0.00001)	(0.0001)
$\Delta(\text{impshare})_{i,t-1}$	0.000	-0.000	-0.000	0.0002**	-0.0002**
	(0.000)	(0.000)	(0.000)	(0.0001)	(0.0001)
					(continued)

Table 7.5 (continued)

	OLS			GMM	
Dependent variable: $\Delta\ln(\text{employment})_t$	(1)	(2)	(3)	(4)	(5)
$\Delta\ln(\text{employment})_{i,t-1}$				−0.334 (0.037)	−0.002 (0.003)
Joint significance tests					
$\Delta oss_{i,t} + \Delta oss_{i,t-1} = 0$	$F(1,93) = 2.37$, p-value = 0.12	$F(1,93) = 1.52$, p-value = 0.22	$F(1,93) = 2.82$, p-value = 0.10	$\chi^2(1) = 5.9$, p-value = 0.01	$\chi^2(1) = 3.88$, p-value = 0.05
$\Delta osm_{i,t} + \Delta osm_{i,t-1} = 0$	$F(1,93) = 1.43$, p-value = 0.23	$F(1,93) = 0.02$, p-value = 0.88	$F(1,93) = 0.14$, p-value = 0.70	$\chi^2(1) = 1.65$, p-value = 0.2	$\chi^2(1) = 0.74$, p-value = 0.39
$\Delta(\text{htech})_{i,t} + \Delta(\text{htech})_{i,t-1} = 0$ (ex post rental prices)	$F(1,93) = 3.36$, p-value = 0.07	$F(1,93) = 5.37$, p-value = 0.02	$F(1,93) = 5.87$, p-value = 0.10		
$\Delta(\text{impshare})_{i,t} +$ $\Delta(\text{impshare})_{i,t-1} = 0$	$F(1,93) = 0.22$, p-value = 0.64	$F(1,93) = 28.0$, p-value = 0.00	$F(1,93) = 28.8$, p-value = 0.00		
H_0: no 2nd order autocorrelation				$z = -0.57$, p-value = 0.57	$z = -0.89$, p-value = 0.37
Sargan test				$\chi^2(20) = 29.35$, p-value = 0.08	$\chi^2(20) = 32.55$, p-value = 0.04
Observations	3,018	3,018	3,018	2,581	2,581
R^2	0.55	0.33	0.33		

Notes: Robust standard errors in parentheses. There are 13 SICs with missing import data, and several SICs that have missing employment data for various years. All columns have year and industry fixed effects. OLS = ordinary least squares; GMM = generalized method of moments.
***Significant at the 1 percent level.
**Significant at the 5 percent level.
*Significant at the 10 percent level.

with and without controlling for output. However, the material offshoring effect has now become insignificant.

Using estimates from table 7.5, the effect from service offshoring on employment is equal to 0.3. Since service offshoring in the manufacturing sector grew by 0.1 percentage point over the sample period, this implies an average loss of 3 percent employment. However, since more service offshoring occurs in industries with relatively small employment, weighted by employment shares of each sector, these estimates imply a fall of total manufacturing employment by only 0.4 of a percent.

7.5   Conclusions

Sourcing service inputs from abroad by U.S. firms is growing rapidly. Although the level of service offshoring is still low compared to material offshoring, this business practice is expected to grow as new technologies make it possible to access cheaper foreign labor and different skills. This has led to concerns that jobs will be transferred from the United States to developing countries. To see if these concerns have any foundation, we estimate the effects of service and material offshoring on manufacturing employment in the United States between 1992 and 2000.

We find there is a small negative effect of less than half a percent on employment when industries are finely disaggregated (450 manufacturing industries). However, this effect disappears at the more aggregated industry level of ninety-six industries, indicating that there is sufficient growth in demand in other industries within these broadly defined classifications to offset any negative effects. This probably reflects the relatively flexible nature of the U.S. labor market that allows for reallocation of labor between industries. The employment effect could be different for other countries with a less flexible labor market.

Our analysis suggests a number of possible avenues for future research. First, improvements in the collection of data at the firm level with information distinguishing between domestic input purchases from imports, combined with detailed skill level data would be a major step forward in making this type of analysis possible. Second, our sample ends in 2000. Because the BLS annual input-output tables were provided up to 2000, extending the measure of service offshoring beyond that year on a consistent basis is not straightforward. However, more could be happening in more recent years, including a continued rise in the share of imported service inputs. When relevant data become available, updating the analysis can provide additional insight. Third, offshoring is likely to have income distribution effects. Feenstra and Hanson (1999) found that material outsourcing explained about 40 percent of the increase in the skill premium in the United States in the 1980s. Given that service offshoring is likely to be more skill-intensive than material offshoring, it will be interesting to see what effects, if any, service offshoring has on the wage skill premium. Disaggregated data by skill would also make it possible to study whether any particular skill groups are relatively more affected.

Appendix

Table 7A.1   Data sources

Variable	Code	Years available	Source
Input/output tables	BLS	1992–2000	BLS
Trade (manufacturing)	HS10 digit	1992–2001	Feenstra
Trade (services)	Balance of Payments	1992–2001	IMF
Output (manufacturing)	SIC 4 digit	1992–2001	BEA
Output (services)	SIC 3 digit	1992–2001	BEA
Value-added per worker	BLS	1992–2000	BLS
Employment	SIC 4 digit	1992–2001	ASM
Payroll	SIC 4 digit	1992–2001	ASM
Capital stock	SIC 4 digit	1992–1996	NBER Productivity Database
	SIC 4 digit	1996–2001	Constructed using investment perpetual method
Capital expenditure	SIC 4 digit	1996–2001	ASM
Investment deflators	SIC 2 digit	1996–2001	BLS
Materials	SIC 4 digit	1992–2001	ASM
Material deflators	SIC 4 digit	1992–1996	NBER Productivity Database
	SIC 4 digit	1997–2001	BEA output deflators with 1992 BEA I/O table

References

Amiti, M., and S.-J. Wei. 2005. Fear of outsourcing: Is it justified? *Economic Policy* 20 (April): 308–48.
———. 2006. Service offshoring and productivity: Evidence from the United States. NBER Working Paper no. 11926. Cambridge, MA: National Bureau of Economic Research, January.
Bartelsman, E. J., and W. Gray. 1996. The NBER manufacturing productivity database. NBER Technical Working Paper no. t0205. Cambridge, MA: National Bureau of Economic Research, October.
Blinder, A. S. 2006. Offshoring: The next industrial revolution? *Foreign Affairs* 85 (2): 113–28.
Ekholm, K., and K. Hakkala. 2005. Effect of offshoring on labor demand: Evidence from Sweden. IUI Working Paper no. 654.
Feenstra, R. C., and G. H. Hanson. 1996. Globalization, outsourcing, and wage inequality. *American Economic Review* vol. LXXXVI: 240–45.

Feenstra, R. C., and G. H. Hanson. 1999. The impact of outsourcing and high technology capital on wages: Estimates for the United States, 1979–1990. *Quarterly Journal of Economics* 114 (3): 907–40.

Hamermesh, D. 1993. Labor Demand. Princeton, NJ: Princeton University Press.

Hanson, G. H., R. J. Mataloni Jr., and M. J. Slaughter. 2003. Expansion abroad and the domestic operations of U.S. multinational firms. University of California, San Diego; BEA; Tuck School of Business at Dartmouth; NBER. Unpublished Manuscript.

Harrison, A. E., and M. S. McMillan. 2005. U.S. multinational activity abroad and U.S. jobs: Substitutes or complements? University of California, Berkeley. Unpublished Manuscript.

Jensen, J. B., and L. Kletzer. 2005. Tradable services: Understanding the scope and impact of services offshoring. In *Brookings trade forum 2005, offshoring white-collar work: The issues and the implications,* ed. L. Brainard and S. M. Collins, Washington, D.C.: Brookings Institution.

Krugman, P. 1995. Growing world trade: Causes and consequences. *Brookings Papers on Economic Activity,* Issue no. 1:327–377. Washington, D.C.: Brookings Institution.

———. 2008. Trade and wages, reconsidered. *Brookings Papers on Economic Activity,* forthcoming.

Lorentowicz, A., D. Marin, and A. Raubold. 2005. Is human capital losing from outsourcing? Evidence for Austria and Poland. CEPR Discussion Paper no. 5344.

Mann, C. L. 2004. Globalization of IT services and white collar jobs: The next wave of productivity growth. *International Economics Policy Briefs* PB 03-11. Institute of International Economics.

Comment   Robert C. Feenstra

This chapter by Mary Amiti and Shang-Jin Wei carries forward from a line of research the authors have been engaged in for several years. In Amiti and Wei (2005) they point out that a number of industrial countries—including the United States—are net *exporters* of business services, so that they should certainly benefit from this activity. In Amiti and Wei (2006), they estimate that the import of business services has enhanced productivity in those industries making the greatest use of service imports. This chapter takes the final step in estimating the employment impact of service imports for the United States.

Before commenting on the specifics of the chapter, I would like to suggest that the nature of outsourcing has changed in the United States, especially when we compare the 1980s with the 1990s. In figure 7C.1, I show the relative wage of nonproduction workers and their relative employment in U.S. manufacturing, from 1979 to 1989. The annual earnings of nonpro-

Robert C. Feenstra is a professor of economics at the University of California, Davis, and a research associate of the National Bureau of Economic Research.

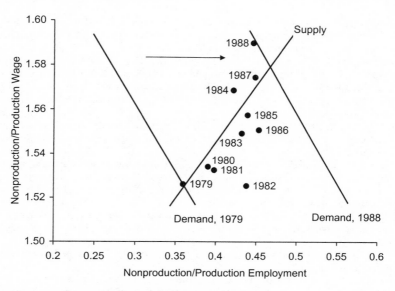

Fig. 7C.1   Nonproduction/production workers, 1980s
Source: National Bureau of Economic Research Productivity Database updated.

duction workers relative to production workers increased steadily during this period, as did the ratio of nonproduction to production workers employed in U.S. manufacturing. The only way that this pattern can be consistent with a demand and supply diagram is if the relative demand curve for skilled labor has increased, as illustrated. There are two explanations for this shift in labor demand during the 1980s: skill-biased technological change (see Berman, Bound, and Griliches 1994; and Berman, Bound, and Machin 1998), and the foreign outsourcing of activities using less-skilled labor (Feenstra and Hanson 1999). Estimates vary as to which of these explanations is the most important, but it is safe to conclude that they both have played a role.

Figure 7C.1 is the picture that launched dozens of research studies, but it is surprising that the picture for the 1990s—shown in figure 7C.2—is not yet familiar. We see that from 1989 to 2000, there continued to be an increase in the relative wage of nonproduction/production labor in U.S. manufacturing, but in addition, there was a *decrease* in the relative employment of these workers. There are two possible explanations suggested by the literature for this shift.

First, it is possible that more-skilled workers were drawn out of manufacturing and into the service sector. Sachs and Schatz (1998) point out that services really are skill-intensive as compared to manufacturing. The characterization of service jobs as flipping hamburgers is not true on average; in fact, the jobs are more likely to be professionals. A second possibility, how-

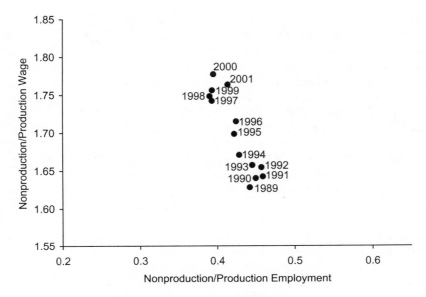

Fig. 7C.2   Nonproduction/production workers, 1990s
Source: National Bureau of Economic Research Productivity Database.

ever, is that figure 7C.2 is a smoking gun for service offshoring from U.S. manufacturing. To the extent that the back-office jobs being outsourced from manufacturing use the lower-paid nonproduction workers, then the offshoring of those jobs could very well *raise the average* wage among non-production workers, while lowering their employment. This hypothesis puts service offshoring at the center of the policy and research debate.

Turning to the contribution by Amiti and Wei, they find that the amount of imported service inputs in the United States is small but growing. Measured as a share of total inputs purchased, imported services were 0.2 percent in 1992 (i.e., two-tenths of 1 percent of total inputs), and grew to 0.3 percent in 2000 (i.e., three-tenths of 1 percent), as shown in their table 7.1.[1] The fact that imported services are small does not prevent them from being important for productivity and employment. In Amiti and Wei (2006), they find that over 1992 to 2000, service outsourcing can explain between 12 and 17 percent of the total increase in productivity in U.S. manufacturing.

In this chapter, a rise in productivity potentially reduces employment, via equation (2): an increase in A_i will reduce L_i, ceteris paribus. Of course, the "all else held equal" may not apply, and as the authors explain, it is pos-

---

1. The columns marked %Δ in table 7.1 are confusing, since they are the percentage changes of numbers that are themselves percentages. Very slight changes in these percentages, especially those for service offshoring that only need to change in the third significant digit, are responsible for the percentage changes that are shown.

sible that *output* Y_i can increase simultaneously with increased A_i due to offshoring. This means there are two opposing effects on employment: the productivity increase that tends to reduce employment, and the rise in output that tends to increase it. To these effects I would add a third, which the authors do not consider in their model—offshoring can change the *relative* demand for unskilled/skilled labor, much as occurred for production/nonproduction workers during the 1980s. That effect lies outside their equations because they model a productivity increase as Hick's neutral in equations (1) through (3), whereas offshoring can actually have a factor-biased impact. Because they do not decompose labor into several skill types, it is impossible to test for this factor-biased effect, however.

Turning to their estimates, the authors find that service offshoring has no significant impact on employment when using ninety-six industries, but does have a small, negative impact on employment when using 450 industries. The authors suggest that we should not be surprised to see differences between the disaggregate and aggregate results: "Because the U.S. labor market is reasonably flexible, one does not need to aggregate sectors very much to find that this employment effect washes out." I agree with that assessment, but would add another caveat: the aggregation of labor into a single category also tends to hide the employment impact of service offshoring, if it operates differentially across skill-groups. It is entirely possible that service offshoring has the greatest effect on nonproduction workers, particularly those at the lower end of nonproduction skills, as suggested by figure 7C.2. Extending their analysis to take into account the impact on different skill groups is an important direction for further research.

References

Amiti, M., and S.-J. Wei. 2005. Fear of outsourcing: Is it justified? *Economic Policy* 20 (April): 308–48.
———. 2006. Service offshoring and productivity: Evidence from the United States. NBER Working Paper no. 11926. Cambridge, MA: National Bureau of Economic Research, January.
Berman, E., J. Bound, and Z. Griliches. 1994. Changes in the demand for skilled labor within U.S. manufacturing: Evidence from the annual survey of manufactures. *Quarterly Journal of Economics* 109 (2): 367–98.
Berman, E., J. Bound, and S. Machin. 1998. Implications of skill-biased technological change: International evidence. *Quarterly Journal of Economics* 113 (4): 1245–80.
Feenstra, R. C., and G. H. Hanson. 1999. The impact of outsourcing and high-technology capital on wages: Estimates for the U.S., 1979–1990. *Quarterly Journal of Economics* 114 (3): 907–40.
Sachs, J. D., and H. J. Shatz. 1998. International trade and wage inequality: Some new results. In *Imports, exports, and the american worker,* ed. S. M. Collins, 215–240. Washington, D.C.: Brookings Institution.

8

Outsourcing and Imported Services in BEA's Industry Accounts

Robert E. Yuskavage, Erich H. Strassner, and
Gabriel W. Medeiros

8.1 Introduction

Outsourcing of professional and support services by U.S. firms, especially goods-producing firms, is one of the factors that has contributed to the steady increase in the service sector's share of the U.S. economy. Outsourced services typically include software production, information and data processing services, computer systems design, professional, scientific, and technical services, and administrative and support services. The impact of the outsourcing trend is clearly seen in the growth of the domestic professional and business services sector, whose value-added share of gross domestic product (GDP) increased from 8.7 percent in 1987 to 11.6 percent in 2000.

After 2000, however, growth slowed sharply in this outsourcing supply sector, with its share of GDP declining to 11.3 percent in 2003 before rebounding to 11.5 percent in 2004. While it is possible that the growth of outsourcing itself slowed during the economic downturn, another possible explanation is that U.S. firms started to substitute imported services for domestic services as part of their outsourcing strategy, thus reducing demand for domestic outsourcing services. In recent years, imports of business, professional, and technical services, while still relatively low, have increased faster than domestic production of similar services. This faster growth may

Robert E. Yuskavage is a senior economist in the office of the Associate Director for Industry Accounts at the Bureau of Economic Analysis. Erich H. Strassner is the chief of the Industry Research Group at the Bureau of Economic Analysis. Gabriel W. Medeiros is an economist in the Industry Research Group at the Bureau of Economic Analysis.

The authors thank Maria Borga, Karen Horowitz, Ned Howenstine, Doug Meade, Sue Okubo, Mark Planting, George Smith, and Obie Whichard, of BEA, for helpful comments on the paper.

be related to the offshore outsourcing development that has received much attention recently from the media, economists, and policymakers.

The growing importance of international transactions in services, especially services enabled by information and communications technology, has also raised questions about the effects of offshore outsourcing on U.S. economic growth, its impact on the output and employment of domestic industries, and the implications for productivity growth. Outsourcing as an economic activity is fundamentally about industry production technology and how business establishments adjust their mix of inputs in response to changes in demand, relative prices, and technology, so it is best studied at the industry level, using time series data on industry output, inputs, and prices. Detailed industry data at the establishment level are important because of the different ways in which producers can meet their needs for inputs of professional and support services.[1] These needs can be met internally (within the establishment), using their own resources, or externally, by contracting out or through other arrangements. External suppliers can be affiliated, either as domestic auxiliaries or foreign affiliates, or they can be unaffiliated, independent domestic or foreign entities.[2] Regardless of supplier affiliation or location, industry data on input cost categories such as energy, materials, and purchased services, combined with data on labor and capital inputs, can help identify the industries that engage in outsourcing and to study how and why outsourcing occurs.

Empirical evidence on the dimensions of outsourcing is quite limited, especially evidence needed to assess the impact of offshore outsourcing on domestic industries. The Bureau of Economic Analysis's (BEA) annual industry accounts, however, provide some insights into how outsourcing affects domestic industries. These accounts provide consistent time series data on the composition of gross output, intermediate inputs, and value added, including quantity and price indexes, for establishment-based industries classified according to the 1997 North American Industry Classification System (NAICS). The detailed time series data are available starting in 1997 and recently were expanded to include estimates of energy, materials, and purchased services intermediate inputs by industry. For this chapter, estimates of the imported portion of purchased services by industry were also developed.

Studies of offshore outsourcing by U.S. firms have primarily addressed its impact on economy-wide measures such as GDP, the balance of pay-

---

1. Establishments are units, such as a plant, mine, store, or office, where productive activities occur. They are classified by industry according to their primary activity. Different establishments owned by the same company can be classified in different industries.

2. Some authors, including van Welsum and Reif (this volume), classify transactions between affiliated parties as "insourcing" rather than outsourcing. This distinction is not important for our purposes, so for convenience, we use outsourcing to mean all purchases of offshored services. See Olsen for a discussion of this issue.

ments, aggregate employment, and business sector productivity (Borga 2005; Government Accountability Office 2004; Kozlow and Borga 2004). Some studies, though, have examined its impact on domestic industries by identifying the occupations that are most affected by outsourcing and determining which industries tend to employ those occupations (e.g., van Welsum and Reif 2005). One study took a different approach, by identifying the domestic industries that were most engaged in providing tradable services that went beyond local markets, and that were thus subject to import competition (Jensen and Kletzer 2005). Studies that address the impact of offshore outsourcing on industry productivity are summarized by Olsen (2006).

This chapter extends the focus on industries by identifying industries that engage in outsourcing and the degree to which their outsourcing needs are met by offshore suppliers. The objectives of this chapter include:

- Explaining the treatment of imported services in BEA's international, national, and industry accounts
- Describing BEA's new framework for measuring purchased services in the industry accounts, including the role of the integrated industry accounts
- Identifying the growth of purchased services as an intermediate input and the effect of imports on that growth, and
- Describing research that uses BEA company data to improve the estimates of imported purchased services by industry.

8.1.1   Overview of Findings

Imports of services in the U.S. economy exceeded $300 billion in 2004 and accounted for nearly 17 percent of total U.S. imports of goods and services. Imports of business, professional, and technical services, the category in BEA's international transactions accounts most closely associated with outsourcing, increased rapidly after 1997 but still only accounted for about 15 percent of imported services. Moreover, only about 30 percent of these outsourcing-related services are currently classified in BEA's industry accounts as comparable to domestic production, and thus able to compete with similar domestic services in the outsourcing market.

In BEA's industry accounts, imports of intermediate purchased services were also relatively small, but they steadily increased as a share of total intermediate purchased services, rising from 2.9 percent in 1997 to 3.6 percent in 2004. Purchased services include those that are closely associated with outsourcing, such as computer, engineering, and accounting services, but also include other purchased services, such as utilities, transportation, communications, finance, and insurance. Outsourcing-related services overall increased as a share of total services purchased by business, rising from 30.8 percent in 1997 to 33.9 percent in 2004. The share of outsourcing-related services attributable to imports also increased during this period, rising from 2.1 percent to 2.7 percent.

The small size of these imported services, especially those currently classified in the industry accounts as competing with domestic production, suggests that import competition played only a small role in the slower growth of the domestic professional and business services (outsourcing) sector after 2000. Slower real output growth and declining employment in this sector are probably better explained by the downturn of 2001 and the decline in demand for certain types of information and communications technology. Further study is required, though, to develop a better understanding of how imported services affect industry output, employment, and contributions to GDP. More research is also needed to determine the sensitivity of these results as to how imported services are classified and distributed in the industry accounts.

8.1.2   Outline of the Chapter

The remainder of this chapter is presented in four sections. Section 8.2 discusses the treatment of imports, particularly imported services, in BEA's international, national, and industry accounts. Section 8.3 discusses the treatment of purchased services generally in BEA's production-oriented industry accounts, how outsourcing-related services are defined, and how imported services are handled within this framework. This section also includes empirical results on the industry distributions of imported services and the contribution of imports to outsourcing. Section 8.4 presents an evaluation of the methodology based on unpublished data from BEA's international accounts, and offers some suggestions for improving the industry estimates of imported purchased services. Section 8.5 is a summary and conclusion.

8.2   Imports in BEA's Accounts

This section provides an overview of how imported services are defined and classified in BEA's international, national, and industry accounts. It begins with the international transactions accounts (ITAs), where these transactions are initially recorded, proceeds to the national income and product accounts (NIPAs), and then concludes with the annual industry accounts (AIAs). Differences among these accounts in concepts and coverage are described and the relationships among the flows in the accounts are briefly explained. An understanding of the relationships among these three accounts is important, because imported services first appear in the ITAs before showing up in the NIPAs and then in the industry accounts.

8.2.1   International Transactions Accounts

The BEA's international transactions accounts (ITAs) provide monthly, quarterly, and annual estimates of transactions between U.S. and foreign residents.[3] The ITAs include a current account, a capital account, and a financial account. The two major components of the current account are (a) exports of goods and services and factor income receipts and (b) imports of goods and services and factor income payments. The difference between these two components, plus net unilateral current transfers, equals the balance on current account. The capital account includes capital transfers, such as debt forgiveness. The two major components of the financial account are (a) changes in net U.S.-owned assets abroad and (b) changes in net foreign-owned assets in the United States. These components are the major source of change in the U.S. net international investment position.

Imports of services in the current account are estimated from a variety of sources, primarily BEA's own direct investment surveys of U.S. and foreign multinational companies (MNCs) and BEA's surveys of U.S. international services transactions between unaffiliated parties. Quarterly and annual estimates of imported services are published for seven broad categories that represent types of services transactions. These categories are direct defense expenditures, travel, passenger fares, other transportation, royalties and license fees, other private services, and U.S. government miscellaneous services. Direct defense expenditures include some goods (mainly materials), supplies, and petroleum products purchased abroad by U.S. military agencies. Other transportation includes some fuels purchased by airline and steamship operators. Additional detail is provided annually.

The BEA's direct investment surveys are mandatory and collect selected data for transactions between the U.S. parents of multinational companies and their foreign affiliates and transactions between the U.S. affiliates of foreign MNCs and their foreign parent companies and certain other affiliated foreign firms. These data play an important role in compiling the ITAs and are complemented with data on transactions between unaffiliated parties to provide a full picture of U.S. international transactions. Because U.S. MNCs are typically very large firms, the combined data for U.S. parents and U.S. affiliates of foreign MNCs account for a significant share of domestic economic activity, especially in the goods-producing sector of the economy. These combined company data, when classified by industry, provide valuable insights into the industry distribution of imported purchased services and are discussed in more detail in section 8.4.

8.2.2   National Income and Product Accounts

The BEA's national income and product accounts (NIPAs) provide quarterly and annual estimates of U.S. production, income, consumption, investment, and saving. The NIPAs include subaccounts for domestic

---

3. Transactions between the United States and its territories, Puerto Rico, and the Northern Mariana Islands are not treated as foreign transactions in the ITAs.

Table 8.1   **Imported services in the NIPAs, 2004 (in billions of dollars)**

Imports of services	301.9
Direct defense expenditures	29.3
Travel	65.6
Passenger fares	23.7
Other transportation	54.2
Royalties and license fees	23.9
Other private services	95.7
Other imports of services	9.5

Note: Exports of services were $355.7 billion in 2004.

product and income, personal income and outlays, government current receipts and expenditures, foreign transactions, and saving and investment. The featured measure from these accounts is GDP, which is a measure of the market value of final goods and services produced in a period. The major categories of final expenditures, which sum to GDP, are personal consumption expenditures, gross private domestic investment, net exports of goods and services, and government consumption expenditures and gross investment.

Net exports are defined as exports less imports. Estimates of trade in goods and services are provided separately for exports and for imports. In calculating GDP as the sum of final expenditures, all imports are subtracted without regard to whether they are consumed in final uses (e.g., as personal consumption expenditures) or in intermediate uses by U.S. industries (e.g., as purchased services or materials). Current-dollar (nominal) imports in the NIPAs are valued in the prices paid to foreign suppliers (foreign port value), which exclude import duties and transportation and insurance costs needed to reach the United States. Quantity and price indexes are prepared quarterly and annually for both exports and imports.

Foreign transactions in the NIPAs are shown in more detail for goods and for services in several of its subaccounts. Imports of services in the NIPAs are slightly larger than in the ITAs, mostly because of a territorial adjustment in the NIPAs that treats purchases by U.S. residents from U.S. territories and Puerto Rico as imports rather than as transactions between domestic parties. Imports of services are shown in NIPA subaccounts for the same seven broad categories of transactions that appear quarterly in the ITAs, except for an "other" category that includes the territorial adjustment. The NIPA foreign transactions subaccounts also provide quantity and price indexes for the seven categories of imported services. Table 8.1 shows the nominal values for these imported services categories for 2004.[4]

4. Estimates provided in this chapter do not include the results of the annual revision of the NIPAs released in July 2006.

8.2.3   Annual Industry Accounts

BEA's annual industry accounts (AIAs) include the integrated GDP-by-industry and annual input-output (I-O) accounts. In these accounts, industries are defined according to the North American Industry Classification System (NAICS). Estimates are published for sixty-one private industries and for four government classifications. The GDP-by-industry accounts feature nominal and real value added by industry estimates. Value added is defined as an industry's gross output (sales or receipts and other operating income) minus its intermediate inputs (energy, materials, and purchased services). Intermediate inputs are acquired from either domestic or foreign sources (imports). Price and quantity indexes of gross output, intermediate inputs, and value added are published for industries, industry groups, and broad sectors in the GDP-by-industry accounts.

The annual I-O accounts provide a time series of detailed, consistent information on the flows of goods and services that comprise industry production processes and that are included in final expenditures. These accounts are presented in standard make-and-use tables and several supplementary tables, and they provide more detail than the GDP-by-industry accounts on the commodities included in gross output and intermediate inputs. The make table shows the commodities (goods and services) that are produced by each industry. The use table shows the commodity inputs to industry production and the commodities that are consumed by final users (see table 8.2).

Commodities are shown along the rows of the use table, and industries and final uses are shown in the columns. Total commodity output (in the right-most column) represents total domestic production of each commodity. The total domestic supply of each commodity (not shown) is the sum of total commodity output less exports of goods and services less imports of goods and services (recorded as negative values) less the change in private inventories. In the industry accounts methodology, commodity supply is distributed to (and completely exhausted) in final uses (GDP) and in intermediate uses by industries. Because final and intermediate uses include imports, the negative values in the imports column ensure that all imports, regardless of use, are subtracted in the final uses measure of GDP.

The commodity composition of imports is calculated as part of the AIAs. Import categories from the NIPAs for both goods and services are disaggregated and distributed among the detailed commodities that comprise the rows of the I-O use table. This distribution closely follows that from the most recent benchmark I-O accounts, which are prepared every five years using detailed data from the economic censuses and other sources. When the domestic supply of detailed commodities, including imports, is allocated among final and intermediate uses, however, no distinction is made based on the source of the commodity. As a result, the values

Table 8.2   The use of commodities by industries, 2004 (in millions of dollars)

Industries	Agriculture, forestry, fishing, and hunting	Mining	Utilities	Construction	Manufacturing	Wholesale trade	Retail trade	Transportation and warehousing	Information	Finance, insurance, real estate, rental, and leasing	Professional and business services
Commodities											
Agriculture, forestry, fishing, and hunting	73,612	1	10	1,024	173,064	3,052	394	9	12	1,452	5,903
Mining	517	42,192	88,407	6,004	229,751	34	23	6,283	1	1,685	179
Utilities	5,680	2,616	174	3,110	50,223	6,786	16,176	3,206	4,911	43,073	16,644
Construction	1,443	67	2,226	1,000	8,139	2,552	5,475	1,511	2,998	30,027	9,875
Manufacturing	51,068	27,690	7,367	241,656	1,405,324	55,902	73,900	75,433	72,256	91,859	89,667
Wholesale trade	11,418	4,494	1,457	30,131	261,318	30,624	10,207	16,405	13,641	11,269	14,670
Retail trade	149	424	74	68,130	13,783	3,153	5,697	2,638	817	13,543	9,628
Transportation and warehousing	7,454	6,778	22,886	15,434	125,974	17,250	22,731	73,268	9,945	27,649	25,689
Information	1,146	737	317	9,673	39,960	17,148	20,114	9,416	217,972	30,704	83,235
Finance, insurance, real estate, rental, and leasing	15,751	23,344	4,217	31,898	117,555	51,604	98,117	33,021	69,088	639,982	142,300
Professional and business services	5,213	22,974	4,665	78,989	337,727	104,861	162,238	53,292	128,400	237,878	330,260
Educational services, health care, and social assistance	17	91	275	117	3,235	881	682	548	2,527	1,131	2,618
Arts, entertainment, recreation, accommodation, and food services	501	596	554	2,141	20,959	6,372	8,216	4,716	16,241	21,374	33,657
Other services, except government	3,209	437	411	9,907	48,527	9,076	10,127	8,102	15,379	24,307	26,569
Government	111	54	174	1,136	3,157	4,149	5,790	1,047	4,672	9,006	14,549
Other inputs[a]	95	1,862	30	611	32,304	14,861	695	18,610	9,403	22,843	6,524
Scrap, used and secondhand goods	1		0	8	20,503	4	405	7	0	−702	12
Total intermediate inputs	177,383	134,354	133,246	500,967	2,891,501	328,308	440,987	307,513	568,265	1,207,078	811,979
Compensation of employees	39,277	43,459	55,432	360,105	915,215	367,855	451,515	219,785	234,115	605,384	944,587
Taxes on production and imports, less subsidies	−4,285	16,264	39,026	6,831	47,637	152,525	164,843	17,097	40,415	240,507	25,315
Gross operating surplus	106,629	112,161	140,804	182,570	457,270	174,361	174,042	96,026	264,209	1,566,992	381,965
Total value added	141,620	171,884	235,262	549,506	1,420,123	694,741	790,400	332,908	538,739	2,412,884	1,351,866
Total industry output	319,003	306,239	368,508	1,050,473	4,311,624	1,023,050	1,231,387	640,421	1,107,004	3,619,962	2,163,845

[a]Includes noncomparable imports, inventory valuation adjustment, and rest-of-the-world adjustments.

of intermediate inputs in the industry accounts include imports, but data are not available to indicate how much of intermediate consumption comes from imports.

An important part of the allocation of imported services to final uses or to the industries that use them as intermediate inputs is the translation of the ITA and NIPA import categories, which are primarily types of expenditures or transactions, into the commodity detail used in the production-oriented industry accounts. Detailed annual data on types of purchased

Educational services, health care, and social assistance	Arts, entertainment, recreation, accommodation, and food services	Other services, except government	Government	Total intermediate use	Personal consumption expenditures	Private fixed investment	Change in private inventories	Exports of goods and services	Imports of goods and services	Government consumption expenditures and gross investment	Total final uses (GDP)	Total commodity output
584	9,547	323	2,513	271,498	48,927		1,197	28,202	−28,013	−1,830	48,483	319,981
10	56	11	10,635	385,788	113	56,493	6,294	5,896	−166,451	1,204	−96,451	289,337
11,887	16,875	6,248	47,529	235,140	205,236			1,054	−1,438		204,851	439,991
8,867	6,714	3,464	48,783	133,140		806,138		69		227,452	1,033,659	1,166,800
124,318	112,134	67,205	246,894	2,742,672	1,428,340	619,523	79,954	566,131	−1,239,721	98,871	1,553,098	4,295,770
18,324	19,437	10,521	29,827	483,743	318,111	87,658	11,354	77,943	23,265	9,908	528,238	1,011,982
3,025	3,763	8,748	25	133,597	959,430	45,868		1			1,005,299	1,138,897
16,595	9,735	5,753	42,171	429,310	154,601	12,609	4,208	70,353	−13,164	1,011	229,618	658,928
37,813	18,735	14,068	67,270	568,307	295,314	57,648	1,808	26,260	−4,548	7,917	384,398	952,705
142,931	69,657	45,876	76,464	1,561,805	1,870,437	98,021		92,228	−30,357		2,030,329	3,592,134
138,006	52,800	45,050	251,386	1,953,738	178,916	167,447		71,811	−11,179	25,173	432,168	2,385,906
12,814	515	721	36,931	63,100	1,610,637			782	−400		1,611,019	1,674,120
23,429	21,967	5,026	24,288	190,035	660,242			805	−167		660,880	850,915
11,037	8,335	6,241	35,329	216,992	420,966		46	182	−2,067		419,126	636,119
14,757	3,317	3,724	9,130	74,772	53,260			257		1,846,923	1,900,439	1,975,212
222	473	267	25,188	133,991	−38,351	−308	−53,650	99,616	−193,971	−976	−187,641	−53,650
2	3	713	13,177	34,133	48,118	−78,454	4,222	10,483	−7,865	266	−23,230	10,902
564,619	354,061	223,957	967,541	9,611,761								
727,119	263,719	193,966	1,271,851	6,693,383								
10,687	48,487	18,691	−14,687	809,353								
171,163	112,131	65,089	226,135	4,231,549								
908,969	424,337	277,746	1,483,299								11,734,285	
1,473,588	778,398	501,703	2,450,840		8,214,296	1,872,643	55,432	1,052,072	−1,676,077	2,215,919		21,346,046

services are obtained from the company surveys conducted for the ITAs and are used to assign imported services to specific I-O commodities. These assignments may be straightforward, based on the nature of the service, or they may be indirect, with allocations made among several commodities based on historical relationships. For example, direct defense expenditures and other government services are allocated entirely to the government sector. The allocation of other categories, such as passenger fares and other transportation, is limited to a small number of transportation services commodities. Payments for the cross-border transport of merchandise and U.S. import duties are included in the domestic port value of merchandise (goods) imports.

A significant portion of imported services, however, is treated in the industry accounts as not having a direct domestic counterpart, either because of the location of the service, its highly specialized nature, or because of the relationship of the supplier to the customer. These imports are currently classified as "noncomparable" in the industry accounts and are shown as a special commodity row in the use table. Examples of noncomparable imports include expenditures by U.S. residents on personal and business travel while abroad, port expenditures abroad by U.S. air and water transportation providers, certain royalties and license fees paid to foreign residents, and payments by U.S. firms to their foreign affiliates or to their foreign parents for unspecified services. While it is possible that some of the imported services that are currently classified as noncomparable have domestic counterparts, especially transactions between affiliated parties, the information available to BEA on the nature of the transaction is not detailed enough to determine the comparable domestic service.

Table 8.3 shows the translation of total imported services from the NIPAs to the annual industry accounts for 2004.

Because most imported goods now have domestic counterparts, noncomparable imports, which have accounted for about 70 percent of imported services in recent years, consist almost entirely of services. Before 1992, noncomparable imports included goods that had no significant domestic counterparts, such as bananas or coffee. Direct defense expenditures, travel, and royalties and license fees are classified entirely as noncomparable imports. Other private services and "other" services are distributed among a wider variety of comparable services, but large portions are treated as noncomparable imports. For example, nearly 80 percent of business, professional, and technical (BPT) services, the largest

Table 8.3   Translation of imported services in the NIPAs to comparable imported services in the annual industry accounts, 2004 (in billions of dollars)

Imports of services, NIPAs	301.9
Less: Coverage adjustment	3.2
Equals: Adjusted imports of services	298.7
Less: Transport and duty adjustment*	64.7
Equals: Imports of services, AIAs	234.0
Less: Noncomparable imports	193.9
Equals: Comparable services imports	40.1

*In the industry accounts, cross-border transport costs and import duties are included in the domestic port value of merchandise imports. Offsetting adjustments are made in wholesale trade and transportation services to ensure that total imports exclude import duties and transport costs paid to U.S. carriers, and that transport costs paid to foreign carriers are not counted twice.

component of other private services, was classified as noncomparable in 2004, mostly because of the highly specialized or unspecified nature of the services provided by foreign affiliates to their U.S. parents or by foreign parents to their U.S. affiliates.[5] All transactions in BPT services between unaffiliated parties, however, are classified as comparable services imports in the industry accounts.

8.3 Purchased Services in BEA's Industry Accounts

As described previously, BEA's annual industry accounts include the integrated GDP-by-industry and annual input-output (I-O) accounts. The annual I-O accounts provide a time series of detailed, consistent information on the flows of goods and services that comprise industry production processes and final expenditures. Estimates of the supply of commodities are prepared at nearly the same level of detail as in the benchmark I-O accounts, and are then aggregated to the less-detailed publication level used for the annual industry accounts. These time series are estimated within the framework of balanced make and use tables and are consistent with the NIPA estimates of final expenditures and industry estimates of gross output and value added. These additional layers of internal consistency in the annual industry accounts increase the overall reliability of the estimates of intermediate inputs by industry.

The AIAs were recently expanded to provide additional information on the composition of intermediate inputs by industry, allowing these accounts to be used to study trends in the use of purchased services inputs. The balanced I-O use table, which shows the commodity composition of intermediate inputs by industry and by final demand category, provides the product detail needed for aggregating estimates of intermediate inputs into cost categories that are useful for economic analysis. The product detail underlying the industry estimates of intermediate inputs has been aggregated into three cost categories—energy, materials, and purchased services. These estimates were prepared by applying a KLEMS production framework to BEA's estimates of industry production.[6] Each of these three cost categories includes both imported and domestically produced goods and services. Intermediate inputs are valued in purchasers' prices, which include domestic transportation costs and wholesale trade margins plus sales and excise taxes.

---

5. Some imported services are classified as noncomparable partly because information is available for direct allocation to the using industries. Otherwise, they would be included in the domestic supply of a comparable commodity and allocated indirectly to using industries. The Bureau of Economic Analysis plans to evaluate this trade-off as part of an overall review of the treatment of imported purchased services in the industry accounts.

6. See Strassner, Medeiros, and Smith. For the most recently updated KLEMS estimates, see http://bea.gov/industry/gdpbyind_data.htm.

The NAICS industry classification system that is used for the AIAs also provides advantages for studying outsourcing in the U.S. economy. The NAICS classification improves on the SIC as a classification system because it more consistently classifies establishments into industries on the basis of similar production processes, recognizes new and emerging industries, and provides greater detail for the services sector, which includes the industries that provide outsourcing services. Unlike the SIC system, NAICS provides separate industry groupings for information-related activities and for professional and business services. In addition, under NAICS, establishments that primarily provide support services to other establishments of the same company (i.e., auxiliaries) are classified according to the type of service they provide, rather than according to the industry of the establishments they serve, as they were under the SIC. Most such auxiliaries are classified in the NAICS professional and business services sector.

8.3.1   Purchased Services Inputs

The newly expanded AIAs allow the growth of services as intermediate inputs, including outsourcing-related purchased services, to be studied more closely after 1997 because, starting with that year, these accounts provide consistent time series data on gross output, intermediate input cost categories, value added, and price and quantity indexes. For the overall economy (all industries), purchased services increased as a share of gross output in each year from 1997 to 2003, before declining in 2004. The increases after 2000, however, were smaller than those between 1997 and 2000.

Purchased services inputs increased from 22.5 percent of gross output in 1997 to 24.8 percent in 2004. (See figure 8.1 and table 8.4.) Similar but less consistent trends appear for private goods-producing industries, which include manufacturing, and for private services-producing industries. For goods-producing industries, the purchased-services share increased from 15.1 percent in 1997 to 16.7 percent in 2002, but then it declined afterward. For services-producing industries, the purchased services share increased from 26.9 percent in 1997 to 29.7 percent in 2000 before declining in 2001 and then remaining flat.

The growth in purchased services inputs as a share of gross output after 1997 may have been due to faster growth in the relative prices of services inputs, faster growth in the use of purchased services relative to other inputs, or a combination of these two factors. Faster growth in the *use* of purchased services is a better indicator of possible outsourcing, because it implies changes in the production process rather than changes in relative input prices. The approximate contributions of these two factors can be found using the KLEMS-based price and quantity indexes. From 1997 to 2004, the quantity index of purchased-services inputs for all industries in-

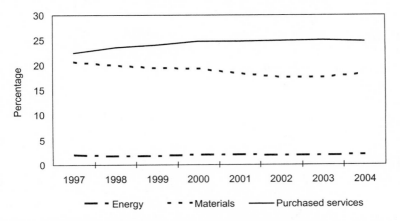

Fig. 8.1   Intermediate inputs as a percentage of all industries' gross output

creased at an average annual rate of 4.7 percent, compared to 3.2 percent for gross output, implying some substitution of purchased services for other inputs. Prices for purchased services inputs increased at about the same rate as gross output prices (1.7 percent). These results suggest that the growth in the share of purchased services reflects substitution among categories of inputs (i.e., changes in the production process) more than changes in the relative prices of inputs. Of course, the substitution toward purchased services may itself have been induced by changes in relative prices.

Outsourcing-Related Purchased Services

Not all of the growth in the output share of purchased services inputs is necessarily due to outsourcing, so it is useful to draw a distinction between outsourcing-related services and other types of purchased services. Because no consensus exists on exactly which types of purchased services constitute outsourcing, this study defines outsourcing-related services somewhat conservatively to include NAICS commodities 5112 (packaged software), 514 (information and data processing services), 54 (professional, scientific, and technical services), and 561 (administrative and support services).[7] An important feature of each of these services is that more than one half of their domestic supply is used by the business sector, either as an intermediate input to production or as a form of business investment, such as capitalized software.

For the most part, these are the types of professional, technical, support,

7. Management of companies and enterprises (NAICS commodity code 55) was not included, mostly because there are no imports. This service could be included in a broader measure of outsourcing since it consists of management oversight services provided to other establishments of the same company.

Table 8.4   Components of current-dollar gross output by industry group as a percentage of gross output

Industry group	1997	1998	1999	2000	2001	2002	2003	2004
All industries	100.0	100.0	100.0	100.0	100.0	100.0	100.0	100.0
Value Added	54.8	55.0	54.8	54.0	55.0	55.7	55.6	55.0
Compensation of employees	30.8	31.6	31.7	31.8	32.3	32.4	32.1	31.4
Taxes on production and imports less subsidies	3.8	3.8	3.7	3.7	3.7	3.9	3.8	3.8
Gross operating surplus	20.2	19.6	19.4	18.5	19.1	19.4	19.7	19.8
Intermediate inputs	45.2	45.0	45.2	46.0	45.0	44.3	44.4	45.0
Energy inputs	2.0	1.7	1.7	2.0	2.0	1.9	1.9	2.0
Materials inputs	20.6	19.8	19.4	19.2	18.2	17.5	17.5	18.2
Purchased-services inputs	22.5	23.5	24.1	24.8	24.8	24.9	25.0	24.8
Private goods-producing industries[a]	100.0	100.0	100.0	100.0	100.0	100.0	100.0	100.0
Value added	37.2	38.1	37.8	38.0	38.4	39.1	39.3	38.1
Compensation of employees	22.0	23.0	23.2	23.7	24.2	24.6	24.2	22.7
Taxes on production and imports less subsidies	1.1	0.9	0.8	0.8	0.9	1.1	1.1	1.1
Gross operating surplus	14.2	14.1	13.8	13.5	13.3	13.4	14.0	14.3
Intermediate inputs	62.8	61.9	62.2	62.0	61.6	60.9	60.7	61.9
Energy inputs	1.9	1.6	1.6	1.7	1.8	1.6	1.7	1.8
Materials inputs	45.8	44.8	44.7	44.6	43.2	42.6	42.5	44.0
Purchased-services inputs	15.1	15.5	15.9	15.7	16.7	16.7	16.5	16.1
Private services-producing industries[b]	100.0	100.0	100.0	100.0	100.0	100.0	100.0	100.0
Value added	63.0	62.3	62.0	60.4	61.6	62.1	61.9	61.7
Compensation of employees	31.4	32.1	32.2	32.2	32.4	32.2	31.7	31.5
Taxes on production and imports less subsidies	6.3	6.2	6.0	5.8	5.7	5.9	5.9	5.9
Gross operating surplus	25.3	24.1	23.8	22.4	23.4	24.0	24.3	24.4
Intermediate inputs	37.0	37.7	38.0	39.6	38.4	37.9	38.1	38.3
Energy inputs	1.9	1.6	1.6	1.9	1.8	1.8	1.8	1.9
Materials inputs	8.3	8.1	7.9	8.0	7.7	7.5	7.5	7.6
Purchased-services inputs	26.9	27.9	28.5	29.7	28.9	28.7	28.8	28.7

Source: U.S. Bureau of Economic Analysis, Annual Industry Accounts.

[a]Consists of agriculture, forestry, fishing, and hunting; mining; construction; and manufacturing.

[b]Consists of utilities; wholesale trade; retail trade; transportation and warehousing; information; finance, insurance, real estate, rental, and leasing; professional and business services; educational services; health care, and social assistance; arts, entertainment, recreation, accommodation, and food services; and other services, except government.

and administrative services that firms can choose either to provide within the same establishment using own-establishment employees or to acquire from external suppliers, either establishments owned by other companies or from their own domestic auxiliaries or foreign affiliates. Moreover, the outsourcing-related inputs defined previously are the types of services that are most vulnerable to import competition, because recent advances in information and communications technology have enabled foreign suppliers to provide these services more effectively and at lower cost. Other major types of services, such as utilities, communications, and finance, are not as likely to be performed within the establishment on an own-account basis.

In the remainder of this chapter, outsourcing-related services are referred to as business, professional, and technical (BPT) services. These services are defined to include the NAICS outsourcing-related services commodities, described previously, plus the portion of noncomparable imports identified as "other private services payments to affiliated foreigners." These noncomparable imports, which are very small relative to the total domestic supply of BPT services, are included because they consist largely of services that are similar in nature to the NAICS services commodities described earlier. Examples of these services include management consulting, public relations, research and development, and custom computer programming.[8]

The BPT services increased as a share of total purchased services, from 30.8 percent in 1997 to 33.9 percent in 2004.[9] This "outsourcing" share of purchased services varies by sector, ranging in 2004 from a high of 58 percent in construction to a low of nearly 7 percent in agriculture, forestry, fishing, and hunting. Among private industries, the second-highest outsourcing share of purchased services was in professional and business services (50 percent). The largest increase in the outsourcing share among private industries was in durable goods manufacturing, whose share rose from 31 percent in 1997 to 37 percent in 2004. Outsourcing-related services are clearly very important in the cost structure of many domestic industries, and they appear to be growing faster than other types of purchased services.

8.3.2   Imported Services Inputs

Purchased services, including outsourcing-related services, can be provided either by resident suppliers (domestic production) or by foreign suppliers (imports). The rapid growth of business, professional, and technical

---

8. Some argue that imports of BPT services from affiliates should not be treated as outsourcing because the transactions occur within the firm. Many of the underlying services, however, could have been performed by the U.S. establishment using its own resources or by other (unaffiliated) domestic establishments.

9. These shares were calculated using unpublished data from BEA's Annual Industry Accounts.

Table 8.5   Imported business, professional, and technical services, industry accounts, 2004 (in billions of dollars)

Business, professional, and technical services	48.1*
Comparable imports	9.8
Purchased software and information services	0.2
Professional, scientific, and technical services	9.4
Administrative and support services	0.2
Noncomparable imports	38.3*

*Includes $6.2 billion in affiliated financial services. These services are not included in the ITA measure of BPT services.

(BPT) services imports in the ITAs suggests that offshore suppliers have contributed to the growth of purchased services and outsourcing in the U.S., and may have slightly gained market share at the expense of domestic suppliers. Imported services, however, are still very small compared to domestic production. For example, from 1997 to 2004, imported BPT services in the ITAs increased at an average annual rate of 10.1 percent, nearly doubling from $20.8 billion to $40.7 billion. By comparison, domestically produced professional and business services increased at an average annual rate of 6.3 percent, from $1,555.5 billion to $2,385.9 billion.

Table 8.5 shows the composition of imported BPT services in the industry accounts for 2004.

For this chapter, the authors disaggregated BEA's published KLEMS-based intermediate input cost categories to obtain estimates, by industry, of the imports included in each category, including purchased services. These annual import matrices were developed because of the lack of actual data on the use of comparable imports by industry. For each comparable commodity used by an industry, the portion attributable to imports was calculated as a percentage of the total purchase value, using the economy-wide share of imports in the total supply of the commodity. For example, if imports represent 40 percent of the domestic supply of semiconductors, then the import matrix estimates assume that imports comprise 40 percent of the value of semiconductors in each industry that uses semiconductors. These import shares were first developed for the benchmark use table using very detailed product data, and they were updated annually at the same level of product detail.[10] Under this methodology, variation in the use of comparable imports by industry is due to variation in the commodity composition of intermediate inputs and variation in the commodity import shares.

10. The Bureau of Economic Analysis has prepared an import matrix for 1997 as a supplement to the 1997 benchmark I-O accounts using similar assumptions about the use of imported commodities. However, the valuation of imports in that matrix is slightly different. For more information, see the BEA website at http://www.bea.gov/industry/more.htm.

Comparable imports at detailed product levels were aggregated, for each industry, into the broad category of purchased services, as defined for the KLEMS estimates, and into the narrower category of outsourcing-related BPT services, as previously defined for this chapter. Nearly all of the non-comparable imports were classified as purchased services in the KLEMS estimates, and a large portion of these were also classified as BPT services. Industry estimates of purchased services and of BPT services are the sums of the comparable and noncomparable imports assigned to these categories. The combined estimates are used in the following to identify the industries that import intermediate services, to describe how their use has changed since 1997, and to provide preliminary measures of the contribution of imports to total purchased services and BPT services.

Industries Using Imported Services

In the industry accounts, imported services for intermediate use increased from $98.5 billion in 1997 to $188.2 billion in 2004. Imports as a share of intermediate purchased services, while still very low, increased from 2.9 percent to 3.6 percent over this period. The four largest imported services, which accounted for 95 percent of total imported intermediate purchased services in 2004, were noncomparable imports (70 percent), insurance carriers and related activities (16 percent), air transportation (5 percent), and miscellaneous professional, scientific, and technical services (4 percent). Imports of other transportation services and selected professional services accounted for the remainder.

Table 8.6 shows the dollar levels for the estimated imported purchased services by industry group for 1997 to 2004, and table 8.7 shows the percentage distribution of industry purchases of imported services. In 2004, finance and insurance consumed the most imported services ($45.0 billion), followed by federal government ($26.6 billion), transportation and warehousing ($23.6 billion), durable goods manufacturing ($17.7 billion), and nondurable goods manufacturing ($16.8 billion). Table 8.7 indicates that some change took place in the industry distribution of imported purchased services over this period. Shares increased for the federal government and for finance and insurance and declined for transportation and warehousing and for information. Manufacturing's share decreased slightly after peaking in 2001.

Another way of identifying industry groups that are significant users of imported purchased services is by examining the share of intermediate purchased services accounted for by imports. This "import intensity" is calculated by dividing an industry's imported purchased services by its total use of intermediate purchased services (table 8.8). In 2004, import intensities ranged from a high of 11.5 percent for transportation and warehousing to a low of 0.3 percent for health care and social assistance and for agriculture. Other private industry groups with relatively high import

Table 8.6   Imported purchased services by industry group, 1997–2004 (in billions of dollars)

Industry group	1997	1998	1999	2000	2001	2002	2003	2004
All industries	98.5	106.1	120.1	134.1	139.1	151.1	164.2	188.2
Private industries	85.7	93.4	105.6	119.3	122.9	131.5	139.5	160.1
Agriculture, forestry, fishing, and hunting	0.1	0.1	0.1	0.2	0.2	0.2	0.2	0.2
Mining	0.8	1.0	0.9	1.1	1.4	1.2	1.5	2.0
Utilities	0.2	0.2	0.2	0.2	0.2	0.2	0.1	0.1
Construction	0.8	0.9	1.0	1.0	1.1	1.1	1.2	1.2
Manufacturing	19.5	21.0	24.5	25.1	31.9	31.9	31.3	34.5
Nondurable goods	8.5	9.3	11.2	13.0	14.3	14.9	14.3	16.8
Durable goods	11.0	11.7	13.4	12.2	17.7	17.0	17.0	17.7
Wholesale trade	6.6	7.6	8.1	9.1	8.8	11.1	10.8	15.9
Retail trade	1.0	1.1	1.3	1.5	1.5	1.5	1.7	1.9
Transportation and warehousing	17.5	17.4	19.0	21.4	20.6	19.9	20.9	23.6
Information	11.8	11.4	11.1	10.5	10.8	10.6	11.1	11.2
Finance, insurance, real estate, rental, and leasing	19.0	23.1	28.1	36.2	32.3	40.2	45.8	53.9
Finance and insurance	16.0	19.8	24.0	29.3	27.3	35.0	38.1	45.0
Real estate and rental and leasing	3.0	3.3	4.0	6.9	5.0	5.3	7.7	8.9
Professional and business services	6.3	7.4	8.8	10.3	11.1	10.7	11.7	12.1
Professional, scientific, and technical services	4.6	5.4	6.5	7.5	8.4	8.1	9.0	9.3
Management of companies and enterprises	0.4	0.4	0.4	0.5	0.6	0.5	0.5	0.5
Administrative and waste management services	1.3	1.6	1.8	2.3	2.1	2.1	2.1	2.2

Educational services, health care, and social assistance	0.9	1.0	1.1	1.3	1.3	1.3	1.5	1.6
Educational services	0.3	0.3	0.3	0.4	0.4	0.3	0.4	0.5
Health care and social assistance	0.7	0.7	0.8	0.9	0.9	1.0	1.1	1.2
Arts, entertainment, recreation, accommodation, and food services	0.7	0.7	0.8	0.9	0.9	0.9	1.0	1.2
Arts, entertainment, and recreation	0.2	0.2	0.2	0.2	0.2	0.2	0.2	0.3
Accommodation and food services	0.5	0.6	0.6	0.7	0.7	0.7	0.8	0.9
Other services, except government	0.4	0.5	0.6	0.7	0.7	0.7	0.7	0.8
Government	12.8	12.7	14.5	14.7	16.2	19.7	24.7	28.1
Federal government	11.9	11.8	13.5	13.5	14.9	18.3	23.2	26.6
State and local government	0.8	0.9	1.0	1.3	1.4	1.4	1.5	1.6
Addenda								
Private goods-producing industries[a]	21.3	23.0	26.5	27.3	34.6	34.3	34.2	37.9
Private services-producing industries[b]	64.4	70.4	79.1	92.0	88.3	97.2	105.3	122.2

Source: Authors' calculations, using unpublished data from BEA's Annual Industry Accounts.

[a]Consists of agriculture, forestry, fishing, and hunting; mining; construction; and manufacturing.

[b]Consists of utilities; wholesale trade; retail trade; transportation and warehousing; information; finance, insurance, real estate, rental, and leasing; professional and business services; educational services; health care, and social assistance; arts, entertainment, recreation, accommodation, and food services; and other services, except government.

Table 8.7   Distribution of imported purchased services by industry group, 1997–2004 (%)

Industry group	1997	1998	1999	2000	2001	2002	2003	2004
All industries	100.0	100.0	100.0	100.0	100.0	100.0	100.0	100.0
Private industries	87.0	88.0	87.9	89.0	88.3	87.0	85.0	85.1
Agriculture, forestry, fishing, and hunting	0.1	0.1	0.1	0.1	0.1	0.1	0.1	0.1
Mining	0.8	0.9	0.7	0.8	1.0	0.8	0.9	1.1
Utilities	0.2	0.2	0.1	0.1	0.2	0.1	0.1	0.0
Construction	0.8	0.8	0.8	0.7	0.8	0.7	0.8	0.7
Manufacturing	19.8	19.8	20.4	18.8	23.0	21.1	19.0	18.3
Nondurable goods	8.6	8.7	9.3	9.7	10.3	9.9	8.7	8.9
Durable goods	11.2	11.1	11.1	9.1	12.7	11.2	10.4	9.4
Wholesale trade	6.7	7.1	6.8	6.8	6.3	7.3	6.6	8.4
Retail trade	1.0	1.0	1.1	1.1	1.0	1.0	1.0	1.0
Transportation and warehousing	17.8	16.4	15.8	15.9	14.8	13.2	12.8	12.5
Information	11.9	10.8	9.2	7.9	7.7	7.0	6.7	6.0
Finance, insurance, real estate, rental, and leasing	19.3	21.8	23.4	27.0	23.2	26.6	27.9	28.6
Finance and insurance	16.3	18.7	20.0	21.8	19.6	23.1	23.2	23.9
Real estate and rental and leasing	3.0	3.1	3.3	5.2	3.6	3.5	4.7	4.7
Professional and business services	6.4	7.0	7.3	7.7	8.0	7.1	7.1	6.4
Professional, scientific, and technical services	4.7	5.1	5.4	5.6	6.1	5.4	5.5	5.0
Management of companies and enterprises	0.4	0.4	0.4	0.3	0.4	0.3	0.3	0.3
Administrative and waste management services	1.3	1.5	1.5	1.7	1.5	1.4	1.3	1.2

Educational services, health care, and social assistance	0.9	0.9	0.9	1.0	0.9	0.9	0.9	0.9
Educational services	0.3	0.3	0.3	0.3	0.3	0.2	0.2	0.3
Health care and social assistance	0.7	0.7	0.7	0.7	0.7	0.6	0.7	0.6
Arts, entertainment, recreation, accommodation, and food services	0.7	0.7	0.7	0.7	0.7	0.6	0.6	0.6
Arts, entertainment, and recreation	0.2	0.2	0.2	0.1	0.2	0.1	0.1	0.1
Accommodation and food services	0.5	0.5	0.5	0.5	0.5	0.5	0.5	0.5
Other services, except government	0.5	0.5	0.5	0.5	0.5	0.4	0.4	0.4
Government	13.0	12.0	12.1	11.0	11.7	13.0	15.0	14.9
Federal government	12.1	11.1	11.2	10.1	10.7	12.1	14.1	14.1
State and local government	0.9	0.9	0.9	0.9	1.0	0.9	0.9	0.8
Addenda								
Private goods-producing industries[a]	21.6	21.7	22.1	20.4	24.9	22.7	20.8	20.1
Private services-producing industries[b]	65.4	66.4	65.8	68.6	63.4	64.3	64.1	64.9

Source: Authors' calculations, using unpublished data from BEA's Annual Industry Accounts.

[a]Consists of agriculture, forestry, fishing, and hunting; mining; construction; and manufacturing.

[b]Consists of utilities; wholesale trade; retail trade; transportation and warehousing; information; finance, insurance, real estate, rental, and leasing; professional and business services; educational services; health care, and social assistance; arts, entertainment, recreation, accommodation, and food services; and other services, except government.

Table 8.8   Imported purchased services as a share of total purchased services by industry group, 1997–2004 (%)

Industry group	1997	1998	1999	2000	2001	2002	2003	2004
All industries	2.9	2.8	2.9	3.0	3.0	3.2	3.3	3.6
Private industries	2.8	2.8	2.9	2.9	3.0	3.2	3.2	3.4
Agriculture, forestry, fishing, and hunting	0.2	0.2	0.3	0.4	0.3	0.4	0.3	0.3
Mining	2.6	3.1	2.9	2.6	2.9	2.8	2.9	3.6
Utilities	0.7	0.6	0.7	0.7	0.9	0.8	0.7	0.7
Construction	0.9	0.9	0.9	0.8	0.9	0.9	0.9	0.9
Manufacturing	3.5	3.6	3.9	3.9	4.8	4.9	4.7	4.8
Nondurable goods	3.5	3.5	4.0	4.4	4.6	4.8	4.7	5.0
Durable goods	3.5	3.6	3.7	3.4	5.0	4.9	4.8	4.6
Wholesale trade	3.9	4.5	4.5	4.4	4.7	5.5	5.3	6.3
Retail trade	0.5	0.5	0.6	0.6	0.6	0.5	0.6	0.6
Transportation and warehousing	10.2	9.3	9.8	10.7	10.7	10.5	10.9	11.5
Information	4.7	3.8	3.3	2.6	2.5	2.4	2.4	2.4
Finance, insurance, real estate, rental, and leasing	2.7	2.9	3.2	3.6	3.4	4.4	4.7	5.2
Finance and insurance	3.9	4.3	4.4	4.6	4.8	6.8	7.1	7.5
Real estate and rental and leasing	1.0	1.0	1.2	1.9	1.3	1.3	1.8	2.0
Professional and business services	1.8	1.8	1.9	1.9	1.9	1.8	1.8	1.8
Professional, scientific, and technical services	2.5	2.4	2.5	2.5	2.4	2.2	2.3	2.2
Management of companies and enterprises	0.4	0.5	0.5	0.5	0.6	0.5	0.5	0.5
Administrative and waste management services	1.6	1.6	1.6	1.7	1.5	1.5	1.5	1.5

Educational services, health care, and social assistance	0.4	0.4	0.4	0.4	0.4	0.4	0.4	0.4
Educational services	0.7	0.6	0.7	0.8	0.7	0.6	0.7	0.8
Health care and social assistance	0.3	0.3	0.3	0.3	0.3	0.3	0.3	0.3
Arts, entertainment, recreation, accommodation, and food services	0.6	0.6	0.6	0.6	0.6	0.6	0.6	0.6
Arts, entertainment, and recreation	0.4	0.4	0.4	0.4	0.4	0.4	0.4	0.4
Accommodation and food services	0.7	0.7	0.7	0.7	0.7	0.6	0.6	0.7
Other services, except government	0.5	0.5	0.6	0.6	0.6	0.6	0.6	0.6
Government	3.6	3.4	3.5	3.3	3.3	3.7	4.2	4.5
Federal government	9.6	9.6	9.9	9.4	9.1	9.6	10.4	10.7
State and local government	0.4	0.4	0.4	0.4	0.4	0.4	0.4	0.4
Addenda								
Private goods-producing industries[a]	2.9	3.0	3.2	3.2	3.9	4.0	3.8	3.9
Private services-producing industries[b]	2.8	2.7	2.8	2.9	2.8	3.0	3.0	3.3

Source: Authors' calculations, using unpublished data from BEA's Annual Industry Accounts.

[a]Consists of agriculture, forestry, fishing, and hunting; mining; construction; and manufacturing.

[b]Consists of utilities; wholesale trade; retail trade; transportation and warehousing; information; finance, insurance, real estate, rental, and leasing; professional and business services; educational services; health care, and social assistance; arts, entertainment, recreation, accommodation, and food services; and other services, except government.

intensities include finance and insurance, wholesale trade, and manufacturing. Increases over time in the import intensity of purchased services may indicate that imported services are being substituted for domestic output.

Industries Using Imported BPT Services

In the industry accounts, imports of estimated BPT services increased from $22.0 billion in 1997 to $48.1 billion in 2004 (table 8.9). By 2004, BPT services accounted for slightly more than one fourth of all imported intermediate purchased services, up from 22 percent in 1997. Shares increased over this period for both the private goods-producing sector, which includes manufacturing, and the private services-producing sector. The industry distribution of imported BPT services is similar to that for all imported purchased services, but there are some important differences (table 8.10). Private industries account for a larger share of the imported BPT services, and these services are more heavily concentrated in the goods-producing sector, especially in durable goods manufacturing.

As with total purchased services, a measure of the import intensity of outsourcing can be calculated by dividing imported BPT services by all purchased BPT services. This measure increased from 2.1 percent in 1997 to 2.7 percent in 2004 (table 8.11). While the import intensity of outsourcing is not as high as that for all imported purchased services, it has demonstrated a steady if irregular upward trend over the period. This trend appears for both the goods-producing and the services-producing sectors. For the goods-producing sector, the import intensity of outsourcing increased from 3.1 percent to 4.0 percent. For the services-producing sector, it increased from 2.0 percent to 2.8 percent. Among the three largest private users of outsourcing services, import intensities were little changed in professional and business services but increased significantly in manufacturing (from 3.8 percent to 4.9 percent) and in finance, insurance, real estate, rental, and leasing (from 3.1 percent to 5.4 percent).

Impact on Output and Value Added

If U.S. firms did substitute imports of services for domestic production after 2000, then we should observe some effect on the output and value added of the U.S. industries that provide outsourcing services. In BEA's annual industry accounts, nominal and real gross output for the professional and business services sector increased rapidly from 1997 to 2000 but then slowed considerably after 2000. Real value added in this sector increased more slowly than for all private services industries and GDP. Gross output prices and value added prices also increased more slowly than in the rest of the economy. As a result, the value added share of GDP originating in the outsourcing sector declined after 2000, from 11.6 percent to 11.5 percent. It is not clear, though, how much of this decline was due to the downturn

Table 8.9   Imported business, professional, and technical services by industry group, 1997–2004 (in billions of dollars)

Industry group	1997	1998	1999	2000	2001	2002	2003	2004
All industries	22.0	24.6	31.4	34.3	39.4	38.7	43.7	48.1
Private industries	21.2	23.7	30.4	33.2	37.7	37.3	41.9	46.0
Agriculture, forestry, fishing, and hunting	0.0	0.0	0.1	0.1	0.1	0.1	0.1	0.1
Mining	0.3	0.3	0.4	0.4	0.5	0.5	0.7	0.8
Utilities	0.1	0.1	0.1	0.1	0.1	0.1	0.0	0.0
Construction	0.4	0.5	0.5	0.5	0.6	0.6	0.7	0.7
Manufacturing	6.1	6.6	8.6	8.0	11.0	10.7	11.4	11.8
Nondurable goods	1.7	1.8	2.4	2.6	3.1	2.9	3.0	3.3
Durable goods	4.5	4.8	6.3	5.4	8.0	7.8	8.3	8.4
Wholesale trade	2.2	2.5	3.1	3.2	3.2	4.1	4.4	6.2
Retail trade	0.5	0.6	0.7	0.7	0.9	0.8	0.9	1.0
Transportation and warehousing	0.9	1.1	1.4	1.3	1.6	1.5	1.7	1.6
Information	2.0	2.2	2.7	3.0	3.7	3.6	3.8	3.5
Finance, insurance, real estate, rental, and leasing	5.0	5.6	7.5	10.1	8.4	8.8	10.5	12.8
Finance and insurance	3.8	4.3	6.0	7.2	6.3	6.8	7.2	9.0
Real estate and rental and leasing	1.1	1.3	1.6	2.9	2.2	2.0	3.3	3.8
Professional and business services	2.9	3.4	4.2	4.7	5.8	5.3	6.2	5.9
Professional, scientific, and technical services	2.2	2.6	3.4	3.8	4.6	4.3	5.1	4.9
Management of companies and enterprises	0.3	0.3	0.3	0.4	0.5	0.3	0.3	0.4
Administrative and waste management services	0.3	0.4	0.5	0.6	0.7	0.6	0.7	0.7

(continued)

Table 8.9   (continued)

Industry group	1997	1998	1999	2000	2001	2002	2003	2004
Educational services, health care, and social assistance	0.4	0.4	0.5	0.5	0.7	0.6	0.7	0.7
Educational services	0.1	0.1	0.1	0.1	0.2	0.1	0.2	0.2
Health care and social assistance	0.3	0.3	0.4	0.3	0.5	0.4	0.5	0.5
Arts, entertainment, recreation, accommodation, and food services	0.3	0.3	0.3	0.3	0.4	0.4	0.4	0.5
Arts, entertainment, and recreation	0.1	0.1	0.1	0.1	0.1	0.1	0.1	0.1
Accommodation and food services	0.2	0.2	0.2	0.2	0.3	0.3	0.3	0.4
Other services, except government	0.2	0.3	0.3	0.3	0.4	0.4	0.4	0.4
Government	0.8	0.9	1.1	1.1	1.7	1.4	1.9	2.1
Federal government	0.5	0.6	0.7	0.7	1.2	0.9	1.3	1.6
State and local government	0.3	0.3	0.4	0.4	0.5	0.4	0.5	0.5
Addenda								
Private goods-producing industries[a]	6.9	7.5	9.7	9.0	12.3	11.9	12.8	13.4
Private services-producing industries[b]	14.3	16.3	20.7	24.3	25.4	25.4	29.0	32.6

Source: Authors' calculations, using unpublished data from BEA's Annual Industry Accounts.

[a]Consists of agriculture, forestry, fishing, and hunting; mining; construction; and manufacturing.

[b]Consists of utilities; wholesale trade; retail trade; transportation and warehousing; information; finance, insurance, real estate, rental, and leasing; professional and business services; educational services; health care, and social assistance; arts, entertainment, recreation, accommodation, and food services; and other services, except government.

Table 8.10   Distribution of imported business, professional, and technical services by industry group, 1997–2004 (%)

Industry group	1997	1998	1999	2000	2001	2002	2003	2004
All industries	100.0	100.0	100.0	100.0	100.0	100.0	100.0	100.0
Private industries	96.3	96.3	96.6	96.9	95.7	96.4	95.8	95.6
Agriculture, forestry, fishing, and hunting	0.2	0.2	0.2	0.2	0.2	0.1	0.2	0.2
Mining	1.3	1.4	1.3	1.2	1.4	1.4	1.5	1.8
Utilities	0.3	0.4	0.2	0.2	0.3	0.2	0.1	0.1
Construction	2.0	2.0	1.7	1.5	1.6	1.5	1.7	1.5
Manufacturing	27.8	26.8	27.5	23.3	28.0	27.7	26.0	24.5
Nondurable goods	7.5	7.4	7.5	7.5	7.8	7.4	6.9	6.9
Durable goods	20.3	19.4	20.0	15.8	20.2	20.3	19.1	17.6
Wholesale trade	10.0	10.2	9.8	9.4	8.1	10.5	10.0	12.9
Retail trade	2.2	2.3	2.1	2.0	2.3	2.0	2.2	2.1
Transportation and warehousing	4.3	4.3	4.3	3.8	4.1	3.8	3.9	3.3
Information	8.9	8.8	8.7	8.8	9.5	9.4	8.8	7.2
Finance, insurance, real estate, rental, and leasing	22.5	22.6	23.9	29.5	21.5	22.7	24.1	26.6
Finance and insurance	17.5	17.5	19.0	20.9	15.9	17.7	16.5	18.7
Real estate and rental and leasing	5.0	5.1	5.0	8.5	5.5	5.0	7.5	7.9
Professional and business services	12.9	13.6	13.4	13.7	14.8	13.6	14.1	12.2
Professional, scientific, and technical services	10.2	10.7	10.7	11.0	11.7	11.1	11.7	10.1
Management of companies and enterprises	1.3	1.3	1.1	1.0	1.3	0.8	0.8	0.8
Administrative and waste management services	1.5	1.6	1.6	1.7	1.8	1.6	1.6	1.4

(continued)

Table 8.10 (continued)

Industry group	1997	1998	1999	2000	2001	2002	2003	2004
Educational services, health care, and social assistance	1.6	1.7	1.5	1.4	1.7	1.5	1.5	1.4
Educational services	0.4	0.4	0.3	0.4	0.4	0.4	0.4	0.3
Health care and social assistance	1.3	1.3	1.1	1.0	1.3	1.1	1.1	1.1
Arts, entertainment, recreation, accommodation, and food services	1.1	1.1	1.0	1.0	1.1	0.9	0.9	1.0
Arts, entertainment, and recreation	0.3	0.3	0.2	0.2	0.3	0.2	0.2	0.2
Accommodation and food services	0.8	0.8	0.8	0.7	0.9	0.7	0.7	0.7
Other services, except government	1.0	1.1	1.0	1.0	1.1	1.0	1.0	0.9
Government	3.7	3.7	3.4	3.1	4.3	3.6	4.2	4.4
Federal government	2.3	2.3	2.2	2.0	2.9	2.4	3.1	3.3
State and local government	1.3	1.4	1.2	1.0	1.3	1.2	1.2	1.1
Addenda								
Private goods-producing industries[a]	31.4	30.3	30.7	26.1	31.2	30.8	29.4	27.9
Private services-producing industries[b]	64.9	66.0	65.9	70.8	64.6	65.7	66.4	67.7

Source: Authors' calculations, using unpublished data from BEA's Annual Industry Accounts.

[a]Consists of agriculture, forestry, fishing, and hunting; mining; construction; and manufacturing.
[b]Consists of utilities; wholesale trade; retail trade; transportation and warehousing; information; finance, insurance, real estate, rental, and leasing; professional and business services; educational services; health care, and social assistance; arts, entertainment, recreation, accommodation, and food services; and other services, except government.

Table 8.11   Imported business, professional, and technical (BPT) services as a share of total BPT services by industry group, 1997–2004 (%)

Industry group	1997	1998	1999	2000	2001	2002	2003	2004
All industries	2.1	2.1	2.4	2.3	2.6	2.5	2.6	2.7
Private industries	2.3	2.2	2.6	2.5	2.8	2.7	3.0	3.0
Agriculture, forestry, fishing, and hunting	1.2	1.2	1.4	1.4	1.7	1.4	1.6	1.7
Mining	4.9	6.4	8.3	5.2	5.2	5.7	6.1	7.4
Utilities	0.8	0.8	1.0	0.8	1.2	0.9	0.9	0.9
Construction	0.8	0.8	0.9	0.8	1.0	0.9	1.0	1.0
Manufacturing	3.8	3.8	4.4	3.9	5.0	4.8	5.1	4.9
Nondurable goods	2.6	2.6	3.1	3.1	3.3	3.0	3.3	3.3
Durable goods	4.6	4.5	5.2	4.5	6.3	6.1	6.3	6.0
Wholesale trade	3.6	4.1	4.5	4.2	4.6	5.5	5.8	6.9
Retail trade	0.8	0.8	0.8	0.8	1.1	0.9	1.0	1.0
Transportation and warehousing	2.1	2.1	2.6	2.6	3.3	3.1	3.6	3.2
Information	2.8	2.5	2.8	2.5	2.9	2.8	2.8	2.5
Finance, insurance, real estate, rental, and leasing	3.1	3.1	3.8	4.4	3.9	4.1	4.7	5.4
Finance and insurance	5.7	5.6	6.3	6.6	6.7	8.1	8.6	9.4
Real estate and rental and leasing	1.2	1.3	1.5	2.4	1.8	1.5	2.4	2.7
Professional and business services	1.7	1.6	1.8	1.7	2.0	1.7	1.9	1.8
Professional, scientific, and technical services	2.5	2.2	2.5	2.4	2.6	2.3	2.5	2.3
Management of companies and enterprises	0.6	0.7	0.7	0.6	1.0	0.6	0.6	0.7
Administrative and waste management services	1.1	1.0	1.1	1.0	1.2	1.0	1.1	1.1

(continued)

Table 8.11   (continued)

Industry group	1997	1998	1999	2000	2001	2002	2003	2004
Educational services, health care, and social assistance	0.5	0.5	0.5	0.5	0.7	0.5	0.5	0.5
Educational services	0.9	0.8	0.9	1.0	1.1	0.9	1.1	1.1
Health care and social assistance	0.4	0.4	0.5	0.4	0.6	0.4	0.5	0.5
Arts, entertainment, recreation, accommodation, and food services	0.8	0.8	0.8	0.8	1.0	0.8	0.9	0.9
Arts, entertainment, and recreation	0.6	0.6	0.6	0.6	0.8	0.6	0.7	0.7
Accommodation and food services	0.9	0.9	0.9	0.9	1.2	0.9	1.0	1.0
Other services, except government	0.8	0.8	0.9	0.8	1.1	0.9	1.0	1.0
Government	0.7	0.7	0.7	0.7	1.0	0.7	0.8	0.8
Federal government	1.0	1.0	1.1	1.1	1.5	0.9	1.1	1.1
State and local government	0.4	0.4	0.4	0.4	0.6	0.4	0.4	0.4
Addenda								
Private goods-producing industries[a]	3.1	3.1	3.6	3.1	4.1	3.9	4.1	4.0
Private services-producing industries[b]	2.0	2.0	2.3	2.4	2.5	2.4	2.6	2.8

Source: Authors' calculations, using unpublished data from BEA's Annual Industry Accounts.

[a]Consists of agriculture, forestry, fishing, and hunting; mining; construction; and manufacturing.

[b]Consists of utilities; wholesale trade; retail trade; transportation and warehousing; information; finance, insurance, real estate, rental, and leasing; professional and business services; educational services; health care, and social assistance; arts, entertainment, recreation, accommodation, and food services; and other services, except government.

in the overall economy after 2000. For example, during the recession of 1990 to 1991, the outsourcing sector's share of GDP declined from 9.8 percent to 9.7 percent before resuming its upward trend in later years.

As previously shown, the growth of purchased services inputs as a share of gross output for U.S. industries since 1997 has primarily been due to the substitution of purchased services for other inputs, such as energy, materials, and labor, rather than relative price change. Other things equal, this would tend to increase demand for the output of domestic services industries. But we have also seen, within the broad category of purchased services and the narrower category of outsourcing-related BPT services, upward trends in the import intensity of these services. The relatively faster growth of imported BPT services could have come partly at the expense of the domestic outsourcing sector. However, the magnitudes of imported purchased services and imported BPT services are not large enough to explain much of the decline in the domestic outsourcing sector. For example, if nominal gross output (sales) for the domestic outsourcing sector and imported BPT services had continued to grow after 2000 at the same faster rates as in 1997 to 2000, then imported BPT services would have accounted for just slightly more than 2 percent of the difference between potential and actual domestic sales after 2000.

8.4   Evaluating the Methodology

This section presents the findings from evaluating some of the assumptions and procedures used by BEA to prepare the estimates of imported purchased services in the industry accounts. These assumptions and procedures affect the classification of imported services, their distribution by industry, and the deflation of imported purchased services for calculating real value added by industry.

8.4.1   Classification

About 70 percent of imported purchased services are classified as noncomparable imports in the industry accounts. Some of these services are clearly noncomparable because they are produced and consumed overseas and are not available for domestic consumption, such as overseas port operations by U.S. air and water carriers and purchases by the U.S. government for overseas operations. However, some other noncomparable services, such as business, professional, and technical services and royalties and license fees, have components that may be comparable to domestically produced services and that could be included in the domestic supply of those services in the industry accounts.

One of the advantages of the current treatment of noncomparable imports for the industry accounts is that data are available from BEA's international investment surveys to assist in the direct assignment of these imported services to the industry that purchases them, thus improving the overall industry distributions of intermediate inputs and value added. The estimates of noncomparable imports for private industries are obtained directly from BEA's mandatory surveys of the U.S. affiliates of foreign companies and the U.S. parents of foreign companies, which are assigned an enterprise-based industry classification by BEA. Otherwise, some noncomparable imported services would be included in the domestic supply, and their allocation among industries would be based on the assumption of a constant import share for each industry. The Bureau of Economic Analysis will investigate options for reducing the size of imports classified as noncomparable, while retaining the distributional advantages of the current procedures.

8.4.2 Industry Distribution

In BEA's industry accounts, estimates of comparable imports by industry, including imported purchased services, are based on the assumption that the economy-wide ratio of imports to total supply (import share) for a comparable good or service applies to each industry that uses the product. This constant-import-share assumption, which is used because of the lack of actual data on the import content of intermediate inputs for individual industries, has been employed in past studies of outsourcing and import substitution for both materials and services (Amiti and Wei provide examples). Variation in the use of comparable imports by industry in the industry accounts thus depends on variation in the use of commodities by industry and in the commodity import share.

Although this assumption is necessary, the import content of specific types of purchased services could vary by industry as a result of factors such as affiliation status, location, product mix, relative prices, or technology. Unfortunately, data have not been available either to test this assumption or to determine the sensitivity of import-related estimates to alternative assumptions. For this chapter, however, we have compiled data on industry-specific purchases of "other private services" and BPT services by combining unpublished industry data from BEA's international accounts on cross-border purchases of services by U.S. firms from both affiliated and unaffiliated parties.

Because multinational companies are typically very large firms, the combined BEA data for U.S. parents and the U.S. affiliates of foreign MNCs account for a significant share of domestic economic activity, especially in the manufacturing sector of the economy. For example, in 2003 the combined value added of U.S. parent companies and U.S. affiliates of foreign companies represented about 25 percent of the value added for all private U.S. industries from BEA's annual industry accounts. For companies classified in manufacturing, the combined value added was 80 percent of the value added for manufacturing in the industry accounts. Because the firms that participate in the BEA surveys are enterprises rather than establishments, however, the industry estimates for manufacturing include the operations of nonmanufacturing establishments that are owned by these companies.

Data collected on BEA's direct investment surveys and surveys of transactions between unaffiliated parties can be used to compile estimates of selected types of imported services purchased by U.S. businesses, classified by industry. Industry estimates reflect the consolidated operations of companies that are engaged in more than one industry. The kind of detail available for imported purchased services classified by the industry of the purchaser varies by the source of the data. For example, data are available on industry purchases of royalties and license fees and of other private services (in total) for affiliated transactions, which account for the majority of the import activity. More detailed data are available on purchases of types of BPT services for transactions between unaffiliated parties.

Table 8.12 compares, at highly aggregated levels, the industry distributions of imported BPT services from the industry accounts with those from the international accounts for the year 2002, which is the reference year for

Table 8.12   **Distribution of imported business, professional, and technical services by private industry group, 2002—International accounts and industry accounts (%)**

Industry group	International accounts	Industry accounts
Private industries	100	100
Manufacturing	32	29
Distributive services[a]	14	17
Information	11	10
Finance and insurance	22	18
Professional and business services	16	14
Other industries[b]	6	12
Addenda		
Private goods-producing industries[c]	33	32
Private services-producing industries[d]	67	68

Source: Authors' calculations, using unpublished data from BEA's International Accounts and Annual Industry Accounts.

[a]Consists of transportation and warehousing; wholesale trade; and retail trade.

[b]Consists of agriculture, forestry, fishing, and hunting; mining; utilities; construction; real estate and rental and leasing; educational services, health care, and social assistance; arts, entertainment, recreation; accommodation, and food services; and other services, except government.

[c]Consists of agriculture, forestry, fishing, and hunting; mining; construction; and manufacturing.

[d]Consists of utilities; wholesale trade; retail trade; transportation and warehousing; information; finance, insurance, real estate, rental, and leasing; professional and business services; educational services, health care, and social assistance; arts, entertainment, recreation, accommodation and food services; and other services, except government.

BEA's next set of benchmark input-output accounts. For transactions between affiliated enterprises, the estimates are based on special tabulations prepared by BEA's International Investment Division (IID).[11] For transactions between unaffiliated parties, IID provided access to databases that allowed the authors to identify and tabulate BPT services directly. The BPT services in the international accounts include some services that are not included in the industry accounts measure, such as leasing, construction, medical services, miscellaneous disbursements, sports and performing arts, and training services. In recent years, however, the totals compare favorably. For example, in 2002 the sum of BPT services plus affiliated financial services from the international accounts was $38.9 billion, and the corresponding sum from the industry accounts was $38.7 billion.[12]

Table 8.12 reveals some important differences in the industry distributions of imported BPT services. Shares for the aggregate private-goods producing and private-services producing sectors are very close, but larger differences arise in the distributions within those broad sectors. For example, the share for the manufacturing nondurable goods sector from the industry accounts (not shown) is only about half of that from the international accounts. Within the services sector, shares from the two sets of accounts differ by relatively large amounts in finance and insurance. Some of the differences, of course, are attributable to the fact that the data from the international accounts are classified by industry on an enterprise basis, whereas data from the industry accounts are classified by industry on an establishment basis.

Within both the goods- and services-producing sectors, some large share differences for industry groups are offset at higher levels of aggregation, suggesting the possibility that the differences are attributable largely to differences in classification. These results indicate that the assumptions underlying the industry distributions of imported BPT services in the industry accounts give reasonable results at aggregate levels, but that improvements are possible at more detailed industry levels. The Bureau of Economic Analysis plans to investigate these differences in more detail, with the goal of obtaining improved industry distributions of imported purchased services in the industry accounts. Better grounding of these assumptions is important, not only for understanding the nature of offshore outsourcing, but also for developing more reliable quantity and price indexes for intermediate purchased services by industry.

11. The Bureau of Economic Analysis' data on affiliated transactions by industry from the international accounts are for other private services (OPS) by industry. The OPS differs from BPT services by the inclusion of affiliated financial services, for which the distribution by industry is not separately available. The measure of BPT services from the industry accounts, however, also includes affiliated financial services, which amounted to $5.4 billion in 2002. This causes the shares for financial services industries to be higher in both distributions.

12. About $2 billion of the total from the international accounts is not allocated by industry.

8.4.3   Deflation Procedures

In BEA's annual industry accounts, a distinction is made between imports and domestic production for the purpose of calculating quantity and price indexes for intermediate inputs as part of the double-deflation method used to calculate real value added by industry. This distinction is made in order to account for differences in the behavior of prices for imported and domestic products when separate price indexes are available. For example, BEA uses a wide variety of price indexes compiled by the BLS International Price Program to deflate merchandise imports in the NIPAs. A composite price index for an intermediate input commodity is computed as a weighted average of its domestic and import price indexes. The weight for the import price index is the share of imports in the total supply of the commodity, and this share is assumed to not vary by industry. This is the same constant-import-share assumption that was used to prepare the annual import matrices for comparable imports.

For imported services, the same deflators that are used to deflate the imported services categories in the NIPAs are also used to deflate the corresponding commodities in the annual industry accounts. For comparable services imports, BEA uses BLS international price indexes, but these are currently available only for passenger fares and for selected components of other transportation services. Other components of transportation services and other comparable nontransportation services are usually deflated with the same price index used to deflate domestic production, such as a BLS producer price index. This procedure assumes that the rate of price change is the same for both imports and domestically produced services. Noncomparable imports that are similar in nature to domestic services, such as financial services, telecommunications, and insurance services, are also deflated with similar domestic price indexes.

Some of the larger categories of noncomparable imports, such as royalties, license fees, and other private services (including noncomparable BPT services) are deflated with a broad measure of price change, the implicit price deflator for final sales to domestic purchasers. Developing price indexes for noncomparable imports is particularly difficult, because large shares of these imports either are a composite of a variety of goods or services or do not represent true arm's length market transactions. For example, direct defense expenditures, travel, and port expenditures abroad consist of a variety of goods and services purchased overseas.[13] A large portion of royalties and license fees and other private services payments to

13. The Bureau of Economic Analysis uses a composite index of foreign consumer price indexes, adjusted for differences in exchange rates, to deflate travel, miscellaneous services, and U.S. students' expenditures abroad. Direct defense expenditures abroad are disaggregated by type of expenditure and deflated with corresponding price indexes for government consumption expenditures.

affiliated parties are most likely not actual market transactions, and thus may raise internal company transfer-pricing issues. Classifying more of the noncomparable imports, where possible, as comparable may result in better real estimates, even if domestic prices are used for the deflation.

From 1997 to 2004, the KLEMS-based price index for imported purchased services increased slightly faster than the domestic purchased services price index (1.9 percent versus 1.6 percent). Prices for imported services increased more slowly than those for domestic services, however, from 1997 to 2000, when the outsourcing sector's share of GDP was rising. Moreover, for the goods-producing sector, in which the import intensity of purchased services increased the most, prices for imported services declined relative to prices for domestic services over the entire period, but especially from 1997 to 2000. During this period, real imported purchased services grew rapidly relative to real domestic services in the goods-producing sector. These estimated effects might be larger, however, if more of the imported purchased services—BPT services in particular—could be deflated with true quality-adjusted price indexes. Catherine Mann (2003) and others have commented on the need for better and more detailed price indexes in order to understand the incentives that U.S. firms face when considering outsourcing. The Bureau of Economic Analysis will continue to work with BLS to improve the price indexes used to deflate both domestic and imported purchased services.

8.5   Summary and Conclusion

In the industry accounts, imports of intermediate purchased services are relatively small but have steadily increased as a share of total intermediate purchased services, rising from 2.9 percent in 1997 to 3.6 percent in 2004. These services include those that are closely associated with outsourcing but also include other purchased services such as transportation, communications, and finance and insurance. Outsourcing-related services, as defined for this chapter, increased as a share of total purchased services, from 30.8 percent in 1997 to 33.9 percent in 2004. The import share of these outsourcing-related services also increased during this period, rising from 2.1 percent to 2.7 percent.

The small size of these imported services, especially those that are classified as competing with domestic production in the industry accounts, suggests that import competition played only a small role in the slower growth of the domestic professional and business services (outsourcing) sector after 2000. Slower real output growth and employment reductions in this sector are probably better explained by the downturn of 2001 and by sluggish demand for information and communications technology. Using industry and occupation data from BLS, Bednarzik (2005) also concluded that services offshoring contributed only modestly to very slow employment growth in the professional and business services sector.

Further study is required to develop a better understanding of how imported services affect industry output, employment, and contributions to GDP. More research is also needed to determine the sensitivity of these results to the assumptions used by BEA for the industry accounts with respect to the classification of imported services and the distribution of these services by using industry. The Bureau of Economic Analysis will continue to review these assumptions and will further investigate company-based data from the international accounts that could help evaluate the assumptions underlying the industry distributions. The bureau will also work with BLS to try to develop improved price indexes for the deflation of imported purchased services in both the national and industry accounts.

References

Amiti, M. and S.-J. Wei. 2006. Service offshoring and productivity: Evidence from the United States. NBER Working Paper no. 11926. Cambridge, MA: National Bureau of Economic Research.

Bednarzik, R. W. 2005. Restructuring information technology: Is offshoring a concern? *Monthly Labor Review* 128 (August):11–21.

Borga, M. 2005. Trends in employment at U.S. multinational companies: Evidence from firm-level data. Presented at Offshoring white-collar work: The issues and the implications. Brookings Institution Trade Forum, Washington, D.C.

Government Accountability Office (GAO). 2004. Current government data provide limited insight into offshoring of services. September 2004, GAO-04-932 International Trade, Washington, D.C.: GPO.

Jensen, B., and L. Kletzer. 2005. Tradable services: Understanding the scope and impact of services offshoring. Presented at Offshoring white-collar work: The issues and the implications. Brookings Institution Trade Forum, Washington, D.C.

Kozlow, R., and M. Borga. 2004. Offshoring and the U.S. balance of payments. Presented at Services offshoring: What do the data tell us? Brookings Institution Workshop, Washington, D.C.

Mann, C. L. 2003. Globalization of IT services and white collar jobs: The next wave of productivity growth. *International Economics Policy Briefs* PB03-11. Washington, D.C.: Institute for International Economics.

Olsen, K. B. 2006. Productivity impacts of offshoring and outsourcing: A review. STI Working Paper 2006/1. Directorate for Science, Technology, and Industry, Organization for Economic Cooperation and Development, Paris.

Strassner, E. H., G. W. Medeiros, and G. M. Smith. 2005. Annual industry accounts: Introducing KLEMS input estimates for 1997–2003. *Survey of Current Business* 85 (September):31–65.

van Welsum, D., and X. Reif. 2005. Potential offshoring: Evidence from selected OECD countries. Presented at Offshoring white-collar work: The issues and the implications. Brookings Institution Trade Forum, Washington, D.C.

Comment   J. Bradford Jensen

As context for my remarks, I should note that I am not all that familiar with BEA's estimation methodologies, but instead do microdata research that would potentially use the detailed estimates described in this paper.

The paper is motivated by the increasing interest in services imports (a.k.a. offshoring or outsourcing), particularly an interest in industry-level detail for imports of business, professional, and technical (BPT) services. The overarching goal of the paper is to address the lack of detailed data on these imported services.

To address this gap, the paper proceeds in several steps. First, it seeks to explain the treatment of purchased service imports in BEA's International Transaction Accounts (ITAs), National Income and Product Accounts (NIPAs), and the Annual Industry Accounts (AIAs). The paper specifically highlights changes in the AIA methodology that provide more detailed estimates of purchased service imports.

Then, the authors turn to the bulk of the effort in the paper—to use existing data to produce new, more detailed estimates of purchased services by industry, BPT services by industry, imported purchased services by industry, and imported BPT services by industry. The authors also evaluate their estimates using unpublished data. Importantly, along the way the authors identify and illuminate the pitfalls of both the approach taken in this paper and the official AIA estimates for some purposes and identify a number of specific caveats.

The paper is interesting and useful. I would like to draw readers' attention to three issues regarding the methodology for producing the estimates in the paper and BEA's AIA estimates. The first issue is not directly taken up in the paper, but is important context to understanding the limitations of the estimates developed in the AIAs and in the paper. The issue is the level of detail that is collected in the ITA survey programs. The principal data collection programs for the imports of services estimates are BEA's surveys of U.S. and foreign multinational companies (MNCs) and BEA's surveys of U.S. international transactions between unaffiliated parties. Please see figure 8C.1, which shows a portion of the BE-10B(LF) from the MNCs survey program, and figure 8C.2, which shows a portion of the BE-20 form, which is from the unaffiliated trade-in-services program.

There are two important things to note on the survey forms. First, the categories included on the form are not as detailed as the categories provided in the AIAs. For example, the MNC form collects only eight categories of BPT service imports. The other thing to note is that the level of

J. Bradford Jensen is an associate professor in the McDonough School of Business, Georgetown University, and a research associate of the National Bureau of Economic Research.

By type — See *Additional Instructions*, pages 21 and 22, at the back of this form for an explanation of how to report each type of service

	1	2	3	4
a. Accounting, auditing, and bookkeeping services 3171				
b. Computer and information services 3172				
c. Financial services 3173				
d. Insurance services — To avoid duplication with other BEA surveys, report only the following: In column (1) report receipts by the U.S. reporter from the foreign insurance affiliate for losses covered by insurance reported in column (3). In column (3) report payments by the U.S. Reporter of premiums for the purchase of primary insurance from the foreign affiliate. 3174				
e. Management, consulting, and public relations services — Include in column (1), expenses allocated by the U.S. Reporter to the foreign affiliate for management, consulting, and public relations services performed by the U.S. Reporter or someone other than the U.S. Reporter and charged to the U.S. Reporter. Exclude the following types of services from this category: Computer consulting services – (include in b.) Management of health care facilities – (include in h.) Consulting engineering services related to actual or proposed construction projects – (include in h.) Public relations services that are an integral part of an advertising campaign (include in h.) 3175				
f. Research, development, and testing services 3176				
g. Transportation 3177				
h. Other services — *Specify primary type(s) of service(s) performed.* 3178				

Fig. 8C.1 BEA form BE-10B(LF) (partial) for affiliated trade

detail in the categories does not match across the survey forms. The unaffiliated form has more, and more detailed, categories. Further, neither of the forms has a one-to-one match to the level of industry detailed in the AIAs. One issue the paper does not discuss, but that is important to understanding the limitations of the estimates produced in both the AIA program and this paper, is how BEA maps information from these two forms to the detailed industry categories for which estimates are produced in the AIA program. Recognizing the nature of the information that is actually collected is very important for understanding the limitations of the estimates produced in the AIAs and in this paper.

The second issue I would like to highlight is one that is directly addressed in the paper, the issue of noncomparables. Imported services are allocated across commodities and across industries. Certain types of imports are, for the purposes of the AIAs, classified as noncomparables and aggregated into a "noncomparables" line in the AIAs. For example, royalties and li-

1. Agricultural services			Schedule A		Schedule B
2. Research, development, and testing services			Schedule A		Schedule B
3. Management, consulting, and public relations services			Schedule A		Schedule B
4. Management of health care facilities			Schedule A		Schedule B
5. Accounting, auditing, and bookkeeping services			Schedule A		Schedule B
6. Legal services			Schedule A		Schedule B
7. Educational and training services			Schedule A		Schedule B
8. Mailing, reproduction, and commercial art			Schedule A		Schedule B
9. Employment agencies and temporary help supply services			Schedule A		Schedule B
10. Industrial engineering services			Schedule A		Schedule B
11. Industrial-type maintenance, installation, alteration, and training services			Schedule A		Schedule B
12. Performing arts, sports, and other live performances, presentations, and events			Schedule A		Schedule B
13. Sale or purchase of rights to natural resources, and lease bonus payments			Schedule A		Schedule B
14. Use or lease of rights to natural resources, excluding lease bonus payments			Schedule A		Schedule B
15. Disbursements to fund news-gathering costs of broadcasters			Schedule A		Schedule B
16. Disbursements to fund news-gathering costs of print media			Schedule A		Schedule B
17. Disbursements to fund production costs of motion pictures			Schedule A		Schedule B
18. Disbursements to fund production costs of broadcast program material other than news			Schedule A		Schedule B
19. Disbursements to maintain government tourism and business promotion offices			Schedule A		Schedule B
20. Disbursements for sales promotion and representation			Schedule A		Schedule B
21. Disbursements to participate in foreign trade shows		Not reportable			Schedule B
22. Premiums paid on purchases of primary insurance		Not reportable			Schedule B
23. Losses recovered on purchases of primary insurance		Not reportable			Schedule B
24. Construction, engineering, architectural, and mining services		Not reportable			Schedule B
25. Merchanting services			Schedule A	Not reportable	
26. Financial services		Not reportable			Schedule C
27. Advertising services			Schedule D		Schedule B
28. Computer and data processing services			Schedule E		Schedule B
29. Data base and other information services			Schedule F		Schedule B
30. Telecommunications services			Schedule G, Part I		Schedule G, Part II
31. Operational leasing services			Schedule H		Schedule B
32. Other private services*			Schedule A		Schedule B

*Other private services (i.e., service number 32) consist of language translation services, security services, collection services, actuarial services, salvage services, satellite photography services, and toxic waste cleanup services.

Fig. 8C.2   BEA form BE-20 (partial) for unaffiliated trade

cense fees are classified as noncomparable. Affiliate trade for unspecified financial, communication, business, professional, and technical services are also classified as noncomparables, while unaffiliated trade in BPT categories are included in comparable trade. As it turns out, the authors report that a significant portion of imported services are assigned to the "noncomparables" line in the AIAs. For example, 80 percent of business, professional, and technical services are classified as noncomparables in 2004. The large share of imported services, particularly BPT services, that are classified as noncomparables is a potentially important caveat on the estimates produced in the paper.

The third methodological issue I would like to highlight is discussed in some detail in the paper. The issue is how BEA allocates purchased services and imported purchased services across "using" industries. The Bureau of Economic Analysis uses purchased input shares from the AIA input-output tables to allocate overall purchased services across "using" industries. They use the economy-wide share of imports/domestic consumption to allocate comparable imports of services across industries. Note that this results in no variation in comparables' import intensity across industries—they all have the economy-wide ratio of imports to domestic purchases for comparable services. For noncomparables, BEA uses unpublished information on a firm's industry from the BE-10 forms to allocate noncomparables across industries.

Beyond the issue of allocation of comparables and noncomparables across industries, the authors identify another issue with the AIA methodology that could potentially impact the usefulness of the estimates for examining trends in imported services. The BEA uses information from the most recent benchmark Input-Output tables, in this case the 1997 Benchmark I-O tables, as the source for the I-O relationship to allocate purchased services across "using" industries. To the extent that purchased service practices have evolved over time across industries, the AIAs will not capture this variation. If firms in an industry have changed their practices for both domestic outsourcing for service inputs and offshored some of their intermediate services provision since 1997, these changes will not be recognized by the estimation methodology. Because of the seemingly rapid changes in these practices, this potential shortcoming could reduce the utility of the estimates for some purposes.

In conclusion, this is a useful paper. It highlights improvements in BEA's AIA program. The paper identifies caveats to using the AIA estimates to investigate changes in purchased service imports and provides new, more detailed estimates of imported BPT services by industry. The authors and BEA should be commended for undertaking the project, and encouraged to pursue it further.

We Can Work It Out
The Globalization of
ICT-Enabled Services

Desirée van Welsum and Xavier Reif

9.1 Introduction

Services now account for around two-thirds of output and foreign direct investment in most developed countries, and for up to 20 to 25 percent of total international trade. The importance of services in international trade remains comparatively modest because many services have only recently become tradable, and many others remain nontradable. Many services are also delivered in ways that would not be captured in the trade flows measured in the Balance of Payments, for example through foreign direct investment (FDI) or the temporary movement of persons. Rapid advances in information and communication technologies (ICTs) and the ongoing global liberalization of trade and investment in services have increased the tradability of many service activities and created new kinds of tradable services. Many services sector activities are thus becoming increasingly internationalized, especially since ICTs enable the production of services to be increasingly location independent. This has led to the globalization of ser-

Desirée van Welsum is an economist in the Directorate for Science, Technology, and Industry of the Organization for Economic Cooperation and Development (OECD). Xavier Reif is an economist at the National Institute of Statistics and Economic Studies (INSEE) in France.

This paper was presented in the CRIW conference on International Services Flows. Disclaimer: The opinions expressed and arguments employed in this paper do not necessarily reflect the official views of the Organisation or of the governments of its member countries. This paper draws on a larger body of work published by the OECD as it becomes available on: http://www.oecd.org/sti/offshoring. We thank Nigel Pain from the OECD Economics Department for his help and advice in preparing this paper. Comments from participants at the CRIW-NBER Conference on International Services Flows (28–29 April 2006, Bethesda, Maryland, U.S.), and in particular Marshall Reinsdorf and our discussant Lori Kletzer, are also gratefully acknowledged. This paper was prepared while Xavier Reif was visiting the OECD.

vices activities and facilitated the ICT-enabled offshoring[1] of services, with associated changes in trade and cross-border investment in service activities and employment patterns.

This chapter builds on earlier work that attempted to quantify the share of employment potentially affected by ICT-enabled offshoring of services (van Welsum and Vickery 2005; van Welsum and Reif 2006b, 2006c). At present there are no official data measuring the extent of offshoring of services, nor of the numbers of jobs lost and created in different locations, so it is necessary to use indirect measures such as data on trade in services, employment data, input-output tables, and trade in intermediates. Evidence from company surveys can also be a useful complement. This chapter combines the information from both trade and employment data to examine the relationship between the share of employment potentially affected by offshoring and other economic and structural factors using some simple descriptive regressions for a panel of OECD economies between 1996 and 2003. Initial estimates of the statistical association between the share of employment potentially affected by service sector offshoring, trade in business services, and foreign direct investment are provided by van Welsum and Reif (2006b, 2006c). In this chapter the model is extended to test whether there are differences in the factors driving the shares of potentially offshorable clerical and nonclerical occupations in total employment. Separate indicators for manufacturing and services foreign direct investment are now also included.

It is important to take care with the interpretation of the results though, as they are not drawn from the empirical testing of a formal theoretical model of the underlying structural relationships. Thus, it is not possible to separate out completely the effects from demand and supply side developments. However, the results provide guidance on the statistical associations that are found to exist between the variables included in these descriptive regressions.

The structure of the rest of this chapter is as follows. A number of different measures of the extent to which services activities have become globalized are discussed in section 9.2. Section 9.3 then summarizes the work undertaken at the Organization for Economic Cooperation and Development (OECD) to obtain estimates of potentially offshorable ICT-using occupations in a number of OECD economies. The fourth section contains the new empirical analysis of the factors associated with the evolution over time of the share of these potentially offshorable occupations in

---

1. Under the definition of offshoring adopted in this chapter, offshoring includes both international outsourcing (where activities are contracted out to independent third parties abroad) and international insourcing (to foreign affiliates). The cross-border aspect is the distinguishing feature of offshoring (i.e., whether services are sourced within the domestic economy or abroad), not whether they are sourced from within the same company or from external suppliers (outsourcing).

total employment. Indicators of international trade and investment, national economic structure, and economy-wide framework factors are all found to be important influences.

9.2 The Globalization of ICT-Enabled Services

9.2.1 Trade in ICT-Enabled Services

The extent of international trade in ICT-related services and business services can be approximated by summing the IMF Balance of Payments categories "computer and information services" and "other business services" (see table 9A.1 in the Appendix for details on which services are included in these categories). Data on computer and information services are not available for all countries. For some, such as India, they are included under "other business services," along with other services.[2] The "other business services" category may have variable shares of information technology (IT) and ICT-enabled services in different countries. We will refer to this category as "business services" from hereon. The data are reported in current USD and can be affected by currency movements.

Most exports of business and computer and information services still originate in OECD countries, close to 80 percent, although their share is slowly declining. The twenty countries that accounted for the largest value shares in 2003, as well as some selected other economies, are shown in figure 9.1. The OECD countries had the top seven shares of these services exports in 2003. Hong Kong, China, India, Singapore, and Israel are the six non-OECD countries in this top twenty. Nevertheless, some countries often mentioned as receiving offshored services activities are experiencing rapid growth in exports (fig. 9.2), although most are starting from very low levels. This reflects, in part, their economic development, but could also be an indication of their confirmation as an "offshoring location."

The increasing importance of trade in services, and of trade in business services and computer and information services in particular, for most countries is also illustrated in table 9.1. In most countries the share of services trade in total trade increased between 1995 and 2003. Business ser-

2. For India, the category "other business services" includes all services except travel, transport, and government services. However, Indian firms are now extensively exporting ICT-enabled services and business process services and the remaining services included in the category are likely to be small in comparison. The data may also include the earnings of Indians working abroad. There are some data quality concerns though, not only for India, but also for China, for example (OECD 2006). Some large discrepancies have been observed in the exports data reported by India, and the imports data from its main trading partners (OECD 2004; GAO 2005). Some of the problems with data on trade in services can be explained by factors such as reporting difficulties, collection methods (company surveys rather than customs records for goods), varying timelines of implementing Balance of Payments (BPM5) methodology and rules, the treatment of certain services categories, and the complexity of the structures and operations of multinational. These issues are being addressed.

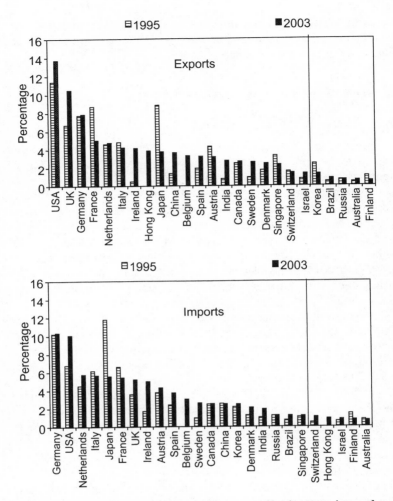

Fig. 9.1 Share of the value of reported total exports of business services and computer and information services, top 20 and selected other countries, 1995 and 2003. Decreasing order of the total reported value share in 2003, percentages.

Source: Authors' calculations based on IMF Balance of Payments Database (August 2005).

Notes: The reported total for all countries does not necessarily correspond to a world total. For some countries, such as India, it is not possible to isolate other business services and computer and information services. As a consequence, for India, the category includes total services, minus travel, transport, and government services (i.e., including construction, insurance, and financial services as well as other business services and computer and information services). The data are in current USD and may therefore be affected by currency movements.

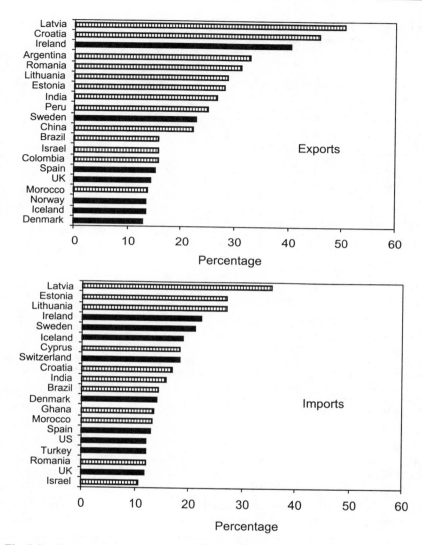

Fig. 9.2   Twenty selected countries with rapid growth, exports and imports, business services, and computer and information services (CAGR 1995–2003)
Source: Authors' calculations based on IMF Balance of Payments Database (August 2005).
Note: Darker shading corresponds to OECD member economies.

vices and computer and information services also tend to account for a relatively large and increasing share of services trade.

Trade in business and computer and information services accounts for a relatively modest, but increasing, share of GDP in most countries (table 9.2). The share tends to be somewhat larger in smaller countries than in

Table 9.1   Relative importance of trade in services and trade in business and computer and
               information services, selected countries, 1995 and 2003 (percentages)

	Exports						Imports					
	S in T		BCIS in T		BCIS in S		S in T		BCIS in T		BCIS in S	
	1995	2003	1995	2003	1995	2003	1995	2003	1995	2003	1995	2003
Australia	23.3	23.1	1.7	3.3	7.3	14.3	23.0	20.0	2.8	2.8	12.3	14.2
Austria	35.8	32.5	13.3	12.2	37.0	37.5	30.1	31.9	11.1	15.0	36.9	47.1
Canada	11.9	13.0	3.1	4.1	26.3	31.8	16.7	17.2	3.3	3.9	20.0	22.5
China	13.0	9.6	2.5	3.8	19.6	39.6	18.6	12.3	5.1	2.5	27.5	20.6
Denmark	23.3	32.9	7.2	12.9	30.8	39.1	24.3	34.0	5.8	11.5	24.0	33.9
Finland	15.5	13.0	6.2	4.4	40.1	34.0	25.4	20.2	10.3	6.8	40.4	33.8
France	23.2	21.4	6.6	5.5	28.6	25.7	19.8	18.8	5.4	5.6	27.1	29.8
Germany	13.3	14.1	3.5	4.5	26.7	32.2	22.4	22.2	4.7	6.1	20.9	27.3
India	17.8	28.3	5.6	16.9	31.3	59.7	21.3	27.4	5.6	9.3	26.4	34.0
Ireland	10.1	29.8	2.8	16.6	27.7	55.6	26.8	50.3	10.8	21.8	40.2	43.3
Italy	20.8	19.4	4.5	5.8	21.6	30.0	22.0	20.6	6.7	7.1	30.3	34.6
Sweden	16.4	23.1	2.7	9.9	16.4	42.9	21.2	25.7	3.1	10.6	14.8	41.1
United Kingdom	24.5	33.2	5.7	11.5	23.4	34.8	20.0	24.5	3.0	4.6	14.8	18.8
United States	27.4	29.8	4.0	6.8	14.5	22.9	15.9	16.9	2.1	3.0	13.0	17.8

Source: Authors' calculations based on IMF Balance of Payments Database (August 2005).
Notes: Where S in T = services trade in total trade; BCIS in T = business and computer and information services in total trade; and BCIS in S = business and computer and information services in services trade. Services trade (S) also includes royalties and license fees. Some of the large shift in "S in T" for Ireland may be explained by changes in this category, which is thought to reflect tax minimization strategies rather than real activity.

larger countries. There was a particularly large increase in the share in Ireland between 1995 and 2003, reflecting Ireland's rapid shift into service activities over that period (Barry and van Welsum 2005).

The trade balance (in current USD) in the sum of business and computer and information services as a percentage of GDP for selected countries in 1995 and 2003 is shown in figure 9.3. The United States have a relatively large and still increasing surplus in trade in these categories, although it is relatively small as a percent of GDP. The United Kingdom also has a large and growing surplus, and the share in GDP is also increasing, in spite of the impression that may be given by the many (media) reports on the extent of offshoring and related imports. Ireland has a surplus looking at the category "computer and information services," but a deficit for the sum of the two ICT-enabled trade categories. More recently released data show that Ireland moves into surplus in 2004. Of the countries shown in the graph, Denmark and the UK have the largest surplus as a percent of GDP.

Table 9.2   **Exports and imports of business and computer and information services as a share of GDP, selected countries, 1995 and 2003 (percentages)**

	Exports		Imports	
	1995	2003	1995	2003
Australia	0.32	0.57	0.57	0.58
Austria	4.97	6.32	4.27	7.64
Canada	1.18	1.58	1.15	1.34
Denmark	2.61	5.84	1.87	4.51
Finland	2.29	1.66	2.99	2.10
France	1.55	1.44	1.15	1.46
Germany	0.87	1.60	1.13	1.96
Ireland	2.09	13.88	6.85	14.88
Italy	1.21	1.46	1.52	1.75
Netherlands	3.08	4.70	2.94	5.10
Sweden	1.03	4.36	1.02	3.92
United Kingdom	1.63	2.96	0.86	1.31
United States	0.43	0.63	0.25	0.42

Source: Authors' calculations based on IMF Balance of Payments Database (August 2005).

9.2.1   FDI in Services

Another indicator of the extent of globalisation of services is given by the stock share of services in total FDI (table 9.3). In most countries, the share of services has increased between 1995 and 2003, and the stock of services tends to account for more than half of the total stock, and up to 88 percent in Germany for inward investment, and up to 82 percent in outward investment in France in 2003. A further indicator of globalization of services is given by the share of this type of FDI in GDP. In all countries, both the total share of FDI (inward and outward) and the share of services FDI in GDP have increased between 1995 and 2003 (table 9.4).

However, most of this FDI in services is not in services that can necessarily be traded with the help of ICTs. The sectors distinguished in the OECD FDI database are listed in table 9A.2. It is difficult to know which category would be most suitable to match the categories used as proxies for ICT-enabled trade in services,[3] but probably the best approximation would be given by "business activities," which can be obtained by subtracting "real estate" from "real estate and business activities." Unfortunately, this breakdown is not widely available (eight countries in the sample, and not

3. "Real estate and business activities" represents section K of ISIC 3 (minus if available "of which real estate"), but the connection is loose between service products and service activities determined for large enterprises. Business services can be provided internally within multinationals with main activities elsewhere (e.g., in manufacturing).

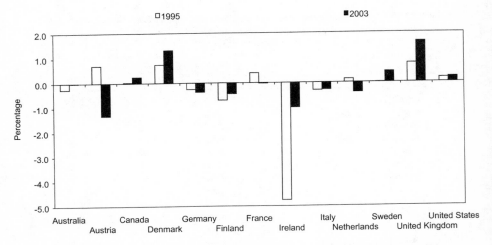

Fig. 9.3   Trade balance in the sum of the categories business and computer and information services, as a percentage of GDP, selected countries, 1995 and 2003 (percentages)

Source: Authors' calculations based on IMF Balance of Payments Database (February 2005).

necessarily for all years considered), but "real estate" tends to account for a relatively small share of that category.

9.3   Employment Potentially Affected by Offshoring

To get an idea of the "outer limits" of employment potentially affected by offshoring, van Welsum and Vickery (2005) calculate the share of people employed who are mainly performing the types of functions that could potentially be carried out anywhere, using data on employment by occupation by industry. The classifications were not harmonized internationally, but the same methodology and rationale were applied to the individual country data sources.[4] As this analysis was carried out in order to

4. The European data are Labor Force Survey data provided by Eurostat. The occupational classification system in those data is the ISCO—International Standard Classification of Occupations, and NACE—the industrial classification system of the European Union—is used for sectoral classification. For the United States, data from the Current Population Survey were used. The Current Population Survey collects information on both the industry and the occupation of the employed and unemployed. However, beginning with data from January 2003, the 1990 Census Industrial Classification System was replaced by one based on the North American Industry Classification (NAICS), and the 1990 Census Occupational Classification was replaced by one derived from the U.S. Standard Occupational Classification (SOC). Further information is available on the website of the U.S. Bureau of Labor Statistics at: http://www.bls.gov/opub/hom/pdf/homch1.pdf (accessed November 2004): Chapter 1: Labor Force Data derived from the Current Population Survey. For Canada, Labour Force Data provided by Statistics Canada were used. The occupational classification is in SOC91. For Australia, data from the Labour Force Survey provided by the Australian Bureau of Sta-

Table 9.3   **The share of FDI in services in total FDI, 1995 and 2003**

	Inward		Outward	
	1995	2003	1995	2003
Australia	47.0	52.7	35.1	34.2
Austria	65.2	76.8	69.9	79.1
Canada	30.7	29.2	40.0	55.1
Denmark	73.4	77.1	64.5	69.6
Finland	39.5	64.9	9.7	13.2
France	67.4	80.5	80.0	81.8
Germany	76.1	88.1	67.6	81.1
Italy	55.8	54.5	63.6	59.1
Netherlands	55.2	63.1	49.5	58.1
Sweden	33.0	38.8	31.7	42.5
United Kingdom	46.6	66.1	40.1	61.7
United States	51.0	62.6	55.2	74.1

Source: Authors' calculations, based on OECD Direct Investment Statistics Database.

Table 9.4   **Share of FDI in GDP, 1995 and 2003**

	Total Inward		Services Inward		Total Outward		Services Outward	
	1995	2003	1995	2003	1995	2003	1995	2003
Australia	25.8	37.9	12.1	20.0	14.2	28.6	5.0	9.8
Austria	7.3	21.0	4.8	16.1	4.9	21.8	3.4	17.3
Canada	21.2	32.1	6.5	9.4	20.3	36.5	8.1	20.1
Denmark	12.1	41.3	8.9	31.8	12.5	42.6	8.0	29.7
Finland	6.5	31.0	2.6	20.1	11.5	46.9	1.1	6.2
France	12.2	29.1	8.2	23.4	13.0	40.3	10.4	32.9
Germany	7.6	27.5	5.8	24.2	10.2	30.4	6.9	24.7
Italy	5.8	12.3	3.2	6.7	8.8	16.3	5.6	9.6
Netherlands	29.4	89.3	16.2	56.4	43.0	103.6	21.3	60.1
Sweden	12.3	39.9	4.1	15.5	29.0	53.3	9.2	22.7
United Kingdom	17.6	33.7	8.2	22.3	26.9	68.4	10.8	42.3
United States	7.3	12.9	3.7	8.1	9.5	16.4	5.3	12.2

Source: Authors' calculations, based on OECD Direct Investment Statistics Database.

obtain an order of magnitude on the share of people employed performing tasks that could potentially be carried out anywhere, no additional assumptions were made as to what proportion of each occupational group was actually likely to be affected by offshoring in practice. Thus, the whole of each selected occupation was then included in the calculations.

Occupations were selected by examining detailed occupational and task

---

tistics were used. The occupational classification is in Australian Standard Classification of Occupations (ASCO), second edition.

descriptions on the basis of the following four criteria, or "offshorability attributes": (a) intensive use of ICTs; (b) an output that can be traded and transmitted in a way that is enabled by ICTs (e.g., via email or the internet); (c) high content of codifiable knowledge; and (d) no face-to-face contact requirements. The occupational selections that resulted from this exercise are reported in tables 9A.3 through 9A.6. For further details on the methodological background see van Welsum and Vickery (2005), and OECD (2004). This analysis, using occupational data for several OECD countries, suggests that around 20 percent of total employment carries out the kinds of functions that are potentially geographically footloose as a result of rapid technological advances in ICTs and the increased tradability of services, and could therefore potentially be affected by international sourcing of IT and ICT-enabled services. Services sectors (such as computer and related activities, financial services, insurance services, and R&D services) tend to have large shares of this type of employment (see van Welsum and Vickery [2005] for rankings of industrial sector by the share of employment potentially affected by offshoring).

Other studies have taken a similar approach. Blinder (2005), and as quoted in Mankiw and Swagel (2005), finds a similar estimate of around 20 percent of total employment potentially affected by offshoring in the United States in 2004. He uses the concept of "personally deliverable services" and "impersonally deliverable services." However, the estimates of employment potentially affected by offshoring vary widely. For example, Bardhan and Kroll (2003) produced estimates of 11 percent of total employment in the United States in 2001 as potentially affected by offshoring, and Forrester Research, as reported by Kirkegaard (2004), up to 44 percent of total employment. The differences in these estimates can be explained by the selection criteria that are applied to the occupational data. Thus, Bardhan and Kroll (2003) only included occupations in which at least some offshoring was already known to have taken place or being planned, yielding a more conservative estimate of the share of employment potentially affected, whereas the Forrester study used less detailed occupational categories resulting in a larger estimate of jobs potentially affected. A different but related approach was taken by Jensen and Kletzer (2005) looking at tradable versus nontradable occupations based on Gini coefficients. The list of tradable occupations they find for the United States overlaps with the list in van Welsum and Vickery (2005) and used in this chapter, but the methodology of Jensen and Kletzer (2005) identifies a larger set of tradable occupations. According to their methodology, around 30 percent of employment in the United States can be considered as tradable. They find little evidence of slower employment growth in tradable occupations (and activities).

The evolution over time of the share of employment potentially affected by offshoring is illustrated in figure 9.4. Even though the levels of these

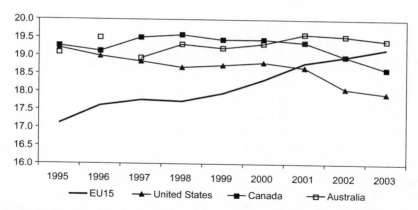

Fig. 9.4   The share of ICT-intensive using occupations potentially affected by off-shoring in total employment: EU15, United States, Canada, and Australia 1995–2003 (percentages)

Source: Author's calculations and van Welsum and Vickery (2005), based on EULFS, U.S. Current Population Survey, Statistics Canada, and Australian Bureau of Statistics (2004/5).

Note: Includes estimates where a full data set was not available. Because of classification changes, the number for the United States for 2003 is also an estimate. There is a break in the data for Australia, with data for 1995 and 1996 in ASCO first edition and subsequent data in ASCO second edition. Due to differences in classifications the levels are not directly comparable.

shares are not directly comparable, the evolution of the trends is interesting. The share of occupations potentially affected by offshoring in the EU15[5] increased from 17.1 percent in 1995 to 19.2 percent in 2003. For Canada it was more or less flat around 19.5 percent until 2001, after which it declined to 18.6 percent by 2003. For the United States, the share declined by more than a percentage point, from 19.2 percent in 1995 to 18.1 percent in 2002.[6] In Australia, the share increased between 1996 and 2001 (except in 1999) but started to decline in 2001.

It is difficult to draw inferences from these trends without further analysis, since the trends are affected by a multitude of factors and it is difficult to separate out the effect of ICTs from the effects of the changes ICTs enable. Nonetheless, the evolutions shown are consistent with some casual observations on the ICT-enabled offshoring that is taking place. For example, Canada serves as an offshoring location, mainly from the United States, but may have become a comparatively less important location recently as other countries such as India have started to emerge. Similarly, Australia has also experienced competition for attracting, or keeping, activities that can be sourced internationally from India and other emerging

5. See van Welsum and Reif (2006c) for the evolution of the share for the individual countries that make up the EU15.

6. The number for 2003 (just under 18 percent) is an estimate as both the occupational and industrial classification systems were changed in 2003 in the United States.

locations in the region. Thus, the declining share in the United States, Canada, and Australia toward the end of the period could be consistent with the offshoring of IT-related and back-office activities (with some potential offshoring having become actual offshoring), even though this is unlikely to account for all of the decline.

Another possible explanation for differences in the evolution of the trends could be different paces of technological change, with a relatively more rapid adoption and integration of new technologies leading to relatively more jobs disappearing as they become automated and/or digitized.[7] The increasing share for the EU15 is compatible with an overall increase in services employment as well as the finding from surveys that European firms tend to offshore within Europe (see Millar [2002] and Marin [2004], for example). The upward trend is broadly similar across the individual countries that make up the EU15 (see van Welsum and Reif 2006c), but at different levels. At least one EU15 country, Ireland, is also a major destination country of offshoring activities from the United States (IT-related activities in particular). And between 2002 and 2005, more jobs were created as a result of activities offshored to Denmark than were eliminated because of offshoring from Denmark to other countries (Jensen, Kirkegaard, and Laugesen 2006). Other factors, such as cyclical developments and changes in labor supply and labor quality, could also be important.

The offshoring phenomenon does not necessarily have to result in a decline in total services employment, though.[8] Many existing services sectors have expanded, new services have emerged, and with ongoing technological developments and services trade liberalization it is likely that yet more are to be created. Furthermore, with the income elasticity of demand of internationally traded services greater than one (e.g., Pain and van Welsum 2004; van Welsum 2004; Mann 2004), rapid growth in countries such as India and China should also lead to reinforced exports from OECD countries. The offshoring phenomenon itself will also create new jobs in the domestic economy. However, it is likely that certain types of occupations will experience slower growth than they otherwise might have done.

As the trends in figure 9.4 are expressed as shares, there are several possibilities to explain changes in these trends. For example, a decline in the

7. A parallel can be drawn here with some of the work undertaken by Autor, Levy, and Murnane (2003) and Levy and Murnane (2004). These authors argue that the tasks most vulnerable to being substituted by technology are those where information processing can be described in rules. If a significant part of a task can be described by rules, this increases the likelihood of the task being offshored, since the task can then be assigned to offshore producers with less risk and greater ease of supervision.

8. The cost savings from offshoring will raise the real income of consumers (who will pay lower prices) and of business owners in countries that import the relatively cheaper offshored services; this higher income will result in some extra demand. External demand is also likely to increase as income in countries providing the offshored services increases. These sources of growing demand will create new jobs that will help to offset the jobs originally offshored.

share could be explained by an absolute decline in the number of people employed in the categories identified as potentially affected by offshoring. Alternatively, it could be that this selection of occupations is growing at a slower pace than total employment. The relatively slower growth of employment potentially affected by offshoring is in fact what explains most of the declines observed in the trends, except for the United States, where the absolute number of people employed in the categories identified as potentially affected by offshoring has declined (table 9A.1 in the Appendix). These observations would therefore tend to support the idea that offshoring may lead to slower growth of employment in occupations potentially affected by offshoring and not necessarily to actual declines in employment.

9.3.1   Disaggregating Employment Potentially Affected by Offshoring

As offshoring and technology may have a different effect on workers with different types of skills (e.g., Autor, Levy, and Murnane 2003), the share of employment potentially affected by offshoring is broken down into two subcategories: clerical and nonclerical occupations potentially affected by offshoring (fig. 9.5 and 9.6). This is important, as the clerical

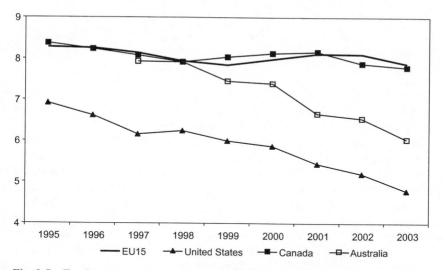

Fig. 9.5   Employment in clerical occupations potentially affected by offshoring as a share of total employment: EU15, United States, Canada, and Australia 1995–2003 (percentages)

Source: Author's calculations and van Welsum and Vickery (2005), based on EULFS, U.S. Current Population Survey, Statistics Canada, and Australian Bureau of Statistics (2004/5).

Notes: The years 1995 and 1996 exclude Finland and Sweden; 1998 excludes Ireland; and 2003 excludes Denmark, Luxembourg, and the Netherlands. Because of classification changes, the number for the United States for 2003 is an estimate. Due to differences in classifications the levels are not directly comparable.

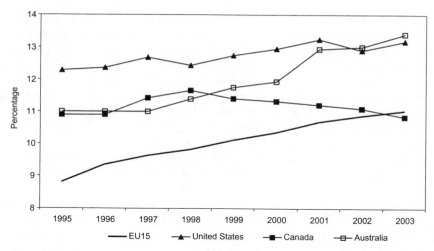

Fig. 9.6   Employment in nonclerical occupations potentially affected by offshoring as a share of total employment: EU15, United States, Canada, and Australia 1995–2003 (percentages)

Source: Author's calculations and van Welsum and Vickery (2005), based on EULFS, U.S. Current Population Survey, Statistics Canada, and Australian Bureau of Statistics (2004/5).

Notes: The years 1995 and 1996 exclude Finland and Sweden; 1998 excludes Ireland; and 2003 excludes Denmark, Luxembourg, and the Netherlands. Because of classification changes, the number for the United States for 2003 is an estimate. Due to differences in classifications the levels are not directly comparable.

group includes the types of jobs that can be substituted for by ICTs (through the digitization and/or automation of certain tasks and types of codifiable knowledge) so a differential pace of adoption and integration of technology can have a different effect across countries.

Looking at the share for each country at the beginning and end of the respective available data periods, it can be seen that for the United States and Australia, and to a lesser extent Canada, there is an obvious decline in the share of potentially offshorable employment. This is consistent both with the destruction of these types of jobs as a result of technological advances and with the offshoring of back-office activities. For the EU15 countries the evidence is more mixed. In some countries a decline in the share can be observed (Austria, Belgium, Germany, Finland, France, Ireland, Netherlands, Portugal), but in other countries there is an increase (Denmark, Spain, Greece, Italy, Luxembourg, Sweden, and the United Kingdom). It is likely that there are different explanations underlying these evolutions; for example, the varying importance of the size of the public sector and the services sector in the economy, and the differential pace of technology adoption and integration. However, it also means that while there are many reports about clerical-type occupations being offshored—in some countries, at least—more still are being created at home. For example, in the UK employment growth in IT and call center occupations potentially affected by offshoring over the period 2001 to 2005 was 8.8 percent compared to 3.2 percent for total employment, in spite of many media reports of these kinds of jobs being offshored. Nevertheless, Computer Weekly (February 2006 issue) reports that the effects of offshoring are now being felt in the IT job market in the UK with more and more IT employers offshoring and outsourcing basic development and programming work.

Even though job displacement from technological progress, in particular in ICTs, may account for at least some of the relative decline in the occupations potentially affected by offshoring, the possibility that some of these jobs have already been offshored cannot be ruled out. For example, Baily and Lawrence (2005) argue that at least some of the declines in low-wage ICT-enabled occupations in the United States, a concept close but not equivalent to the group of clerical workers identified previously, took place as a result of activities being shifted overseas. Looking at IT specialist occupations, they also find that the net loss of computer programmers in the United States was most likely the result of offshoring. Nevertheless, even the largest projections of jobs to be offshored, as often reported in the media, are in fact relatively small compared to annual job churning in OECD labor markets.

In the short run, labor-augmenting technical progress (associated with innovations and improvements in ICTs) and international outsourcing of tasks may both reduce the level of domestic employment for a given level of domestic output. In the longer-term, both may enhance productivity and the competitiveness of the firm, enabling an increase in output and hence employment. So distinguishing between two effects is difficult when looking at a single country. Looking across countries, as in the following models, it could be argued that improvements in ICTs are common to all countries and are picked up by the time dummies included in the following regressions. If so, observed differences in employment patterns must be due to other factors, such as the extent of offshoring.

Appendix tables 9A.3 through 9A.6 illustrate the occupations that have been included as "potentially affected by offshoring," and which of those are considered as "clerical" occupations. The following two graphs illustrate the evolution over time of the share of these clerical occupations and nonclerical occupations in total employment.

The three-year averages for the share of clerical occupations in the occupations potentially affected by offshoring are shown in table 9.5. The share of potentially offshorable employment accounted for by clerical occupations varies widely across countries, from over 60 percent in Italy and Portugal to around 30 percent in Australia, Ireland, Sweden, the United Kingdom, and the United States.

Table 9.5   The share of clerical occupations in employment potentially affected by offshoring, three-year averages, 1995–2003 (percentages)

	Clerical in offshoring		
	1995–1997	1998–2000	2001–2003
Australia	41.9	39.3	32.8
Canada	42.6	41.2	41.8
United States	34.5	32.2	28.1
Austria	44.6	42.5	39.7
Belgium	38.0	36.7	33.2
Germany	49.1	44.8	42.3
Denmark	38.9	38.3	37.6
Spain	55.7	53.3	51.3
Finland	31.6	30.6	26.6
France	42.0	39.9	36.2
Greece	46.6	51.4	51.5
Ireland	22.0	33.0	30.8
Italy	65.8	62.8	61.9
Luxembourg	57.9	51.9	48.6
Netherlands	42.8	39.4	39.7
Portugal	63.8	67.8	62.9
Sweden	30.3	28.8	28.0
United Kingdom	33.8	31.7	32.9

Source: Author's calculations, based on EULFS, U.S. Current Population Survey, Statistics Canada and Australian Bureau of Statistics (2004/5).

Note: Three years or as many as available. Includes estimates where a full data set was not available. Due to differences in classifications the levels of the shares are not directly comparable between the European and non-European countries.

9.4 Empirical Analysis

The empirical work in this chapter extends and refines the models estimated by van Welsum and Reif (2006b, 2006c) in an attempt to identify the key factors associated with the share of economy-wide employment that is potentially offshorable in the United States, Canada, Australia, and nine European Union member states[9] over the period 1996 to 2003.

In the empirical model, the share of employment that is potentially offshorable is related to a set of factors controlling for international openness, the national economic structure, and economy-wide framework influences. The controls for openness include indicators of exports and imports of business services and a number of different measures of foreign direct investment (FDI) stocks. The controls for economic structures are the shares of services and high-tech industries in GDP, and the share of ICT

9. The EU15 countries excluding Belgium, Greece, Ireland, Luxembourg, Spain, and Portugal. The choice of countries is determined by the availability of the necessary data.

investments in total gross fixed capital formation. Finally, economy-wide framework factors are controlled for by the inclusion of the OECD product market regulation indicator, trade union density and an indicator of human capital. Each of these series is described in greater detail below.[10] The choice of variables is motivated by findings from a vast background literature, including studies of the factors determining the overall share of the service sector in the economy, studies of services sector employment, and studies of the effect of trade and technology on employment. See van Welsum and Reif (2006b) for details.

The empirical work in this chapter extends and improves the model used by van Welsum and Reif (2006b, 2006c) in two ways. First, the dependent variable is disaggregated into potentially offshorable clerical and nonclerical occupations (see figures 9.5 and 9.6), permitting a test of whether there are common influences on both. Secondly, there is an improved treatment of the FDI data used in the regression analysis. In the earlier papers use was made of only the aggregate stocks of inward and outward FDI. In this chapter more disaggregated data are used for FDI, allowing tests to be undertaken of whether FDI in manufacturing has similar effects to FDI in market services.

Ideally, it would be appropriate to begin with a simple structural model of the factors affecting the relative demand for all potentially offshorable ICT-using occupations. Using the first-order marginal productivity conditions from an (unknown) production function with two types of labor (ICT and non-ICT using labor), such a model might be expected to include measures of the relative output and relative wages of ICT-using occupations. Control variables might also be included to pick up possible differences in the extent of (labor-augmenting) technical progress in the two broad types of occupations. As in the literature on the demand for skilled and unskilled labor, possible controls are indicators for both trade and technology.

Unfortunately, while it is possible to control for output and technology effects directly, data on occupational wages are not readily available in most countries at the level of detail required. Their effect can be captured only indirectly by including a number of variables that can be expected to have an influence on real wages. It should be noted that although it is not possible to estimate a full structural model, the estimates we show are not

10. Even though GDP per capita was found to be associated with the share of services sector employment (Messina 2004) it is not included in the regressions in this chapter. In a time series context it does not make sense to include the level of GDP per capital in a regression of an ultimately bounded variable. The first difference of GDP per capital was tested at an early stage of the empirical analysis, but was found to be insignificant and is thus dropped from the model reported in this chapter. This is not necessarily surprising as the countries in sample all have relatively high levels of GDP per capita. Nevertheless, with the exception of Austria, the countries with a relatively low share of potentially offshorable employment are also those with a comparatively lower level of GDP per capita. Time dummies pick up common cyclical effects.

a pure reduced form model either, since potentially endogenous current dated terms in output and/or trade and technology remain in the model.

9.4.1 Description of the Data

Trade effects are approximated by including both imports and exports of other business and computer and information services as a share of GDP.[11] The idea of trade related displacement would suggest that imports may have a negative association with the share of potentially offshorable occupations ("exporting jobs"), while exports should have a positive relationship (increase in demand). The FDI measures used in this chapter are the net outward stock of FDI in manufacturing and in services as a share of national GDP.[12] The predictions from the literature are ambiguous about the overall direction of the relationship between FDI and the share of employment potentially affected by offshoring, and it is quite possible that the effects may vary according to the characteristics of particular types of potentially offshorable employment and the sectors in which FDI takes place, just as the relationship between trade and FDI depends on the level of aggregation (Pain and van Welsum 2004; van Welsum 2004).

The share of services sector[13] value added in total value added and the share of high-tech industries[14] value added in total value added are included as indicators of the industrial structure of the economy.[15] Other things being equal, the larger the share of the services sector in the economy, the larger the aggregate demand for ICT-using occupations are expected to be. The share of ICT investment[16] in total national gross fixed capital formation is also included in order to approximate technology

11. The trade data are from IMF Balance of Payments statistics and GDP is taken from the OECD ANA database.

12. The foreign direct investment data are taken from the OECD Direct Investment Statistics Database. For Denmark and Sweden it was necessary to interpolate missing stock data using the available information on the composition of investment flows.

13. ISIC Rev.3 categories 50-99: 50-55: Wholesale and retail trade; repairs; hotels and restaurants; 60-64: Transport, storage, and communications; 65-74: Finance, insurance, real estate, and business services; 75-99: Community, social and personal services.

14. ISIC Rev.3 categories: 2423: pharmaceuticals; 30: office, accounting, and computing machinery; 32: radio, television, and communication equipment; 33: medical, precision, and optical instruments; 353: aircraft and spacecraft.

15. These are taken from the OECD STAN database; missing values have been estimated using the "60-Industry Database" from the Groningen Growth and Development Centre of the University of Groningen (Netherlands), available at http://www.ggdc.net/dseries/60-industry.html (last accessed 28 April, 2005).

16. ISIC Rev.3 categories: 30: office, accounting, and computing machinery; 3130: Insulated wire and cable; 3210: Electronic valves and tubes and other electronic components; 3220: Television and radio transmitters and apparatus for line telephony and line telegraphy; 3230: Television and radio receivers, sound or video recording or reproducing apparatus, and associated goods; 3312: Instruments and appliances for measuring, checking, testing, navigating and other purposes; 3313: Industrial process control equipment; 5150: Wholesale of machinery, equipment, and supplies; 6420: Telecommunications; 7123: Renting of office machinery and equipment (including computers); 72: computer and related activities.

adoption and integration. The ICT investment data are from an unpublished OECD database based on national account sources.

It is possible that the intensity of product market competition may influence the speed at which new technologies are adopted and the subsequent use made of them to adjust employment and labor tasks. An OECD indicator of anticompetitive product market regulations is thus included as a control in the regressions. This measure is an average of separate indicators of regulation in selected nonmanufacturing industries.[17] A lower value of the aggregate indicator suggests that regulations are less restrictive and that there is a higher degree of competitive pressures in the economy. Other things being equal, there should be a negative relationship between this variable and the share of potentially offshorable employment. Messina (2005) includes a measure of entry-barriers to the creation of new firms in the economy as an indicator of product market regulations and finds a significant and negative effect on the share of services sector employment.

Two additional economy-wide structural variables are included to capture institutional and supply-side influences on (unobserved) real wages—union density and human capital. Trade union density indicators may of course provide information about the degree of flexibility in national labor markets, as well as the relative strength of workers in wage bargaining.[18] A number of existing papers suggest that union density rates are inversely related to the growth of service sector occupations. For example, Messina (2004) finds that a fall in union density rates is associated with an increase in services sector employment.[19] Similarly, Nickell, Redding, and Swaffield (2004) find evidence that countries with higher levels of employment protection were slower in reallocating resources from declining sectors (agriculture, manufacturing, and other production) into the services sector, possibly because stronger employment protection makes labor shedding in declining sectors more costly. The analysis in this chapter does not consider employment at the sectoral level, but an analogy can be drawn as labor market inflexibilities are likely to affect occupational shifts as well as sectoral changes. The *a priori* effect of this variable is ambiguous though, as it can both prevent a reallocation of resources into ICT-intensive using occupations, and hinder the speed at which existing ICT-intensive using jobs can be transferred abroad. In the latter case, the share of potentially

17. The original version of these data is described in Nicoletti and Scarpetta (2003), with subsequently updated series available at: http://www.oecd.org/document/1/0,2340,en_2649_34117_2367297_1_1_1_1,00.html

18. The data on trade union density rates come from OECD Labor Force Statistics Indicators and OECD Employment Outlook 2004 (table 3.3). Factors other than union density rates, including union coverage and hiring and firing restrictions, may also be important but are not included here.

19. The interpretation of this result is that lower union density rates facilitate the reallocation of labor between sectors. An alternative explanation is that union density rates are simply lower in the service sector.

offshorable occupations in total employment will be at a higher level than it would otherwise have been.

Human capital is approximated by the average years of education per person in the population of working age[20] (de la Fuente and Doménech 2002a, 2002b; OECD 2003). It is expected that this variable should be positively related to the share of potentially offshorable occupations, since higher levels of human capital are positively correlated with the supply of ICT-literate people in the workforce. Such increases in supply should help to restrain the growth of real wages of workers in ICT occupations and hence support demand. Nickell, Redding, and Swaffield (2004) find a strong positive effect of increases in educational attainment on the output share of the "other services" sector in the economy in Australia, Canada, France, Italy, Japan, the Netherlands, Sweden, Germany, the United Kingdom, and the United States.[21]

Thus, the final specification used in the empirical work has the basic form:

$$(1) \left(\frac{OFF_j}{EMP}\right) = \alpha_i + \beta_1\left(\frac{X}{GDP}\right)_{it} + \beta_2\left(\frac{M}{GDP}\right)_{it} + \beta_3\left(\frac{NETMFDI}{GDP}\right)_{i,t-1}$$

$$+ \beta_4\left(\frac{NETSFDI}{GDP}\right)_{i,t-1} + \beta_5 ICTIRAT_{i,t-1} + \beta_6 SERVICES_{i,t-1}$$

$$+ \beta_7 HITECH_{i,t-1} + \beta_9 PMR_{i,t} + \beta_{10} UNIONS_{t-1}$$

$$+ \beta_{11} HK_{i,t-1} + \varepsilon_{it}$$

where the dependent variable is the share of potentially offshorable employment of type j in total employment in country i, X and M are exports and imports of business and computer information services, NETMFDI and NETSFDI are the net outward stocks of manufacturing and services FDI, ICTRAT is the share of ICT investments in total investment, SERVICES and HITECH are the share of service sector output and hi-tech sector output in GDP, PMR is the product market regulation indicator, UNIONS denotes union density and HK denotes human capital. All the GDP share variables use data at current prices. The reported regressions also include country-specific fixed effects, capturing otherwise unobserved factors specific to each country that do not vary over time, and annual time dummies, capturing otherwise unobserved effects that are common to all countries in each year.

---

20. Although the main differences between countries are cross-sectional, there is sufficient variation over time to allow this variable to be included in the empirical analysis (see table 9.7).

21. But in the sector "business services" they found a greater role for changes in relative prices.

This model is estimated using three different measures of the dependent variable—total potentially offshorable employment, potentially offshorable clerical employment, and potentially offshorable nonclerical employment. The equations for the two subcategories are estimated jointly to improve the efficiency of the estimates by allowing for potential correlations in the respective equation variances. Joint estimation also allows tests to be undertaken for common parameters in both equations.

As the two subcategories sum to total potentially offshorable employment, and the same explanatory factors are used in all three equations, the coefficients in the jointly-estimated clerical and nonclerical equations will sum to those in the equation for the aggregate measure. The main advantage of estimating the equations for the individual categories is thus to establish whether different factors affect the different types of occupations. It does not provide an alternative picture of the factors driving the evolution of total potentially offshorable employment.

9.4.2 Results

The results from using fixed effects, simultaneous equation, and instrumental variables estimation techniques are shown in table 9.6. Estimation for the basic fixed-effect single and multivariate regression models is for a sample of twelve countries over 1996 to 2003. The multivariate instrumental variables estimates (by 3SLS) are for the same countries, but over 1997 to 2003.

An initial set of results using total potentially offshorable employment as the dependent variable is shown in column (1). The results from simultaneous estimation of equations for the clerical and nonclerical components are reported in column (2). Although a joint test for common parameters in both equations is strongly rejected (p-value = 0.00), the imposition of common parameters on four explanatory factors—product market regulation, imports of business and computer services, human capital, and the share of hi-tech industries in GDP—cannot be rejected (p-value = 0.42). The results from imposing these restrictions and discarding one highly insignificant variable are shown in column (3).

The final column of table 9.6 shows the results obtained from estimating the simultaneous equation model in (3) by three-stage least squares (3SLS). This combines an instrumental variable approach to produce consistent estimates and generalized least squares to account for the correlation structure in the disturbances across equations. A year is dropped from the estimation period to allow higher order lagged variables to be used as instruments. All current dated terms, with the exception of the product market regulation indicator, are instrumented in column (4), as is the lagged ICT investment ratio, to allow for the possibility that it is acting as a proxy lagged dependent variable. The 3SLS model results have a similar pattern to those from the simultaneous equation models, though

Table 9.6 Factors associated with the share of employment that is potentially offshorable

Dependent variable	[1]	[2]		[3]		[4]	
	Total	Nonclerical	Clerical	Nonclerical	Clerical	Nonclerical	Clerical
$(X/GDP)_t$	1.1504 (7.6)**	0.7310 (7.0)**	0.4194 (4.6)**	0.6776 (8.4)**	0.4586 (6.5)**	1.0390 (4.4)**	0.7891 (3.4)**
$(M/GDP)_t$	−0.4457 (2.8)**	−0.2763 (2.5)**	−0.1693 (1.8)*	−0.2108 (2.8)**	−0.2108 (2.8)**	−0.5278 (2.0)**	−0.5278 (2.0)**
$(NETMFDI/GDP)_{t-1}$	−0.0012 (0.1)	0.0395 (1.9)**	−0.0408 (3.2)**	0.0498 (2.5)**	−0.0457 (3.8)**	0.0352 (1.4)	−0.0518 (3.3)**
$(NETSFDI/GDP)_{t-1}$	0.0543 (3.8)**	0.0422 (3.1)**	0.0121 (1.3)	0.0386 (3.0)**	0.0137 (1.5)	0.0380 (2.7)**	0.0153 (1.7)*
$ICTIRAT_{t-1}$	0.1876 (3.5)**	0.1918 (4.7)**	−0.0042 (0.1)	0.2036 (6.2)**		0.3079 (4.7)**	
$SERVICES_{t-1}$	0.0994 (1.8)*	0.1590 (3.4)**	−0.0596 (2.1)**	0.1540 (3.7)**	−0.0578 (2.0)**	0.1621 (3.2)**	−0.0330 (0.9)
$HTECH_{t-1}$	0.4833 (2.3)**	0.3315 (2.1)**	0.1518 (1.3)	0.2063 (2.2)**	0.2063 (2.2)**	0.2232 (1.7)*	0.2232 (1.7)*
PMR_t	−0.5642 (2.9)**	−0.3206 (2.0)**	−0.2436 (2.0)**	−0.2803 (2.9)**	−0.2803 (2.9)**	−0.4208 (2.8)**	−0.4208 (2.8)**
$UNIONS_{t-1}$	−0.0472 (1.1)	−0.0978 (2.4)**	0.0506 (1.9)*	−0.0936 (2.4)**	0.0495 (1.8)*	−0.1114 (2.3)**	0.0363 (1.1)
HK_{t-1}	2.0099 (3.8)**	0.8028 (2.3)**	1.2072 (4.7)**	1.0833 (4.4)**	1.0833 (4.4)**	1.0210 (3.4)**	1.0210 (3.4)**
$\bar{R}^2$	0.966	0.984	0.987	0.983	0.987	0.981	0.987
Standard error	0.502	0.319	0.238	0.321	0.238	0.342	0.243
Mean of dependent variable	18.61	11.39	7.23	11.39	7.23	11.39	7.23
Estimation method	OLS	MVR	MVR	3SLS		MVR	

Notes: (X/GDP) is the share of exports of other business and computer and information services in GDP, (M/GDP) is the share of imports of other business and computer and information services in GDP, NETMFDI/GDP (NETSFDI/GDP) i is the net stock of outward foreign investment in manufacturing (services) as a share of GDP, ICTIRAT is the share of ICT investment in total fixed investment, SERVICES is the share of the services sector in total value added, HTECH is the share of high-tech industries in total value added, PMR is a product market regulations indicator, UNIONS denotes the trade union density rate, and HK is the average years of education per person. Country fixed effects and annual time dummies are included in all regressions. Heteroscedastic-consistent t-statistics are in parentheses.

**Denotes a coefficient significant at the 5% level.

*Denotes a coefficient significant at the 10% level.

there are some differences in the magnitude and significance of the coefficients.

The following subsections discuss the estimation results for the international openness variables, the economic structure variables and the economy-wide framework variables in turn.

International Openness

International trade and the FDI measures are both found to be significant. In contrast to earlier findings, the coefficient on imports of business and computer and information services is negatively signed, implying that increasing imports are associated with a reduction in the share of potentially offshorable occupations at the aggregate level, with similar-sized effects on both types of potentially offshorable employment. Exports of business and computer information services are found to have a positive and significant association with the share of employment potentially affected by offshoring—as expected. The impact on potentially offshorable nonclerical employment is significantly larger than that for potentially offshorable clerical employment, as can be seen from the results in columns (2) to (4). Although the trade variables may be endogenous, especially if companies' decisions about international sourcing and employment are made simultaneously, the basic findings remain even in the 3SLS estimates in which the trade variables are treated as endogenous.

The results for the two net outward FDI measures vary across the different occupational categories and the different econometric techniques. In the single equation for total potentially offshorable employment column (1) only the net services FDI variable is significant, with a higher net outward stock of services FDI being positively associated with the share of potentially offshorable employment. The simultaneous equation estimates show that this effect largely arises from a positive association with potentially offshorable nonclerical occupations. The impact on clerical occupations is significant only in the 3SLS estimates, and even then the coefficient is significant only at the 10 percent level. This result is consistent with a scenario where skill intensive headquarter services (e.g., management, R&D, marketing, design) continue to be provided from the home country, at least initially, while there is a reduced need for administrative support functions when relatively more of the activity is located abroad.

The net outward manufacturing FDI stock does not have a significant overall impact on the aggregate share of potentially offshorable employment. The simultaneous equation estimates show that this arises because there are offsetting effects on clerical and nonclerical occupations. In particular, an increase in the net outward manufacturing FDI stock is associated with a decline in the employment share of potentially offshorable clerical occupations and an *increase* in the employment share of potentially offshorable nonclerical occupations. This latter effect is significant in the simultaneous equation estimates in (2) and (3), but not in the 3SLS estimates. The same type of scenario of a relative increase in the need for highly skilled headquarter services combined with a reduced need for clerical-type occupations could again explain this result, with the negative effect on the latter stronger in this case.

A common element of the findings for both FDI variables is that they are associated with a rise in the share of nonclerical occupations relative to the share of clerical occupations. This is consistent with other studies that have found that outward FDI is positively associated with a rise in the relative demand for skilled labor in the home economy (see, e.g., Head and Ries [2002]).

There are many different factors that might be reflected in the coefficients on the FDI variables. It is also the case that FDI data can, at times, be a poor measure of the actual scale of activities that multinational companies undertake. However, as shown in van Welsum and Reif (2006b, 2006c), the inclusion of FDI variables does not significantly bias the coefficients on the other explanatory factors.

Economic Structure

The share of ICT investment in gross fixed capital formation, the share of services in GDP and the share of high-tech industries in GDP are all significantly positively associated with the share of employment potentially affected by offshoring (column [1]), as might be expected. However, there are noticeable differences in their effects on clerical and nonclerical ICT-using occupations.

The ICT investment term has a significant positive association only with nonclerical occupations—as shown in (2), the coefficient on this term in the clerical occupations terms is not significant and is thus discarded in (3) and (4). This means the share of nonclerical to clerical is rising. However, there is no sign that, overall, ICTs are having a destructive effect on ICT-using clerical occupations. Furthermore, improvements in ICTs are common to all countries, suggesting that observed differences in employment patterns must be due to other factors, such as the extent of offshoring.

The service sector share has a significant positive association with nonclerical occupations, but a small negative association with ICT-using clerical occupations. The latter effect is statistically significant in the simultaneous equation models shown in columns (2) and (3), but not in the 3SLS estimates. The initial estimates also suggest that the share of high-tech output in GDP matters mainly for the nonclerical employment share (see [2]), but it is not possible to reject the imposition of a common coefficient in the clerical and nonclerical employment equations, with the resulting estimate being statistically significant, as shown in (3).

Table 9.7   **Effects of a one standard deviation increase in the explanatory variables**

	Sample mean	Standard deviation	Effect on share of potentially offshorable occupations in employment (% points)	
			Nonclerical	Clerical
(X/GDP)	2.43%	0.50	0.34	0.23
(M/GDP)	2.34%	0.51	−0.11	−0.11
(NETMFDI/GDP)	3.82%	2.06	0.10	−0.09
(NETSFDI/GDP)	1.93%	2.60	0.10	—
(ICTIRAT)	19.84%	1.82	0.37	—
SERVICES	69.35%	1.11	0.17	−0.06
HTECH	2.45%	0.27	0.06	0.06
PMR+	2.46	0.45	0.13	0.13
UNIONS+	39.16%	1.64	0.15	−0.08
HK	11.99 years	0.18	0.20	0.20

Notes: For variables indicated with a +, a one standard deviation decrease is shown. These results use the coefficients from model [3] in table 9.6.

Economy-Wide Framework Factors

A reduced level of anticompetitive product market regulations and a higher level of human capital are both found to be positively associated with the aggregate share of potentially offshorable occupations in total employment. Both of these factors encourage the adoption and usage of ICT technologies. Subsequent tests indicated that both also have similar effects on the two types of ICT-using occupations, with common coefficients being imposed on these terms in the estimates shown in column (3) and column (4).

Union density is not found to be significantly related to the aggregate share of potentially offshorable occupations in total employment. However, it does appear to affect the composition of this share, having a negative association with the share of nonclerical occupations and a positive association with the share of clerical occupations, although the latter effect is not significant in the 3SLS estimates. These results suggest that higher levels of union density act to slow the general adjustment that is taking place from clerical to nonclerical occupations in all the economies, included in the sample used in this chapter.

Finally, the impact of a one standard deviation change in the statistically significant explanatory factors on the nonclerical and clerical employment shares is illustrated in table 9.7 using the coefficient estimates from the results reported in model (3) in table 9.6.[22] It is important to note that such

---

22. The findings when using model [4] in table 9.1 are generally similar, but the effects of changes in the explanatory factors are usually a little larger.

changes are only partial effects, with all other factors being held constant. Use of standard deviation changes enables the effects of changes in different factors to be more easily compared. The standard deviations are the average of the individual within-sample standard deviations for each of the twelve countries.[23]

9.5   Conclusion

This chapter extends and improves previous models (van Welsum and Reif 2006b, 2006c) by distinguishing between different types of employment potentially affected by offshoring and by disaggregating the FDI variable into manufacturing and services sectors. The results suggest it is important to make these distinctions. Contrary to the results in previous work, we now find a negative association between employment in offshorable occupations and the share of imports of business and computer and information services in GDP. The effects of four of the explanatory variables (net outward manufacturing, ICT investment, the comparative size of the services sector, and trade union density) also vary according to the type of potentially offshorable employment. Separating out the effects of ICTs from the effects of ICT-enabled changes remains a challenge given data availability. However, technological changes in ICTs are likely to be common to the countries included in the analysis, suggesting that differences in observed employment patterns are due to other factors.

The analysis suggests that the share of exports of business services in GDP, the share of ICT investment in total investment, the share of the service sector in GDP, and improvements in human capital have all been especially important factors behind the general upward tendency in the share of employment in potentially offshorable nonclerical occupations. The remaining variables considered also help to raise the employment share, with the exception of the share of imports of business services in GDP.

The exports to GDP ratio and human capital also help to raise the share of employment in potentially offshorable clerical occupations, as does the share of hi-tech output in GDP and reductions in product market regulations. However, these factors have been offset by rising imports of business services, the decline in trade union densities, and the rising share of services in GDP.

Overall, the principal findings appear to be robust to changes in estima-

23. The use of average within-country sample standard deviations is necessary because of the scale of differences in some factors across countries and the feasible extent to which some policies may be changed. Calculations with the cross-country standard deviation, whether evaluated using the full sample of observations or a cross-section at a particular point in time, can also be especially problematic when using indicator variables whose upper or lower limit is bounded.

tion techniques and specifications of the model. Indicators of international trade and investment, the structure of national economies, and economy-wide framework factors are all important for understanding the cross-country pattern of the share of potentially offshorable occupations in total employment. Although the development of corresponding data sources for the relative wages of the various types of occupations would help to separate out demand and supply-side influences more clearly, the results from the descriptive regressions in this chapter provide useful guidance for both policy development and for further work in this area.

Further work in this area could follow a number of paths to improve understanding of the effects of international sourcing. A major area would be to strive to improve the occupational selections, for example, by coordinating with work undertaken in the United States (e.g., Blinder 2005; Jensen and Kletzer 2005). Controlling for differences in ICT-content of occupations, over time and across countries, would be another extension. Further separating out the effects of technology on occupations from those of offshoring should also be explored. Finally, the impact of variables such as the size of the public sector and the importance of SMEs in the economy should also be examined.

International harmonization of the definition of offshoring and the data classifications, as well as data collection itself, would greatly enhance the scope for the formulation of consistent and sound policy recommendations and would enhance the scope for comparison of the various studies on the effects of offshoring.

Appendix

Table 9A.1   **Detailed analysis of the U.S. occupational data**

Looking at the year-on-year change in the occupational data for the United States (1995–2002) at the level of the individual occupations shows:

- All of the occupations selected as potentially affected by offshoring experienced at least one year-on-year decline.
- Forty-five out of the sixty-seven occupations included in the U.S. selection experienced an absolute decline between 2001 and 2002, as did the overall selection of occupations potentially affected by offshoring and total employment.
- The overall selection of occupations potentially affected by offshoring experienced three absolute declines between 1995–2002; to compare the individual occupations against the overall selection, the following forty-seven occupations experienced at least three absolute declines:

Accountants and auditors	23	Economists	166
Architects	43	Urban planners	173
Metallurgical and materials engineers	45	Authors	183
Mining engineers	46	Technical writers	184
Petroleum engineers	47	Editors and reporters	195
Engineers, electrical and electronic	55	Air traffic controllers	227
Engineers, industrial	56	Computer programmers	229
Engineers, mechanical	57	Supervisors and Proprietors, Sales Occupations	243
Marine and naval architects	58	Insurance sales occupations	253
Engineers, n.e.c.	59	Real estate sales occupations	254
Operations and systems researchers		Supervisors, computer equipment operators	304
and analysts	65	Computer operators	308
Actuaries	66	Peripheral equipment operators	309
Statisticians	67	Secretaries	313
Physicists and astronomers	69	Typists	315
Chemists, except biochemists	73	Transportation ticket and reservation agents	318
Atmospheric and space scientists	74	File clerks	335
Geologists and geodesists	75	Payroll and timekeeping clerks	338
Physical scientists, n.e.c.	76	Billing clerks	339
Biological and life scientists	78	Cost and rate clerks	343
Forestry and conservation scientists	79	Telephone operators	348
Medical scientists	83	Bank tellers	383
Librarians	164	Data-entry keyers	385
Archivists and curators	165	Statistical clerks	386

Note: The estimates for 2003 show a further absolute decline in the selection of occupations potentially affected by offshoring.

Table 9A.2   **IMF balance of payments categories**

7.	Computer and information services
7.1	Computer services
7.2	Information services
7.2.1	News agency services
7.2.2	Other information provision services
9.	Other business services
9.1	Merchanting and other trade-related services
9.1.1	Merchanting
9.1.2	Other trade-related services
9.2	Operational leasing services
9.3	Miscellaneous business, professional, and technical services
9.3.1	Legal, accounting, management consulting, and public relations
9.3.1.1	Legal services
9.3.1.2	Accounting, auditing, bookkeeping, and tax consulting services
9.3.1.3	Business and management consulting, and public relations
9.3.2	Advertising, market research, and public opinion polling
9.3.3	Research and development
9.3.4	Architectural, engineering, and other technical services
9.3.5	Agricultural, mining, mining, and on-site processing services
9.3.5.1	Waste treatment and depollution
9.3.5.2	Agricultural, mining, and other on-site processing services
9.3.6	Other business services
9.3.7	Services between related enterprises, n.i.e.

Source: OECD (2002).

Table 9A.3   **Sectors distinguished in the OECD Direct Investment Statistics Database**

Primary sector

Agriculture and Fishing
Mining and Quarrying
of which: Extraction of petroleum and gas

Manufacturing

of which: Food products
                Total textile and wood activities
                Total petroleum, chemical, rubber, plastic products
                Total metal and mechanical products
                Total machinery, computers, RTV, communication
                Total vehicles and other transport equipments

Service sector

Electricity, Gas, and Water
Construction
Trade and Repairs
Hotels and Restaurants
Transports, Communication
of which: Total land, sea, and air transport
                Telecommunications
Financial Intermediation
of which: Monetary intermediation
                Other financial intermediation
                of which: Financial holding companies
                Insurance and activities auxiliary to insurance
                Total other financial intermediation and insurance activities
Real Estate and Business Activities
of which: Real estate
Other Services
Unallocated
Total

Table 9A.4 **Europe: Occupations potentially affected by offshoring**

3 Digit ISCO-88
123: Other specialist managers
211: Physicists, chemists, and related professionals
212: Mathematicians, statisticians, and related professionals
213: Computing professionals
214: Architects, engineers, and related professionals
241: Business professionals
242: Legal professionals
243: Archivists, librarians, and related information professionals
312: Computer associate professionals
341: Finance and sales associate professionals
342: Business services agents and trade brokers
343: Administrative associate professionals
411: Secretaries and keyboard-operating clerks
412: Numerical clerks
422: Client information clerks

Source: van Welsum and Vickery (2005), based on EULFS (2004).
Note: Occupations in last four lines have been classified as clerical.

Table 9A.5   **United States: Occupations potentially affected by offshoring**

CPS categories

Occupation	Code	Occupation	Code
Accountants and auditors	23	Archivists and curators	165
Underwriters	24	Economists	166
Other financial officers	25	Urban planners	173
Management analysts	26	Authors	183
Architects	43	Technical writers	184
Aerospace engineer	44	Editors and reporters	195
Metallurgical and materials engineers	45	Air traffic controllers	227
Mining engineers	46	Computer programmers	229
Petroleum engineers	47	Tool programmers, numerical control	233
Chemical engineers	48	Supervisors and proprietors, sales occupations	243
Nuclear engineers	49	Insurance sales occupations	253
Civil engineers	53	Real estate sales occupations	254
Agricultural engineers	54	Securities and financial services sales occupations	255
Engineers, electrical and electronic	55		
Engineers, industrial	56	Sales occupations, other business services	257
Engineers, mechanical	57	Supervisors, computer equipment operators	304
Marine and naval architects	58	Supervisors, financial records processing	305
Engineers, n.e.c.	59	Chief communications operators	306
Surveyors and mapping scientists	63	Computer operators	308
Computer systems analysts and scientists	64	Peripheral equipment operators	309
Operations and systems researchers and analysts	65	Secretaries	313
Actuaries	66	Typists	315
Statisticians	67	Transportation ticket and reservation agents	318
Mathematical scientists, n.e.c.	68	File clerks	335
Physicists and astronomers	69	Records clerks	336
Chemists, except biochemists	73	Bookkeepers, accounting, and auditing clerks	337
Atmospheric and space scientists	74	Payroll and timekeeping clerks	338
Geologists and geodesists	75	Billing clerks	339
Physical scientists, n.e.c.	76	Cost and rate clerks	343
Agricultural and food scientists	77	Billing, posting, and calculating machine operators	344
Biological and life scientists	78	Telephone operators	348
Forestry and conservation scientists	79	Bank tellers	383
Medical scientists	83	Data-entry keyers	385
Librarians	164	Statistical clerks	386

Source: van Welsum and Vickery (2005), based on U.S. Current Population Survey.
Note: Occupations Secretaries through Statistical clerks have been classified as clerical.

Table 9A.6   **Canada: Occupations potentially affected by offshoring**

		SOC91 Canada	
A121	Engineering, science, and architecture managers	C012	Chemists
A122	Information systems and data processing managers	C013	Geologists, geochemists, and geophysicists
A131	Sales, marketing and advertising managers	C014	Meteorologists
A301	Insurance, real estate, and financial brokerage managers	C015	Other professional occupations in physical sciences
A302	Banking, credit, and other investment managers	C021	Biologists and related scientists
A303	Other business services managers	C031	Civil engineers
A311	Telecommunication carriers managers	C032	Mechanical engineers
A312	Postal and courier services managers	C033	Electrical and electronics engineers
A392	Utilities managers	C034	Chemical engineers
B011	Financial auditors and accountants	C041	Industrial and manufacturing engineers
B012	Financial and investment analysts	C042	Metallurgical and materials engineers
B013	Securities agents, investment dealers, and traders	C043	Mining engineers
B014	Other financial officers	C044	Geological engineers
B022	Professional occupations in business services to management	C045	Petroleum engineers
B111	Bookkeepers	C046	Aerospace engineers
B112	Loan officers	C047	Computer engineers
B114	Insurance underwriters	C048	Other professional engineers, n.e.c.
B211	Secretaries (except legal and medical)	C051	Architects
B212	Legal secretaries	C052	Landscape architects
B213	Medical secretaries	C053	Urban and land use planners
B214	Court recorders and medical transcriptionists	C054	Land surveyors
B311	Administrative officers	C061	Mathematicians, statisticians, and actuaries
B312	Executive assistants	C062	Computer systems analysts
B412	Supervisors, finance, and insurance clerks	C063	Computer programmers

(continued)

Table 9A.6   (continued)

		SOC91 Canada	
B512	Typists and word processing operators	C152	Industrial designers
B513	Records and file clerks	C172	Air traffic control occupations
B514	Receptionists and switchboard operators	E012	Lawyers and Quebec notaries
B521	Computer operators	E031	Natural and applied science policy researchers, consultants and program officers
B522	Data entry clerks	E032	Economists and economic policy researchers and analysts
B523	Typesetters and related occupations	E033	Economic development officers and marketing researchers and consultants
B524	Telephone operators	F011	Librarians
B531	Accounting and related clerks	F013	Archivists
B532	Payroll clerks	F021	Writers
B533	Tellers, financial services	F022	Editors
B534	Banking, insurance, and other financial clerks	F023	Journalists
B553	Customer service, information, and related clerks	F025	Translators, terminologists, and interpreters
B554	Survey interviewers and statistical clerks	G131	Insurance agents and brokers
C011	Physicists and astronomers		

Source: van Welsum and Vickery (2005), based on Statistics Canada.

Note: Occupations B211, B212, B213, B214, B311, B312, B412, B512, B513, B514, B522, B524, B531, B532, B533, B534, B553, and B554 have been classified as clerical.

Table 9A.7   Australia: Occupations potentially affected by offshoring

	ASCO 4-digit		
1221	Engineering managers	2521	Legal professionals
1224	Information technology managers	2522	Economists
1231	Sales and marketing managers	2523	Urban and regional planners
1291	Policy and planning managers	2534	Journalists and related professionals
2111	Chemists	2535	Authors and related professionals
2112	Geologists and geophysicists	3211	Branch accountants and managers (financial institution)
2113	Life scientists	3212	Financial dealers and brokers
2114	Environmental and agricultural science professionals	3213	Financial investment advisers
2115	Medical scientists	3294	Computing support technicians
2119	Other natural and physical science professionals	3392	Customer service managers
2121	Architects and landscape architects	3399	Other managing supervisors (sales and service)
2122	Quantity surveyors	5111	Secretaries and personal assistants
2123	Cartographers and surveyors	5911	Bookkeepers
2124	Civil engineers	5912	Credit and loans officers
2125	Electrical and electronics engineers	5991	Advanced legal and related clerks
2126	Mechanical, production, and plant engineers	5993	Insurance agents
2127	Mining and materials engineers	5995	Desktop publishing operators
2211	Accountants	6121	Keyboard operators
2212	Auditors	6141	Accounting clerks
2221	Marketing and advertising professionals	6142	Payroll clerks
2231	Computing professionals	6143	Bank workers
2292	Librarians	6144	Insurance clerks
2293	Mathematicians, statisticians, and actuaries	6145	Money market and statistical clerks
2294	Business and organization analysts	8113	Switchboard operators
2299	Other business and information professionals	8294	Telemarketers
2391	Medical imaging professionals		

Source: van Welsum and Vickery (2005), based on Australian Bureau of Statistics.

Note: Occupations 5111, 5991, 6121, 6141, 6142, 6143, 6144, 6145, and 8113 have been classified as clerical.

References

Autor, D. H., F. Levy, and R. J. Murnane. 2003. The skills content of recent technological change: An empirical exploration. *Quarterly Journal of Economics* 118 (4): 1279–1333.

Baily, M. N., and R. Z. Lawrence. 2005. What happened to the great U.S. job machine? The role of trade and electronic offshoring. *Brookings Papers on Economic Activity*, Issue no. 2:211–84. Washington, D.C.: Brookings Institution.

Bardhan, A. D., and C. Kroll. 2003. The new wave of outsourcing. University of California Berkeley, Fisher Center for Real Estate and Urban Economics, Fisher Center Research Report no. 1103.

Barry, F., and D. van Welsum. 2005. Services FDI and offshoring into Ireland. Paper prepared for the Panel session on ICT-enabled offshoring: Country experience and business perspectives. OECD Working Party on the Information Economy. June, Paris. Available at www.oecd.org/sti/offshoring.

Blinder, A. S. 2005. Fear of offshoring. Center for Economic and Policy Research (CEPS) Working Paper no. 119, December.

de la Fuente, A., and R. Doménech. 2002a. Educational attainment in the OECD, 1960–1995. Centre for Economic Policy Research, Discussion Paper no. 3390.

———. 2002b. Human capital in growth regressions: How much difference does data quality make? An update and further results. Centre for Economic Policy Research, Discussion Paper no. 3587.

Head, K., and J. Ries. 2002. Offshore production and skill upgrading by Japanese manufacturing firms. *Journal of International Economics* 58 (1): 81–105.

Jensen, J. B., and L. Kletzer. 2005. Tradable services: Understanding the scope and impact of services offshoring. Institute for International Economics Working Paper no. WP05-9, September.

Jensen, P. D. Ø., J. F. Kirkegaard, and N. S. Laugesen. 2006. Offshoring in Europe: Evidence of a two-way street from Denmark. Institute for International Economics Working Paper no. WP06-3, June.

Kirkegaard, J. F. 2004. Outsourcing: stains on the white collar? Institute for International Economics, Washington, D.C. Unpublished Manuscript.

Levy, F., and R. J. Murname. 2004. *The new division of labor.* New York: Princeton University Press and the Russell Sage Foundation.

Mankiw, N. G., and P. Swage. 2005. The economics and politics of offshore outsourcing. American Enterprise Institute for Public Policy Research Working Paper no. 122, December.

Mann, C. L. 2004. The U.S. current account, new economy services and implications for sustainability. *Review of International Economics* 12 (2): 262–76.

Marin, D. 2004. A nation of poets and thinkers: Less so with Eastern enlargement? Austria and Germany. University of Munich, Department of Economics Discussion Paper no. 2004-06, April.

Messina, J. 2005. Institutions and service employment: A panel study for OECD countries. *Labour: Review of Labour Economics and Industrial Relations* 19 (2): 343–72.

Millar, J. 2002. Outsourcing practices in Europe. STAR Issue Report 27. Available at www.databank.it/star/list_issue/e.html.

Nickell, S., S. Redding, and J. Swaffield. 2004. The uneven pace of deindustrialisation in the OECD. Paper prepared for the OECD Workshop on Services. 15–16 November, Paris.

Organization for Economic Cooperation and Development (OECD). 2002 *The manual on statistics on international trade in services.* Joint publication of the

United Nations, the International Monetary Fund, the OECD, the European Commission, the United Nations Conference on Trade and Development, and the World Trade Organization. Available at www.oecd.org/std/trade-services.

———. 2003. *The sources of economic growth in OECD countries.* Paris: OECD.

———. 2004. *OECD information technology outlook 2004.* Paris: OECD.

———. 2006. *OECD information technology outlook 2006.* Paris: OECD.

Pain, N., and D. van Welsum. 2004. International production relocation and exports of services. *OECD economic studies* 38 (2004/1): 68–94.

van Welsum, D. 2004. In search of "offshoring": Evidence from U.S. imports of services. Birkbeck Economics Working Paper 2004 no. 2. London: Birkbeck College.

van Welsum, D., and G. Vickery, 2005. Potential offshoring of ICT-intensive using occupations. DSTI Information Economy Working Paper, DSTI/ICCP/IE(2004)19/FINAL, OECD, Paris. Available at: http://www.oecd.org/sti/offshoring.

van Welsum, D., and X. Reif. 2006a. Potential impacts of international sourcing on different occupations. DSTI Information Economy Working Paper, DSTI/ICCP/IE(2006)1/FINAL, OECD, Paris. Available at http://www.oecd.org/sti/offshoring.

———. 2006b. Potential offshoring: Evidence from selected OECD countries. In *The Brookings trade forum 2005: Offshoring white-collar work—the issues and implications,* ed. S. Collins and L. Brainard, 165–202. Washington, D.C.: Brookings Institution.

———. 2006c. The share of employment potentially affected by offshoring: An empirical investigation. DSTI Information Economy Working Paper, DSTI/ICCP/IE(2005)8/FINAL, OECD, Paris. Available at http://www.oecd.org/sti/offshoring.

U.S. Government Accountability Office (GAO). 2005. International trade—U.S. and India data on offshoring show significant differences. GAO-06-116, Report to Congressional Committees, October, Washington, D.C.

Comment   Lori G. Kletzer

Much is new in thinking about services. The evolution in thinking about services trade was first a broadening from nontradable to tradable. Measuring services trade is now a task of considerable energy and importance, as evidenced by the chapters in this conference volume. From the labor market side, thinking about tradable services is very much linked to the current debate about offshoring. The intensity of the offshoring debate is often seen in claims and questions such as, "is your job next?"

This chapter takes on the question of the potential offshoring of jobs, specifically information and communication technology (ICT)-enabled occupations. These jobs are at the heart of the offshoring debate. The chapter is part of a research program, by van Welsum and coauthors, to quan-

Lori G. Kletzer is a professor of economics at the University of California, Santa Cruz.

tify the share of employment potentially affected by ICT-enabled offshoring (see van Welsum and Vickery [2005a, 2005b] and van Welsum and Reif [2006]). The authors are to be commended for their cross-country approach. Within the developed countries of the Organization for Economic Cooperation and Development (OECD), there appears to be interesting variation in the time-series pattern of the share of employment in these ICT-enabled occupations. Despite the use of the word offshoring, the analysis itself is not really about offshoring; it is about developing a set of jobs potentially affected by offshoring.

To develop the list of occupations, the authors start with job characteristics uniformly mentioned in the offshoring literature as the characteristics of offshorability: (a) intensive use of ICTs (to produce output); (b) output that can be traded or transmitted by ICTs (ICT-enabled services); (c) high codifiable knowledge content (little tacit, nonroutine, implicit knowledge); and (d) no face-to-face (customer) contact.[1] Through mostly subjective judgment, with some limited use of occupational descriptions, a set of occupations is drawn up for Europe (as the EU15), the United States, Canada, and Australia (these are reported in tables 9A.3 through 9A.6). Harmonizing the occupations across countries presents a challenge that the authors handle well.

In this type of analysis, much emphasis is, and should be, in the details of the lists. Just which jobs are potentially offshorable, due to their ICT-enabled characteristics? Focusing on table 9A.3, for the United States, many jobs conform to our priors on the type of work that seems offshorable (e.g., typists; bookkeepers, accounting, and auditing clerks; telephone operators; data entry keyers). Other occupations are more questionable, such as librarians, tellers, and secretaries. These last three occupations, while working with computers and using information, all involve either face-to-face work with the public or with the "boss."[2] Air traffic controllers seem also unlikely to be offshorable, despite the claim by the authors that in Europe, an airport's air traffic controllers can be located up to 1,000 km away from the site.

As is often the case, a more general and objective methodology is often preferred to the subjective judgment approach. Jensen and Kletzer (2006) use a novel methodology, based on geographic concentration of occupational employment to derive a distinction between tradable and nontradable occupations.

The figures present some interesting comparisons. The share (in total employment) of ICT-enabled occupations (potentially affected by offshoring) is rising in the EU15, declining in the United States and Canada, and

---

1. See Bardhan and Kroll (2003) and Blinder (2005) for a discussion of these characteristics.
2. This statement is based on a preliminary analysis in Kletzer (2006).

is flat in Australia, over the period 1995 to 2003. Separating clerical (seen as lower-skill) from nonclerical yields a potentially important difference: the share of clerical ICT-enabled occupations is rather sharply declining in the United States and Australia, while basically flat in EU15 and Canada. The share of nonclerical (seen as higher skill) occupations is rising in EU15, Australia, and the United States, while basically flat in Canada. Can the declines be due to offshoring? Certainly, but the ICT technology itself (through word processing and accounting software, voice-recognition software, and the internet) is likely to play a very large role. In this sense, we are back to the trade versus technology debate, last seen in the many papers on international competition and the decline of manufacturing employment.[3]

The chapter goes on to examine the time-series pattern of the share of ICT-enabled occupations (potentially affected by offshoring), in a regression setting. The authors recognize their specification to be somewhat ad hoc, based loosely in the literature on trade and employment, and some common sense. They model the share of employment that is potentially offshorable (total, as well as clerical separate from nonclerical) as related to: international openness (exports and imports of Business, Computer, and Information Services [BCIS] as a share of GDP); national economic structure (shares of services and high-tech industries in GDP; share of ICT investment in total gross fixed investment); and economy-wide framework influences (OECD product market regulation indicator, union density, human capital). The authors acknowledge that potentially endogenous factors are used as independent variables (exports and imports being the best examples). The objective is to arrive at some correlations, not test a causal model. The results are consistent with most priors, yielding few surprises. Most significantly, employment in potentially offshorable occupations is positively associated with exports of BCIS; negatively associated with imports of BCIS; positively associated with the share of ICT investment (for nonclerical ICT-enabled employment); positively associated with share of services in GDP (nonclerical); positively associated with share of high-tech output; negatively associated with anticompetitive product market regulations; positively associated with human capital; and negatively associated with union density.

Interestingly, by these measures, the United States should have a high share of potentially offshorable employment, not a low and declining share. A natural question then is whether the U.S. share is low because of offshoring. That is possible, but for all the OECD countries it seems more important to ask if declining share could be due to technological change. That is, ICT substituting for clerical employment.

As the research moves forward, a challenge will be to directly include

---

3. The literature is large. See Feenstra (2000) and Kletzer (2002) for references.

offshoring in the empirical specification. One way to think about the issue is that domestic ICT-enabled employment is a combination of two separable measures. The first is the one modeled by the authors, *potential* ICT-enabled services employment. That employment is a function of demand (exports, investment, imports, services output, technology) and supply (human capital, technology). The second measure is offshorable employment, where we might model the activity of offshoring as a function of technology, foreign wages, foreign labor quality, and other relative costs of remote services production, including managerial needs. Actual domestic ICT-enabled services employment equals potential ICT services employment minus offshorable employment. An implication of this thinking is that in the authors' current specification offshoring (actual) is a missing variable.

The empirical challenges in this type of research are considerable. The authors are to be commended on their cross-country approach. Much research in this area focuses on the United States, yet as revealed in the tables and figures, there is variation across the industrial countries, and this variation should be exploited in our research.

References

Bardhan, A. D., and C. A. Kroll. 2003. The new wave of outsourcing. Fisher Center Research Reports, no. 1103. Fisher Center for Real Estate and Urban Economics. Berkeley: University of California.

Blinder, A. 2005. Fear of offshoring. CEPS Working Paper no. 119, December.

Feenstra, R. C., ed. 2000. *The impact of international trade on wages.* Chicago: University of Chicago Press.

Jensen, J. B., and L. G. Kletzer. 2006. Tradable services: Understanding the scope and impact of services offshoring. In *Brookings trade forum 2005, offshoring white-collar work*, ed. S. M. Collins and L. Brainard, 75–134. Washington, D.C.: Brookings Institution.

Kletzer, L. G. 2002. *Imports, exports, and jobs: What does trade mean for employment and job loss?* Kalamazoo, MI: W. E. Upjohn Institute for Employment Research.

———. 2006. The scope of tradable services and the task content of offshorable services jobs. University of California, Santa Cruz. Unpublished Manuscript, April.

van Welsum, D., and X. Reif. 2006. Potential offshoring: Evidence from selected OECD countries. In *Brookings trade forum 2005, offshoring white-collar work*, ed. S. M. Collins and L. Brainard, 165–194. Washington, D.C.: Brookings Institution.

van Welsum, D., and G. Vickery. 2005a. New perspectives on ICT skills and employment. DSTI Information Economy Working Paper, DSTI/ICCP/IE (2004)10/FINAL. Paris: OECD.

———. 2005b. Potential offshoring of ICT-intensive using occupations. DSTI Information Economy Working Paper, DSTI/ICCP/IE(2004)19/FINAL. Paris: OECD.

IV

Topics in the Measurement of Price and Productivity

10

The Contribution of Multinational Corporations to U.S. Productivity Growth, 1977–2000

Carol Corrado, Paul Lengermann, and Larry Slifman

10.1 Introduction and Background

Concomitant with the surge in productivity growth in the United States since 1995 has been a surge in research on productivity. Before the productivity step-up had become fully evident, Corrado and Slifman (1999) focused attention on productivity by major sector as well as on problems in measuring productivity and their implications for the performance of productivity in the mid-1990s.[1] Later, others began to concentrate on the role of information technology (IT)—examining the productivity of the producers of IT equipment as well as the users of IT equipment. The research often used growth accounting as the organizing principle for analysis, and was conducted using both detailed industry-level data (Jorgenson and Stiroh 2000) and macroeconomic time series data at only the broadest levels of disaggregation (Oliner and Sichel 2000).

But IT is not the only important economic force that has been influenc-

Carol Corrado is senior advisor and research director in economics at The Conference Board. Paul Lengermann is an economist in the Division of Research and Statistics of the Board of Governors of the Federal Reserve System. Larry Slifman is senior associate director of the Division of Research and Statistics of the Board of Governors of the Federal Reserve System.

This paper was prepared for the NBER/CRIW Conference on International Service Flows, held April 28–29, 2006. Earlier versions were given at the NBER Productivity Workshop (July 2005) and the OECD Workshop on the Impact of Multinational Enterprises on Productivity Growth (November 2003). We are grateful to Ray Mataloni and William Ziele of the BEA for helpful conversations and special tabulations. We thank Marshall Reinsdorf and other participants at the conference and workshops for helpful comments, and Niels Burmester, Brian Rowe, and Sarit Weisburd for research assistance.

The views expressed in this paper are those of the authors and should not be attributed to the Board of Governors of the Federal Reserve System or other members of its staff.

1. The research by Corrado and Slifman was initially circulated in late 1996.

ing productivity growth in recent years. In particular, many companies reportedly have been able to achieve significant efficiencies by reorganizing the way they conduct their operations. Meanwhile, business has become increasingly global in its nature, with globalization arguably a significant part of the enhanced organizational efficiencies.[2]

Many studies that have examined the link between globalization and productivity have looked at the productivity of multinational corporations (MNCs). The emphasis in this literature is on foreign-owned MNCs in the host country. Using microeconomic data, two questions often addressed are whether the host-country operations of foreign-owned firms are more productive than the operations of domestically owned firms in the host country and whether the higher productivity creates favorable spillovers in the host country (see Keller 2004 for a review of the recent literature).[3] Doms and Jensen (1998a and 1998b) broadened the scope of this research strain to look at both foreign-owned and domestically owned MNCs and to inquire whether country of ownership matters.[4] Their results, which are based on microeconomic data, suggest that for productivity growth country of ownership does not matter: "It is not the fact that the plants are foreign owned that is important . . . rather, it is the fact that the plants are owned by multinational corporations that seems important." (251)[5]

In this chapter, we attempt to merge these research strains by measuring the contribution of MNCs to the aggregate productivity record of the United States. While we cannot examine the causal linkages between specific characteristics of MNCs and their higher productivity as carefully as most microlevel studies, we can move beyond such studies—which typically focus on the manufacturing sector—to assess the importance of MNCs in the macroeconomy. Toward this end, we first develop a consistent database of information from 1977 to 2000 on the activities of foreign-owned operations in the United States and the domestic activities of U.S.

2. Lipsey, Blomstrom, and Rumstetter (1998) document the growth of internationalized production in world output.
3. Mechanisms by which this might occur include learning externalities through labor training and turnover (Fosfurie, Motta, and Rønde 2001), technology transfer (Griffith, Harrison, and Van Reenen 2004), and the provision of high-quality intermediates (Rodriguez-Clare 1996). Haskel, Pereira, and Slaughter (2004) present evidence in support of a positive spillover effect in the United States, though the implied economic magnitudes are fairly small relative to the subsidies paid to attract foreign direct investment (FDI). Keller and Yeaple (2003) find that spillovers are much larger, accounting for 11 percent of U.S. manufacturing productivity growth between 1987 and 1996. In the United Kingdom, Griffith, Redding, and Simpson (2003) conclude there is a significant positive spillover from FDI, while Aitken and Harrison (1999) find a negative relationship between FDI and the productivity of domestic plants in Venezuela.
4. Howenstein and Zeile (1994) use similar data but focus on comparing foreign-owned establishments to U.S.-owned establishments. While foreign-owned establishments pay higher wages and are more productive, this appears to be due largely to differences in industry mix, plant scale, and occupational mix.
5. More recently, Criscuolo and Martin (2003) document a similar "MNC effect" in the U.K. manufacturing sector, while Griffith, Redding, and Simpson (2004) provide evidence of an MNC productivity advantage in the U.K. service sector.

firms that have foreign operations. Then we integrate that database with a more standard productivity database covering all establishments of all industries operating in the United States (Bartelsman and Beaulieu 2003, 2007) and examine the contribution of the MNC sector to overall labor productivity growth in the United States. We look at labor productivity *growth* because, even though studies of MNC performance based on microeconomic data have tended to identify effects on the *level* of productivity, if these underlying productivity-enhancing effects are spreading and/or filtering in over time, productivity aggregates will be affected in terms of growth rates (as well as levels).

Although our final analysis is relatively straightforward—indeed, most of the hard work of this study involved the integration of the various data sets—we nevertheless believe our findings are quite striking. Specifically, although the MNC sector accounts for only 40 percent of the output of nonfinancial corporations (NFCs) between 1977 and 2000, MNCs appear to have accounted for *more than three-fourths* of the increase in NFC labor productivity over this period. Moreover, MNCs account for *all* of the NFC sector's pickup in labor productivity growth in the late 1990s; accordingly, they account for *more than half* of the much-studied acceleration in aggregate productivity.[6] And, while MNCs involved in the production of IT contributed significantly toward this acceleration, MNCs in other manufacturing and nonmanufacturing industries contributed significantly as well.

10.2   Why Might MNCs Have Better Productivity Performance than Other Firms?

Although the aggregate nature of our analysis does not allow for an examination of the specific sources of the MNC productivity advantage, there has recently been a great deal of microlevel research on the link between global engagement and firm productivity. Such work has focused mostly on two main factors—characteristics of the plants and cross-border integration of operations.

In terms of plant characteristics, MNCs tend to be larger than domestic plants, they are more capital intensive, and they use more advanced technology (Doms and Jensen 1998). All else equal, these characteristics tend to be associated with higher labor productivity—in part because of the greater amount of capital per worker and in part because size and technology can enhance the organizational efficiency of a plant.[7] Several

6. "Aggregate" refers to all U.S. nonfarm private businesses.

7. In a similar vein, Bernard and Jensen (1995) document the superior productivity of exporters. Bernard and Jensen (1999) examine whether highly productive firms select into export markets or whether exporting boosts productivity, and find more compelling evidence for the former. Baldwin and Gu (2003), however, find that export participation in Canada *is* associated with improved productivity and argue this is due to a learning effect associated with export activity.

recent general equilibrium models propose that global engagement—either through trade or as an MNC—is a consequence rather than a cause of higher productivity. In these models, heterogeneity in firm productivity is exogenously determined (Melitz 2003; Helpman, Melitz, and Yeaple 2004). As such, only the most highly productive firms can afford the costs of becoming a multinational by establishing a foreign affiliate.

Alternatively, MNCs may be able to enhance their organizational efficiency through their ability to integrate their operations across borders. Indeed, intra-MNC trade by U.S.-owned MNCs has risen steadily over time, accounting for 22 percent of total U.S. exports in 2002, and 16 percent of total imports (Mataloni 2004).[8] Such vertical integration between parents and affiliates allows MNCs to take advantage of international factor price differentials as a means of holding down unit costs of production.[9] In addition, outsourcing to foreign affiliates may also allow the parent to organize overall production processes more efficiently (Hanson, Mataloni, and Slaughter 2001).

Finally, internationalized production by MNCs may serve as a conduit for the transfer of knowledge between parents and affiliates, thereby contributing to higher productivity.[10] For instance, Criscuolo, Haskel, and Slaughter (2005) find that MNCs generate more ideas than their purely domestic counterparts, not only because they use more researchers, but also because they draw on a larger stock of ideas through their "intra-firm worldwide pool of information." More generally, cross-border integration enables firms to spread firm-specific intangible assets (R&D, for example) across geographical boundaries. Blomström, and Ramstetter (1998) make this point.[11] This spreading of intangible assets, input production, and final processing across borders occurs prominently, for example, in industries that manufacture electronic and electrical equipment.

10.3   The Data

Overview

The primary data on U.S. multinational companies come from two surveys conducted by the Bureau of Economic Analysis (BEA). The survey of

8. All trade by U.S.-owned MNCs—that is, trade with unrelated entities as well as with affiliates—as a share of total exports and imports was 58 percent and 37 percent, respectively, in 2002 (Mataloni 2004). Hanson, Mataloni, and Slaughter (2001), Borga and Zeile (2004), and Bernard, Jensen, and Schott (2005) all provide evidence of the increasing use of parent-to-affiliate outsourcing over time.

9. For example, Hanson, Mataloni, and Slaughter (2005) discuss how the growth of overall world trade has been driven in large part by the rapid growth of trade in intermediate inputs by MNCs. Among their main findings are that demand for imported inputs is higher when affiliates face lower trade costs, lower wages for less-skilled labor, and lower corporate income tax rates.

10. Coe, Helpman, and Hoffmaister (1997) make a similar point with regard to the productivity benefits of international trade.

11. See also Grossman and Helpman (1991), Howitt (2000), and Griffith, Redding, and van Reenan (2005).

U.S. Direct Investment Abroad (USDIA) provides information on the operations of U.S.-headquartered multinational companies (parents), while the survey of Foreign Direct Investment in the United States (FDIUS) provides information on operations of foreign companies operating in the United States (affiliates). The surveys contain much data on the domestic activities of parents and affiliates—data such as total sales, gross product (value added), capital spending, R&D spending, compensation of employees, and employment. The BEA tabulates the data by industry of the parent or affiliate. Periodically, BEA also shows the sales and employment of parents (or affiliates) by industry of sales.

One major advantage of the data from these surveys is that they are designed to yield measures aligned with National Income and Product Account (NIPA) concepts. For example, the published figures for the gross product of nonbank parents of U.S. multinational companies are conceptually consistent with the NIPA figures for the gross product, or value added, of all businesses.[12] Because of the conceptual consistency, therefore, these data can be integrated with other relevant productivity data in order to conduct growth accounting exercises.

Creating a Multinational Corporate (MNC) Sector

Corrado and Slifman (1999) highlighted the value of looking at the economy not only by industry but also by sector—for example, corporate and noncorporate, financial and nonfinancial. In particular, they focused their analysis on productivity trends in the *nonfinancial corporate (NFC) sector.* This chapter carries that approach one step further by dividing the nonfinancial corporate sector into two distinct sectors: MNCs and domestically oriented firms. These sectoral data are then disaggregated into key industry sub-divisions. Each survey's results were therefore first adjusted to be conceptually consistent with this general approach. Results for nonbank finance and insurance MNCs were excluded to obtain data on nonfinancial activities, and results for real estate were excluded to approximate results for corporations.[13]

Because we are interested in creating an MNC sector and studying its contribution to overall U.S. productivity growth, the published BEA survey data need further development, and they need to be integrated with broader aggregates to perform growth accounting for the overall U.S. economy. Fortunately, a tool exists to readily carry out the development and integration: the Federal Reserve Board Productivity Data System (Bartelsman and Beaulieu 2003, 2007). This is a system that contains all

12. Indeed, these data are inputs to the NIPAs; see Mataloni 1995.
13. The BEA reported to us that in the USDIA survey for 2000, corporate gross product and compensation was 99 percent of total gross product and virtually all of compensation. For FDIUS, corporations accounted for 91 percent of gross product and 95 percent of total compensation.

the aggregate and industry-level data typically used by productivity researchers, organized within a highly structured database. The system also contains specialized tools to manipulate and analyze the data. After adding the relevant USDIA and FDIUS data issued by BEA to the productivity data system, we used many of its tools to help carry out such tasks as balancing, concording, deflation, and aggregation.[14] The routines in the system also facilitate the calculation of capital stocks and capital services, although we do not create such measures for the MNC sector in this study.

Before the USDIA and FDIUS data could be combined and used for productivity analysis, we had to deal with several important measurement issues. The Appendix describes the methods we used in full. Here we present a brief overview.

Survey Overlap

As we define it, the MNC sector refers to the U.S. activities of multinational corporations operating in the United States. Accordingly, we need to combine data on the activities of parents from the USDIA survey with data on activities of U.S. affiliates from the FDIA survey. In the spirit of the Doms and Jensen results, the combined data from the USDIA and FDIUS surveys provide information on the activities of MNCs in the United States regardless of country of ownership.

However, some firms that are technically U.S. parents are actually under the control of a foreign parent company. Accordingly, some firms in the USDIA data are also captured in the FDIUS survey. The overlap of firms in the two surveys prevents us from simply adding together the results of the two surveys. Because we want to combine the data from both surveys, we need to adjust for the overlap.

The overlap arises because some U.S. affiliates of foreign companies engage in foreign direct investment that is attributed to U.S. affiliates. For survey purposes this makes some U.S. affiliates both a U.S. parent and a U.S. affiliate; accordingly, the company is counted in both the FDIUS survey (as a U.S. affiliate of a foreign company) and in the USDIA survey (as a U.S. parent of a foreign affiliate.) As an example, suppose a Japanese automaker sets up a foreign affiliate in the United States. That U.S. affiliate then sets up a parts-producing subsidiary in Canada that only serves the U.S. affiliate. The Canadian parts-producing facility is considered to be foreign direct investment by a U.S. entity, which, by definition, makes the U.S. affiliate of the Japanese company a U.S. parent of the Canadian affiliate. As a result, the U.S. affiliate will be counted in both surveys: as a U.S. affiliate of a Japanese parent in the FDIUS survey, and as a U.S. parent of a Canadian affiliate in the USDIA survey.

---

14. For example, we used the biproportional balancing tools to help fill in missing observations and the concordance tools to put all the industry estimates on a consistent industry classification basis.

How big is the overlap? As it turns out, a substantial number of foreign affiliates operating in the United States have their own foreign affiliates. According to BEA, when measured in terms of gross product, about 45 percent of the activities of U.S. affiliates during 2000 took place at companies that had their own foreign affiliates. These U.S. parent foreign affiliates, however, represent only a small part of the overall number of U.S. parents. Again using gross product as the metric, the activities of U.S. parent foreign affiliates were only 11 percent of the gross product of all U.S. parents.[15] Moreover, these ratios have been relatively unchanged over time (see Appendix table 10A.3).

In order to adjust for the overlap, we obtained from the BEA special tabulations of the activities of those U.S. parents that are also affiliates of foreign companies and, hence, counted in both surveys. Because of concerns at the BEA regarding the disclosure of information about individual survey respondents, the data on overlap firms are only available for all nonbank industries and all manufacturing industries, and only for 1990 on. However, the BEA also provided us with industry-level information on the number of U.S. parent companies that are also foreign affiliates. As described in the Appendix, we used the information from these special tabulations and the concording and balancing tools of the FRB productivity system to create industry-level overlap data so that U.S. parent-foreign affiliates are only counted once when we combine the results of the two surveys.

Level of Consolidation

Another issue with these data is that they are collected at the overall company level. For many multinational corporations, the company level is a very aggregate level of consolidation by industry. Most industry-level data used for productivity analysis are collected at the establishment (or plant) level. Thus, the activities of a company that produces in more than one industry (say, home appliances and jet engines) will have the activities of its individual plants allocated to the relevant industry. In contrast, data for the MNC surveys are collected for a group of enterprises under common control (referred to as "a consolidated business enterprise"). This can lead to serious problems in classifying the data by industry, because in most tabulations, all of the operations of a given U.S. parent or foreign affiliate are assigned to one primary industry, even if the parent or affiliate has secondary activities in other industries. In order to get around this problem, we constructed our own establishment estimates from the consolidated MNC data. The method is described in detail in the Appendix.

---

15. According to the BEA, "in 2000, U.S. parents that were in turn controlled by foreign parents accounted for 9 percent of the gross product of all U.S. parents." (Mataloni 2002, 117, footnote 8.) The difference between the published number and the 11 percent figure that we cite reflects that, in our calculations, a foreign affiliate is defined as a U.S. business with 10 percent or more foreign ownership, whereas the figure cited by Mataloni is for majority-owned foreign affiliates.

Essentially, however, we use the periodic information provided by BEA on sales and employment of affiliates or parents (as appropriate) by industry of sales. As noted by Zeile (1999, 29), "these data . . . approximate the disaggregation of the data for all U.S. businesses by industry of establishment." We apply the employment/sales shares to the consolidated data to create establishment estimates.

Industry Classification

The BEA's USDIA and FDIUS survey data for recent years use the North American Industry Classification System (NAICS) to group results by industry, whereas data for earlier periods apply various issues of the Standard Industrial Classification (SIC) system. We converted the more recently published NAICS-based data to the SIC system, which (as of the initial writing of this paper) BEA still used for its U.S. industry-level data on gross product and gross product prices.

Deflators

The data in the two MNC surveys are collected in current dollars (except, of course, employment). However, for productivity analysis it is necessary to have data measured in real terms, that is, adjusted to remove the effects of price changes. Mataloni (1997) describes one method for deflating current dollar figures that relies on producer prices indexes (PPIs) by industry. However, PPIs alone are imperfect as deflators for industry gross product; PPIs are appropriate for gross *output,* but a gross *product* price should represent an implicit price for gross output less intermediate inputs. As an alternative, therefore, we used the deflators published by the BEA for gross product originating by industry. Real GDP by industry is computed using the double-deflation method, in which separate estimates of real gross output and intermediate inputs are combined in a Fisher chain-type quantity-index-number formula (Yuskavage 1996). These deflators are for all establishments in an industry, not just those owned by MNCs. By applying these deflators to the data from the MNC surveys, we are assuming that within a given industry establishments owned by MNCs and non-MNCs had the same product composition, input composition, and price behavior over time.

10.4   Method of Analysis

Much of the recent literature on the post-1995 pickup in U.S. productivity growth disaggregates the data into IT-producing and IT-using sectors. This chapter adds a new dimension: specifically, we consider the role of MNCs. As indicated previously, we do this by looking separately at the role of U.S. parents and foreign affiliates. Then, in the spirit of the findings in Doms and Jensen, we combine the data to create a single MNC sector for

Table 10.1   **U.S. gross domestic product of nonfarm private businesses,* by sector (percent of total)**

	1977	1989	1995	2000	2002
Nonfinancial corporations	70.5	68.8	67.7	66.7	65.6
MNC Sector**	25.5	24.2	24.7	28.6	26.2
Parents**	23.5	19.3	19.4	22.1	19.7
Affiliates of foreign companies	2.0	4.9	5.3	6.6	6.5
Domestically oriented	45.0	44.6	43.0	38.1	39.3
Financial corporations	4.6	6.3	7.4	9.0	9.2
Noncorporate business	25.0	24.9	24.9	24.3	25.3

*Calculated using gross domestic income, excludes government enterprises.

**Excludes U.S. parent companies that are also affiliates of foreign companies.

the U.S. economy. As far as we know, this is the first time the data have been combined consistently to create time series for a single MNC sector.

Following the approach of Corrado and Slifman (1999), we disaggregate the overall U.S. economy into an economically meaningful group of sectors and subsectors. We do this to examine the contribution of individual sectors to overall productivity growth. The ratios of each sector's gross product to the gross product of all U.S. nonfarm private businesses—the sector's contribution to the total (unduplicated) value of production by business—help unravel the role of each sector in the productivity decomposition. As may be seen in table 10.1, we estimate that the MNC sector accounts for about 25 percent of U.S. nonfarm private business (NFPB) gross product (or value added). Although the MNC share fell off a bit in the early 1990s, it subsequently rebounded and, all told, has been relatively stable for the period shown.

The relative stability in the MNC share masks important developments within both the MNC and corporate sectors, however. As may be seen, the value added by financial corporations has been rising steadily over the period, whereas the share of overall value added accounted for by nonfinancial corporations has fallen off. The drop is in the domestically oriented share: it was 45 percent in 1977 but was under 40 percent by 2002, with much of the drop occurring after 1995. Within the MNC sector, the share of value added accounted for by U.S. parents has declined, while the share attributed to foreign affiliates increased from 2 percent in 1977 to 6.5 percent in 2002. All told, the MNC sector currently is about 40 percent of the nonfinancial corporate sector.

Table 10.2 looks deeper within the nonfinancial corporate and MNC sectors. As may be seen, 43 percent of MNC gross product in 2000 originated in manufacturing. This is nearly 20 percentage points below the share observed in 1977, with the decline being offset by rising MNC concentration in services industries and in wholesale and retail trade. While the proportion of output originating in manufacturing is roughly equiva-

Table 10.2   Nonfinancial corporate gross product by industry* (percent of total)

	MNCs			Domestically oriented	Total
	Parents	Foreign affiliation	Total		
2000	100.0	100.0	100.0	100.0	100.0
Manufacturing	42.5	44.9	43.0	15.5	19.2
High tech	5.7	3.1	5.1	0.6	1.7
Manufacturing, except high tech	36.8	41.7	38.0	14.9	17.5
Nonmanufacturing	57.5	55.1	57.0	84.5	80.8
Wholesale and retail trade	13.6	24.5	16.1	34.4	20.0
Services	15.9	13.3	15.3	26.9	21.4
Transp., commun., and util.	18.9	9.5	16.8	10.1	10.2
Other	9.1	7.8	8.8	13.1	29.3
1995	100.0	100.0	100.0	100.0	100.0
Manufacturing	49.9	49.8	49.8	20.9	22.2
High tech	5.4	3.8	5.0	1.7	2.0
Manufacturing, except high tech	44.5	46.0	44.8	19.2	20.2
Nonmanufacturing	50.1	50.2	50.2	79.1	77.8
Wholesale and retail trade	11.4	22.5	13.8	32.5	19.8
Services	12.0	9.2	11.4	23.8	19.6
Transp., commun., and util.	19.8	8.7	17.4	12.3	11.0
Other	7.0	9.8	7.6	10.6	27.4
1989	100.0	100.0	100.0	100.0	100.0
Manufacturing	53.7	52.4	53.5	22.6	23.8
High tech	5.9	4.2	5.6	1.3	1.9
Manufacturing, except high tech	47.8	48.2	47.9	21.3	21.8
Nonmanufacturing	46.3	47.6	46.5	77.4	76.2
Wholesale and retail trade	9.5	21.8	12.0	32.4	20.0
Services	9.5	7.3	9.0	19.8	17.9
Transp., commun., and util.	19.5	4.8	16.5	12.9	10.9
Other	7.8	13.7	9.0	12.3	27.4
1977	100.0	100.0	100.0	100.0	100.0
Manufacturing	61.1	59.6	61.0	28.5	29.1
High tech	3.4	5.5	3.5	0.9	1.3
Manufacturing, except high tech	57.7	54.1	57.5	27.6	27.8
Nonmanufacturing	38.9	40.4	39.0	71.5	70.9
Wholesale and retail trade	10.4	26.3	11.6	31.0	21.0
Services	4.4	2.6	4.3	12.7	12.3
Transp., commun., and util.	15.7	3.7	14.8	14.4	11.3
Other	8.3	7.9	8.3	13.4	26.3

*Excludes corporate farms

lent for U.S. parents and affiliates of foreign companies, it appears that U.S. parents maintain a somewhat larger presence in IT equipment. In non-manufacturing, however, a larger proportion of the output of foreign affiliates is concentrated in wholesale and retail trade, while the proportion of output originating in the transportation, communications, and public utilities group is larger for U.S. parents.

10.5   Results for Labor Productivity

Our results for the sectoral decomposition of labor productivity are shown in tables 10.3 through 10.6. Labor productivity estimates were calculated as follows. In each year, sectoral labor productivity levels (LP_i) were defined as real value added (Y_i) per total hours worked of all persons (H_i): $LP_i = Y_i/H_i$. Aggregate labor productivity growth can therefore be decomposed as follows:

$$d \ln LP = \underbrace{\sum_i \overline{w}_i d \ln LP_i}_{\text{direct contributions}} + \underbrace{\left(\sum_i \overline{w}_i d \ln H_i - d \ln H \right)}_{\text{reallocation of hours}}$$

where $\overline{w}_i$ is the two-period average of each industry's share of nominal gross product. The first term on the right hand side measures the direct contributions to aggregate labor productivity, that is, the share weighted sum of the labor productivity growth rates for individual industries and sectors. The second term on the right-hand side captures an indirect contribution owing to the reallocation of hours across sectors. This contribution is positive when, on balance, the change in hours is positive for sectors where gross product shares exceed hours shares (Stiroh 2002).

As may be seen in table 10.3, the rate of change in NFPB output per hour averaged 1.5 percent per year from 1977 to 2000 in the United States.[16] We estimate that the growth of output per hour in the MNC sector averaged 3.2 percent per year during the same period, or more than twice the NFPB average. As indicated in table 10.4, the MNC sector accounted for more than half of the overall gain in labor productivity.

The sectoral decomposition by subperiod also reveals interesting developments: From 1977 to 1989 and, to a lesser extent, from 1989 to 1995, gains in MNC sector productivity accounted for a goodly portion of the overall increase in output per hour. The pickup in productivity in the late 1990s, however, was generally widespread across the individual sectors shown. Even so, according to our sectoral hierarchy, and as can be seen by comparing the two right-hand columns, the MNC sector contributed significantly (about .75 percentage point) to the 1.2 percentage point pickup in NFPB output per hour during the late 1990s.

Because output per hour varies by industry, part of the MNC productivity story in the late 1990s could be explained by differences between the industry mix of the MNC sector compared with that of all nonfinancial corporations or total nonfarm businesses. As is well known, the production of IT equipment was a major source of the rapid gains in U.S. productivity in the late 1990s (see Jorgensen and Stiroh 2000, Oliner and Sichel

---

16. This figure differs slightly from the official figures for U.S. labor productivity issued by the BLS in that our measure is derived from the income side of the national accounts while the BLS measure is derived from the product side. In addition, our measure excludes the output of government enterprises.

Table 10.3   Growth of labor productivity—nonfarm private businesses, by sector (percent change, average annual rate)

	1977–1989	1989–1995	1995–2000
Nonfarm private business	0.9	1.6	2.8
Nonfinancial corporations	1.2	1.6	2.6
MNCs	2.5	2.7	5.6
Parents	2.8	2.8	6.0
Affiliates of foreign companies	0.6	2.4	4.5
Domestically oriented	0.6	1.0	0.5
Financial corporations	–0.0	0.3	0.4
Nonfarm noncorporate businesses	0.1	0.4	0.7

Note: Nonfarm private business output is calculated using gross domestic income.

Table 10.4   Contributions to the growth of labor productivity—nonfarm private businesses, by sector (percentage points, annual rate)

	1977–1989	1989–1995	1995–2000
Nonfarm private business	0.9	1.6	2.8
Nonfinancial corporations	0.9	1.1	1.8
MNCs	0.6	0.7	1.5
Parents	0.6	0.5	1.2
Affiliates of foreign companies	–0.0	0.1	0.3
Domestically oriented	0.3	0.4	0.2
Financial corporations	–0.0	0.3	0.4
Nonfarm noncorporate businesses	0.1	0.4	0.7
Memo: Reallocation of Hours	0.0	0.0	–0.1

Note: Nonfarm private business output is calculated using gross domestic income.

2000, among others), and the IT equipment-producing sector has a relatively large MNC share.

Tables 10.5 and 10.6 present a broad industry cut of the productivity results for nonfinancial corporations. As may be seen, this decomposition is consistent with the extraordinary productivity change in the production of IT equipment accounting for part of the story for the pickup in MNC and nonfinancial corporate labor productivity in the late 1990s. The decomposition also shows, however, that the pickup in MNC productivity was based more broadly in other manufacturing and nonmanufacturing industries. Meanwhile, the aggregate domestically oriented sector did not contribute to the pickup in nonfinancial corporate labor productivity in the late 1990s, a result driven mainly by the poor performance of its manufacturing component.[17] Moreover, while there is some evidence that reallocation of hours contributed to the pickup, its contribution is nevertheless quite small.

17. As shown in table 10.2, domestically oriented manufacturers have a very small IT share, and the IT versus non-IT decomposition of this sector is not shown.

Table 10.5   **Growth of labor productivity—Nonfinancial corporations, by subsector and industry (percentage change, average annual rate)**

	1977–2000	1977–1989	1989–1995	1995–2000
Nonfinancial corporations	1.6	1.2	1.6	2.6
MNCs	3.2	2.5	2.7	5.6
Manufacturing	4.1	3.3	2.5	7.8
IT equipment	25.0	20.0	19.5	45.3
Other manufacturing	2.0	1.8	0.8	3.9
Nonmanufacturing	2.3	1.4	2.9	3.6
Domestically oriented	0.7	0.6	1.0	0.5
Manufacturing	1.0	1.6	2.6	-2.3
Nonmanufacturing	0.3	0.0	0.5	1.1

Table 10.6   **Contributions to the growth of labor productivity—Nonfinancial corporations, by subsector and industry (percentage points, annual rate)**

	1977–2000	1977–1989	1989–1995	1995–2000
Nonfinancial corporations	1.6	1.2	1.6	2.6
MNCs	1.3	0.9	1.0	2.2
Manufacturing	0.8	0.7	0.5	1.4
IT equipment	0.4	0.3	0.4	0.9
Other manufacturing	0.4	0.3	0.1	0.6
Nonmanufacturing	0.4	0.2	0.5	0.8
Domestically oriented	0.4	0.4	0.6	0.3
Manufacturing	0.1	0.3	0.4	-0.3
Nonmanufacturing	0.2	0.0	0.2	0.5
Memo: Reallocation of hours	0.1	0.1	0.0	0.2

Of course, some of the MNC contribution to the productivity pickup could be due to the reallocation of value added among MNC components rather than a faster rate of productivity growth for the underlying MNC subsectors and industries. As shown in table 10.1 and table 10.2, the MNC share of nonfinancial corporate value added rose during the late 1990s owing to the ongoing expansion of MNCs into nonmanufacturing industries. Table 10.7 shows a standard decomposition of the pickup in nonfinancial corporate labor productivity during this period into "within" and "between" effects. The within effect measures how much of the pickup in labor productivity growth can be attributed to faster productivity growth for individual sectors when their weights are held fixed at the average for the two periods, while the between effect measures how much of the pickup can be attributed to rising weights for sectors with above-average labor productivity growth in both periods.[18]

18. Specifically, the within effect is calculated as $\sum_i 0.5 * (\overline{w}_{i,1989-1995} + \overline{w}_{i,1995-2000}) * (d \ln LP_{i,1995-2000} - d \ln LP_{i,1989-1995})$ and the between effect as $\sum_i 0.5 * (d \ln LP_{i,1995-2000} + d \ln LP_{i,1989-1995}) * (\overline{w}_{i,1989-1995} - \overline{w}_{i,1995-2000})$.

Table 10.7   Decomposition of the acceleration of labor productivity growth—
Nonfinancial corporations, by sector and industry (percentage points,
annual rate)

	Acceleration	Within effect	Between effect
Nonfinancial corporations	1.05	1.05	0.00
MNCs	1.26	1.10	0.16
Manufacturing	0.96	0.97	−0.01
IT equipment	0.54	0.50	0.04
Other mfg.	0.50	0.50	−0.01
Nonmanufacturing	0.28	0.15	0.13
Domestically oriented	−0.30	−0.27	−0.03
Manufacturing	−0.61	−0.60	0.00
Nonmanufacturing	0.29	0.30	−0.01

As may be seen, about half of the contribution of nonmanufacturing MNCs to the productivity acceleration in the late 1990s can be attributed to their rising weight (the between effect).[19] The absolute size of this effect, however, is quite small, and suggests that the reallocation of value added is not a big part of the MNC productivity story.

To summarize, between 1977 and 2000, labor productivity growth in the MNC sector consistently outpaced that of the nonfinancial corporate sector as a whole, with the gap widening noticeably during the second half of the 1990s. A final question, therefore, is whether the pickup in MNC productivity growth has continued more recently. Unfortunately, at this stage it is not possible to know for sure. Although more recent, consistent data for both U.S. parents and foreign affiliates are available through 2005, methodologically consistent industry-level estimates only extend through 2001.[20] As such, only "back-of-the-envelope" estimates can currently be made based on an extrapolation of the output and hours series for major sectors (i.e., nonfinancial corporations and nonfarm business) using published estimates from the BEA and BLS and making an assumption about the survey overlap and growth rate of deflators.[21]

With this caveat in mind, the results in tables 10.8 and 10.9 suggest that MNCs were disproportionately affected by the onset of the 2001 recession. Indeed, we estimate that output per hour in the MNC sector fell at an an-

19. Also note that, although the average rate of labor productivity growth for nonmanufacturing MNCs was below that of manufacturing MNCs, it still exceeded the average rate for the nonfinancial corporate sector as a whole.

20. The FRB productivity database that we use was built from the BEA's previous system of GDP-by-industry data, which extends only through 2001 and is not methodologically consistent with BEA's more recently released measures; see Moyer et al. (2004).

21. Specifically, the back-of-the-envelope estimates derive real value added for our consolidated MNC sector by holding the overlap share constant from 2002 on and extrapolating changes in the price deflator for MNC gross product and major subcomponents by BEA's deflator for all nonfinancial corporations. Substituting reasonable, alternative assumptions does not materially alter the resulting back-of-the-envelope estimates.

Table 10.8   **Growth of labor productivity—Nonfinancial corporations, by subsector (percentage change, average annual rate)**

	2000–2005	2000–2002	2002–2005
Nonfinancial corporations	3.0	3.0	2.9
MNCs	2.9	–1.5	6.0
Parents	2.1	–3.6	6.0
Affiliates	5.9	5.9	6.0

Note: These MNC figures are not integrated with those for nonfinancial corporations at the industry level, as are figures for prior years shown in previous tables.

Table 10.9   **Contributions to the growth of labor productivity—Nonfinancial corporations, by subsector (percentage points, annual rate)**

	2000–2005	2000–2002	2002–2005
Nonfinancial corporations	3.0	3.0	2.9
MNCs	1.2	–0.8	2.5
Parents	1.0	–0.5	1.9
Affiliates	0.2	–0.3	0.6

Note: These MNC figures are not integrated with those for nonfinancial corporations at the industry level, as are the figures for prior years shown in previous tables.

nual rate of 1.5 percent between 2000 and 2002, even while productivity for the nonfinancial corporate sector as a whole continued to rise briskly. Interestingly, the weakness in the MNC sector appears to have been driven entirely by U.S. parents. Indeed, labor productivity growth for foreign affiliates accelerated further between 2000 and 2002. The productivity declines for U.S. parents have proved temporary, however, and probably reflected particular circumstances in a number of industries where U.S. parents have a significant presence. This includes the cyclically sensitive durable goods manufacturing industries—such as motor vehicles and high-tech—as well as telecommunications services. In contrast, the activities of foreign affiliates are more highly concentrated in less cyclical industries, such as retail and wholesale trade. In summary, the extended back of the envelope results do not change our findings for 1977 to 2000—namely, that multinational corporations have made outsized contributions to the growth of aggregate labor productivity in the United States.

10.6   Conclusions

In this chapter we have begun to investigate the role played by the U.S. operations of multinational corporations in the overall performance of the U.S. economy, especially in the late 1990s. We identify these corporations as a separate segment of the economy—we call it the MNC sector—and we develop labor productivity estimates for this sector.

While progress has been made regarding the contribution of MNCs to aggregate trade flows and employment growth, much less is known about the significance of MNCs for overall productivity growth. This omission from the literature seems particularly glaring when one considers the substantial body of microlevel research on the link between global engagement and productivity at the firm level. We therefore hope that the results in this chapter will complement this microlevel work by placing the superior performance of MNCs into a broader perspective.

Using the tools and procedures in the FRB productivity data system, the new productivity estimates were developed by integrating information from BEA's surveys of multinational operations with conventional productivity data in a consistent fashion. The resulting data set permits the decomposition of labor productivity along MNC/non-MNC, legal form of organization, and major industry lines for the period 1977 to 2000. The results clearly slice the U.S. aggregate productivity data in a novel way and, we hope, confirm the utility of our approach.

The results, which were foreshadowed by the Doms and Jensen findings, confirmed the important role played by multinational corporations in the *aggregate* productivity record of the U.S. economy. The sector (as we define it) accounts for more than 25 percent of the gross product of all nonfarm private businesses and about 40 percent of nonfinancial corporate gross product. Nonetheless, the sector accounted for more than *half* of the increase for all nonfarm private businesses and *all* of the increase in the labor productivity of nonfinancial corporations in the late 1990s.

Of course, our estimates may be sensitive to some of the assumptions we were forced to make when constructing our integrated data set. For example, by applying the industry-level deflators published by the BEA to both MNCs and domestically oriented firms, we are implicitly assuming that, within a given industry, establishments owned by MNCs and non-MNCs had the same product composition, input composition, and price behavior over time. If, instead, value-added deflators actually rose less rapidly for MNCs, then clearly our estimate of real output growth for MNCs would be too low, meaning their contribution to productivity growth could be even larger. Given the literature on the organizational efficiencies afforded by the integration of MNC operations across borders, such a scenario certainly seems plausible.

Another issue that merits further investigation is the extent to which transfer pricing may influence BEA's measures of value added and thereby the interpretation of our results.[22] Transfer pricing is not supposed to dis-

---

22. Because profits data are used in the construction of value added, any tendency for foreign-owned affiliates to underreport profits by shifting them out of the United States via transfer pricing will lower our estimate of the contribution of MNCs to productivity growth. By the same logic, if U.S. parents use transfer pricing to shift profits from abroad back to the United States, then our productivity results for MNCs will be overstated.

tort official statistics because tax regulations generally require that intrafirm transactions be valued at arms-length prices. Nevertheless, intercountry differences in tax rates almost certainly create incentives to deviate from this standard. Moreover, intra-MNC trade in intermediates accelerated in the second half of the 1990s, suggesting the possibility of at least some role for distortions due to transfer pricing. However, Mataloni (2000) finds little evidence that transfer pricing has unduly impacted BEA's industry-level profits data for MNCs.[23] Although Mataloni's results are not dispositive on the issue, we do not think that our results are being *systematically* biased by transfer pricing.[24]

In sum, our work establishes new stylized facts about the contribution of multinational corporations to the growth of aggregate labor productivity. Previous research finds that the cross-border integration of business operations and certain MNC characteristics—namely, organizational efficiencies in inputs and large investments in firm-specific intangible assets such as R&D—confer a productivity advantage to MNCs at the firm level. By establishing the quantitative significance of this finding in a broader context (the growth of output per hour in the overall economy), we underscore the importance of the operations of multinational corporations—for example, their growing role in trade in services—in the overall economic performance of the United States.

Data Appendix

Overview and Data Sources

As described in the text, the data on U.S. multinationals come from two surveys conducted annually by the Bureau of Economic Analysis (BEA). The survey of U.S. Direct Investment Abroad (USDIA) provides information on the operations of U.S.-headquartered multinationals (parents), while the survey of Foreign Direct Investment in the United States (FDIUS) provides information on the operations of U.S.-based affiliates of foreign-owned multinationals (affiliates). Throughout our analysis, a foreign affiliate is defined as a U.S. business with 10 percent or more foreign

23. Mataloni (2000) considers the relationship between the share of sales accounted for by intra-MNC imports and the gap between the rate of return on assets of foreign-owned nonfinancial companies and that of U.S.-owned companies, under the logic that that the greatest opportunities to shift profits using transfer prices exists for foreign-owned affiliates, with a larger share of sales accounted for by intra-firm imports.

24. Even at the more-detailed company level, Mataloni (2000) finds only limited results. A recent study that looks at microdata for *exports alone* finds significant differences between prices for arms-length versus related-party sales (Bernard, Jensen, and Schott 2006), but we have no way of determining the overall impact of this finding on BEA's measures of *profits and value added* for MNCs.

ownership. Information on majority-owned foreign affiliates is also available in more recent BEA publications but does not appear in the earlier surveys. See Mataloni (2002) and Zeile (1999) for detailed descriptions of the methodologies for the two surveys.

We used the following variables in our analysis: gross product (value added), employment, compensation, and sales. Hours worked by employees are not measured in either survey and had to be estimated (see section on establishment-level estimates for U.S. parents and foreign affiliates, following). Table 10A.1 presents the source for each of these variables in each survey and in each year. As shown in the table, while most of these data can be downloaded directly from the BEA website, several older series are only available as tables in selected BEA publications; a subset of these are only available in paper format and therefore had to be scanned into the FRB Productivity Data System.

Our analysis was performed for the period of 1977 to 2000. An annual time series is available for 1994 to 2000. Prior to this, the variables of interest are only available for both surveys in 1977, 1982, and 1989. Although data now exist for both surveys through 2004, the Bartelsman and Beaulieu database with which we integrate the MNC surveys ends in 2001.[25] Because 2001 is a recession year, we chose not to include it in our analysis.

Industrial Classification and Concordances

The industrial classification of both surveys varies over time, complicating efforts to combine them into a consistent time series. For example, the FDIUS survey switched away from the 1987 Standard Industrial Classification system (SIC87) to the 1997 North American Industry Classification System (NAICS) beginning with its 1997 Benchmark Survey. The USDIA survey transitioned to NAICS in its 1999 Benchmark Survey. In addition, the level of industry detail varies over time, across variables, and across surveys.

Because of these classification issues, considerable effort was spent concording the data to a level of detail common to both surveys in all years under consideration. The standard that we ultimately chose is based on the BEA's SIC87-based Gross Product Originating (GPO) industry data. These data also formed the basis of the work by Bartelsman and Beaulieu. In that work, the authors broke out computers (SIC 357), communications equipment (SIC 366), and semiconductors (SIC 367) from Industrial Machinery and Equipment (SIC 35) and Electronic and Other Electric Equipment (SIC 36) in order to permit an improved focus on the high-tech sector. We adopted the resulting industrial hierarchy, which they called the "GPO87HT" hierarchy, and which is shown in table 10A.2. The sixty-four industries in the first column are the "atoms," or finest level of detail,

25. The Bartelsman and Beaulieu database (2007) is consistent with the 2002 Annual Revision to the National Income and Product Accounts.

Table 10A.1   Data sources and industrial classification

Variable	Year	Source for U.S. parents (USDIA Survey)	Source for foreign affiliates (FDIUS Survey)
Gross product	1977, 1982, 1989	Survey of Current Business, Feb. 1994	Survey of Current Business, June 1990
	1994–2000	BEA website	BEA website
Employment	1977	U.S. Direct Investment Abroad, 1977	BEA website
	1982	U.S. Direct Investment Abroad: 1982 Benchmark Survey	BEA website
	1989, 1994–2000	BEA website	BEA website
Sales	1977	U.S. Direct Investment Abroad, 1977	BEA website
	1982	U.S. Direct Investment Abroad: 1982 Benchmark Survey	BEA website
	1989, 1994–2000	BEA website	BEA website
Compensation	1977	U.S. Direct Investment Abroad, 1977	BEA website
	1982	U.S. Direct Investment Abroad: 1982 Benchmark Survey	BEA website
	1989, 1994–2000	BEA website	BEA website
Sales and employment by industry of sales	1980	None	BEA website
	1982	U.S. Direct Investment Abroad: 1982 Benchmark Survey	none
	1989	U.S. Direct Investment Abroad: 1989 Benchmark Survey	BEA website
	1992	None	BEA website
	1993	None	BEA website
	1994	U.S. Direct Investment Abroad: 1994 Benchmark Survey	BEA website
	1995	None	BEA website
	1996	None	BEA website
	1997	None	BEA website
	1998	None	BEA website
	1999	U.S. Direct Investment Abroad: 1999 Benchmark Survey	BEA website
	2000	None	BEA website

Table 10A.2   The "GPO87HT" industrial hierarchy for the nonfarm private business (NFPB) sector

Level 1 Code and description		Level 2	Level 3	Level 4	Level 5
E10	Metal mining	**Mining**	xxx	Non-Mfg.	NFPB
E12	Coal mining	**Mining**	xxx	Non-Mfg.	NFPB
E13	Oil and gas extraction	**Mining**	xxx	Non-Mfg.	NFPB
E14	Nonmetallic minerals, except fuels	**Mining**	xxx	Non-Mfg.	NFPB
E24	Lumber and wood products	**Lumber, wood and furniture**	Mfg. excl. High Tech	Mfg.	NFPB
E25	Furniture and fixtures	**Lumber, wood and furniture**	Mfg. excl. High Tech	Mfg.	NFPB
E32	**Stone, clay, and glass products**	xxx	Mfg. excl. High Tech	Mfg.	NFPB
E33	**Primary metal industries**	xxx	Mfg. excl. High Tech	Mfg.	NFPB
E34	**Fabricated metal products**	xxx	Mfg. excl. High Tech	Mfg.	NFPB
E35X	**Other machinery**	xxx	Mfg. excl. High Tech	Mfg.	NFPB
E36X	**Other electrical machinery**	xxx	Mfg. excl. High Tech	Mfg.	NFPB
E371	**Motor vehicles and equipment**	xxx	Mfg. excl. High Tech	Mfg.	NFPB
E372T9	**Other transportation equipment**	xxx	Mfg. excl. High Tech	Mfg.	NFPB
E38	**Instruments and related products**	xxx	Mfg. excl. High Tech	Mfg.	NFPB
E39	**Miscellaneous manufacturing industries**	xxx	Mfg. excl. High Tech	Mfg.	NFPB
E20	**Food and kindred products**	xxx	Mfg. excl. High Tech	Mfg.	NFPB
E21	**Tobacco products**	xxx	Mfg. excl. High Tech	Mfg.	NFPB
E22	Textile mill products	**Textile and apparel**	Mfg. excl. High Tech	Mfg.	NFPB
E23	Apparel and other textile products	**Textile and apparel**	Mfg. excl. High Tech	Mfg.	NFPB
E26	**Paper and allied products**	xxx	Mfg. excl. High Tech	Mfg.	NFPB
E27	**Printing and publishing**	xxx	Mfg. excl. High Tech	Mfg.	NFPB
E28	**Chemicals and allied products**	xxx	Mfg. excl. High Tech	Mfg.	NFPB
E29	**Petroleum and coal products**	xxx	Mfg. excl. High Tech	Mfg.	NFPB
E30	Rubber and miscellaneous plastics products	**Rubber and leather**	Mfg. excl. High Tech	Mfg.	NFPB
E31	Leather and leather products	**Rubber and leather**	Mfg. excl. High Tech	Mfg.	NFPB
E15T7	**Construction**	xxx	xxx	Non-Mfg.	NFPB
E49	Electric, gas, and sanitary services	**Transportation and communications**	xxx	Non-Mfg.	NFPB
E40	Railroad transportation	**Transportation and communications**	xxx	Non-Mfg.	NFPB
E41	Local and interurban passenger transit	**Transportation and communications**	xxx	Non-Mfg.	NFPB
E42	Trucking and warehousing	**Transportation and communications**	xxx	Non-Mfg.	NFPB
E44	Water transportation	**Transportation and communications**	xxx	Non-Mfg.	NFPB

Code	Description	Category	Sector	Type	
E45	Transportation by air	**Transportation and communications**	xxx	Non-Mfg.	NFPB
E46	Pipelines, except natural gas	**Transportation and communications**	xxx	Non-Mfg.	NFPB
E47	Transportation services	**Transportation and communications**	xxx	Non-Mfg.	NFPB
E481A2A9	Telephone and telegraph	**Transportation and communications**	xxx	Non-Mfg.	NFPB
E483A4	Radio and television	**Transportation and communications**	xxx	Non-Mfg.	NFPB
E50A1	**Wholesale trade**	xxx	Trade	Non-Mfg.	NFPB
E52T9	**Retail trade**	xxx	Trade	Non-Mfg.	NFPB
E60	Depository institutions	**Finance**	FIRE	Non-Mfg.	NFPB
E61	Nondepository institutions	**Finance**	FIRE	Non-Mfg.	NFPB
E62	Security and commodity brokers	**Finance**	FIRE	Non-Mfg.	NFPB
E63	**Insurance carriers**	xxx	FIRE	Non-Mfg.	NFPB
E64	Insurance agents, brokers, and service	xxx	FIRE	Non-Mfg.	NFPB
E65hs	Nonfarm housing services	**Real estate**	FIRE	Non-Mfg.	NFPB
E65re	Other real estate	**Real estate**	FIRE	Non-Mfg.	NFPB
E67	**Holding and other investment offices**	xxx	FIRE	Non-Mfg.	NFPB
E70	Hotels and other lodging places	**Services**	xxx	Non-Mfg.	NFPB
E72	Personal services	**Services**	xxx	Non-Mfg.	NFPB
E73	Other business services	**Services**	xxx	Non-Mfg.	NFPB
E75	Auto repair, services, and parking	**Services**	xxx	Non-Mfg.	NFPB
E76	Miscellaneous repair services	**Services**	xxx	Non-Mfg.	NFPB
E78	Motion pictures	**Services**	xxx	Non-Mfg.	NFPB
E79	Amusement and recreation services	**Services**	xxx	Non-Mfg.	NFPB
E80	Health services	**Services**	xxx	Non-Mfg.	NFPB
E81	Legal services	**Services**	xxx	Non-Mfg.	NFPB
E82	Educational services	**Services**	xxx	Non-Mfg.	NFPB
E83	Social services	**Services**	xxx	Non-Mfg.	NFPB
E86	Membership organizations	**Services**	xxx	Non-Mfg.	NFPB
E84A7A9	Other services	**Services**	xxx	Non-Mfg.	NFPB
E357	**Computers and related equipment**	High Technology	xxx	Mfg.	NFPB
E366	**Communications equipment**	High Technology	xxx	Mfg.	NFPB
E367	**Semiconductors**	High Technology	xxx	Mfg.	NFPB
E91b	Federal government enterprises	Govt. enterprises	xxx	Non-Mfg.	NFPB
E92b	State and local government enterprises	Govt. enterprises	xxx	Non-Mfg.	NFPB

Note. Bold industries represent the finest level of detail available in our final MNC database.

available in the GPO87HT hierarchy. The tools of the FRB Productivity Data System permit values associated with these atoms (for instance, gross product or employment) to be aggregated to higher level subaggregates (columns 2 through 5) as well as the total for the entire nonfarm private business sector (column 6).

Using the tools of the FRB Productivity Data System, we created numerous industrial hierarchies, called "metadata," to analyze the MNC surveys and ultimately concord all variables of interest to industries contained within the GPO87HT hierarchy. Often this was accomplished by first concording variables to an intermediate industrial hierarchy common to a subset of years or surveys.[26]

Unfortunately, while the level of detail we created for the manufacturing sector is typically at the two-digit level, we could not carve out a correspondingly fine level of detail for the services, mining, or transportation and communications industries. As such, the atom-level industries in our final MNC database do not always correspond to those in the GPO87HT hierarchy. Rather, the twenty-nine shaded industries in table 10A.2 denote the MNC-level atoms that ultimately fed into our analysis.

Sectoral Classification

Corrado and Slifman (1999) highlighted the importance of studying productivity not only by industry but also by legal form of organization, specifically along noncorporate, nonfinancial corporate, and financial corporate lines. Bartelsman and Beaulieu (2007) adopted this sectoral approach as well but implemented it for each industry in the GPO data. In this chapter, we make the additional step of breaking out the nonfinancial corporate sector into two distinct parts: an MNC sector and a domestically oriented sector. The MNCs are further divided into parents and foreign affiliates. Figure 10A.1 shows the sectoral hierarchy that we developed for each industry in the nonfarm private business sector:

Data on nonbank finance and insurance companies were excluded from our MNC database so that we could focus on the nonfinancial activities of multinationals. The real estate industry was also excluded in order to focus more directly on multinational corporations. The number of noncorporate multinationals is small but concentrated in this industry.

Constructing a Database for U.S. Parents

As noted in the text, the 1999 and 2000 USDIA surveys are classified on a NAICS97 basis, meaning it was necessary to concord these data to an SIC87 basis in order to make them time-series compatible with the older surveys. Before doing this, however, a few additional steps were necessary.

---

26. The complete metadata for any of these hierarchies and concordances are available upon request.

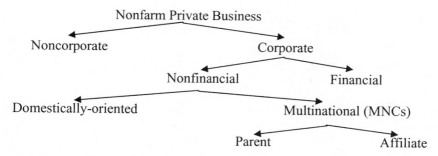

Fig. 10A.1   Sectoral hierarchy

First, beginning with the release of the revised 1999 survey, BEA began including U.S. parents with very small affiliates abroad, that is, affiliates with assets, sales, and net income less than $7 million (Mataloni 2002). These new parents represented 3.8 percent of gross product, 6.1 percent of the employment, and 2.7 percent of the capital expenditures in 1999. We rescaled the industry level data in 1999 to remove the published aggregate contribution of small parents. These level-adjusted values were then extrapolated forward to 2000 based on the growth rate of the unadjusted (i.e., officially published) estimates. In doing this, we implicitly assumed that small parents grew at the same rate as the larger parents.

Second, we corrected an apparent reclassification of an unnamed firm (or firms) from the computers and peripheral equipment manufacturing industry (N334) to the computer systems design and related services industry (N5415). Recall that the BEA assigns all of the operations of a U.S. parent to a primary industry based on a breakdown of the parent's sales. It appears that the primary industry designation of a large company (or several companies) with sales in both N334 and N5415 changed between the initial release for 1999 and when the 1999 data were revised as part of the 2000 release.[27]

Finally, we addressed the overlap issue. As noted in the text, the BEA provided us with special tabulations for 1990 to 2002 of the activities of those U.S. parents that are also affiliates of foreign companies and thus counted in both surveys. Because of concerns about the disclosure of information about individual survey respondents, these tabulations were made at a highly aggregate level, specifically all nonbank industries, manufacturing, and non-manufacturing.

Table 10A.3 presents these tabulations expressed as a percentage of the published values for the USDIA survey. For example, in 2000 the activities

---

27. Specifically, we averaged the absolute difference for each series between the original and revised 1999 values, subtracted this from computer systems, and added it to computers. For 2000, we followed the same procedure, using the 1999 shares to apply to the 2000 values.

Table 10A.3   U.S. parent companies also affiliates of foreign companies (percent of USDIA survey values)

	Sales	Capital expenditures	R&D expenditures	Gross product	Employee compensation	Employment
			All industries			
1990	13.0	15.8	12.8	n.a.	10.4	9.9
1991	12.9	14.1	11.3	n.a.	10.6	10.2
1992	13.0	14.4	11.5	n.a.	10.7	9.9
1993	12.7	13.7	11.7	n.a.	10.2	9.1
1994	13.8	12.9	10.7	10.3	10.6	9.1
1995	13.3	12.7	9.9	10.0	10.2	9.1
1996	13.6	13.3	9.8	10.2	10.4	9.1
1997	13.5	13.0	10.1	10.3	10.5	8.9
1998	14.7	17.3	11.8	10.9	11.6	9.8
1999	14.8	18.5	13.9	10.8	11.8	9.8
2000	15.4	17.1	14.8	11.3	13.3	10.6
			Manufacturing			
1990	17.1	24.3	13.9	n.a.	13.5	13.4
1991	16.9	21.1	n.a.	n.a.	13.6	13.6
1992	16.4	19.5	n.a.	n.a.	13.5	13.4
1993	15.8	17.2	12.4	n.a.	13.1	12.3
1994	15.9	16.2	11.5	13.7	13.0	12.3
1995	14.7	14.8	10.5	12.8	12.1	11.5
1996	15.4	14.5	9.7	12.6	11.8	11.4
1997	15.1	15.8	10.2	13.0	12.1	11.9
1998	17.9	26.2	12.2	15.1	14.7	13.8
1999	18.4	26.0	15.1	14.4	14.9	14.4
2000	16.8	18.2	16.2	12.1	15.3	14.5
			Nonmanufacturing			
1990	9.1	9.1	5.9	n.a.	6.0	6.0
1991	9.3	8.8	n.a.	n.a.	6.5	6.4
1992	9.7	10.7	n.a.	n.a.	6.7	6.0
1993	9.7	11.0	6.0	n.a.	6.4	5.6
1994	12.0	10.4	6.0	6.5	7.5	6.0
1995	12.1	10.9	5.4	6.9	7.8	6.7
1996	11.9	12.4	10.1	7.6	8.6	7.0
1997	12.2	11.3	8.8	7.7	8.6	6.6
1998	12.0	11.4	8.6	6.9	8.4	6.7
1999	11.8	13.1	7.8	7.4	9.0	6.8
2000	14.2	16.3	9.0	10.5	11.4	8.0

Note: n.a. = not applicable.

of foreign affiliates that are also counted as U.S. parents accounted for 11 percent of the gross product and 13 percent of the employee compensation in the USDIA survey. The BEA also provided us with more detailed industry-level information on the number of U.S. parent firms in 2000 that were also foreign affiliates. After reviewing these data, we made a few additional adjustments, roughly doubling the overall manufacturing share for motor vehicles and parts, chemicals, petroleum refining, and stone, clay, and glass, and halving the overall manufacturing share for semiconductors, miscellaneous manufacturing, and furniture. We then made overlap adjustments for 1977, 1982, 1989, and 1994 to 1998 using the same special tabulations. Overlap adjustments for 1977, 1982, and 1989 were based on the tabulations for 1994.

Constructing a Database on Foreign Affiliates

For 1977, 1982, and 1989, all key variables except for gross product were concorded to the GPO87HT hierarchy. Gross product data for this period are organized according to a different industrial hierarchy, which in turn is different from the one used for all variables from 1992 to 1996. Moreover, the level of industry detail for 1977 to 1986 is limited (sixteen categories) compared to 1987 to 1989 (seventy-seven categories). We therefore used the detailed industry shares for 1987 to fill in the gaps in 1986, and then repeated this process back to 1977. All data were then concorded to the GPO87HT hierarchy.

For 1992 to 1996, data for all key variables were published at a slightly more disaggregate level than the corresponding USDIA estimates for 1994 to 1998. This necessitated an additional concordance in order to ultimately convert them to the GPO87HT hierarchy.

Data for 1997 to 2000 were published on a NAICS basis, and it was necessary to concord them to an SIC87 basis in order to make them time-series compatible with the pre-1997 FDIUS surveys. We used the same time-invariant concordance that was applied to the USDIA surveys in 1999 and 2000. The data were then concorded to the GPO87HT hierarchy.

Establishment-Level Estimates for U.S. Parents and Foreign Affiliates

We constructed our establishment-level estimates using periodic information from the BEA on sales and employment of affiliates or parents broken out by industry of sales. As shown in table 10A.1, for the USDIA survey, these data are only available in the benchmark surveys years for 1982 forward. For the FDIUS survey, the data are available annually for 1987 to 2000 but are not available in any previous years except for 1980.[28]

Unfortunately, unlike the firm-level data, the data on sales- and employment-by-industry-of-sales include information on banking, meaning the total values in the two types of files do not match. In addition, two categories—central administrative offices and a residual, "not specified" industry—only exist for the sales- and employment-by-industry-of-sales variables. We therefore implemented an iterative biproportional fitting or "RASing" procedure to adjust these values and ensure that they matched

---

28. In addition, because no data on high-tech industries are available in 1980, they were estimated using weights derived from the 1987 file.

the totals implied by the firm-based data. Ratio variables were then constructed of employment (or sales) in the industry of sales to employment (or sales) at the firm level.

Because data for sales- and employment-by-industry-of-sales were published on a NAICS97 basis in 1999 for the USDIA and in 1997 to 2000 for the FDIUS, we first had to remove the contributions of the additional parents that began to appear in the USDIA survey in this year, following the same approach described previously before concording them to a GPO87HT basis.

Finally, we applied the establishment-to-firm ratios to the firm-level, overlap-adjusted estimates in order to generate our establishment-level estimates. For the USDIA data, because these ratios only exist for 1982, 1989, and 1999, we applied the 1982 ratio to the 1977 firm-level data, the 1994 ratio to the 1995 and 1996 firm-level data, and the 1999 ratio to firm-level data to 1997 to 2001. For the FDIUS data, because these ratios do not exist in 1977 and 1982, we applied the 1980 ratios to both years.

Combining the Parent and Affiliate Databases

Having concorded both surveys to a single, time-series-consistent industrial hierarchy, addressed the overlap problem in the USDIA survey, and generated estimates on an establishment basis, we combined the data from the two surveys into a consolidated MNC database. We then merged this dataset with the Bartlesman and Beaulieu industry-level estimates for the nonfinancial corporate sector. Thus, for each industry, the resulting data set contained values for parents, affiliates, and the entire nonfinancial corporate sector. We estimated hours worked for parents and affiliates as the product of their employment and the average workweek in the corresponding industry for the nonfinancial corporate sector as a whole.[29] Values for the entire MNC sector in each industry are simply the sum of the corresponding parent and affiliate values. Values for domestically oriented nonfinancial corporations were calculated residually.[30]

As discussed in the text, we applied the gross product deflators generated by Bartlesman and Beaulieu for industries in the nonfinancial corporate sector to the *atom-level* parent, affiliate, and domestically oriented industries in our MNC database (i.e., the twenty-nine shaded industries in table 10A.2). Thus, in our analysis, chain aggregation of these atom-level deflators to higher-level subaggregates such as high tech, manufacturing excluding high tech, and nonmanufacturing provides the sole source of price

---

29. These hours estimates were then controlled to published totals for the nonfinancial corporate sector.

30. In a very small number of cases, the resulting values for the non-MNC sector were actually negative. In such instances, we calculated the domestically oriented as a very small fraction of the total nonfinancial corporate value and adjusted the MNC values accordingly.

Table 10A.4 Sectoral estimates of employee hours and real gross product

	Parents	Affiliates	MNC	NMNC	NFC	FC	COR	XCOR	BUS
1977									
Employee Hours:									
Gross domestic product	30,863	2,230	33,093	56,479	89,572	4,010	93,582	29,672	123,254
Nonfarm Business	30,863	2,230	33,093	56,479	89,572	4,010	93,582	24,438	118,020
Manufacturing	18,871	1,475	20,346	19,492	39,838	0	39,838	1,283	41,121
High Technology Industries	1,011	110	1,121	539	1,660	0	1,660	20	1,679
Manufacturing, except High Tech	17,860	1,365	19,225	18,953	38,178	0	38,178	1,264	39,442
Nonmanufacturing	11,992	755	12,748	36,987	49,734	4,010	53,745	23,154	76,899
Real Gross Product:									
Gross domestic product	685,616	60,335	747,995	1,457,904	2,210,918	305,990	2,499,951	1,065,389	3,553,215
Nonfarm Business	685,616	60,335	747,995	1,457,904	2,210,918	305,990	2,499,951	985,165	3,473,079
Manufacturing	368,429	34,716	405,980	366,936	772,022	0	772,022	16,960	788,267
High Technology Industries	1,030	633	1,389	991	2,309	0	2,309	1	2,236
Manufacturing, except High Tech	473,076	36,367	507,024	416,161	922,311	0	922,311	20,369	941,145
Nonmanufacturing	315,840	25,596	340,649	1,085,459	1,428,398	305,990	1,712,391	964,091	2,668,746
2000									
Employee Hours:									
Gross domestic product	36,032	12,028	48,060	95,276	143,336	5,481	148,817	38,249	187,066
Nonfarm Business	36,032	12,028	48,060	95,276	143,336	5,481	148,817	33,220	182,036
Manufacturing	15,171	5,643	20,814	19,617	40,431	0	40,431	1,395	41,826
High Technology Industries	1,385	382	1,767	655	2,422	0	2,422	62	2,484
Manufacturing, except High Tech	13,786	5,260	19,047	18,962	38,009	0	38,009	1,333	39,342
Nonmanufacturing	20,861	6,385	27,246	75,658	102,905	5,481	108,386	31,824	140,210
Real Gross Product:									
Gross domestic product	1,752,905	503,859	2,256,787	2,871,566	5,121,125	637,192	5,761,391	1,846,462	7,605,677
Nonfarm Business	1,752,905	503,859	2,256,787	2,871,566	5,121,125	637,192	5,761,391	1,754,303	7,513,077
Manufacturing	807,780	228,800	1,035,219	464,266	1,493,420	0	1,493,420	72,202	1,566,247
High Technology Industries	333,765	36,626	368,978	60,177	429,452	0	429,452	11,111	440,516
Manufacturing, except High Tech	593,233	201,627	794,918	407,271	1,200,331	0	1,220,331	64,395	1,264,933
Nonmanufacturing	943,762	274,797	1,218,581	2,405,737	3,625,490	637,192	4,264,410	1,683,942	5,946,905

Note: Employee hours reported in thousands; real gross product reported in thousands of 1996 dollars. NMNC = Domestically Oriented; NFC = Nonfinancial Corporations; FC = Financial Corporations; COR = Corporate Business; XCOR = Nonfarm Corporate Business; BUS = Nonfarm Private Business. Parents + Affiliates = MNC; MNC + NMC = NFC; NFC + FC = COR; COR + XCOR = BUS.

variation across parents, affiliates, and domestically oriented firms in any given industry in the nonfinancial sector.

Because the deflators are Fisher indexes, chain aggregation requires values for both prices and quantities in adjoining years. This posed a problem because, prior to 1994, we only have nominal gross product data for parents and affiliates at infrequent intervals. It was therefore necessary to estimate nominal gross product in years adjacent to 1977, 1982, and 1989. To do so, we implemented an iterative proportional fitting procedure that ensured these estimates summed to known totals (i.e., nonfinancial corporate gross product in each atom-level industry) and were consistent with the various accounting identities in our sectoral hierarchy (i.e., MNC = Parent + Affiliate; Nonfinancial Corporate = MNC + domestically oriented). We exploited the availability of nonfinancial corporate gross product and gross product deflators in the adjacent years and used values for parents and affiliates in 1977, 1982, and 1989 as starting values. Finally, we combined all relevant data on MNCs and nonfinancial corporations with data on the noncorporate, financial corporate, and government sectors to complete our analysis dataset.

Table 10A.4 presents our sectoral estimates of employee hours and real gross product in both 1977 and 2000 for selected aggregates and subaggregates. Estimates for all other years and variables as well as for atom-level industries are available on request.

References

Aitken, B., and A. Harrison. 1999. Do domestic firms benefit from foreign direct investment? Evidence from Venezuela. *American Economic Review* 89 (3): 605–18.

Baldwin, J. R., and W. Gu. 2003. Export-market participation and productivity performance in Canadian manufacturing. *Canadian Journal of Economics* 36 (3): 634–57.

Bartelsman, E. J., and J. J. Beaulieu. 2003. A user's guide to the Federal Reserve productivity data system. Mimeograph. Board of Governors of the Federal Reserve System.

———. 2007. A consistent accounting of U.S. productivity growth. In *Hard-to-measure goods and services,* ed. E. R. Berndt and C. R. Hulten, 449–82. Studies in Income and Wealth, vol. 67. Chicago: University of Chicago Press.

Bernard, A. B., and J. B. Jensen. 1995. Exports, jobs, and wages in U.S. manufacturing: 1976–1987. *Brookings Paper on Economics Activity, Microeconomics:* 67–119.

———. Exceptional exporter performance: Cause, effect, both? *Journal of International Economics* 47 (1999): 1–25.

Bernard, A. B., J. B. Jensen, and P. K. Schott. 2005. Importers, exporters, and multinationals: A portrait of firms in the U.S. that trade goods. NBER, Working Paper no. 11404. Cambridge, MA: National Bureau of Economic Research.

————. 2006. Transfer pricing by U.S.-based multinational firms. NBER Working Paper no. 12493. Cambridge, MA: National Bureau of Economic Research.

Borga, M., and W. Zeile. 2004. International fragmentation of production and the intrafirm trade of U.S. multinational companies. BEA Working Paper no. 2004-02. Washington, D.C.: Bureau of Economic Analysis.

Coe, D. T., E. Helpman, and A. W. Hoffmaister. 1997. North-South R&D spillovers. *Economic Journal, Royal Economic Society* 107 (Jan.):134–49.

Corrado, C., and L. Slifman. 1999. Decomposition of productivity and unit costs. *American Economic Review* 89 (2): 328–32.

Criscuolo, C., J. E. Haskel, and M. J. Slaughter. 2005. Global engagement and the innovation activities of firms. NBER Working Paper no. 11479. Cambridge, MA: National Bureau of Economic Research.

Criscuolo, C., and R. Martin. 2005. Multinationals and U.S. productivity leadership: Evidence from Great Britain. CEP Discussion Paper no. dp0672.

Doms, M. E., and J. B. Jensen. 1998a. Comparing wages, skills, and productivity between domestically and foreign-owned manufacturing establishments in the United States. In *Geography and ownership as bases for economic accounting,* 235–58. ed. R. E. Baldwin, R. E. Lipsey, and J. David Richardson, Studies in Income and Wealth, Volume 59. Chicago: University of Chicago Press.

Fosfuri, A., M. Motta, and T. Rønde. 2001. Foreign direct investment and spillovers through workers' mobility. *Journal of International Economics* 53 (1): 205–22.

Griffith, R., R. Harrison, and J. Van Reenen. 2004. How special is the special relationship? Using the impact of R&D spillovers on U.K. firms as a test of technology sourcing. Center for Economic Performance Discussion Paper no. 659.

Griffith, R., S. Redding, and H. Simpson. 2003. Productivity convergence and foreign ownership at the establishment level. Center for Economic Policy Research Working Paper no. 3765.

————. 2004. Foreign ownership and productivity: New evidence from the service sector and the R&D lab. *Oxford Review of Economic Policy* 20 (3): 440–56.

Griffith, R., S. Redding, and J. Van Reenen. 2004. Mapping the two faces of R&D: Productivity growth in a panel of OECD industries. *Review of Economics and Statistics* 86 (4): 9883–95.

Grossman, G., and E. Helpman. 1991. *Innovation and growth in the world economy.* Cambridge, MA: MIT Press.

Hanson, G. H., R. J. Mataloni, Jr., and M. J. Slaughter. 2001. Expansion strategies of U.S. multinational firms. In *Brookings Trade Forum 2001,* ed. D. Rodrik and S. Collins, 245–94. Washington, D.C.: Brookings Institution.

————. 2005. Vertical production networks in multinational firms. *Review of Economics and Statistics* 87 (4): 664–78.

Haskel, J., S. Pereira, and M. J. Slaughter. 2004. Does inward foreign direct investment boost the productivity of domestic firms? NBER Working Paper no. 8724. Cambridge, MA: National Bureau of Economic Research.

Helpman, E., M. J. Melitz, and S. R. Yeaple. 2004. Export versus FDI heterogeneous firms. *American Economic Review* 94 (1): 300–316.

Howenstine, N. G., and W. J. Zeile. 1994. Characteristics of foreign-owned U.S. manufacturing establishments. In *Survey of Current Business,* 34–59. U.S. Commerce Department: Bureau of Economic Analysis.

Howitt, P. 2000. Endogenous growth and cross-country income differences. *American Economic Review* 90 (4): 829–46.

Jorgenson, D. W., and K. J. Stiroh. 2000. U.S. economic growth in the new millennium. *Brookings Papers on Economic Activity* 2000 (1): 125–211.

Keller, W. 2004. International technology diffusion. *Journal of Economic Literature* 42:752–82.

Keller, W., and S. R. Yeaple. 2003. Multinational enterprises, international trade, and productivity growth: Firm level from the United States. NBER Working Paper no. 9504. Cambridge, MA: National Bureau of Economic Research.

Lipsey, R. E., M. Blomström, and E. D. Ramstetter. 1998. Internationalized production in world output. In *Geography and ownership as bases for economic accounting,* ed. R. E. Baldwin, R. E. Lipsey, and J. D. Richardson, 83–135. Studies in Income and Wealth, vol. 59. Chicago: University of Chicago Press.

Mataloni, R. J. Jr. 1995. A guide to BEA statistics on U.S. multinational companies. In *Survey of Current Business,* 38–55. U.S. Commerce Department: Bureau of Economic Analysis.

———. 1997. Real gross product of U.S. companies' majority-owned foreign affiliates in manufacturing. In *Survey of Current Business,* 8–17. U.S. Commerce Department: Bureau of Economic Analysis.

———. 2000. An examination of the low rates of return of foreign-owned U.S. companies. In *Survey of Current Business,* 55–73. U.S. Commerce Department: Bureau of Economic Analysis.

———. 2002. U.S. multinational companies: Operations in 2000. In *Survey of Current Business,* 111–22. U.S. Commerce Department: Bureau of Economic Analysis.

———. 2004. U.S. multinational companies: Operations in 2002. In *Survey of Current Business,* 10–29. U.S. Commerce Department: Bureau of Economic Analysis.

Mataloni, R. J. Jr., and D. R. Yorgason. 2002. Operations of U.S. multinational companies: Preliminary results from the 1999 benchmark survey. In *Survey of Current Business,* 24–54. U.S. Commerce Department: Bureau of Economic Analysis.

Melitz, M. J. 2003. The impact of trade on aggregate industry productivity and intra-industry reallocations. *Econometrica* 71 (6): 1695–1725.

Moyer, B. C., M. A. Planting, M. Fahim-Nadar, and S. K. S. Lum. 2004. Preview of the comprehensive revision of the annual industry accounts. In *Survey of Current Business,* 38–51. U.S. Commerce Department: Bureau of Economic Analysis.

Oliner, S. D., and D. E. Sichel. 2000. The resurgence of growth in the late 1990s: Is information technology the story? *Journal of Economic Perspectives* 14:3–22.

Rodriguez-Clare, A. 1996. Multinationals, linkages, and economic development. *American Economic Review* 86 (4): 852–73.

Stiroh, K. J. 2002. Information technology and the U.S. productivity revival: What do the industry data say? *American Economic Review* 92 (5): 1559–76.

Yuskavage, R. E. 1996. Improved estimates of gross product by industry, 1959–94. In *Survey of Current Business,* 133–53. U.S. Commerce Department: Bureau of Economic Analysis.

Zeile, W. J. 1999. Foreign direct investment in the United States: Preliminary results from the 1997 benchmark survey. In *Survey of Current Business,* 21–54. U.S. Commerce Department: Bureau of Economic Analysis.

Comment   Raymond J. Mataloni Jr.

One of the often cited benefits of foreign direct investment is to raise labor productivity by combining the multinational firms' capital and proprietary assets (such as advanced technologies or management and marketing techniques) with the skill and effort of the national labor force. Rising labor productivity may occur in home as well as host countries and is widely regarded to be of central importance in improving the standard of living in both developed and less-developed countries. With regard to less-developed countries, Surjit Bhalla observed succinctly that, to alleviate poverty, per capita economic "growth is sufficient, period" (Loungani 2002).

In this chapter, Corrado, Lengermann, and Slifman demonstrate just how important multinational firms have been in advancing one country's economic growth. Through careful analysis involving creative combinations and adjustments of various data sets from the Bureau of Economic Analysis (BEA), they find some remarkable patterns underlying U.S. productivity growth. During the 1980s and 1990s, the labor productivity of U.S. operations of nonfinancial multinational firms grew twice as fast as that of other nonfinancial U.S. corporations. The authors also find the contribution of multinationals to have been especially strong in the late 1990s, when these firms accounted for *all* of the acceleration in labor productivity of nonfinancial U.S. corporations.[1] While a number of firm-level studies have demonstrated the productivity-enhancing effects of foreign direct investment, few other studies have quantified these effects at a national level.

Through a number of adjustments and extensions, the authors significantly increased the analytical value of the underlying source data. These adjustments and extensions are clever and reveal a high degree of familiarity with the source data. Although they require the use of assumptions and therefore undoubtedly lack some precision, the assumptions are reasonable and the resulting estimates can support the broad macroeconomic analysis in the chapter.

The authors' estimates of the labor productivity of the multinational sector are based on data on the value added and employment of U.S. parent companies of U.S. multinational companies and of U.S. affiliates of foreign multinational companies. Because there is some overlap between U.S. parent companies and U.S. affiliates in the BEA data, the authors had to remove the overlap by attributing the value added of those firms that were in both data sets to only one of the two groups of firms—U.S. affiliates. The

Raymond J. Mataloni Jr. is an economist in the Research Branch of the Balance of Payments Division, U.S. Bureau of Economic Analysis.

1. This does not imply that only multinational firms had accelerated growth in labor productivity, because some firms undoubtedly had a deceleration in labor productivity growth.

overlap consists of U.S. affiliates that, in turn, own a foreign affiliate; a common example is a foreign-owned U.S. manufacturer that owns a factory in Canada or Mexico. The authors used special BEA industry-level tabulations of value added of firms belonging to both groups to make the adjustment.

A second extension of the BEA source data was the production of the first comprehensive time series estimates of the value added of U.S. parents and U.S. affiliates classified by line of business. The BEA's estimates of the value added of these firms are classified by the main industry of the enterprise (company), rather than by the individual lines of business within the enterprise. For diversified firms, classification by industry of enterprise may not always be indicative of the scope of the underlying activities of the firms. In order to create estimates classified on a line-of-business basis, the authors reclassified the BEA value added data based on related line-of-business data collected in the BEA surveys. The resulting estimates were classified in a manner consistent with the value added estimates for all U.S. firms.

The authors' third extension of the BEA source data was to place the industrial classification of U.S. parents, U.S. affiliates, and other U.S. firms on a Standard Industrial Classification (SIC) basis for the entire period covered by the study. Beginning with 1997 data for U.S. affiliates and 1999 data for U.S. parent companies, BEA's data on multinational U.S. firms are classified by the North American Industry Classification System (NAICS) rather than according to the SIC. The authors converted the NAICS-based data to a SIC basis by developing a concordance between the NAICS and SIC codes.

A fourth extension of the BEA source data was to remove the effects of price inflation from the estimates of value added of U.S. parents and U.S. affiliates. As noted by the authors, BEA has produced estimates of the real value added of foreign affiliates of U.S. companies but this has not yet been done for U.S. parents or U.S. affiliates. The authors developed their estimates of real value added using industry-level deflators for all U.S. business establishments from BEA's Industry Economic Accounts.

A final step was to estimate the number of hours worked by the employees of U.S. parents and U.S. affiliates. The authors produced these estimates by applying the average number of hours worked, by industry, from BEA's National Income and Product Accounts, to data on the number of employees of U.S. parents and U.S. affiliates. Using this estimate of hours worked as the denominator and the estimate of real value added as the numerator, the authors constructed their estimates of labor productivity. The resulting estimates represent the first such labor productivity estimates for U.S. parent companies and the first such time-series estimates for U.S. affiliates of foreign companies.

The estimation of real value added and labor input created through these extensions of the source data allowed the authors to generate industry-level productivity estimates for multinational U.S. firms and to compare them to similar estimates for domestically oriented firms. One important contribution of this research is the authors' ability to distinguish patterns that reflect industry-specific conditions from patterns associated with multinationality. For example, the authors are able to attribute the fact that the multinational sector was disproportionately affected by the 2001 recession to the industry mix of the firms.

A possible extension of the authors' research would be to explore some of the factors underlying the patterns they have identified in the labor productivity estimates. One way to approach this question would be to calculate a broader measure of productivity, such as total factor productivity, in order to isolate the effect of increased output per unit of labor input from the effect of increased capital input per worker. Another approach would be to try to correlate some of the firm characteristics that are expected to influence productivity with firms' actual productivity growth. The authors identify several possible influences, such as international fragmentation of the production chain, the transfer of knowledge between domestic and foreign units of multinational companies, and increased capital spending—particularly for information technology equipment. This research could be supported by BEA's firm-level data on the operations of U.S. multinational companies and of U.S. affiliates of foreign companies. The data include, for example, measures of cross-border trade between U.S. parent companies and their foreign affiliates and between U.S. affiliates and their foreign parent companies, measures of R&D conducted by U.S. parents and foreign affiliates, and measures of capital spending by U.S. multinational companies and by U.S. affiliates of foreign companies.

I would like to end by noting recent steps that the BEA has taken to maintain and expand its estimates of value added of U.S. parent companies and of U.S. affiliates of foreign companies in order to facilitate this type of research, and other recent BEA steps to support studies of the sources of U.S. productivity growth. Last fall, the Bureau updated its annual enterprise-level estimates of the value added of multinational U.S. firms. The BEA, in conjunction with the Census Bureau, will also soon be releasing establishment-level estimates of the value added of U.S. affiliates in manufacturing for 2002 based on a link to the plant-level data collected by the U.S. Census Bureau.[2] In addition to updating and expanding its data on value added of multinational U.S. firms, BEA has taken other steps to support research on the sources of U.S. productivity growth. Recent initiatives

2. Establishment-level estimates of the value added of U.S. affiliates have been previously published for the years 1988 to 1992, and for 1997. For details about these publications, see the section "Establishment from BEA-Census Link" of the International Investment Division Product Guide, which is available on the BEA website (www.bea.gov) under "International," "About International."

have been focused on improving the measurement of investment in intangible assets and on understanding the effect of this type of investment on U.S. economic growth. One major initiative is the recently updated R&D satellite account for the United States (see Okubo et al. [2006]). Later this year, the BEA will update these estimates and will present options for adding an international dimension to the satellite account using BEA data on the operations of U.S. multinational firms. A related initiative is the Bureau's R&D Link Project, in conjunction with the National Science Foundation and the U.S. Bureau of the Census. It will involve matching the BEA data for U.S. parent companies and U.S. affiliates with R&D data for all U.S. companies collected by the Census Bureau.[3]

References

Loungani, P. 2002. Interview with Surjit Bhalla: Growth, poverty, inequality—getting the facts right. *IMF Survey* 31 (October): 335–36.
Okubo, S., C. A. Robbins, C. E. Moylan, B. K. Sliker, L. I. Schultz, and L. S. Mataloni. 2006. BEA's 2006 Research and development satellite account: Preliminary estimates of R&D for 1959–2002 and effect on GDP and other measures. *Survey of Current Business* 86 (December): 14–44.

3. A plan of action for this project is available on the BEA website at www.bea.gov/bea/di/FinalReportPublic.pdf.

Contributors

Mary Amiti
International Research Function
Federal Reserve Bank of New York
33 Liberty Street
New York, NY 10045

Maria Borga
Bureau of Economic Analysis
U.S. Department of Commerce
1441 L Street, NW
Washington, D.C. 20230

Carol Corrado
The Conference Board
845 Third Avenue
New York, NY 10022

Robert C. Feenstra
Department of Economics
University of California, Davis
One Shields Avenue
Davis, CA 95616

C. Fritz Foley
Harvard Business School
Soldiers Field
Boston, MA 02163

Harry Grubert
Office of Tax Policy
Department of the Treasury
1500 Pennsylvania Avenue, NW
Washington, D.C. 20220

Gordon H. Hanson
IR/PS 0519
University of California, San Diego
9500 Gilman Drive
La Jolla, CA 92093-0519

J. Bradford Jensen
McDonough School of Business
Georgetown University
Washington, D.C. 20057

Wolfgang Keller
Department of Economics
University of Colorado at Boulder
Boulder, CO 80309-0256

Lori G. Kletzer
University of California, Santa Cruz
Department of Economics
439 Engineering 2 Bldg.
1156 High Street
Santa Cruz, CA 95064

Paul Lengermann
Federal Reserve Board
20th Street and Constitution Avenue,
    NW
Washington, D.C. 20551

Robert E. Lipsey
NBER
365 Fifth Avenue, 5th Floor
New York, NY 10016-4309

Raymond J. Mataloni Jr.
U.S. Department of Commerce
Bureau of Economic Analysis
1441 L Street, NW
Washington, D.C. 20230

Phillip McCalman
Department of Economics
University of California, Santa Cruz
Santa Cruz, CA 95064

Gabriel W. Medeiros
Bureau of Economic Analysis
U.S. Department of Commerce
1441 L Street, NW
Washington, D.C. 20230

Francisco Moris
Division of Science Resources
    Statistics
National Science Foundation
4201 Wilson Boulevard, Suite 965
Arlington, VA 22230

John Mutti
Department of Economics
Grinnell College
Grinnell, IA 50112

Xavier Reif
National Institute of Statistics and
    Economic Studies (INSEE)
18, Boulevard Adolphe-Pinard
75675 Paris Cedex 14, France

Marshall Reinsdorf
Bureau of Economic Analysis
U.S. Department of Commerce
1441 L Street, NW
Washington, D.C. 20230

J. David Richardson
Department of Economics
347 Eggers Hall
Syracuse University
Syracuse, NY 13244-1090

Carol A. Robbins
Bureau of Economic Analysis
U.S. Department of Commerce
1441 L Street, NW
Washington, D.C. 20230

Matthew Slaughter
Tuck School of Business
Dartmouth College
100 Tuck Hall
Hanover, NH 03755

Larry Slifman
Federal Reserve Board
20th Street and Constitution Avenue,
    NW
Washington, D.C. 20551

Erich H. Strassner
Bureau of Economic Analysis
U.S. Department of Commerce
1441 L Street, NW
Washington, D.C. 20230

Desirée van Welsum
Organization for Economic
    Cooperation and Development
    (OECD)
STI/SPD
2, rue André Pascal
75775 Paris Cedex 16 France

Shang-Jin Wei
Graduate School of Business
Columbia University
Uris Hall, Room 619
3022 Broadway
New York, NY 10027-6902

Chong Xiang
Department of Economics
Purdue University
403 West State Street
West Lafayette, IN 47907-2056

Robert E. Yuskavage
Bureau of Economic Analysis
U.S. Department of Commerce
1441 L Street, NW
Washington, D.C. 20230

Author Index

Subject Index